Study Guide
Volume I

Louis D. Rossi, CCSI
Louis R. Rossi, CCIE, CCSI
Thomas Rossi, CCSI

Genium Publishing Corp.
One Genium Plaza
Schenectady, NY 12304

CCIEprep.com Study Guide, Volume 1

Printed in Canada

10 9 8 7 6 5 4 3 2

ISBN 1-89-091108-9

This publication is available at special quantity discounts for use as a business premium or as a text within educational institutions or corporate training programs. For more information, please write to Genium Publishing Corporation, Sales Department, One Genium Plaza, Schenectady, NY 12304, or e-mail sales@genium.com.

Disclaimer

Extreme care has been taken in preparation of this work. However, neither the publisher nor the authors shall be responsible or liable for any errors, omissions, or damages resulting in connection with or arising from the use of any of the information in this book. With this work, the publisher and author are supplying information but are in no way attempting to provide engineering or other professional services.

Contents

Foreword

This is Volume 1 of what is anticipated to be a continuing series of Study Guides. It includes information that has appeared or will appear at the CCIEprep.com website (http://www.ccieprep.com). Each month, sixty model questions and four model laboratory and trouble-shooting scenarios are posted at the website. It is the author's intention to release subsequent volumes of this Study Guide at the rate of one every 12 to 16 months.

Included in this Study Guide are the questions (approximately 300) and scenarios (approximately 20) that have appeared at the site from June through November of 1998. Also included are a portion of the new questions and scenarios scheduled to appear at the site during the next five months. Discounts have been made available to networking professionals who wish to both purchase the Study Guide and Subscribe to the website so that they are not being charged twice for the same information. See the back of the book for a coupon for purchase of a six-month or one-year subscription to the CCIEprep.com website at a significant discount.

CCIEprep.com's website and this Study Guide are not in anyway connected with, or endorsed by Cisco Systems, Inc. Therefore, Cisco Systems, Inc. is not in any way responsible for the accuracy or reliability of any information, data, opinions, advice, or statements that appear in this reference.

The authors' of this Study Guide strongly recommend that networking professionals use Cisco products, attend Cisco-related training courses, and pursue Cisco networking certifications.

The following is a list of trademarks currently used by Cisco Systems, Inc. that have been registered with the United States Patent and Trademark Office.

AccessPath, Any to Any, AtmDirector, ClickStart, ControlStream, DAGAZ, Fast Step, FireRunner, IGX, IOS, JumpStart, Kernel Proxy, LoopRunner, MGX, Natural Network Viewer, NetRanger, NetSonar, Packet, PIX, Point and Click Internetworking, Policy Builder, RouteStream, Secure Script, SMARTnet, SpeedRunner, Stratm, StreamView, The Cell, TrafficDirector, TransPath, VirtualStream, VlanDirector, Workgroup Director, and Workgroup Stack are trademarks™. BPX, Catalyst, Cisco, Cisco IOS, Cisco Systems, Enterprise/Solver, EtherChannel, FastHub, ForeSight, FragmentFree, IP/TV, IPX, LightStream, MICA, Phase/IP, StrataSphere, StrataView Plus, and SwitchProbe are registered trademarks® of Cisco Systems, Inc. in the U.S. and certain other countries. All other trademarks mentioned in this document are the property of their respective owners.

Acknowlegements

In 1968 I was introduced into the world of computers. A few years later, armed with my Atari 400, I taught my two boys the BASIC language. For the last 20 years I have been trying to stay ahead of them. Let me take this opportunity to announce to the world "UNCLE." The battle is over, and I lost.

There are no words that can express the joy of communicating with your grown children almost every day, talking about business and life. Almost 30 years ago, I entered the teaching field to be able to spend more time with my kids, I guess it worked out pretty good for me. Thanks guys for keeping me inspired to attain new levels of knowledge.

I never realized what an all-consuming task it is to complete a book. I would like to thank my wife Annette, the love of my life. For the past several months I have been obsessed with the CCIEprep.com website, this book, and my training, which did not leave a whole lot of time for her and I. Thanks Annette for all your support and patience.

Who knows how we end up doing what we do in life? I am happy that no one told my parents that I would grow up to be a teacher, they might have died of a heart attack at an early age. I was not the best student, to put things kindly. My parents taught me the value of learning and instilled in me that you don't give up just because something is difficult. Thanks Mom and Dad for always supporting my far-out ideas.

Last spring I came up with the idea that I would like to write a couple of books and did not have the slightest idea of how to begin. I would like to thank my brother-in-law Mike Cinquanti and the staff at Genium for putting me on the right track. They've done a wonderful job of producing and marketing this book and have also marketed CCIEprep.com to be one of the most successful computer-related web sites on the Internet. Thanks, Mike, and the entire Genium staff for your dedication to the success of the CCIEprep.com family of services and products.

Thanks goes out to all the guys at Capernaum, John, Steve, Phil and Will for taking care of CCIEprep.com and continuing to put up with my Italian temper. I can't help it; blame my mom!

Thank you Rich Stanley for sending me several CCNA questions when I was buried with my CCIEprep.com responsibilities. I would also like to thank the thousands of students I have had the pleasure to teach and train over the years. If it was not for you sitting in those seats every week, I don't know what I would have done with my life.

I need to apologize to my friends that I have ignored over the past several months, Bert, Chris, Big and Little T, Beano, Baginga, Gary, Kevin, Kim, Kit, Dennis, Doug, Mike, Brian, Jen, Mina and the gang at B. Merrell's and the Outback of Tallahassee. Keep the Sam Smith and Fosters on ice. I will be there soon!

Last but not least I need to thank Larry Cody. Several years ago I was struggling doing application training. Lou Jr. was teaching high school chemistry and dealing with unruly kids. Tommy was "working for the man" as an aerospace engineer. Larry gave me a call, suggesting I look at the Certified Novell Instructor certification. That phone call not only changed my life, but the lives of my children, and for that I will be ever grateful.

Thank you Larry, and thank you all!

— Lou Rossi

I would like to express my gratitude to the many people who have helped us through the long and tedious process of completing this book.

First and foremost I would like to thank the person who had an idea in early 1998 of helping students with the most difficult certification in the Internetworking industry, my Father. It was his innovative thinking that led to CCIEprep.com and eventually this book, with more to follow.

Second, I would like to thank Michael Cinquanti of Genium Publishing, who also happens to be my Uncle. He has supported us and CCIEprep from the very beginning. It is his marketing skill that has generated the millions of hits on CCIEprep.com, the web page.

I would also like to thank my Wife, Kimberly. She has been very patient with me these last several months as I have had a hectic teaching schedule coupled with hours of writing. My gratitude also goes to my Mother, who has endured hours of her son's constant conversations of the Internetworking Industry. She has always listened intently, no matter how dull the conversations became.

I would also like to mention those people that I learn the most from, my students. Their constant questions and comments make me a better Network Engineer, and, for that, I thank them.

I would finally like to thank the rest of my family for always being supportive and patient with my incredibly hectic schedule and boring conversations with my Father and Brother. Just imagine what Thanksgiving dinner is like!

Thank You.

— Louis R. Rossi

I would like to thank God for the talent that he has given us. Without His presence, no work I could ever accomplish would provide fulfillment.

CCIEprep.com is my father's brainchild, and I owe him a great debt of gratitude for his countless sleepless nights (not that he EVER sleeps!). He has poured over questions and taken more than a few exams to provide unsurpassed quality. For this, I thank him.

My brother is one of the highest caliber network engineers in the country. I thank him for his invaluable knowledge and experience.

I would also like to thank my staff at Capernaum, which has done an innovative and professional job while bringing the web site concept to reality.

Lastly, I have to thank my newly wed wife, Kit. She has just begun to learn what she has married into, yet this hasn't stopped her!

— Tom Rossi

Introduction

Welcome to CCIEprep.com the book!

Inside this book you will find 600 hand-crafted questions and 31 lab and trouble-shooting scenarios.

Are these questions the actual questions from the exams? NO, but the questions and explanations have been crafted in such a way as to provide you with the information needed to get the question right on the real exam.

In many cases we provide not only answers to these questions; we also provide complete explanations. When you are studying for the exam, our explanations are just as important as the questions and answers, so don't skim over the explanations.

Each one of CCIEprep.com questions contains a code. This code will help the exam candidate (that's you) prepare for specific exams. See Appendix B for a complete explanation of the coding system.

If you are studying with our CD-ROM you can simply choose the exam you wish to take, or build your own study session by selecting questions that are coded for categories and protocols in which you need the most help. Some questions that appear on the CD-ROM have slightly different answer choices than the choices presented in the book. We had to change some of these choices based upon limitations of the test engine.

If you don't have the CD-ROM available, (Let's say you are going shopping with your wife, and it's too cumbersome and nerdy to take along your laptop) just slip this book under your arm and (while she is shopping her heart away) you can study for your next exam.

Each chapter is laid out in such a way to identify the different Cisco exams. Page numbers start over in each chapter. Use the handy tabs to find the chapter you want.

For the CCIE written exam study ALL the questions!

About the Exams

All of Cisco's tests are of standard type, meaning you can skip a question and go back to it later on.

Scoring is a straight percentage, unlike Novell and other exams you may have taken in the past.

In most cases the questions are multiple choice; however, there are some exams that do have a few fill-in-the-blank questions.

The tests are only given at Drake centers, but don't assume that you can take a Cisco test at the same testing center you have taken your Microsoft or Novell exams. Check to make sure when you call to register for the exam.

The number to call to register for a Cisco exam is 1-800-204-EXAM (3926). If you are located in another country, check out the Cisco website for phone numbers.

Test Taking Recommendations

- Keep moving; don't get hung up on a question
- If you don't know an answer, skip the question and go back to it later.
- Read the entire question and formulate an answer before looking at the choices.
- As a general rule don't "second guess" yourself.
- Cisco expects answers based on the Cisco materials.
- You can complain all you want about the fairness or the accuracy of the questions and answers, but it will do you no good, it's the world according to Cisco.

Accuracy of our information

Cisco does change certifications and exams from time-to-time, so check with Cisco before taking an exam to be certain of all exam numbers and objectives.

My sons and I have spent hours going over all of the questions and explanations in this book, but I am sure there will be some problems with a few questions, answers, or explanations. We will post a forum at CCIEprep.com to deal with these issues.

I hope you all enjoy this book and find it helpful in achieving your life's objectives. Cisco certifications are valuable to you, your employer and your family. Obtaining these certifications is not easy, but what value would they have if they were? With persistence and dedication you can achieve your goals.

Good luck to you all!

Knowledge is power.
Power is independence.

Thank you,

— Lou Rossi (the Dad)

Chapter One
OSI Model Questions

Many Cisco certification exams include sample OSI Model questions. You should not attempt any exam without knowing the OSI layered model. This first chapter is dedicated to OSI Model-related questions, answers, and explanations.

When using this Study Guide's CD-ROM to study and/or test your knowledge of the OSI Model, you will need to select the "CCNA" or "CCIE" option at the *select exam* window. You must then select *study session*, and select all questions with the category "O". There are currently a total universe of 33 questions available for this category.

Question 1–1. [OxNx] When discussing the subject of Multiplexing or Demultiplexing, the concept of a **Port Number** is best described by which one of the following statements?

a) A method of ensuring the delivery of data in the correct encapsulation format for the receiving host
b) The assembly of data from different layers of the OSI model into separate data streams, identified by port numbers
c) A method of distinguishing the data from different applications as it travels over a single data stream
d) The numbering system used to identify the data portion of an outgoing (multiplexing) or incoming (demultiplexing) data segment

Question 1–2. [OxNx] What is the major difference between the Ethernet version 2 frame and the 802.3 frame?

a) 802.3 frame uses a two-byte Length field where Ethernet describes type.
b) 802.3 frame uses a two-byte field for sequence numbers where Ethernet describes Type.
c) Ethernet uses a 802.2 header to describe type.
d) Ethernet uses a SNAP header.
e) There is no major difference.
f) None of the above.

Question 1–3. [OxNx] Frames are converted to Bits at which layer?

a) Application Layer 7
b) Presentation Layer 6
c) Session Layer 5
d) Transport Layer 4
e) Network Layer 3
f) Data Link Layer 2
g) Physical Layer 1

Question 1–4. [OxNx] When a Destination Service Access Point (DSAP) and Source Service Access Point (SSAP) are set to AA:

a) All stations with AA contained in their MAC addresses would receive this frame.
b) All stations would receive this frame, because it acts like a broadcast.
c) The encapsulated protocol contained in the frame must be IP.
d) The encapsulated protocol contained in the frame is proprietary.
e) None of the above

Question 1–5. [OxNx] The first segment of the "Three-Way Handshake" will most likely carry an ACK of (Choose the best answer):

a) 1
b) The SEQ number of the remote host "plus" 1
c) 0
d) There is no ACK.
e) A randomly generated number

Question 1–6. [OxNx] Which of the following layers defines network addressing and determines the best path?

a) Application Layer 7
b) Presentation Layer 6
c) Session Layer 5
d) Transport Layer 4
e) Network Layer 3
f) Data Link Layer 2
g) Physical Layer 1

Question 1–7. [OxNx] Which one of the following describes the process of a TCP/IP host learning a remote host MAC address?

a) ARP (Address Resolution Protocol)
b) SLARP (Serial Line Address Resolution Protocol)
c) RARP (Reverse Address Resolution Protocol)
d) IARP (Inverse Address Resolution Protocol)
e) MOP (Maintenance Operation Protocol)

Question 1–8. [OxNx] Which of the following layers sends and receives binary information?

a) Application Layer 7
b) Presentation Layer 6
c) Session Layer 5
d) Transport Layer 4
e) Network Layer 3
f) Data Link Layer 2
g) Physical Layer 1

Question 1–9. [OxNx] Which of the following are reasons for the OSI model?

a) Standardizes interfaces
b) Allows modular engineering
c) Standardizes Interfaces
d) Facilitates learning and teaching
e) All of the above.

1. OSI Model

Question 1–10. [OxNx] The Media Access Control (MAC) address is made up of the following two parts.

a) Vendor Code
b) Network Address
c) Host Address
d) Serial Number
e) No such address

Question 1–11. [OxNx] With a connection-oriented service a host will ACK (Acknowledge) with (Answer all that apply):

a) The last (SEQ) sequence number received from the remote host
b) The next expected (SEQ) sequence number from the remote host
c) The last ACK number from the remote host
d) The current SEQ number from the remote host "plus" 1
e) None of the above

Question 1–12. [OxNx] The establishment of a window during a session setup allows for which of the following? (Choose two.)

a) Multiple data segments to be sent before the **sender** requires an acknowledgement.
b) Multiple frame types to be sent over the same media type.
c) Multiple data segments to be sent before the **receiver** requires an acknowledgement.
d) Separate data streams from different hosts to a common host.
e) More efficient use of the available bandwidth.

Question 1–13. [OxPx] Which of the following best describes the IEEE standard 802.4? (Choose all that apply.)

a) Created in large part to satisfy the LAN needs of factories
b) Describes a Token Bus LAN
c) Describes a CSMA/CD media access method
d) Describes a Token Ring LAN
e) Describes a Metropolitan Area Network (MAN)

Question 1–14. [OxNx] What is the purpose of the 802.3 Subnet Access Protocol (SNAP) format?

a) To make ethernet perform faster
b) To identify the length of the frame
c) To identify proprietary protocols
d) To allow windowing
e) To allow flow control

Question 1–15. [OxNx] The presentation layer of the OSI model is primarily responsible for which of the following? (Choose two.)

a) Ensuring reliable end-to-end communications by using connection oriented protocols
b) Providing code formatting and conversion such as EBCDIC to ASCII
c) Managing encryption of data
d) Coordinating applications such as NFS and SQL as they interact on different hosts
e) Providing support for the intelligent segmentation and reassembly of upper-layer application data streams

Question 1–16. [OxNx] Which statement is true of the Datalink OSI layer ?

a) 802.3 is the MAC sub layer.
b) No such thing
c) MAC sublayer provides the connection to the network layer.
d) MAC sublayer uses SAPS to access the network layer.
e) SAP sublayer uses the MAC layer to access the LAN medium.

Question 1–17. [OxNx] Segments are converted to Datagrams at which layer?

a) Application Layer 7
b) Presentation Layer 6
c) Session Layer 5
d) Transport Layer 4
e) Network Layer 3
f) Data Link Layer 2
g) Physical Layer 1

Question 1–18. [OxNx] Which of the following applications requires the connection-oriented layer four protocol, TCP? (Choose all that apply.)

a) Telnet
b) FTP
c) TFTP
d) SNMP
e) None of the above

Question 1–19. [OxNx] Which of the following statements does NOT define a purpose of the OSI Reference Model? (Choose one.)

a) To define standard interfaces for plug-and-play compatibility and multi-vendor integration
b) To constrain or define the implementation of network functions
c) To allow areas to evolve more quickly by preventing changes in one area from impacting other areas
d) To allow engineers to design and develop in a modular fashion
e) To make it easier to understand the complexity of internetworking

1. OSI Model

Question 1–20. [OxNx] Which of the following could be a feature of a connection-oriented service?

a) Flow Control
b) "Three-Way" hand shake
c) Error checking
d) Windowing
e) All of the above

Question 1–21. [OxPx] IEEE 802.2 is described at which layer?

a) Physical Layer 1
b) Data-Link Layer 2
c) Network Layer 3
d) Transport Layer 4

Question 1–22. [OxPx] Which of the following best describes the IEEE standard 802.6? (Choose all that apply.)

a) Created in large part to satisfy the LAN needs of factory concerns
b) Describes a Token Bus LAN
c) Describes a CSMA/CD media access method
d) Describes a Token Ring LAN
e) Describes a Metropolitan Area Network (MAN)

Question 1–23. [OxNx] Handshaking is a technique found primarily at which layer of the OSI model?

a) The Session layer during outgoing communications
b) The Data-link layer during Token ring framing
c) The Network layer if a connection oriented protocol is being used
d) The Transport layer when connection oriented UDP is being used
e) The Transport layer when TCP is being used

Question 1–24. [OxNx] Which one of the following layers "best" describes the ability of the upper layers to gain independence over LAN media access?

a) Application Layer 7
b) Presentation Layer 6
c) Session Layer 5
d) Transport Layer 4
e) Network Layer 3
f) Data Link Layer 2
g) Physical Layer 1
h) MAC sublayer
i) LLC sublayer

Question 1–25. [OxNx] Which of the following layers provides end to end connections?

a) Application Layer 7
b) Presentation Layer 6
c) Session Layer 5
d) Transport Layer 4
e) Network Layer 3
f) Data Link Layer 2
g) Physical Layer 1

Question 1–26. [OxNx] Simple Network Management Protocol uses what numeric value, in decimal, of the destination port field of the User Datagram Protocol (UDP) header?

a) 20
b) 21
c) 23
d) 69
e) 161

Question 1–27. [OxNx] Which of the following layers controls access to the media?

a) Application Layer 7
b) Presentation Layer 6
c) Session Layer 5
d) Transport Layer 4
e) Network Layer 3
f) Data Link Layer 2
g) Physical Layer 1

Question 1–28. [OxNx] Raw data is converted to segments at which layer?

a) Application Layer 7
b) Presentation Layer 6
c) Session Layer 5
d) Transport Layer 4
e) Network Layer 3
f) Data Link Layer 2
g) Physical Layer 1

Question 1–29. [OxNx] Which of the following layers defines data representation?

a) Application Layer 7
b) Presentation Layer 6
c) Session Layer 5
d) Transport Layer 4
e) Network Layer 3
f) Data Link Layer 2
g) Physical Layer 1

1. OSI Model

Question 1–30. [OxNx] During a TFTP transfer using Cisco routers, what is the numeric value, in decimal, of the destination port field of the User Datagram Protocol (UDP) header?

a) 96
b) 47
c) a random number above 1024
d) 69
e) none of the above

Question 1–31. [OxNx] Which of the following layers would most likely provide connection oriented service?

a) Application Layer 7
b) Presentation Layer 6
c) Session Layer 5
d) Transport Layer 4
e) Network Layer 3
f) Data Link Layer 2
g) Physical Layer 1

Question 1–32. [OxNx] Datagrams are converted to frames at which layer?

a) Application Layer 7
b) Presentation Layer 6
c) Session Layer 5
d) Transport Layer 4
e) Network Layer 3
f) Data Link Layer 2
g) Physical Layer 1

Question 1–33. [OxPx] Connectionless Network Protocol (CLNP) is a service at which layer?

a) Physical Layer 1
b) Data-Link Layer 2
c) Network Layer 3
d) Transport Layer 4
e) Session Layer

Answer 1–1.
  c) **A method of distinguishing the data from different applications as it travels over a single data stream**

Answer 1–2.
  a) **802.3 frame uses a two-byte Length field where Ethernet describes type.**

Bob Metcalf usually gets named as the man who invented ethernet, he was working for XEROX at the time. In this original ethernet frame from the 1970s there was a two-byte field describing type. The IEEE took the two byte field and used it to describe length. IEEE uses SSAP, DSAP and sometimes SNAP to describe type.

Answer 1–3.
  g) **Physical Layer 1**

Answer 1–4.
  d) **The encapsulated protocol contained in the frame is proprietary.**

Refer to the following capture:

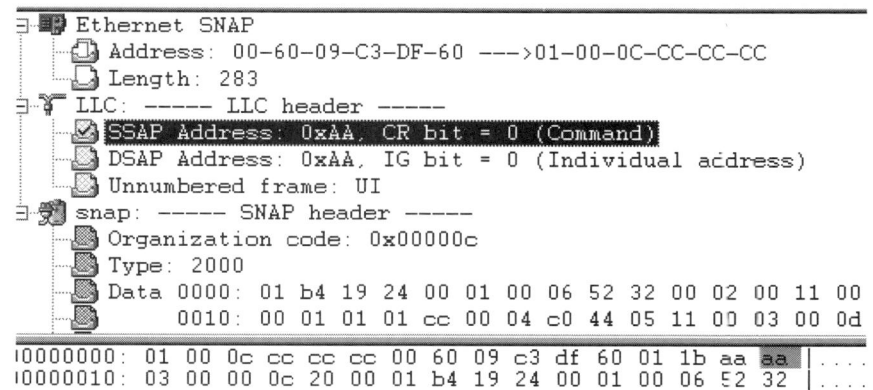

The above capture is Cisco's proprietary Cisco Discovery Protocol (CDP).

Answer 1–5.
  c) **0**

Below is an example of the first part of a Three-Way Handshake.

```
   ......□  Ethernet II Protocol Type: IP
☐ Ƴ Internet Protocol
      ...□  Version(MSB 4 bits): 4
      ...□  Header length(LSB 4 bits): 5 (32-bit word)
   ⊞-□  Service type: Precd=Routine,Delay=Normal,Thrput=Normal,Reli=Normal
      ...□  Total length: 44 (Octets)
      ...□  Fragment ID: 17159
   ⊞-□  Flags: Do not fragment,Last fragment,Offset=0 (0x00)
      ...□  Time to live: 32 seconds/hops
      ...□  IP protocol type: TCP (0x06)
      ...□  Checksum: 0xBF98
      ...□  IP address 172.20.0.3 ->172.20.0.1
      ...□  No option
☐ ▩ IP Transmission Control Protocol
      ...□  Port 1074 ---> Telnet
      ...□  Sequence Number: 39635900
      ...□  Acknowledgement Number: 0
      ...□  Header Length(MSB 4 bits): 6 (32-bit word)
      ...□  Reserved(LSB 4 bits): 0
   ⊞-□  Code: SYN,
      ...□  Window: 8192
      ...□  Checksum: 0x4D98
      ...□  Urgent Pointer: 0x0000
      ...□  TCP Option: 020405B4
```

In this first part of the handshake, take note of the Sequence and Acknowledgement numbers. Since this is the first part of the handshake the ACK is 0. The host initiating this connection-oriented conversation can not acknowledge a number that has not been received. This is the key factor in creating an access list that provides the ability to telnet out, but not allow the outside world to telnet in. The key word "established" means permit only those packets where the ACK is non-zero.

Answer 1–6.
   e)   Network Layer 3

Answer 1–7.
   a)   ARP (Address Resolution Protocol)

Below is an ARP request: Take note of the destination MAC address!

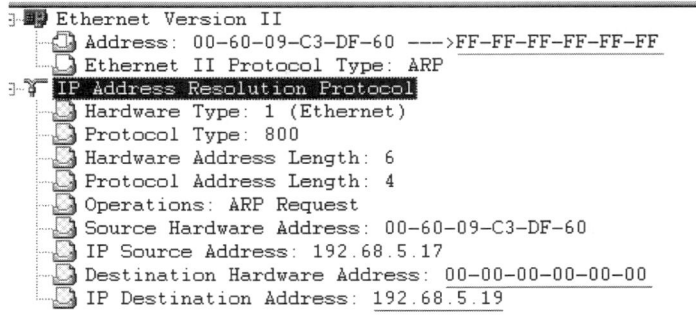

```
☐ ▣ Ethernet Version II
      ...□  Address: 00-60-09-C3-DF-60 --->FF-FF-FF-FF-FF-FF
      ...□  Ethernet II Protocol Type: ARP
☐ Ƴ IP Address Resolution Protocol
      ...□  Hardware Type: 1 (Ethernet)
      ...□  Protocol Type: 800
      ...□  Hardware Address Length: 6
      ...□  Protocol Address Length: 4
      ...□  Operations: ARP Request
      ...□  Source Hardware Address: 00-60-09-C3-DF-60
      ...□  IP Source Address: 192.68.5.17
      ...□  Destination Hardware Address: 00-00-00-00-00-00
      ...□  IP Destination Address: 192.68.5.19
```

Followed by an ARP reply:

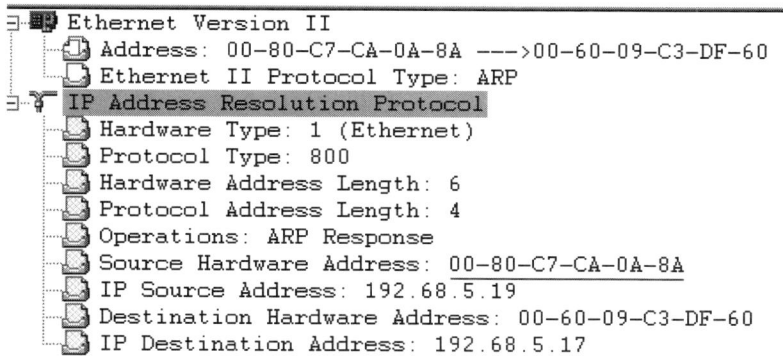

```
Ethernet Version II
    Address: 00-80-C7-CA-0A-8A --->00-60-09-C3-DF-60
    Ethernet II Protocol Type: ARP
IP Address Resolution Protocol
    Hardware Type: 1 (Ethernet)
    Protocol Type: 800
    Hardware Address Length: 6
    Protocol Address Length: 4
    Operations: ARP Response
    Source Hardware Address: 00-80-C7-CA-0A-8A
    IP Source Address: 192.68.5.19
    Destination Hardware Address: 00-60-09-C3-DF-60
    IP Destination Address: 192.68.5.17
```

Notice that the reply includes the source MAC address.

Answer 1–8.
  g) **Physical Layer 1**

Answer 1–9.
  e) **All of the above.**

Answer 1–10.
  a) **Vendor Code**
  d) **Serial Number**

The MAC address consists of 48 bits. The first 24 bits are the Vendor code or the Organizational Unique Identifier (OUI) number. The IEEE assigns these addresses to each vendor. It is the responsibility of each vendor to make sure that each card produced has a unique serial number. A vendor may have more than one Vendor Code.

Has anyone ever caught a vendor in a screw up?
When would a user ever know if there has been a screw up by a vendor?

Some Examples of OUI numbers:

```
CISCO     00 00 0c xx xx xx
Novell    00 00 1b xx xx xx
3COM      02 60 8c xx xx xx
```

Take note of the organizational code below:

```
Ethernet SNAP
    Address: 00-60-09-C3-DF-60 --->01-00-0C-CC-CC-CC
    Length: 283
LLC: ----- LLC header -----
    SSAP Address: 0xAA, CR bit = 0 (Command)
    DSAP Address: 0xAA, IG bit = 0 (Individual address)
    Unnumbered frame: UI
snap: ----- SNAP header -----
    Organization code: 0x00000c
    Type: 2000
    Data 0000: 01 b4 19 24 00 01 00 06 52 32 00 02 00 11 00
         0010: 00 01 01 01 cc 00 04 c0 44 05 11 00 03 00 0d

0000000: 01 00 0c cc cc cc 00 60 09 c3 df 60 01 1b aa aa |....
0000010: 03 00 00 0c 20 00 01 b4 19 24 00 01 00 06 52 32 |....
```

Answer 1–11.
b) **The next expected (SEQ) sequence number from the remote host**
d) **The current SEQ number from the remote host "plus" 1**

Following are three captures that clearly show the ACK and SEQ numbers of a three-way handshake.

First Part

```
Ethernet II Protocol Type: IP
Internet Protocol
    Version(MSB 4 bits): 4
    Header length(LSB 4 bits): 5 (32-bit word)
    Service type: Precd=Routine,Delay=Normal,Thrput=Normal,Reli=Normal
    Total length: 44 (Octets)
    Fragment ID: 17159
    Flags: Do not fragment,Last fragment,Offset=0 (0x00)
    Time to live: 32 seconds/hops
    IP protocol type: TCP (0x06)
    Checksum: 0xBF98
    IP address 172.20.0.3 ->172.20.0.1
    No option
IP Transmission Control Protocol
    Port 1074 ---> Telnet
    Sequence Number: 39635900
    Acknowledgement Number: 0
    Header Length(MSB 4 bits): 6 (32-bit word)
    Reserved(LSB 4 bits): 0
    Code: SYN,
    Window: 8192
    Checksum: 0x4D98
    Urgent Pointer: 0x0000
    TCP Option: 020405B4
```

Second Part

```
Internet Protocol
    Version(MSB 4 bits): 4
    Header length(LSB 4 bits): 5 (32-bit word)
    Service type: Precd=Routine,Delay=Normal,Thrput=Normal,Reli=Normal
    Total length: 44 (Octets)
    Fragment ID: 0
    Flags: May be fragmented,Last fragment,Offset=0 (0x00)
    Time to live: 255 seconds/hops
    IP protocol type: TCP (0x06)
    Checksum: 0x639F
    IP address 172.20.0.1 ->172.20.0.3
    No option
IP Transmission Control Protocol
    Port Telnet ---> 1074
    Sequence Number: 1891894733
    Acknowledgement Number: 39635901
    Header Length(MSB 4 bits): 6 (32-bit word)
    Reserved(LSB 4 bits): 0
    Code: ACK,SYN,
    Window: 2144
    Checksum: 0xEE95
    Urgent Pointer: 0x0000
    TCP Option: 020405B4
    Frame Padding : (2 bytes)
```

Third Part

```
Ethernet Version II
    Address: 00-80-C7-CA-0A-8A --->00-60-09-C3-DF-60
    Ethernet II Protocol Type: IP
Internet Protocol
    Version(MSB 4 bits): 4
    Header length(LSB 4 bits): 5 (32-bit word)
    Service type: Precd=Routine,Delay=Normal,Thrput=Normal,Reli=Normal
    Total length: 40 (Octets)
    Fragment ID: 17415
    Flags: Do not fragment,Last fragment,Offset=0 (0x00)
    Time to live: 32 seconds/hops
    IP protocol type: TCP (0x06)
    Checksum: 0xBE9C
    IP address 172.20.0.3 ->172.20.0.1
    No option
IP Transmission Control Protocol
    Port 1074 ---> Telnet
    Sequence Number: 39635901
    Acknowledgement Number: 1891894734
    Header Length(MSB 4 bits): 5 (32-bit word)
    Reserved(LSB 4 bits): 0
    Code: ACK,
    Window: 8760
    Checksum: 0xEC7A
    Urgent Pointer: 0x0000
```

Answer 1–12.
   a) **Multiple data segments to be sent before the sender requires an acknowledgement.**
   e) **More efficient use of the available bandwidth.**

1. Answers

Answer 1–13.
  a) **Created in large part to satisfy the LAN needs of factories**
  b) **Describes a Token Bus LAN**

Answer 1–14.
  c) **To identify proprietary protocols**

The following is a capture of a proprietary protocol.

Can you identify the vendor? (That's easy.)
Can you identify the protocol? (That's a little harder.)

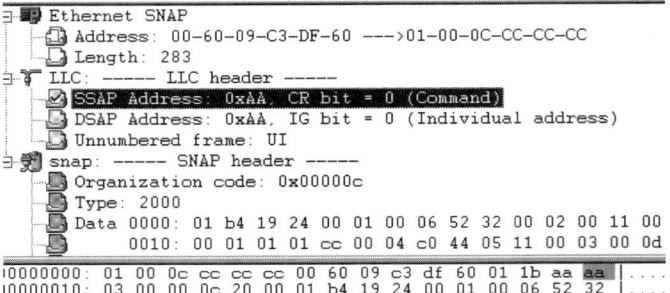

```
Ethernet SNAP
   Address: 00-60-09-C3-DF-60 --->01-00-0C-CC-CC-CC
   Length: 283
LLC: ----- LLC header -----
   SSAP Address: 0xAA, CR bit = 0 (Command)
   DSAP Address: 0xAA, IG bit = 0 (Individual address)
   Unnumbered frame: UI
snap: ----- SNAP header -----
   Organization code: 0x00000c
   Type: 2000
   Data 0000: 01 b4 19 24 00 01 00 06 52 32 00 02 00 11 00
        0010: 00 01 01 01 cc 00 04 c0 44 05 11 00 03 00 0d

0000000: 01 00 0c cc cc cc 00 60 09 c3 df 60 01 1b aa aa |....
0000010: 03 00 00 0c 20 00 01 b4 19 24 00 01 00 06 52 32 |....
```

Answer 1–15.
  b) **Providing code formatting and conversion such as EBCDIC to ASCII**
  c) **Managing encryption of data**

Answer 1–16.
  a) **802.3 is the MAC sub layer.**

The IEEE subdivided the data link layer into two sublayers.

1) MAC Media Access Control, which provides access to the LAN media
2) LLC Logical Link Control, which provides protocols media independent access.

Answer 1–17.
  e) **Network Layer 3**

Answer 1–18.
  a) **Telnet**
  b) **FTP**

TFTP and SNMP use layer 4 UDP.

Answer 1–19.
  b) **To constrain or define the implementation of network functions**

Answer 1–20.
  e) **All of the above**

Answer 1–21.
  b) **Data-Link Layer 2**

Answer 1–22.
  e) **Describes a Metropolitan Area Network (MAN)**

Answer 1–23.
  e) **The Transport layer when TCP is being used**

Answer 1–24.
  i) **LLC sublayer**

Answer 1–25.
  d) **Transport Layer 4**

Answer 1–26.
  e) **161**

Answer 1–27.
  f) **Data Link Layer 2**

Answer 1–28.
  d) **Transport Layer 4**

Answer 1–29.
  b) **Presentation Layer 6**

Answer 1–30.
  d) **69**

Here is a sampling of other port numbers and the application they are associated with. The first eight of these protocols are automatically forwarded through the router by using the "helper-address" command:

Trivial File Transfer (TFTP) (port 69)
Domain Name System (port 53)
IEN-116 Name Server (port 42)
Time service (port 37)
NetBIOS Name Server (port 137)
NetBIOS Datagram Server (port 138)
BootP client (port 68)
BootP server (port 67)
TACACS service (port 49)
Simple Mail Transfer Protocol (port 25)
File Transfer Protocol (port 20)
File Transfer Protocol (port 21)

Simple Network Management Protocol (port 161)

Answer 1–31.
  d) Transport Layer 4

Answer 1–32.
  f) Data Link Layer 2

Answer 1–33.
  c) Network Layer 3

OSI offers both a connectionless and a connection-oriented network layer service. The connectionless service is described in ISO 8473 or CLNP.

The connection-oriented service or CONS is described in ISO 8208

You may also have heard of Connectionless Network Service (CLNS) in conjunction with CLNP. CLNS describes a service provided to the transport layer in which a request to transfer data receives "best effort" delivery.

Chapter Two
CCNA Questions

This chapter contains questions modeled after those that appear on the Cisco Certified Network Associate (CCNA) exam (exam #640-407). Also presented are the answers and explanations for the model questions. The OSI Model questions addressed in Chapter One should also be studied before taking the CCNA exam.

The actual exam consists of 70 questions. There is a 90-minute time limit for taking this exam, and you must score at least 68 percent to pass. The cost for taking the actual exam is $100.00 per attempt. The objectives of this exam are available as a PDF file at

    http://www.cisco.com/warp/public/10/wwtraining/certprog/lan/programs/ccna_course.html.

When using this Study Guide's CD-ROM to study and/or test your knowledge of questions modeled after those you are likely to encounter on a CCNA exam, you will need to select "CCNA" at the *select exam* window and then select either the *study session* or *simulated exam* option.

If you select the *study session* option, you'll be able to designate the category and protocol of the questions you want to review. You will also be able to choose the number of questions you want presented during the *study session*.

When you select the *simulated exam*, the program will present you with a simulated CCNA exam containing 70 questions that address objectives covered by the exam. The program will automatically set a time limit of 90 minutes for you to complete the exam. When you've finished, or the time has elapsed, the program will calculate your score and help you evaluate your performance within the specific categories and protocols covered by the exam.

There are a total universe of over 160 model CCNA exam questions in this reference. Each time you request a CCNA *simulated exam* using the CD-ROM, 70 questions will be chosen randomly from this universe.

Question 2–1. [CxNx] Which of the following are true regarding passwords on a Cisco router?

a) All passwords can be encrypted.
b) All passwords can be entered using the set-up dialogue.
c) A password can be set before a user can enter the privileged mode.
d) A password can be set for individual lines.
e) TACACS or Radius password authentication can be used.

Question 2–2. [RINx] Which one of the following best describes the address 192.16.17.7/30?

a) This is a host address.
b) This is a broadcast address.
c) This is a wire address.
d) This is a subnet address.
e) This is a multi-cast address.

Question 2–3. [CxNx] NVRAM is best described as: (Choose one.)

a) A location to run the active configuration from
b) A location to run the power on diagnostics from
c) A location to store a backup copy of the router configuration file
d) The source of commonly used configuration commands
e) The primary source of the Cisco IOS

Question 2–4. [RxNx] Which of the following routing protocols are Distance Vector protocols: (Choose two.)

a) IP RIP IPX RIP Cisco EIGRP.
b) IP RIP IPX RIP Cisco IGRP.
c) Cisco EIGRP Cisco IGRP IPX RIP.
d) OSPF Cisco IGRP Apple RTMP.
e) IP RIP Apple RTMP Cisco IGRP IPX RIP.

Question 2–5. [RINx] What Cisco feature of RIP will reduce convergence time?

a) Cisco uses full horizons as opposed to split horizons.
b) The hold-down timer is not activated.
c) Event-triggered updates are used.
d) Infinity is 10 instead of 16.
e) There is no Cisco feature to enhance the performance of IP RIP.

Question 2–6. [CxNx] Cisco uses a naming convention to identify frame types. Which four of the following mappings are correct?

a) cisco_II (Cisco name) & Ethernet_II (common name)
b) arpa (Cisco name) & Ethernet_II (common name)
c) sap (Cisco name) & Ethernet_802.3 (common name)
d) sap (Cisco name) & Ethernet_802.2 LLC (common name)
e) Novell Ether (Cisco name) & Ethernet_802.2 LLC (common name)
f) cisco_802 (Cisco name) & Ethernet_802.2 LLC (common name)
g) snap (Cisco name) & Token Ring Snap (common name)
h) snap (Cisco name) & Ethernet_SNAP (common name)

Question 2–7. [CINx] What is the maximum number of IP routing protocols that can be configured on a Cisco router?

a) 1
b) 2
c) 3
d) 4
e) As many as you want.

Question 2–8. [CxNx] Which statements best describe the message-of-the-day banner (motd)? (Choose two.)

a) The motd will be displayed each time a user initially accesses the router.
b) The motd will be displayed only if a user enters into privileged mode on the router.
c) The motd will be displayed at all terminals connected to the router.
d) The motd will be displayed only if the user enters setup mode.
e) The motd will be displayed only to users listed in the motd access list.

Question 2–9. [RINx] IP subnetting provides the ability to: (Choose the best answers.)

a) Conserve major network IP addresses
b) Construct a hierarchical addressing scheme
c) Make networking more complicated so we can make more money
d) Gain access to the intranet
e) None of the above

Question 2–10. [RxNx] Some of the problems associated with Distance Vector protocols are: (Choose four.)

a) The bandwidth consumed by the initial flooding
b) The count-to-infinity problem
c) The time it takes for all routers to converge
d) The frequent sending of LSP announcements to all routers
e) Routing loops
f) The periodic broadcasts of routing tables

Question 2–11. [CxNx] The prompt "Router (config-if)#" indicates that commands entered at this prompt will affect: (Choose one.)

a) All serial interfaces on the router
b) All Ethernet interfaces on the router
c) All interfaces on the router
d) Only the specific interface chosen in the previous command
e) Only the interfaces that are config enabled on this router

Question 2–12. [xINx] What would be the maximum number of hosts that a class C address could support assuming that the default subnet mask was used? (Choose one.)

a) 65534
b) 255
c) 254
d) 16777214
e) 1024
f) 2048

Question 2–13. [CINx] Refer to the following access list. Which line denies 172.16.10.5 to FTP to 172.18.1.1?

```
L1: deny icmp host 172.16.10.5 host 172.18.1.1 echo (4 matches)
L2: deny icmp host 172.16.10.5 host 172.19.10.2 echo
L3: deny udp host 172.16.10.5 host 172.19.10.2 eq snmp
L4: deny udp host 172.16.10.5 host 172.19.18.1 eq snmp
L5: permit ip host 172.16.10.5 host 172.19.10.2
L6: permit tcp any any eq telnet (6 matches)
L7: permit udp any any eq tftp
```

a) L1
b) L2
c) L3
d) L4
e) L5
f) L6
g) L7
h) None of the above

Question 2–14. [RXNx] Which one of the following is true as it pertains to IPX RIP Load Balancing?

a) The parallel paths must have the same hop count.
b) The parallel paths must have the same bandwidth.
c) The parallel paths must have the same clock rate.
d) The parallel paths must have the same tick count and the same hop count.
e) None of the above.

Question 2–15. [RXNx] Which of the following are true of the IPX addressing scheme:

a) The total address length is 24 bits.
b) The address has a network and a host part.
c) It is hierarchical in nature.
d) The host part is the MAC address of the host.
e) All of the above.

Question 2–16. [RINx] The role of RARP in an IP over Ethernet network is best described by: (Choose one.)

a) Is used to resolve a MAC address to an IP address
b) Is used to resolve an Ethernet NET number to Token Ring number
c) Is used to resolve an IP address to a MAC address
d) Is used to resolve Ethernet NET numbers to the major IP network number
e) RARP is used only on Token Ring networks.

Question 2–17. [xxNx] Which of the following statements describe "SAP"? (Choose all that apply.)

a) Service Advertising Protocol, a Novell protocol used to advertise services
b) Service Access Points, used by the OSI model to communicate between adjacent layers
c) Service Appletalk Protocol, used to advertise Appletalk services
d) Service Any Protocol, used to advertise all protocol services
e) All of the above

Question 2–18. [CxNx] Assuming the default Administrative Distance, which one of the following lists the routing protocols from most reliable to least reliable?

a) Static routes, IGRP, OSPF, EIGRP, RIP
b) Static routes, IGRP, OSPF, RIP, EIGRP
c) Static routes, EIGRP, IGRP, OSPF, RIP
d) Static routes, EIGRP, OSPF, IGRP, RIP
e) Static routes, IGRP, EIGRP, OSPF, RIP

Question 2–19. [RANx] Which of the following are true of an Appletalk address?

a) The total address length is 24 bits.
b) The address has a network and a host part.
c) It is hierarchical in nature.
d) The node part is usually the MAC address of the host.
e) All of the above.

Question 2–20. [FxNx] Using the results of the following show command, which statement is true?

```
Router_A#sh frame map
Serial0 (up): ip 65.62.245.2 dlci 100(0x64,0x1840), dynamic,
              broadcast,, status defined, active
```

a) Router_A learned the next hop address of 65.62.245.2 through a static route configuration.
b) Router_A learned the next hop address of 65.62.245.2 through a routing protocol.
c) Router_A learned the next hop address of 65.62.245.2 through ARP.
d) Router_A learned the next hop address of 65.62.245.2 through RARP.
e) Router_A learned the next hop address of 65.62.245.2 through Inverse ARP.

Question 2–21. [FINx] Given the following configuration for Router A, what group of commands will yield the proper configuration for Router F?

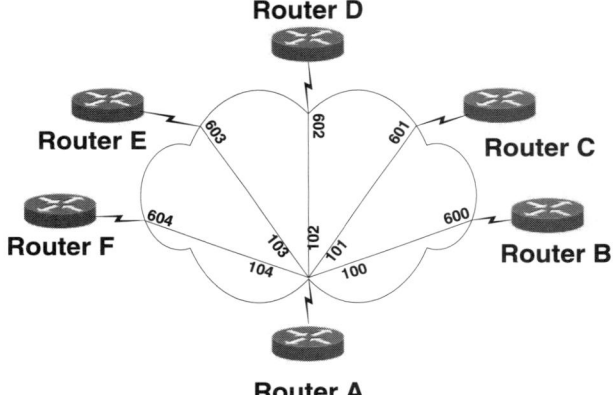

Frame Relay, unlike X.25, does not retransmit. Frame Relay was developed over digital services with a high reliability rate of 99%. If there is an error, Host A must do the retransmission.

The diagram represents a frame-relay network with PVCs configured for a hub and spoke design with corresponding DLCI numbers. Assume all connections are with the serial 0 interface.

```
Router_a(config)#interface s0
Router_a(config-if)#encapsulation frame-relay
Router_a(config-if)#frame-relay lmi-type ansi
Router_a(config-if)#interface s0.1 point-to-point
Router_a(config-if)#ip address 172.16.5.1 255.255.255.0
Router_a(config-if)#frame-relay interface-dlci 100
Router_a(config-if)#interface s0.2 point-to-point
Router_a(config-if)#ip address 172.16.2.1 255.255.255.0
Router_a(config-if)#frame-relay interface-dlci 101
Router_a(config-if)#interface s0.3 point-to-point
Router_a(config-if)#ip address 172.16.3.1 255.255.255.0
Router_a(config-if)#frame-relay interface-dlci 102
Router_a(config-if)#interface s0.4 point-to-point
Router_a(config-if)#ip address 172.16.4.1 255.255.255.0
Router_a(config-if)#frame-relay interface-dlci 103
Router_a(config-if)#interface s0.5 point-to-point
Router_a(config-if)#ip address 172.16.1.1 255.255.255.0
Router_a(config-if)#frame-relay interface-dlci 104
```

I. Command Group I:

```
Router_f(config)#interface s0
Router_f(config-if)#encapsulation frame-relay
Router_f(config-if)#frame-relay lmi-type ansi
Router_f(config-if)#ip address 172.16.1.6 255.255.255.192
Router_f(config-if)#frame-relay map ip 172.16.1.1 604
```

II. Command Group II:

```
Router_f(config)#interface s0
Router_f(config-if)#encapsulation frame-relay
Router_f(config-if)#frame-relay lmi-type ansi
Router_f(config-if)#interface serial 0.1 point-to-point
Router_f(config-if)#ip address 172.16.1.6 255.255.255.0
```

III. Command Group III:

```
Router_f(config)#interface s0
Router_f(config-if)#encapsulation frame-relay ietf
Router_f(config-if)#frame-relay lmi-type cisco
Router_f(config-if)#ip address 172.16.1.6 255.255.255.0
Router_f(config-if)#frame-relay map ip 172.16.1.1 104
```

IV. Command Group IV:

----

2. CCNA

```
Router_f(config)#interface s0
Router_f(config-if)#encapsulation frame-relay
Router_f(config-if)#frame-relay lmi-type ansi
Router_f(config-if)#ip address 172.16.1.6 255.255.255.0
Router_f(config-if)#frame-relay map ip 172.16.1.1 604
```

V. Command Group V:

```
Router_f(config)#interface s0
Router_f(config-if)#encapsulation frame-relay
Router_f(config-if)#frame-relay lmi-type ansi
Router_f(config-if)#interface serial 0.1 point-to-point
Router_f(config-if)#ip address 172.16.1.6 255.255.255.0
Router_f(config-if)#frame-relay map ip 172.16.1.1 104
```

a) Command Group I above
b) Command Group II above
c) Command Group III above
d) Command Group IV above
e) Command Group V above

Question 2–22. [CxNx] Setting the lowest four bits of the configuration register to a value of 0x101 would force the router to: (Choose one.)

a) Boot the IOS from the nearest TFTP server
b) Boot the IOS from NVRAM
c) Load the running configuration from the nearest TFTP server
d) Load the running configuration from ROM
e) Boot the IOS from ROM
f) Examine NVRAM for boot system commands

Question 2–23. [CxNx] Which of the following statements are true as they relate to the configuration line:

```
frame-relay lmi-type cisco
```

a) This line is not necessary.
b) The next hop address may have LMI type cisco configured.
c) The next hop address may have LMI type ansi configured.
d) The next hop address may have LMI type q933a configured.
e) All of the above.
f) None of the above.

Question 2–24. [RINx] The address included in the access-list 1 refers to a: (Refer to the following diagram and configuration.)

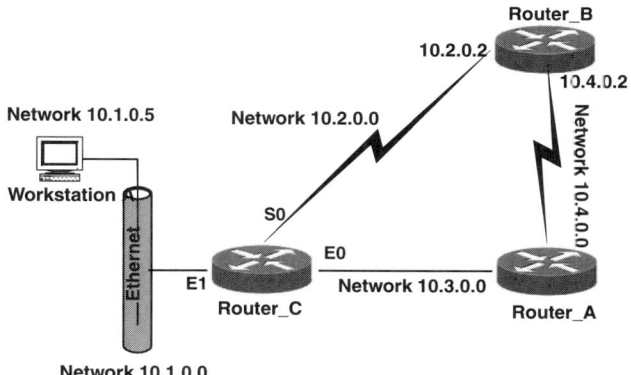

```
Current configuration:
!
version 11.2
!
hostname Router_C
!
interface Ethernet0
 ip address 10.3.0.3 255.255.0.0
!
interface Ethernet1
 ip address 10.1.0.3 255.255.0.0
 ip policy route-map thisway
!
interface Serial0
 ip address 10.2.0.1 255.255.0.0
 clockrate 38400
!
interface Serial1
 no ip address
 shutdown
!
router ospf 100
 network 10.0.0.0 0.255.255.255 area 0
!
no ip classless
access-list 1 permit 10.1.0.5
route-map thisway permit 10
 match ip address 1
 set interface Serial0
!
line con 0
line aux 0
line vty 0 4
 login
```

```
!
end

Router_C#sh ip route
Codes: C - connected, S - static, I - IGRP, R - RIP, M - mobile, B - BGP
       D - EIGRP, EX - EIGRP external, O - OSPF, IA - OSPF inter area
       N1 - OSPF NSSA external type 1, N2 - OSPF NSSA external type 2
       E1 - OSPF external type 1, E2 - OSPF external type 2, E - EGP
       i - IS-IS, L1 - IS-IS level-1, L2 - IS-IS level-2, * - candidate default
       U - per-user static route, o - ODR

Gateway of last resort is not set

     10.0.0.0/16 is subnetted, 3 subnets
C       10.2.0.0 is directly connected, Serial0
C       10.3.0.0 is directly connected, Ethernet0
O       10.4.0.0 [110/74] via 10.3.0.1, 00:00:13, Ethernet0
```

a) Destination host
b) Source host
c) Source or destination host
d) Source subnet
e) Destination subnet

Question 2–25. [CxNx] When in enhanced editing mode, you can move to the beginning of a command line by pressing:

a) <Ctrl><A>
b) <Ctrl><E>
c) <Esc><B>
d) <Esc><F>
e) <Ctrl><B>
f) <Ctrl><F>

Question 2–26. [CxNx] Which of the following are true?

a) The default is to send debug output to the console screen.
b) To view debug output from a telnet session, the "terminal monitor" command must be used.
c) If the "logging buffered" command is used, the debug output would be sent to RAM and can be viewed with the "show log" command
d) If the "no console logging" command were configured, output would be sent to a telnet session.
e) All of the above

Question 2–27. [CxNx] Reverse Address Resolution Protocol (RARP) is the process:

a) Where an IP host resolves its IP address by broadcasting its MAC address to the network, and a RARP server assigns it an IP address.
b) Where an IP host resolves its MAC address by broadcasting to the local network its IP address.
c) Where an IP host tries to resolve the MAC address of a destination by sending a network broadcast. The destination responds to the broadcast with its MAC address.
d) Where an IP host resolves a destination IP address by sending a broadcast on the local network, and the destination host responds with its IP address.
e) There is no such process.

Question 2–28. [CINx] Refer to the following access list. Which is true about the access-list number?

```
L1: deny icmp host 172.16.10.5 host 172.18.1.1 echo (4 matches)
L2: deny icmp host 172.16.10.5 host 172.19.10.2 echo
L3: deny udp host 172.16.10.5 host 172.19.10.2 eq snmp
L4: deny udp host 172.16.10.5 host 172.19.18.1 eq snmp
L5: permit ip host 172.16.10.5 host 172.19.10.2
L6: permit tcp any any eq telnet (6 matches)
L7: permit udp any any eq tftp
```

a) Ranges between 1-99
b) Ranges between 100-199
c) Ranges between 101-199
d) Ranges between 101-200
e) Ranges between 100-200

Question 2–29. [RxNx] Some possible methods for reducing the problems associated with Distance Vector protocols are: (Choose four.)

a) Defining a maximum
b) Using hold-down timers
c) Reducing the maximum size of an LSP
d) Scheduling updates
e) Split Horizon
f) Route poisoning

2. CCNA

Question 2–30. [FINx] Given the following configuration for Router A, what group of commands will yield the proper configuration for Router F?

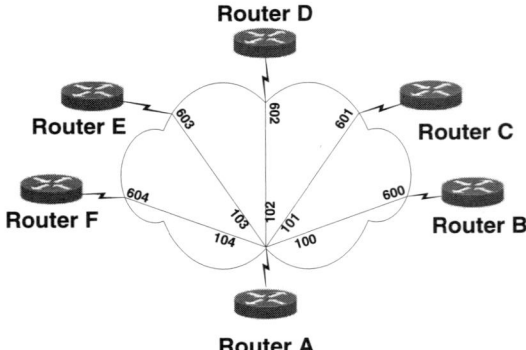

Router D

Router E

Router C

Router F

Router B

Router A

Frame Relay, unlike X.25, does not retransmit. Frame Relay was developed over digital services with a high reliability rate of 99%. If there is an error, Host A must do the retransmission.

The diagram represents a frame-relay network with PVCs configured for a hub and spoke design with corresponding DLCI numbers. Assume all connections are with the serial 0 interface.

```
Router_a(config)#interface s0
Router_a(config-if)#encapsulation frame-relay ietf
Router_a(config-if)#frame-relay lmi-type ansi
Router_a(config-if)#frame-relay map ip 172.16.1.2 100
Router_a(config-if)#frame-relay map ip 172.16.1.3 101
Router_a(config-if)#frame-relay map ip 172.16.1.4 102
Router_a(config-if)#frame-relay map ip 172.16.1.5 103
Router_a(config-if)#frame-relay map ip 172.16.1.6 104
Router_a(config-if)#ip address 172.16.1.1 255.255.255.0
```

I. Command Group I:

```
Router_f(config)#interface s0
Router_f(config-if)#encapsulation frame-relay
Router_f(config-if)#frame-relay lmi-type ansi
Router_f(config-if)#ip address 172.16.1.6 255.255.255.0
Router_f(config-if)#frame-relay map ip 172.16.1.1 104
```

II. Command Group II:

```
Router_f(config)#interface s0
Router_f(config-if)#encapsulation frame-relay
Router_f(config-if)#frame-relay lmi-type ansi
Router_f(config-if)#ip address 172.16.1.6 255.255.255.0
```

```
Router_f(config-if)#frame-relay map ip 172.16.1.1 104 ietⁱ
```

III. Command Group III:

```
Router_f(config)#interface s0
Router_f(config-if)#encapsulation frame-relay
Router_f(config-if)#frame-relay lmi-type ansi
Router_f(config-if)#ip address 172.16.1.6 255.255.255.0
Router_f(config-if)#frame-relay map ip 172.16.1.1 604
```

IV. Command Group IV:

```
Router_f(config)#interface s0
Router_f(config-if)#encapsulation frame-relay
Router_f(config-if)#frame-relay lmi-type ansi
Router_f(config-if)#ip address 172.16.1.6 255.255.255.0
Router_f(config-if)#frame-relay map ip 172.16.1.1 604 ietf
```

V. Command Group V:

```
Router_f(config)#interface s0
Router_f(config-if)#encapsulation frame-relay ietf
Router_f(config-if)#frame-relay lmi-type ansi
Router_f(config-if)#ip address 172.16.1.6 255.255.255.0
Router_f(config-if)#frame-relay map ip 172.16.1.1 104
```

a) Command Group I above
b) Command Group II above
c) Command Group III above
d) Command Group IV above
e) Command Group V above

Question 2–31. [RINx] Given the following address and mask, what would be the broadcast address of the subnet?

172.16.0.125/20

a) 172.16.15.255
b) 172.16.0.255
c) 172.16.255.255
d) 255.255.255.255
e) None of the above

Question 2–32. [RxNx] Split Horizon is a technique for: (Choose the best answer.)

a) Preventing a bridge from sending frames to a network segment that does not contain the destination host
b) Limiting the number of times a frame can loop through a set of routers until it reaches a predetermined maximum
c) Preventing a router from sending an update back to a router it just received the update from.
d) Increasing Time to Convergence.

Question 2–33. [CxNx] A caret symbol (^) inserted into a failed command indicates which of the following. (Choose one.)

a) Numeric data is required for this command.
b) The point in a command where you can simply press return to complete the syntax string.
c) The point in a command where you have entered an incorrect command, keyword or argument.
d) The point in a command where you must enter a required value.
e) This is a normal indicator for any failed command.

Question 2–34. [CxNx] Given the following dialog what is the most logical command that the user should use next?.

```
Router_B#sh art
            ^
% Invalid input detected at '^' marker.
```

a) show art
b) sh ar ?
c) show arap
d) sh ar?
e) Can not be determined

Question 2–35. [xINx] What two protocols would be needed to send a host unreachable message to a source host? (Choose two.)

a) IP
b) ARP
c) FTP
d) ICMP
e) RARP
f) SNMP

Question 2–36. [FxNx] Regarding the following configuration, which of the following are true?

```
Current configuration:
!
version 11.3
no service password-encryption
```

```
!
hostname Router_A
!
enable secret 5 $1$.s1R$iaEqZxLnYJo2QlZi8UNaO0
enable password ccnaprep
!
ipx routing 0010.7b15.bd41
!
interface Tunnel0
 no ip address
 ipx network FAD
 tunnel source Serial0/0
 tunnel destination 65.62.245.2
!
interface Ethernet0/0
 ip address 172.17.10.1 255.255.255.0
 no ip mroute-cache
 ipx network BAD
 no cdp enable
!
interface Serial0/0
 ip address 65.62.245.1 255.255.255.0
 encapsulation frame-relay
 no ip mroute-cache
 frame-relay lmi-type cisco
!
interface TokenRing0/0
 no ip address
 no ip mroute-cache
 shutdown
 ring-speed 16
 no cdp enable
!
interface FastEthernet1/0
 no ip address
 no ip mroute-cache
 shutdown
 no cdp enable
!
ip classless
no cdp run
!
line con 0
 exec-timeout 0 0
line aux 0
line vty 0 4
 password ccieprep
 login
end
```

2. CCNA

a) Since there is no DLCI configured, this configuration will not work.
b) Since there is no frame map statement, this configuration will not work.
c) IP is being tunneled in IPX.
d) The tunnel interface should have an IP address.
e) None of the above.

Question 2–37. [CINx] Which of the following commands could be used to view the configured access list 150?

a) show access-group
b) show ip interface
c) show interface
d) show access-list
e) show access-list 150

Question 2–38. [RxNx] Which of the following would NOT appear in a routing table?

a) Next hop address
b) Interface Port references
c) MAC address
d) Network Address
e) Metrics

Question 2–39. [CxNx] A caret symbol (^) inserted into a failed command indicates which of the following. (Choose one.)

a) That numeric data is required for this command
b) The point in a command where you can simply press return to complete the syntax string
c) The point in a command where you have entered an incorrect command, keyword or argument
d) The point in a command where you must enter a required value
e) This is a normal indicator for any failed command.

Question 2–40. [CxNx] What passwords cannot be set in the setup dialogue?

a) User mode password
b) Privilege mode password
c) Virtual terminal mode(vty) password
d) Secret enable password
e) All passwords can be set using the setup dialogue.

Question 2–41. [RxNx] Which statement is NOT true about link state protocols:

a) Link state advertisements are sent to all routers in an area.
b) Each router executes the SPF algorithm.
c) Link state routers keep a topological database of the network.
d) Link state routers include the originating router's routing table.
e) Link state routers know of possible alternate paths to a particular network.

Question 2–42. [RINx] Which should be the subnet mask for a class C address if 58 hosts are required?

a) 255.255.255.192
b) 255.255.192.0
c) 0.0.0.192
d) 255.255.255.62
e) None of the above

Question 2–43. [xxNx] What is the result of the command?

```
access-list 101 permit tcp any 172.16.0.0 0.0.255.255 established
```

a) Telnet sessions will be permitted regardless of the source address.
b) Telnet sessions will be denied regardless of the source address.
c) Telnet sessions will be denied if initiated from any address other than 172.16.0.0 network.
d) Telnet sessions will be permitted to the 172.16.0.0 network only.
e) Telnet sessions will be denied to the 172.16.0.0 network only.

Question 2–44. [RXNx] The metric used by IPX RIP is:

a) Hops
b) Ticks
c) Cost
d) Ticks and hops
e) None of the above.

Question 2–45. [RxNx] In order to communicate throughout an internetwork, which of the following are required. (Choose two.)

a) The use of a routable protocol such as NetBEUI or LAT
b) A hierarchical naming scheme server such as DNS
c) A host file at each communicating device
d) A two part network addressing scheme such as Network/Host
e) The use of a routable protocol such as IP or IPX
f) The use of a routable protocol such as TCP or IPX

Question 2–46. [SxNx] Name three reasons why VLAN's should be created.

a) Moves, Adds and Changes are made simpler.
b) There is less administrative overhead.
c) The switch can route between VLANS.
d) It limits broadcasts domains.
e) The router can switch faster.

2. CCNA

Question 2–47. [CxNx] Which of the following are methods for configuring a Cisco Router?

a) copying a configuration file from a TFTP server
b) configuring manually from the command line interface (CLI)
c) downloading a configuration file from an RCP server
d) using the copy and paste feature of a multitasking operating system
e) all of the above

Question 2–48. [CxNx] What is stored in NVRAM of a Cisco Router?

a) Stores a copy of the Cisco IOS for when the router boots.
b) Stores a configuration file for when the router boots.
c) Stores the routing tables used by the router to make forwarding decisions.
d) Stores the running version of the configuration file.
e) Cisco Routers do not have NVRAM.

Question 2–49. [CxNx] What would be the proper command to set a bandwidth of 56K for a serial interface? (Choose one.)

a) Router# bandwidth 56000
b) Router (config) #bandwidth 56000
c) Router (config-if) #bandwidth 56,000
d) Router (config-if) #bandwidth 56
e) Router (config-if) #bandwidth T1

Question 2–50. [RXNx] An IPX Layer 3 address has two components. What are they? (Choose the best answers.)

a) Mask
b) Network portion
c) Internal network
d) MAC address
e) Host portion

Question 2–51. [ExNx] If Host A sends a packet to Host B over ethernet, and Host B is not active:

a) The packet will time out.
b) The packet will be removed by Host A.
c) The NVRAM of Host B will remove the packet.
d) The packet will "die" when it reaches the terminator.
e) The packet will be removed by the token monitor.

Question 2–52. [CINx] Refer to the following access list. The network would be best served if this list was placed:

```
L1: deny icmp host 172.16.10.5 host 172.18.1.1 echo (4 matches)
L2: deny icmp host 172.16.10.5 host 172.19.10.2 echo
L3: deny udp host 172.16.10.5 host 172.19.10.2 eq snmp
L4: deny udp host 172.16.10.5 host 172.19.18.1 eq snmp
L5: permit ip host 172.16.10.5 host 172.19.10.2
L6: permit tcp any any eq telnet (6 matches)
L7: permit udp any any eq tftp
```

a) Close to 172.16.10.5
b) Close to 172.18.1.1
c) Close to 172.19.10.2
d) It does not matter where this list is placed.
e) Can not determined from information given

Question 2–53. [CxNx] Which is generally true of the location of access-lists? (Choose all that apply.)

a) Standard lists will most likely be placed close to the destination.
b) Standard lists will most likely be placed close to the source.
c) Extended lists will most likely be placed close to the destination.
d) Extended lists will most likely be placed close to the source.
e) It does not matter.

Question 2–54. [xINx] What would the class and major network be for the IP address 191.12.45.254? (Choose one.)

a) Class B, 191.12.45.0
b) Class B, 191.12.0.0
c) Class C, 191.12.45.0
d) Class C, 191.12.0.0
e) Class C, 255.255.255.0
f) Class B, 255.255.0.0

Question 2–55. [CxNx] Assume a 2514 has all interfaces configured with IP RIP, Appletalk RTMP, and IPX RIP. How many layer 3 addresses will be configured?

a) 4
b) 6
c) 8
d) 3
e) 12

2. CCNA

Question 2–56. [CxNx] A prompt such as "Router_A>" indicates you are in what mode? (Choose one.)

a) Privileged mode
b) Session mode
c) Console mode
d) User mode
e) Setup mode
f) Configuration mode

Question 2–57. [CxNx] Which answer describes the possible locations from which the operating system would be loaded at system initialization? (Choose one.)

a) NVRAM, TFTP Server, ROM
b) NVRAM, TFTP Server, RAM
c) TFTP Server, FTP Server, ROM
d) Flash memory, TFTP Server, ROM
e) NVRAM, Flash memory

Question 2–58. [xINx] A Telnet session to a remote host would be addressed to what port number at the remote host? (Choose one.)

a) UDP port 53
b) TCP port 53
c) UDP port 21
d) TCP port 21
e) UDP port 161
f) TCP port 23

Question 2–59. [RxNx] Which of the following statements are true about hold down timers. (Choose three.)

a) A hold-down timer will be released if the router receives an update indicating a better route.
b) A hold-down timer will not be released if the router receives an update indicating a poorer route.
c) A hold-down timer will not be released if the router receives an update indicating a better route.
d) Hold-down times are configurable by the administrator.
e) The purpose of a hold-down timer is to smooth out updates on a congested network.

Question 2–60. [RINx] Host 192.16.10.30/27 is connected to what subnet?

a) 192.16.10.0
b) 192.16.10.27
c) 192.16.10.16
d) 192.16.10.32
e) 192.16.10.28

Question 2–61. [CxNx] What is the standard encapsulation method used by Cisco routers for the Internet Protocol (IP) on its Ethernet interfaces?

 a) SNAP
 b) ARPA
 c) NOVELL-ETHER
 d) DARPA
 e) Ethernet_802.3

Question 2–62. [RINx] An IP address is made up of what three components?

 a) Major network address
 b) Mask
 c) Subnet address
 d) Host address
 e) MAC address

Question 2–63. [RINx] At what layer of the OSI model does ICMP operate?

 a) The Application layer
 b) The Data link layer
 c) The Physical layer
 d) The Network layer
 e) The Transport layer
 f) The Session layer

Question 2–64. [RxNx] Select all the characteristics of a Distance Vector routing protocol. (Choose two.)

 a) All routers construct an overall view of the internetwork from their perspective.
 b) Routers broadcast their routing table at periodic intervals.
 c) Routers broadcast only the changes to the internetwork that they have become aware of.
 d) Routers discover the best path to destination networks based on accumulated metrics from each neighbor.
 e) During the initial discovery, all routers send LSPs to all other routers.
 f) Updates to the routing tables are usually triggered by topology changes.

Question 2–65. [BxNx] What is the purpose of spanning tree?

 a) Prevents bridging loops
 b) Prevents routing loops
 c) Cisco supported feature that can be used per VLAN
 d) Can be initiated on any routed interface
 e) All of the above

Question 2–66. [FINx] Given the following configuration for Router A, what group of commands will yield the proper configuration for Router F?

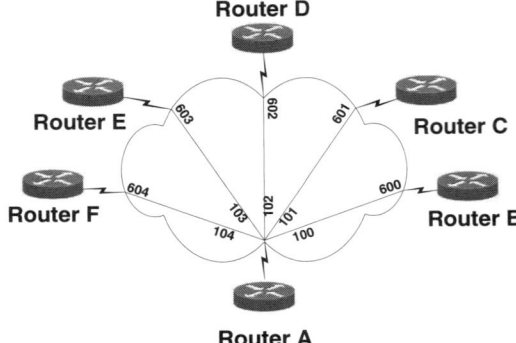

Router D

Router E

Router C

Router F

Router B

Router A

Frame Relay, unlike X.25, does not retransmit. Frame Relay was developed over digital services with a high reliability rate of 99%. If there is an error, Host A must do the retransmission.

The diagram represents a frame-relay network with PVCs configured for a hub and spoke design with corresponding DLCI numbers. Assume all connections are with the serial 0 interface.

```
Router_a(config)#interface s0
Router_a(config-if)#encapsulation frame-relay
Router_a(config-if)#frame-relay lmi-type cisco
Router_a(config-if)#frame-relay map ip 172.16.1.2 100 ietf
Router_a(config-if)#frame-relay map ip 172.16.1.3 101 ietf
Router_a(config-if)#frame-relay map ip 172.16.1.4 102 ietf
Router_a(config-if)#frame-relay map ip 172.16.1.5 103 ietf
Router_a(config-if)#frame-relay map ip 172.16.1.6 104 ietf
Router_a(config-if)#ip address 172.16.1.1 255.255.255.0
```

I. Command Group I:

```
Router_f(config)#interface s0
Router_f(config-if)#encapsulation frame-relay ietf
Router_f(config-if)#frame-relay lmi-type ansi
Router_f(config-if)#ip address 172.16.1.6 255.255.255.0
Router_f(config-if)#frame-relay map ip 172.16.1.1 604
```

II. Command Group II:

```
Router_f(config)#interface s0
Router_f(config-if)#encapsulation frame-relay
Router_f(config-if)#frame-relay lmi-type ansi
```

```
Router_f(config-if)#ip address 172.16.1.6 255.255.255.0
Router_f(config-if)#frame-relay map ip 172.16.1.1 104 ietf
```

III. Command Group III:

```
Router_f(config)#interface s0
Router_f(config-if)#encapsulation frame-relay ietf
Router_f(config-if)#frame-relay lmi-type ansi
Router_f(config-if)#ip address 172.16.1.6 255.255.255.0
Router_f(config-if)#frame-relay map ip 172.16.1.1 104
```

IV. Command Group IV:

```
Router_f(config)#interface s0
Router_f(config-if)#encapsulation frame-relay
Router_f(config-if)#frame-relay lmi-type ansi
Router_f(config-if)#ip address 172.16.1.6 255.255.255.0
Router_f(config-if)#frame-relay map ip 172.16.1.1 604
```

V. Command Group V:

```
Router_f(config)#interface s0
Router_f(config-if)#encapsulation frame-relay ietf
Router_f(config-if)#frame-relay lmi-type ansi
Router_f(config-if)#ip address 172.16.1.6 255.255.255.0
Router_f(config-if)#frame-relay map ip 172.16.1.1 104
```

a) Command Group I above
b) Command Group II above
c) Command Group III above
d) Command Group IV above
e) Command Group V above

Question 2–67. [CxNx] Under what conditions will a router enter setup mode? (Choose one.)

a) If no configuration file can be found
b) If the present configuration file is newer than the one attempting to load
c) If the present configuration file is older than the one attempting to load
d) By manually entering setup mode from the user prompt
e) By manually entering setup mode from the configuration load prompt
f) By manually entering setup mode from the system load prompt

Question 2–68. [RxNx] On an IP over Ethernet network, when one host sends data to another host, which statement is most correct? (Choose one.)

a) Actual communication is between IP addresses.
b) Actual communication is from IP address on the sender to MAC address on the receiver.
c) Actual communication is between physical addresses.
d) Actual communication is from MAC address on the sender to IP address on the receiver.
e) On an Ethernet network, all communication is via either broadcasts or multicasts.

Question 2–69. [CINx] Which command(s) will display the host file?

a) show ip hosts
b) show ip host
c) show host
d) sh hosts
e) display host

Question 2–70. [xINx] TCP "source" port number(s): (Choose the one that best describes.)

a) Depends on the application being accessed on the destination host.
b) Depends on the application running on the source host.
c) Are usually assigned by the source host, and are typically some number greater than 1023.
d) Are assigned by the source host and are usually one of the "well known" port numbers.
e) Must be negotiated by the sender and receiver during session setup.

Question 2–71. [RxNx] Which of the following are benefits of segmenting with routers?

a) Increases bandwidth available to nodes
b) Controls broadcasts
c) Increases the size of the frames
d) Reduces the number of collisions
e) None of the above

Question 2–72. [FxNx] Assuming the configuration below, which of the following commands can be used to verify Frame Relay operation: (Choose three.)

```
interface Serial0/0
 ip address 172.16.10.1 255.255.255.0
 encapsulation frame-relay
 no ip mroute-cache
 cdp enable
 frame-relay interface-dlci 200
 frame-relay lmi-type cisco
```

a) show frame-dlci
b) show fr ma
c) show frame-relay lmi
d) show frame int s0/0
e) show interface serial 0/0

Question 2–73. [xxNx] Which of the following are true of standard half-duplex Ethernet circuitry?

a) It is alternate one-way communication.
b) The receive (RX) is wired directly to the transmit (TX) of the remote station.
c) The transmit (TX) is wired directly to the receive (RX) of the remote station.
d) Collisions are not possible.
e) Both stations can transmit simultaneously.

Question 2–74. [RINx] Given the IP address of 193.243.12.43 and a subnet mask of 255.255.255.128, what is the subnet address?

a) 194.243.12.32
b) 193.243.0.0
c) 194.243.12.43
d) 193.243.12.128
e) None of the above.

Question 2–75. [CXNx] Which of the following are true of the following configuration statement? (Choose 2.)

```
Router_A(config)#access-list 950 permit -1 log
```

a) This is an IPX access list.
b) This is an IP extended access list.
c) This is an appletalk access-list.
d) All matches will be logged.
e) This is not a legal command.

Question 2–76. [CxNx] After the configuration command is used, when does it become effective?

a) Immediately
b) After the router is rebooted
c) After you exit the configuration mode
d) Depends on the change that is made
e) All of the above

Question 2–77. [RINx] Refer to the information below. According to the routing table of Router_C, the best path to Network 10.4.0.0 is out:

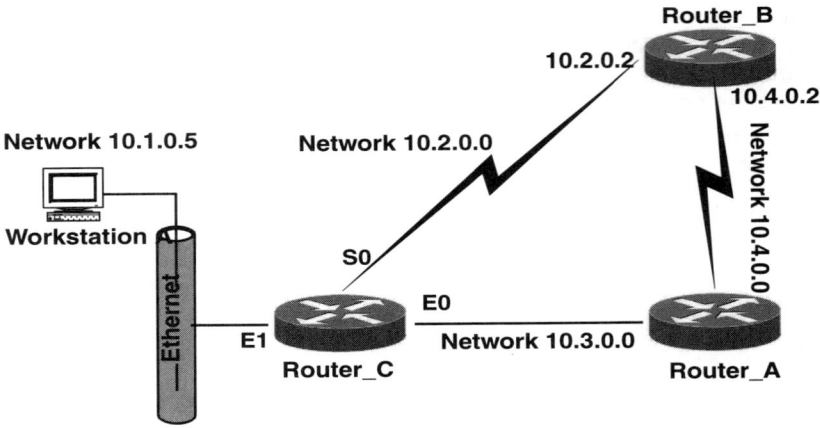

```
Current configuration:
!
version 11.2
!
hostname Router_C
!
interface Ethernet0
 ip address 10.3.0.3 255.255.0.0
!
interface Ethernet1
 ip address 10.1.0.3 255.255.0.0
 ip policy route-map thisway
!
interface Serial0
 ip address 10.2.0.1 255.255.0.0
 clockrate 38400
!
interface Serial1
 no ip address
 shutdown
!
router ospf 100
 network 10.0.0.0 0.255.255.255 area 0
!
no ip classless
access-list 1 permit 10.1.0.5
route-map thisway permit 10
 match ip address 1
 set interface Serial0
!
line con 0
line aux 0
line vty 0 4
```

```
  login
  !
end

Router_C#sh ip route
Codes: C - connected, S - static, I - IGRP, R - RIP, M - mobile, B - BGP
       D - EIGRP, EX - EIGRP external, O - OSPF, IA - OSPF inter area
       N1 - OSPF NSSA external type 1, N2 - OSPF NSSA external type 2
       E1 - OSPF external type 1, E2 - OSPF external type 2, E - EGP
       i - IS-IS, L1 - IS-IS level-1, L2 - IS-IS level-2, * - candidate default
       U - per-user static route, o - ODR

Gateway of last resort is not set

     10.0.0.0/16 is subnetted, 3 subnets
C        10.2.0.0 is directly connected, Serial0
C        10.3.0.0 is directly connected, Ethernet0
O        10.4.0.0 [110/74] via 10.3.0.1, 00:00:13, Ethernet0
```

a) E0
b) E1
c) S0
d) E0 or S0
e) Can't be determined.

Question 2–78. [RxNx] What commands will list all protocols that are currently being routed? (Choose all that apply.)

a) show ip protocol
b) show protocol
c) show run
d) show start
e) All of the above

Question 2–79. [CxNx] What command correctly displays the running configuration file?

a) show configuration
b) show running-configuration file
c) show active-configuration file
d) write terminal
e) all of the above

Question 2–80. [xINx] The size of a window in a TCP segment establishes what? (Choose one.)

a) The maximum number of bytes that a single frame may not exceed
b) The allowable bandwidth for this TCP session
c) The number of octets that the receiver must be willing to accept
d) The number of 32-bit words in the header
e) The number of octets that the sender is willing to accept

Question 2–81. [CxNx] Where are power on diagnostics for the router stored? (Choose one.)

a) In Flash memory
b) In RAM
c) In ROM
d) In ROM or Flash memory
e) In NVRAM

Question 2–82. [RINx] How many subnets are possible with a Class C address and a subnet mask of 255.255.255.252?

a) 32
b) 30
c) 60
d) 62
e) 4

Question 2–83. [CxNx] Where is the active configuration file of the router stored? Choose one.

a) In NVRAM
b) In RAM
c) In ROM
d) In Flash memory
e) In ROM or RAM

Question 2–84. [CxNx] The line console 0 command could be used to: (Choose one.)

a) Establish a telnet session with a remote router.
b) Set a login password on the console terminal.
c) Set a login password for an incoming telnet session.
d) Set a password to restrict access to privileged EXEC mode.
e) Establish a session on the console terminal.

Question 2–85. [CxNx] Which commands will display the IP addresses of all interfaces on a Cisco router? (Choose all that apply.)

a) show ip route
b) show ip address
c) show ip interface
d) show interface
e) display ip addresses

Question 2–86. [CxNx] Which command would be used to establish a password for the privileged EXEC mode? (Choose one.)

a) line console 0
b) line vty 0 4
c) set enable
d) set enable-password
e) enable-password

Question 2–87. [RxNx] Which of the following is NOT a ROUTING protocol:

a) OSPF
b) RIP
c) IPX
d) EIGRP
e) NLSP

Question 2–88. [RINx] What is the purpose of TTL?

a) To prevent routing loops
b) To prevent Timely Telnet Losses
c) To remind engineers that life is short
d) To prevent IP datagrams from living long and fruitful lives
e) To prevent IP datagrams that are caught in a routing loop from traversing the network forever.

Question 2–89. [RXNx] The Serial 0/0 IPX encapsulation of Router_A is: (Refer to the following diagram and configurations.)

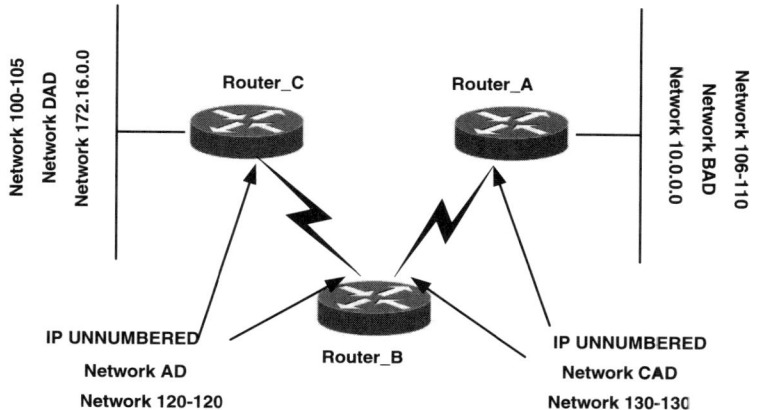

```
Router_C#sh run
Building configuration...

Current configuration:
!
version 11.2
!
hostname Router_C
!
!
appletalk routing
ipx routing 0060.09c3.df60
!
interface Ethernet0
 ip address 172.16.1.1 255.255.255.0
```

```
 appletalk cable-range 100-105 103.243
 appletalk zone right
 ipx network DAD
!
interface Ethernet1
 no ip address
 shutdown
!
interface Serial0
 ip unnumbered Ethernet0
 appletalk cable-range 120-120 120.17
 appletalk zone left
 ipx network AD
 clockrate 56000
!
interface Serial1
 no ip address
 shutdown
!
router igrp 100
 network 172.16.0.0
!
no ip classless
!!
line con 0
line aux 0
line vty 0 4
 login
!
end

Router_B#sh run
Building configuration...

Current configuration:
!
version 11.3
no service password-encryption
!
hostname Router_B
!
!
appletalk routing
ipx routing 0007.7816.fe54
!
interface Loopback0
 ip address 172.17.1.1 255.255.255.0
!
interface Serial0
 ip unnumbered Loopback0
 no ip mroute-cache
 appletalk cable-range 130-130 130.81
 appletalk zone right
 ipx network CAD
```

```
 no fair-queue
!
interface Serial1
 ip unnumbered Loopback0
 appletalk cable-range 120-120 120.125
 appletalk zone left
 ipx network AD
!
interface Serial2
 no ip address
 shutdown
!
interface Serial3
 no ip address
 shutdown
!
interface TokenRing0
 no ip address
 shutdown
!
interface BRI0
 no ip address
 shutdown
!
router igrp 100
 network 172.17.0.0
!
ip classless
!
!
!
!
line con 0
line aux 0
line vty 0 4
 login
!
end

Router_A#sh run
Building configuration...

Current configuration:
!
version 11.3
no service password-encryption
!
hostname Router_A
!
!
appletalk routing
ipx routing 0010.7b15.bd41
!
```

```
interface Ethernet0/0
 ip address 10.1.1.1 255.255.255.0
 appletalk cable-range 106-110 106.17
 appletalk zone left
 ipx network BAD
!
interface Serial0/0
 ip unnumbered Ethernet0/0
 no ip mroute-cache
 appletalk cable-range 130-130 130.37
 appletalk zone right
 ipx network CAD
 clockrate 56000
!
interface TokenRing0/0
 no ip address
 shutdown
 ring-speed 16
!
interface FastEthernet1/0
 no ip address
 shutdown
!
router igrp 100
 network 10.0.0.0
!
ip classless
!!
line con 0
line aux 0
line vty 0 4
 login
!
end
```

a) Novell-ether
b) SAP
c) ARPA
d) SNAP
e) Can not be determined
f) HDLC

Question 2–90. [CxNx] Which of the following ASICs is responsible for Fast EtherChannel?

a) EARL
b) SAINT
c) SAGE
d) EBC
e) SAMBA

Question 2–91. [CxNx] Which of the following commands will display the contents of the IP ARP cache of your Cisco router?

a) show ip arp cache
b) show ip route
c) show ip arp
d) show arp
e) There is no way to display the ARP cache.

Question 2–92. [RxNx] Some problems associated with Link State protocols are: (Choose two.)

a) The size of routing table broadcasts
b) The amount of memory and processing required
c) The count-to-infinity problem
d) The longer time for convergence as compared to Distance Vector protocols
e) The bandwidth consumed by the initial link state flood

Question 2–93. [xINx] In a TCP acknowledgment, the ack number refers to: (Choose one.)

a) A sequential number beginning with 1, and incremented by 1 with each exchange, that identifies this exchange of packets as being complete
b) The number of the packet expected next
c) The number of the packet expected next, plus 1
d) A number agreed upon at session establishment, which will be used by the receiver to indicate a successful exchange of packets
e) TCP does not use acknowledgments.

Question 2–94. [xINx] Which one of the following masks has the nickname of the "serial mask"?

a) 255.255.255.192
b) 255.255.255.224
c) 255.255.255.240
d) 255.255.255.248
e) 255.255.255.252

Question 2–95. [RINx] What is the range of IP addresses that have been allocated for IP Multicasting?

a) 224.0.0.0 to 255.0.0.0
b) 224.0.0.0 to 240.0.0.0
c) 240.0.0.0 to 255.255.255.254
d) 224.0.0.0 to 239.255.255.255
e) None of the above

Question 2–96. [CxNx] If the access-group command is configured on an interface and there is no access-list created which of the following is most correct?

a) An error message will appear.
b) The command will be executed and deny all traffic out.
c) The command will be executed and permit all traffic out.
d) The command will be executed and permit all traffic in and out.
e) The command will be executed and deny all traffic in and out.

Question 2–97. [RxNx] Which of the following is most correct?

a) IP is to TCP as IPX is to SPX.
b) RTMP is to Appletalk as IP RIP is to IP.
c) NLSP is to IPX as OSPF is to IP.
d) No other choices are correct

Question 2–98. [RINx] On an IP over Token Ring network, which answer best describes the role of ARP? (Choose one.)

a) ARP is used to map an IP address to a MAC address.
b) ARP is used to map Ring numbers to IP addresses.
c) ARP is used to map Ring numbers to MAC addresses of the hosts on that ring.
d) ARP is used to map a MAC address to an IP address.
e) ARP is not used on Token Ring networks.

Question 2–99. [xINx] What statement about the IP address 0.10.10.10 is most correct? (Choose one.)

a) This a Class A address.
b) This a reserved private address.
c) For a Class A address, indicates "this route."
d) This is not a legal address.
e) This address can only be used for a network that is not exposed to the Internet.

Question 2–100. [RxNx] What routing protocols are configured? (Refer to the following diagram and configurations.)

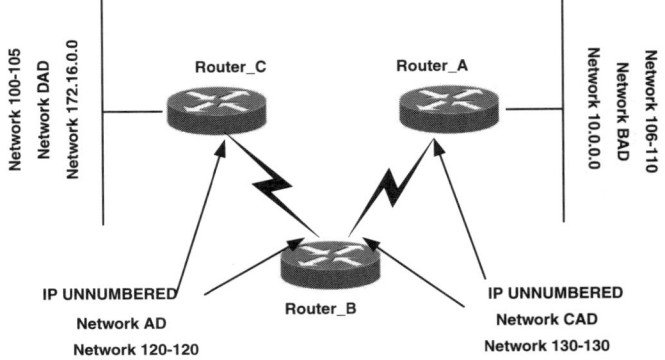

```
Router_C#sh run
Building configuration...

Current configuration:
!
version 11.2
!
hostname Router_C
!
!
appletalk routing
ipx routing 0060.09c3.df60
!
interface Ethernet0
 ip address 172.16.1.1 255.255.255.0
 appletalk cable-range 100-105 103.243
 appletalk zone right
 ipx network DAD
!
interface Ethernet1
 no ip address
 shutdown
!
interface Serial0
 ip unnumbered Ethernet0
 appletalk cable-range 120-120 120.17
 appletalk zone left
 ipx network AD
 clockrate 56000
!
interface Serial1
 no ip address
 shutdown
!
router igrp 100
 network 172.16.0.0
!
no ip classless
!!
line con 0
line aux 0
line vty 0 4
 login
!
end

Router_B#sh run
Building configuration...

Current configuration:
!
version 11.3
```

```
no service password-encryption
!
hostname Router_B
!
!
appletalk routing
ipx routing 0007.7816.fe54
!
interface Loopback0
 ip address 172.17.1.1 255.255.255.0
!
interface Serial0
 ip unnumbered Loopback0
 no ip mroute-cache
 appletalk cable-range 130-130 130.81
 appletalk zone right
 ipx network CAD
 no fair-queue
!
interface Serial1
 ip unnumbered Loopback0
 appletalk cable-range 120-120 120.125
 appletalk zone left
 ipx network AD
!
interface Serial2
 no ip address
 shutdown
!
interface Serial3
 no ip address
 shutdown
!
interface TokenRing0
 no ip address
 shutdown
!
interface BRI0
 no ip address
 shutdown
!
router igrp 100
 network 172.17.0.0
!
ip classless
!
!
!
!
!
line con 0
line aux 0
line vty 0 4
 login
```

```
 !
end

Router_A#sh run
Building configuration...

Current configuration:
 !
version 11.3
no service password-encryption
 !
hostname Router_A
 !
 !
appletalk routing
ipx routing 0010.7b15.bd41
 !
interface Ethernet0/0
 ip address 10.1.1.1 255.255.255.0
 appletalk cable-range 106-110 106.17
 appletalk zone left
 ipx network BAD
 !
interface Serial0/0
 ip unnumbered Ethernet0/0
 no ip mroute-cache
 appletalk cable-range 130-130 130.37
 appletalk zone right
 ipx network CAD
 clockrate 56000
 !
interface TokenRing0/0
 no ip address
 shutdown
 ring-speed 16
 !
interface FastEthernet1/0
 no ip address
 shutdown
 !
router igrp 100
 network 10.0.0.0
 !
ip classless
 !!
line con 0
line aux 0
line vty 0 4
 login
 !
end
```

a) EIGRP, IGRP, RIP
b) IGRP RTMP IPX NLSP
c) IPX RIP, IGRP, RTMP
d) EIGRP, RTMP, IPX RIP
e) IPX RIP, IGRP

Question 2–101. [xINx] Which of the following would most likely use the protocol UDP? (Choose four.)

a) DNS
b) FTP
c) TFTP
d) TELNET
e) SNMP
f) NFS
g) SMTP

Question 2–102. [RINx] Which statements about IP numbers are correct? (Choose four.)

a) An IP number can be used to identify a ring in a Token Ring network.
b) An IP number can be used to identify a serial interface in a router.
c) An IP number can be used to identify a logical Ethernet network.
d) An IP address must be unique only on the logical network where it exists.
e) All bits of an IP number are assigned by InterNIC and may not be modified.
f) An IP address may be 8, 16, 24, or 32 bits long depending upon class.
g) An IP number can be used to identify a Host on a remote logical network.

Question 2–103. [CxNx] To enter global configuration mode from the console for the local router, you would enter which command? (Choose one.)

a) "configure terminal" from the user prompt
b) "configure monitor" from the privileged prompt
c) "configure terminal" from the privileged prompt
d) "configure monitor" from the user prompt
e) "configure running configuration" from the privileged prompt

Question 2–104. [CxNx] What is the default route on an IP network? (Choose one.)

a) This is the route that will be chosen first by IP for delivery of a datagram.
b) The address of the nearest downstream neighbor in a Token ring network.
c) At the router, it is the route used to direct frames for which the next hop has not been explicitly listed in the routing table.
d) Any static route listing in a routing table.
e) When all conditions are equal, the best route for delivery of IP datagrams.

Question 2–105. [xINx] The Class addresses that an administrator would most likely assign to a host are: (Choose one.)

a) Class A and B addresses only
b) Class A, B, C and D addresses
c) Class A, B, C, D and E addresses
d) Class A, B, and C addresses
e) None of the above.

Question 2–106. [SxNx] The Catalyst 5000 uses which switching mode?

a) Cut-through
b) Store and forward
c) Fast switching
d) Choice a and b
e) Choice a and c

Question 2–107. [RxNx] Which of the following are benefits of a Link-State routing protocol? (Choose all that apply.)

a) Allows the use of a more robust addressing scheme.
b) Allows for a larger scalable network
c) Reduces convergence time
d) Allows "supernetting"
e) All of the above.

Question 2–108. [CINx] Which of the following are true about the configuration line below?

```
Router_A(config)#ip route 172.17.10.0 255.255.255.0 172.16.10.1 255
```

a) If Router_A receives a packet with a destination IP subnet address of 172.17.10.0, the packet will be placed on the 172.16.10.0 wire.
b) If Router_A receives a packet with a destination IP subnet address of 172.16.10.1, the packet will be sent to 172.17.10.0.
c) If Router_A receives a packet with a destination IP subnet address of 172.17.10.0, the packet will be sent to 172.16.10.1 (if there is no dynamic entry in the routing table).
d) 255 is the cost to get to the 172.16.10.0 network.
e) 255 is the Administrative Distance (AD).

2. CCNA

Question 2–109. [CxNx] Which of the following explains the correct definition of administrative distance as it pertains to Cisco's IOS?

a) The process by which routers select an administrator for an autonomous system.
b) The process where a router will select the best path to a destination network.
c) The process where a router will distance itself from other routers due to its lack of administrative experience.
d) The process where a router will prioritize routing protocols so that, in the event two routing protocols have conflicting next hop addresses, the routing protocol with the lowest administrative distance will take priority.
e) The process where a router will prioritize routing protocols so that in the event two routing protocols have conflicting next hop addresses, the routing protocol with the highest administrative distance will take priority.

Question 2–110. [CxNx] If the command "show cdp nei det" were entered at Router_B, which of the following would be true? (Choose the best answers.)

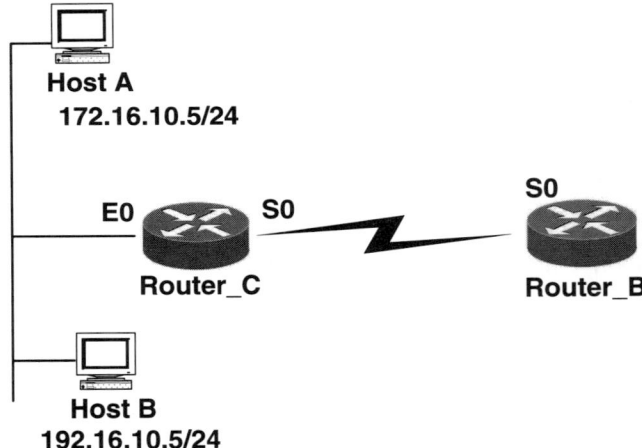

a) This is an illegal command. An error would occur.
b) All the addresses of Router_C would be listed.
c) The serial 0 address of Router_C would be listed.
d) No secondary IP address information would be listed.
e) None of the above.

Question 2–111. [FxNx] BECN and FECN are:

a) Used to provide keepalives in a Frame Relay environment
b) Used to provide error checking in a Frame Relay environment
c) Used to provide congestion information in a Frame Relay environment
d) Used to provide flow control parameters in a Frame Relay environment
e) BECN and FECN are not used in a Frame Relay environment.

Question 2–112. [FINx] Given the following configuration for Router A, what group of commands will yield the proper configuration for Router F?

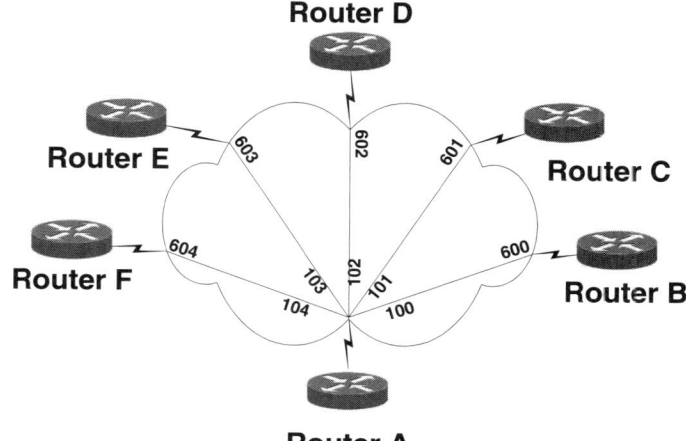

Router D

Router E

Router C

Router F

Router B

Router A

Frame Relay, unlike X.25, does not retransmit. Frame Relay was developed over digital services with a high reliability rate of 99%. If there is an error, Host A must do the retransmission.

The diagram represents a frame-relay network with PVC's configured for a hub and spoke design with corresponding DLCI numbers. Assume all connections are with the serial 0 interface.

```
Router_a(config)#interface s0
Router_a(config-if)#encapsulation frame-relay
Router_a(config-if)#frame-relay lmi-type ansi
Router_a(config-if)#frame-relay map ip 172.16.1.2 100
Router_a(config-if)#frame-relay map ip 172.16.1.3 101
Router_a(config-if)#frame-relay map ip 172.16.1.4 102
Router_a(config-if)#frame-relay map ip 172.16.1.5 103
Router_a(config-if)#frame-relay map ip 172.16.1.6 104
Router_a(config-if)#ip address 172.16.1.1 255.255.255.0
```

I. Command Group I:

```
Router_f(config)#interface s0
Router_f(config-if)#encapsulation frame-relay
Router_f(config-if)#frame-relay lmi-type ansi
```

II. Command Group II:

```
Router_f(config)#interface s0
Router_f(config-if)#encapsulation frame-relay
Router_f(config-if)#frame-relay lmi-type ansi
Router_f(config-if)#ip address 172.16.1.6 255.255.255.0
```

III. Command Group III:

```
Router_f(config)#interface s0
Router_f(config-if)#encapsulation frame-relay
Router_f(config-if)#frame-relay lmi-type ansi
Router_f(config-if)#ip address 172.16.1.6 255.255.255.0
Router_f(config-if)#frame-relay map ip 172.16.1.1 104
```

IV. Command Group IV:

```
Router_f(config)#interface s0
Router_f(config-if)#encapsulation frame-relay
Router_f(config-if)#frame-relay lmi-type ansi
Router_f(config-if)#ip address 172.16.1.6 255.255.255.0
Router_f(config-if)#frame-relay map ip 172.16.1.1 604
```

V. Command Group V:

```
Router_f(config)#interface s0
Router_f(config-if)#encapsulation frame-relay
Router_f(config-if)#frame-relay lmi-type ansi
Router_f(config-if)#ip address 172.16.1.6 255.255.255.0
Router_f(config-if)#frame-relay map ip 172.16.1.6 604
```

a) Command Group I above
b) Command Group II above
c) Command Group III above
d) Command Group IV above
e) Command Group V above

Question 2–113. [xINx] The protocol IP is best described as: (Choose one.)

a) Determines the data link address for known MAC addresses
b) Determines network addresses when data link addresses are known
c) Provides connectionless, best effort delivery routing of datagrams
d) Provides connection oriented, reliable delivery of datagrams
e) Provides connection oriented, best effort delivery routing of datagrams

Question 2–114. [RxNx] Which one of the following is true concerning IPX load balancing?

a) Activated by default
b) Must be configured
c) IPX does not load balance
d) Requires a Novell File Server
e) None of the above

Question 2–115. [FxNx] Which statements are true about the DLCI for interface serial 0 in the following configuration?

```
Current configuration:
!
version 11.3
no service password-encryption
!
hostname Router_A
!
enable secret 5 $1$.s1R$iaEqZxLnYJo2QlZi8UNaO0
enable password ccnaprep
!
ipx routing 0010.7b15.bd41
!
interface Tunnel0
 no ip address
 ipx network FAD
 tunnel source Serial0/0
 tunnel destination 65.62.245.2
!
interface Ethernet0/0
 ip address 172.17.10.1 255.255.255.0
 no ip mroute-cache
 ipx network BAD
 no cdp enable
!
interface Serial0/0
 ip address 65.62.245.1 255.255.255.0
 encapsulation frame-relay
 no ip mroute-cache
 frame-relay lmi-type cisco
!
interface TokenRing0/0
 no ip address
 no ip mroute-cache
 shutdown
 ring-speed 16
 no cdp enable
!
interface FastEthernet1/0
 no ip address
 no ip mroute-cache
 shutdown
```

```
  no cdp enable
!
ip classless
no cdp run
!
line con 0
 exec-timeout 0 0
line aux 0
line vty 0 4
 password ccieprep
 login
end
```

a) The default DLCI of 16 will be used.
b) Can not be determined from configuration given.
c) There is no DLCI configured, and this configuration will not work.
d) There is no DLCI configured, and this configuration will work.
e) The same as the DLCI used on the remote side.

Question 2–116. [CxNx] Which of the following keystrokes will move the cursor to the beginning of the previous word?

a) <Ctrl><A>
b) <Ctrl><B>
c) <Ctrl><F>
d) <Ctrl><E>
e) <Esc><B>

Question 2–117. [FINx] Given the following configuration for Router A, what group of commands will yield the proper configuration for Router F?

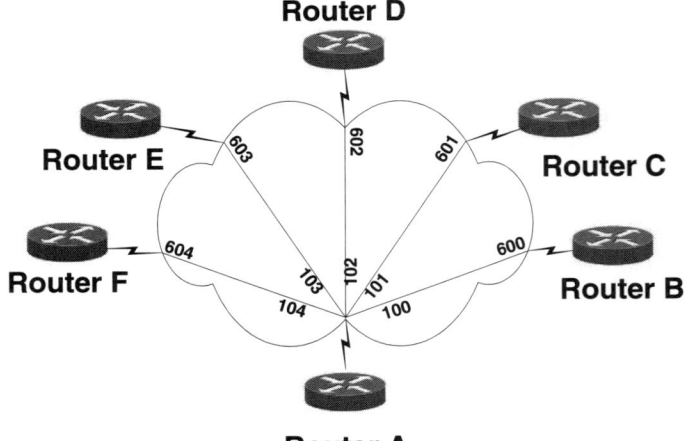

Frame Relay, unlike X.25, does not retransmit. Frame Relay was developed over digital services with a high reliability rate of 99%. If there is an error, Host A must do the retransmission.

The diagram represents a frame-relay network with PVCs configured for a hub and spoke design with corresponding DLCI numbers. Assume all connections are with the serial 0 interface.

```
Router_a(config)#interface s0
Router_a(config-if)#encapsulation frame-relay ietf
Router_a(config-if)#frame-relay map ip 172.16.1.2 100
Router_a(config-if)#frame-relay map ip 172.16.1.3 101
Router_a(config-if)#frame-relay map ip 172.16.1.4 102
Router_a(config-if)#frame-relay map ip 172.16.1.5 103
Router_a(config-if)#frame-relay map ip 172.16.1.6 104
Router_a(config-if)#ip address 172.16.1.1 255.255.255.0
```

I. Command Group I:

```
Router_f(config)#interface s0
Router_f(config-if)#encapsulation frame-relay
Router_f(config-if)#frame-relay lmi-type ansi
```

II. Command Group II:

```
Router_f(config)#interface s0
Router_f(config-if)#encapsulation frame-relay
Router_f(config-if)#frame-relay lmi-type ansi
Router_f(config-if)#ip address 172.16.1.6 255.255.255.0
Router_f(config-if)#frame-relay map ip 172.16.1.1 104
```

III. Command Group III:

```
Router_f(config)#interface s0
Router_f(config-if)#encapsulation frame-relay
Router_f(config-if)#frame-relay lmi-type cisco
Router_f(config-if)#ip address 172.16.1.6 255.255.255.0
Router_f(config-if)#frame-relay map ip 172.16.1.1 104
```

IV. Command Group IV:

```
Router_f(config)#interface s0
Router_f(config-if)#encapsulation frame-relay
```

```
Router_f(config-if)#frame-relay lmi-type cisco
Router_f(config-if)#ip address 172.16.1.6 255.255.255.0
Router_f(config-if)#frame-relay map ip 172.16.1.1 604
```

a) Command Group I above
b) Command Group II above
c) Command Group III above
d) Command Group IV above
e) None of the above.

Question 2–118. [xINx] The protocol ICMP is best described as: (Choose one.)

a) Helps IP by determining the data link addresses for known IP addresses
b) Resolves MAC addresses to IP addresses
c) Resolves IP addresses to MAC addresses
d) Adds a reliable connection-oriented service to IP
e) Helps IP by providing control and messaging capabilities

Question 2–119. [CxNx] What would be the proper command to set a DCE clock rate of 56k for a serial interface? (Choose one.)

a) Router# clockrate 56000
b) Router (config) # clockrate 56000
c) Router (config-if) # clockrate 56k
d) Router (config-if) #clock rate 56k
e) Router (config-if) #clock rate 56000
f) Router (config-if) #clockrate 56000

Question 2–120. [CxNx] Which of the following are true of access lists?

a) Access list should have at least one permit statement.
b) The last configured line should always be a permit statement.
c) Every access-list will implicitly deny all traffic.
d) Access-lists are processed top down.
e) All of the above.

Question 2–121. [RxNx] Which statement best describes a "Triggered Update"? (Choose two.)

a) A method of setting a specific time for route tables to be exchanged.
b) A triggered update is a new routing table that is sent to neighbor routers based upon some change.
c) Triggered updates in conjunction with hold-down timers help prevent routing loops
d) Triggered updates cannot be used if hold-downs are also being used.
e) With triggered updates, nodes are prevented from sending messages every time they notice a change in their routing tables.

Question 2–122. [RxNx] Which of the following are link state routing protocols? (Choose all that apply.)

a) IP
b) OSPF
c) RIP
d) EIGRP
e) IS-IS

Question 2–123. [RINx] What does the condition of Serial 0 down & protocol up represent ?

a) The interface is disconnected but keep alives are being received.
b) The interface is working properly but keep alives are not being received.
c) The interface is bad and should be replaced.
d) The interface is working correctly.
e) Condition not possible.

Question 2–124. [CxNx] Which of the following information will "show cdp neighbors detail" reveal? (Choose all that apply.)

a) Router Platform
b) All layer 3 addresses limited to one per protocol
c) IOS version
d) Incoming and outgoing port
e) IP address only
f) IP address and mask
g) Router Name

Question 2–125. [ExNx] Collisions occur when:

a) Multiple packets are placed on a serial link.
b) Multiple stations listen for traffic and transmit at the same time.
c) Multiple tokens are on a ring simultaneously.
d) Beaconing process takes place.

Question 2–126. [CxNx] When are the files stored in NVRAM transferred to RAM? (Choose two.)

a) When the command "Load NVRAM" is executed
b) Whenever the router is powered on
c) Whenever the command "copy start run" is executed
d) Whenever the command "copy run start" is executed
e) Whenever the command "show startup-config" is executed
f) Whenever the command "show running-config" is executed

2. CCNA

Question 2–127. [CxNx] The following statement would deny traffic from what subnets?

```
Router_B(config)#access-list 101 deny tcp 10.1.8.0 0.0.7.255 192.16.5.0
0.0.0.255
```

a) 10.1.8.0
b) 10.1.15.0
c) 10.1.0.0
d) 10.1.16.0
e) Choice a and b

Question 2–128. [CxNx] Of the following commands, identify the correct one for clearing the IP ARP table in memory of the router.

a) clear ip arp-cache
b) clear ip arp-table
c) clear arp-cache
d) clear arp-table
e) clear arp-ram

Question 2–129. [xINx] Which protocols are best described as connection-oriented and reliable? (Choose two.)

a) UDP
b) IP
c) TCP
d) IPX
e) TCP over IP
f) UDP over IP

Question 2–130. [xINx] The way that TCP uses acknowledgements is best referred to as: (Choose one.)

a) Expectational
b) Sequential
c) Current
d) Sliding
e) Incremental

Question 2–131. [CxNx] What will be the correct command on a Cisco router to set the IP address of an interface assuming you are at the "router(config-if)#" prompt?

a) ip address 1.1.1.1 255.255.255.0
b) ip address 1.1.1.1
c) ip 1.1.1.1
d) ip 1.1.1.1 255.255.255.0
e) none of the above

Question 2–132. [CxNx] Which of the following is not stored in RAM of a Cisco 2500 series router? (Choose all that apply.)

a) Routing Tables
b) The running-configuration file
c) The startup-configuration file
d) The running version of the Cisco IOS
e) The protocol software

Answer 2–1.
   a) **All passwords can be encrypted.**
   c) **A password can be set before a user can enter the privileged mode.**
   d) **A password can be set for individual lines.**
   e) **TACACS or Radius password authentication can be used.**

The following is an example of encrypting all passwords:

Before Password encryption:

```
Router#sh ru
%SYS-5-CONFIG_I: Configured from console by consolen
Building configuration...

Current configuration:
!
version 11.3
no service password-encryption
!
hostname Router
!
```
enable password ccieprep
```
!
[OUTPUT OMMITTED]

line con 0
line aux 0
line vty 0 4
```
 password ccnaprep
```
 login
!
end
```

After encrypting all passwords:

Router(config)#service password-encryption

```
Router#sh run
Building configuration...

Current configuration:
!
version 11.3
```
service password-encryption
```
!
hostname Router
!
```
enable password 7 020507520E161D245C
```
!

[OUPUT OMMITTED]
```

```
!
line con 0
line aux 0
line vty 0 4
 password 7 1306141C0A1C162F3B
 login
!
end
```

Cisco routers can also participate in TACACS authentication:

Refer to the following:

```
Router(config)#enable ?
  last-resort  Define enable action if no TACACS servers respond
  password     Assign the privileged level password
  secret       Assign the privileged level secret
  use-tacacs   Use TACACS to check enable passwords
```

Answer 2–2.
 b) This is a broadcast address.

Answer 2–3.
 c) A location to store a backup copy of the router configuration file

Answer 2–4.
 b) IP RIP IPX RIP Cisco IGRP.
 e) IP RIP Apple RTMP Cisco IGRP IPX RIP.

Answer 2–5.
 c) Event-triggered updates are used.

Cisco uses triggered updates with IP RIP in addition to the periodic updates.

Refer to the following outline that organizes the major routing protocols. Details of these routing protocols are will be addressed in later editions.

I Interior Routing Protocols
  A. Distance Vector
    1. RIP
    2. Cisco's IGRP
    3. Novell's IPX RIP
    4. Appletalk RTMP

  B. Link State
    1. OSPF
    2. IS-IS
    3. NLSP

  C. Hybrid
    1. Cisco's EIGRP

II Exterior Routing Protocols
   A. BGP4

To distinguish between Distance Vector and Link State, answer the following three questions:

What does the routing protocol talk?
When does the routing protocol talk?
Who does the routing protocol talk?

Distance Vector talks the entire routing table to directly connected neighbors (less split horizon) periodically! Link State talks just the state of the link to all neighbors when the state of the link changes. Use the following question to differentiate between distance vector and link state routing protocols:

What protocol are you using if your mother calls you every night to let you know that everyone in the family is alive?

Suppose you make an agreement with your mother to call you just when there is a death in the family?

Suppose Mom dies?

That's what hello packets are used for!

Answer 2–6.
   b) arpa (Cisco name) & Ethernet_II (common name)
   d) sap (Cisco name) & Ethernet_802.2 LLC (common name)
   g) snap (Cisco name) & Token Ring Snap (common name)
   h) snap (Cisco name) & Ethernet_SNAP (common name)

Frame type naming has been an area of confusion since Novell chose to use a frame type of 802.3 which differs from the IEEE 802.3 frame type format. This was compounded when Novell changed their default frame type from 802.3 to 802.2. Cisco has further confused this area by choosing another proprietary naming scheme. Here is a chart that matches some common frame type names to the frame type names used by Cisco and Novell.

Common name	Novell name	Cisco name
Ethernet 2	Ethernet_II	arpa
IEEE 802.3	Ethernet_802.2	sap
IEEE 802.3 with SNAP	Ethernet_SNAP	snap
Ethernet	Ethernet_802.3	Novell-ether
IEEE 802.5 with SNAP	Token_ring	snap

Note that Cisco can use the name snap to define two different frame types because these names are assigned to either a Token Ring or an Ethernet interface. In doing this the frame type name means something different to the router depending upon the interface type it is assigned to.

Answer 2–7.
  e) **As many as you want.**

Cisco Routers have no limitation as to the number of IP routing protocols that can be configured.

Answer 2–8.
  a) **The motd will be displayed each time a user initially accesses the router.**
  c) **The motd will be displayed at all terminals connected to the router.**

Refer to the following example:

```
Router_B(config)#banner motd #
Enter TEXT message.  End with the character '#'.
This will be the message of the day
#
Router_B(config)#^Z

Router_B#
%SYS-5-CONFIG_I: Configured from console by console

Router_B>exit

Router_B con0 is now available

Press RETURN to get started.

This will be the message of the day

Router_B>
```

Answer 2–9.
  a) **Conserve major network IP addresses**
  b) **Construct a hierarchical addressing scheme**

Answer 2–10.
  b) **The count-to-infinity problem**
  c) **The time it takes for all routers to converge**
  e) **Routing loops**
  f) **The periodic broadcasts of routing tables**

Answer 2–11.
  d) **Only the specific interface chosen in the previous command**

Answer 2–12.
  c) **254**

A class C address provides us with a maximum of 8 host bits, which is, of course, the fourth octet.

The formula of $2^n - 2$ (where n is the total number of host bits) provides us with the total number of hosts.

The reason why we subtract two addresses from the total number of hosts is as follows:

- When all the host bits are set to 0, the resulting address is the address of the wire.
- When all the host bits are set to 1, the resulting address represents the broadcast address.

Now, using our formula, $2^8 - 2 = 256 - 2 = 254$

Answer 2–13.
   h) None of the above

The implicit deny statement at the end of the access list will deny all traffic that is not explicitly permitted.

Answer 2–14.
   d) The parallel paths must have the same tick count and the same hop count.

IPX RIP uses TICK and HOP count as a metric. The metric over parallel paths must be the same, also remember that load balancing is not on by default as it is with IP RIP. Use the ipx maximum-paths command to configure load balancing.

Before Maximum paths is configured

```
Router_B#sh ipx route
Codes: C - Connected primary network,
 c - Connected secondary network, S - Static, F - Floating static,
 L - Local (internal), W - IPXWAN, R - RIP, E - EIGRP, N - NLSP,
 X - External, A - Aggregate, s - seconds, u - uses,
 U - Per-user static

3 Total IPX routes. Up to 2 parallel paths and 16 hops allowed.

No default route known.

C         BAD (HDLC),          Se1
C         DAD (HDLC),          Se0
R         CAD [07/01] via      DAD.0060.09c3.df60,     4s, Se0

Router_B(config)#ipx maximum-paths ?
  <1-64>  Number of paths

Router_B(config)#ipx maximum-paths 2

Router_B#sh ipx route
Codes: C - Connected primary network,
 c - Connected secondary network, S - Static, F - Floating static,
 L - Local (internal), W - IPXWAN, R - RIP, E - EIGRP, N - NLSP,
 X - External, A - Aggregate, s - seconds, u - uses,
 U - Per-user static
```

2. Answers

```
3 Total IPX routes. Up to 2 parallel paths and 16 hops allowed.

No default route known.

C         BAD (HDLC),         Se1
C         DAD (HDLC),         Se0
R         CAD [07/01] via     DAD.0060.09c3.df60,     6s, Se0
                        via     BAD.0060.09c3.df60,     6s, Se1
```

Answer 2–15.

b) The address has a network and a host part.
d) The host part is the MAC address of the host.

The following is an example of an IPX ping:

```
Router_B#ping ipx CAD.0060.09c3.df60
Type escape sequence to abort.
Sending 5, 100-byte IPX cisco Echoes to CAD.0060.09c3.df60, timeout is 2
  seconds
!!!!!
Success rate is 100 percent (5/5), round-trip min/avg/max = 4/6/8 ms
```

CAD is the network address represented in hex. The network address can contain 8 HEX digits or 32 bits. 0060.09c3.df60 is a MAC address, which is 12 HEX digits or 48 bits.

Answer 2–16.

a) Is used to resolve a MAC address to an IP address

Reverse Address Resolution Protocol (RARP) is used when a host has its Layer 2 address and is trying to find its Layer 3 address. A diskless workstation, for instance, may send an RARP for a Layer 3 address.

Answer 2–17.

a) Service Advertising Protocol, a Novell protocol used to advertise services
b) Service Access Points, used by the OSI model to communicate between adjacent layers

Answer 2–18.

c) Static routes, EIGRP, IGRP, OSPF, RIP

The lower the number, the more reliable the information.

Protocol	AD
Static	0 or 1
EIGRP	90
IGRP	100
OSPF	110
RIP	120
BGP	180

Answer 2–19.
  a) **The total address length is 24 bits.**
  b) **The address has a network and a host part.**

The following is a portion of a router configuration:

```
interface Serial1
 no ip address
 appletalk cable-range 106-110 106.59
 appletalk zone rightserial
 clockrate 4000000
```

In the above example the router acquired the address 106.59. The router first picked a cable-range value (network number) of 106 (It could have chosen anything between 106 and 110.). After the cable range was chosen, it picked a host address of 59. The choices for the host address range from 1-252. Of course the Appletalk host will send probes to be certain that no one else has chosen that address.

Answer 2–20.
  e) **Router_A learned the next hop address of 65.62.245.2 through Inverse ARP.**

Inverse Address Resolution Protocol will resolve remote layer 3 addresses.

Answer 2–21.
  d) **Command Group IV above**

```
Router_f(config)#interface s0
Router_f(config-if)#encapsulation frame-relay
Router_f(config-if)#frame-relay lmi-type ansi
Router_f(config-if)#ip address 172.16.1.6 255.255.255.0
Router_f(config-if)#frame-relay map ip 172.16.1.1 604
```

There are several configuration parameters that must be checked to answer these frame relay questions.

LMI
Does not have to match end-to-end. This is communication between the local router and the local frame relay switch.

Encapsulation
This parameter needs to match end-to-end.

Frame map statement
The ip address here needs to be the next hop address, and the DLCI number needs to be the local DLCI.

The local DLCI for Router F is 604.
The next hop address is Router A 172.16.1.1.
Encapsulation of Router A is IETF.
Encapsulation of all our choices is Cisco.

The local DLCI for Router F is 604.
The next hop address is Router A 172.16.1.1.
Encapsulation is Cisco the default.

Answer 2–22.
  e) **Boot the IOS from ROM**

Refer to the following example:

```
Router_B>en
Router_B#conf t
Enter configuration commands, one per line.  End with CNTL/Z.
Router_B(config)#config-reg 0x101
Router_B(config)#^Z
Router_B#rel
%SYS-5-CONFIG_I: Configured from console by cons
Router_B#reload

System configuration has been modified. Save? [yes/no]: y
Building configuration...
[OK]
Proceed with reload? [confirm]

%SYS-5-RELOAD: Reload requested
System Bootstrap, Version 11.0(10c)XB1, PLATFORM SPECIFIC RELEASE SOFTWARE
  (fc1)

Copyright (c) 1986-1997 by cisco Systems
2500 processor with 6144 Kbytes of main memory

            Restricted Rights Legend

Use, duplication, or disclosure by the Government is
subject to restrictions as set forth in subparagraph
(c) of the Commercial Computer Software - Restricted
Rights clause at FAR sec. 52.227-19 and subparagraph
(c) (1) (ii) of the Rights in Technical Data and Computer
Software clause at DFARS sec. 252.227-7013.

            cisco Systems, Inc.
            170 West Tasman Drive
            San Jose, California 95134-1706

Cisco Internetwork Operating System Software
IOS (tm) 3000 Bootstrap Software (IGS-BOOT-R), Version 11.0(10c)XB1, PLATFORM
  SP
ECIFIC RELEASE SOFTWARE (fc1)
Copyright (c) 1986-1996 by cisco Systems, Inc.
Compiled Wed 10-Sep-97 13:06 by phester
Image text-base: 0x01010000, data-base: 0x00001000

cisco 2521 (68030) processor (revision K) with 6144K/2048K bytes of memory.
```

2. Answers

```
Processor board ID 06170381, with hardware revision 00000003
X.25 software, Version 2.0, NET2, BFE and GOSIP compliant.
Basic Rate ISDN software, Version 1.0.
1 Token Ring/IEEE 802.5 interface.
2 Serial network interfaces.
2 Low-speed serial(sync/async) network interfaces.
1 ISDN Basic Rate interface.
32K bytes of non-volatile configuration memory.
16384K bytes of processor board System flash (Read/Write)

Press RETURN to get started!

[OUTPUT OMMITTED]

Cisco Internetwork Operating System Software
IOS (tm) 3000 Bootstrap Software (IGS-BOOT-R), Version 11.0(10c)XB1, PLATFORM
  SP
ECIFIC RELEASE SOFTWARE (fc1)
Copyright (c) 1986-1996 by cisco Systems, Inc.
Compiled Wed 10-Sep-97 13:06 by phester
%LINK-5-CHANGED: Interface Serial2, changed state to administratively down
%LINK-5-CHANGED: Interface Serial3, changed state to administratively down
%LINK-5-CHANGED: Interface TokenRing0, changed state to administratively down
This will be the message of the day

Router_B(boot)>
```

The boot prompt above signifies that the IOS was loaded from ROM.

Answer 2–23.
  e) All of the above.

The LMI type is locally significant only. LMI is communication between the local router and the local frame relay switch. The remote router and the remote frame relay switch can be using another LMI type.

The following configuration shows a switch between a network using two different LMI types:

```
Current configuration:
!
version 11.3
no service password-encryption
!
hostname Router_B
!
enable secret 5 $1$eZ3D$vnTjKaCLtbSCcMF1mGzZm0
enable password cnaprep
!

frame-relay switching
isdn switch-type ntt
!
```

```
interface Serial0
 no ip address
 no ip mroute-cache
 shutdown
 no fair-queue
 clockrate 4000000
!
interface Serial1
  encapsulation frame-relay
 no ip mroute-cache
 keepalive 15
 clockrate 2000000
 frame-relay lmi-type ansi
 frame-relay intf-type dce
 frame-relay route 100 interface Serial2 200
!
interface Serial2
 encapsulation frame-relay
 frame-relay lmi-type cisco
 no ip mroute-cache
 keepalive 15
 clockrate 115200
 frame-relay intf-type dce
 frame-relay route 200 interface Serial1 100
!

[OUTPUT OMMITTED]
```

Answer 2–24.
  b) Source host

Answer 2–25.
  a) <Ctrl><A>

Answer 2–26.
  e) All of the above

Answer 2–27.
  a) Where an IP host resolves its IP address by broadcasting its MAC address to the network, and a RARP server assigns it an IP address.

Choice c describes Address Resolution Protocol (ARP). A host never has to resolve its own MAC address. The MAC address is burned into the Network Interface card. When the host is booted the MAC address will be loaded into memory.

Answer 2–28.
  b) Ranges between 100-199

The format of the above list defines it as an extended access list.

```
Router_C[Config)#access-list ?
  <1-99>        IP standard access list
  <100-199>     IP extended access list
  <1000-1099>   IPX SAP access list
  <1100-1199>   Extended 48-bit MAC address access list
  <1200-1299>   IPX summary address access list
  <200-299>     Protocol type-code access list
  <300-399>     DECnet access list
  <400-499>     XNS standard access list
  <500-599>     XNS extended access list
  <600-699>     Appletalk access list
  <700-799>     48-bit MAC address access list
  <800-899>     IPX standard access list
  <900-999>     IPX extended access list
```

Answer 2–29.

  a) Defining a maximum
  b) Using hold-down timers
  e) Split Horizon
  f) Route poisoning

Answer 2–30.

  d) Command Group IV above

```
Router_f(config)#interface s0
Router_f(config-if)#encapsulation frame-relay
Router_f(config-if)#frame-relay lmi-type ansi
Router_f(config-if)#ip address 172.16.1.6 255.255.255.0
Router_f(config-if)#frame-relay map ip 172.16.1.1 604 ietf
```

There are several configuration parameters that must be checked to answer these frame relay questions.

LMI
Does not have to match end-to-end. This is communication between the local router and the local frame relay switch.

Encapsulation
This parameter needs to match end-to-end.

Frame map statement
The ip address here needs to be the next hop address, and the DLCI number needs to be the local DLCI.

The local DLCI for Router F is 604.
The next hop address is Router A 172.16.1.1.
Encapsulation of Router A is IETF.
Encapsulation of all our choices is Cisco.

The local DLCI for Router F is 604.

The next hop address is Router A 172.16.1.1.
Encapsulation is IETF.

Answer 2–31.
  a) **172.16.15.255**

The definition of the broadcast address is when all the host bits are set to 1. In the above
example a /20 identifies the 255.255.240.0 mask. In other words, we can say that the first 20 bits
of the IP address identify the network and the subnet. Since there are 32 bits in an IP address,
that must mean there are 12 host bits.

The broadcast address is defined by setting these 12 host bits to one.

Take a look at the third and fourth octet.

IP Address   0   1

128	64	32	16	8	4	2	1	128	64	32	16	8	4	2	1
0	0	0	0	0	0	0	0	0	0	0	0	0	0	0	1

128	64	32	16	8	4	2	1	128	64	32	16	8	4	2	1
0	0	0	0	1	1	1	1	1	1	1	1	1	1	1	1

Broadcast Address   15   255

Answer 2–32.
  c) **Preventing a router from sending an update back to a router it just received the
       update from.**

Answer 2–33.
  c) **The point in a command where you have entered an incorrect command, keyword
       or argument.**

An example follows:

```
R2#sh clack
       ^
% Invalid input detected at '^' marker.

Router_B>sh cl?
WORD   clock
```

Answer 2–34.
  d) **sh ar?**

The user has either mistyped a character or he is not sure what the command should be.
Refer to the following:

```
Router_B#sh ar?
WORD   arap   arp
```

If "show ar ?" were to be used, it would be ambiguous.

```
Router_B#sh ar ?
% Ambiguous command:   "sh ar "
```

Answer 2–35.
  a) **IP**
  d) **ICMP**

ICMP is a helper protocol for IP to deliver messages. Some ICMP messages are Destination Unreachable, Source Quench, Echo and Address Request. Each of these ICMP messages is carried in IP datagrams.

Answer 2–36.
  e) **None of the above.**

A DLCI need not be configured because the switch will announce its DLCI. Inverse ARP will resolve remote layer 3 addresses, so, in this case, it is not necessary to configure a frame map.

IPX is being tunneled in IP.

The tunnel interface does not require an IP address, just an IPX address in our case. The tunnel on the other side needs to have the same IPX network address.

Answer 2–37.
  d) **show access-list**
  e) **show access-list 150**

Review the show commands below:

```
Router_A#sh access-list
IPX extended access list 950
   permit any log
Extended IP access list 120
    deny ip host 172.16.10.2 any log
    permit ip any any log
Extended IP access list 150
    deny ip any 172.16.5.0 0.0.0.255
    permit ip any any

Router_A#show access-list 150
Extended IP access list 150
    deny ip any 172.16.5.0 0.0.0.255
    permit ip any any
```

The "show interface" command conveys whether or not the access list has been set on the interface, but it will not show you the access-list.

Answer 2–38.
c) MAC address

A router is a device that operates at layer 3 where logical addresses are used, not physical addresses. A switch or a bridge would contain MAC addresses in the bridge table.

Answer 2–39.
c) The point in a command where you have entered an incorrect command, keyword or argument

Refer to the example below:

```
Router_B#cong t
             ^
% Invalid input detected at '^' marker.
```

Answer 2–40.
a) User mode password

The setup dialogue is shown below. Notice that you must be in the privilege mode to use the setup dialogue.

```
Notice: NVRAM invalid, possibly due to write erase.
        --- System Configuration Dialog ---

At any point you may enter a question mark '?' for help.
Use ctrl-c to abort configuration dialog at any prompt.
Default settings are in square brackets '[]'.
Would you like to enter the initial configuration dialog? [yes]:

First, would you like to see the current interface summary? [yes]:

Any interface listed with OK? value "NO" does not have a valid configuration

Interface        IP-Address      OK? Method Status   Protocol
-------------    -------------   --- ------ ------   --------
Ethernet0        unassigned      NO  unset  up       up
Ethernet1        unassigned      NO  unset  up       down
Serial0          unassigned      NO  unset  down     down
Serial1          unassigned      NO  unset  down     down

Configuring global parameters:

  Enter host name [Router]: Router_C

The enable secret is a one-way cryptographic secret used
instead of the enable password when it exists.

  Enter enable secret: ccie

The enable password is used when there is no enable secret
and when using older software and some boot images.
```

```
Enter enable password: ccieprep
Enter virtual terminal password: cnaprep
Configure SNMP Network Management? [yes]: n
Configure LAT? [no]: n
Configure AppleTalk? [no]: n
Configure DECnet? [no]: n
Configure IP? [yes]: n
Configure CLNS? [no]: n
Configure IPX? [no]: n
Configure Vines? [no]: n
Configure XNS? [no]: n
Configure Apollo? [no]: n
Configure bridging? [no]: n

Configuring interface parameters:

Configuring interface Ethernet0:
  Is this interface in use? [yes]: n

Configuring interface Ethernet1:
  Is this interface in use? [yes]: n

Configuring interface Serial0:
  Is this interface in use? [yes]: n

Configuring interface Serial1:
  Is this interface in use? [yes]: n

 [OUTPUT  OMMITTED]
```

To set the user password follow the script below:

```
Router_C>en
Router_C#conf t
Enter configuration commands, one per line.  End with CNTL/Z.
Router_C(config)#line 0
Router_C(config-line)#login
Router_C(config-line)#password cisco
```

Answer 2–41.
  d) Link state routers include the originating router's routing table.

Choice d is not true because during the flooding stage neighbor routers communicate their directly connected networks. They DO NOT communicate routing tables, as a Distance Vector routing protocol would.

Answer 2–42.
  a) 255.255.255.192

To calculate the number of hosts or networks use the formula 2^n-2 where n is the number of bits that will be used to describe the host or the network. To answer this question we first have

to determine how many host bits we would need to have at least 62 unique combinations. Using our formula we need to have 6 host bits (2^6-2 = 64-2 = 62). This would leave us with 2 network bits. Therefore the mask is 192 in the fourth octet.

Answer 2–43.
  c) **Telnet sessions will be denied if initiated from any address other than 172.16.0.0 network.**

The secret to this question is the key word "established." Established means that the packet will be permitted unless it is the first part of the three way handshake. Recall that when we initiate a TCP connection we have no ACK. How can we acknowledge a sequence number from the other side when we have not established a session with him?

Answer 2–44.
  d) **Ticks and hops**

Ticks are used initially if there is a tie then hops are used.
Default tick count is 1 for a LAN connection and 6 for a serial connection.

Answer 2–45.
  d) **A two part network addressing scheme such as Network/Host**
  e) **The use of a routable protocol such as IP or IPX**

Explanation: Since an internetwork is made up of multiple logical networks with hosts on each of those networks, a two-part addressing scheme is required so that each can be identified. For example, IP uses a 32-bit number, which is really at least two separate numbers, one part for the network and one part for the host on that network. In an IP number such as 131.108.25.165, the major network portion is 131.108, and, assuming we are not subnetting, the host portion is 25.165. Both IP and IPX provide such a two part addressing scheme.

But protocols such as NetBEUI or LAT do not provide addressing at layer 3 and therefore are unable to distinguish between different logical networks. As a result they are not routable.

Answer 2–46.
  a) **Moves, Adds and Changes are made simpler.**
  b) **There is less administrative overhead.**
  d) **It limits broadcasts domains.**

If a workstation moves there is a good chance the move is within the same VLAN. If we have a good design of a single subnet within each VLAN there will be no need to reconfigure the workstation with a new layer 3 address. Each VLAN defines a broadcast domain.

Answer 2–47.
  e) **all of the above**

It is possible to configure a Cisco Router using any of the methods listed.

Answer 2–48.
 b) Stores a configuration file for when the router boots.

NVRAM stores the startup-configuration file of the router. It is this file that is used as the initial running-configuration after a router boots.

Answer 2–49.
 d) Router (config-if) #bandwidth 56

Refer to the following example:

```
Router_C(config-if)#bandwidth ?
  <1-10000000>  Bandwidth in kilobits
```

Answer 2–50.
 b) Network portion
 e) Host portion

An IPX address is made up of two parts. The network portion is assigned by the Novell administrator. The Host portion is, in most cases, the MAC address of the host. The MAC address is a Layer 2 address

Answer 2–51.
 d) The packet will "die" when it reaches the terminator.

Answer 2–52.
 a) Close to 172.16.10.5

In general we want to place extended access lists close to the source to prevent eventually denied traffic from travelling our network.

Answer 2–53.
 a) Standard lists will most likely be placed close to the destination.
 d) Extended lists will most likely be placed close to the source.

A standard list will only check the source address. It makes no difference where the packet is going. If you place a standard list close to the source you could very well be denying that traffic to go to other destinations. An extended list can be placed close to the source because we can permit or deny traffic based upon the source and destination address. This insures that only traffic we wish to have denied is denied.

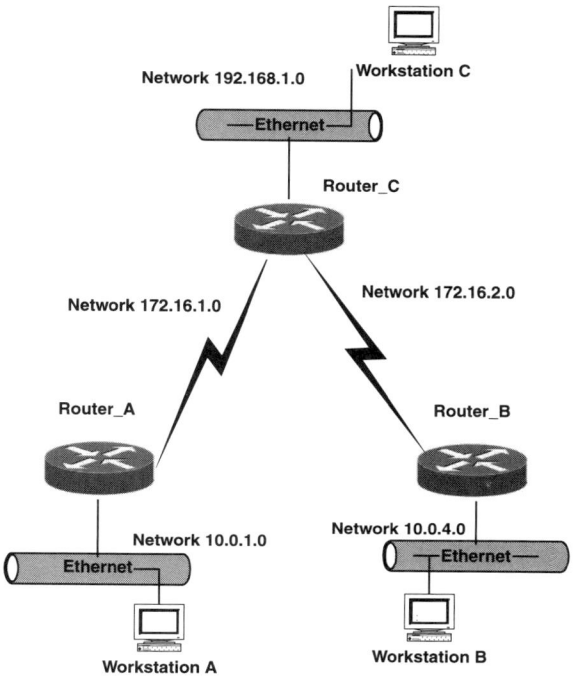

Suppose we created a policy that stated Workstation A will be denied access to network 10.0.4.0. This policy implies that Workstation A will be permitted access to all other networks, and we will assume this to be the case.

If we place a standard list on the outgoing serial interface of Router_A then Workstation A would be denied access to 192.168.1.0. On the other hand a extended access list on the outgoing serial interface of Router_A will work just fine because we can identify the destination 10.0.4.0. We will have more questions in the future that will help you to understand this concept.

Answer 2–54.
   b) Class B, 191.12.0.0

First Octet Rules:

- If the first bit is 0, it's a Class A address.
- If the first two bits are10, it's a Class B address.
- If the first three bits are 110 and the value is less than 224, it's a class C address.
- No address can have a value of zero (0) in the first octet.
- The address of 127 will be reserved for loopback addresses.
- Addresses with a value of 10 will be reserved for private use.

The above rules provide us with the following ranges:

Class A   1 - 126

2. Answers

Class B　　128 - 191
Class C　　192 - 223

Answer 2–55.
  e) **12**

A Cisco 2514 has four interfaces. Each protocol will carry its own layer 3 address for each interface. The tricky part to this question is knowing that a 2514 has four interfaces.

The Cisco Design exams and the CMTD exam are where you might run across questions that will require you to know the different Cisco platforms.

Answer 2–56.
  d) **User mode**

Answer 2–57.
  d) **Flash memory, TFTP Server, ROM**

Answer 2–58.
  f) **TCP port 23**

In the capture below NetXray interpolates the data and shows a source port of 1074 to a destination port of telnet. Refer to the data below the highlighted portion. 0x17 is $1 * 16^1 + 7 * 16^0 = 23$.

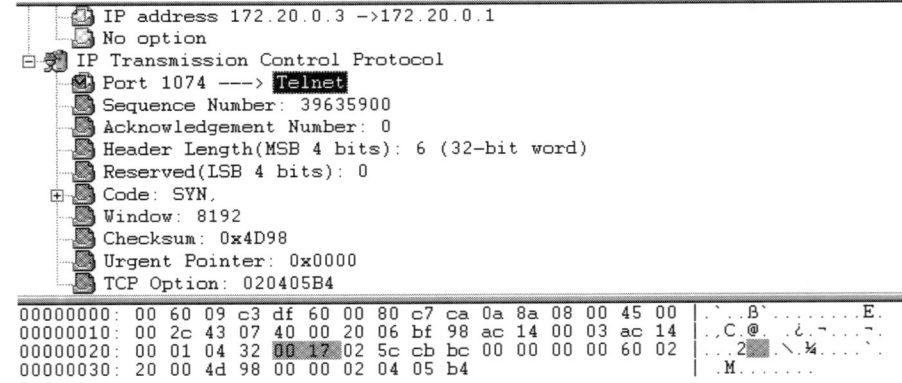

Answer 2–59.
  a) **A hold-down timer will be released if the router receives an update indicating a better route.**
  b) **A hold-down timer will not be released if the router receives an update indicating a poorer route.**
  d) **Hold-down times are configurable by the administrator.**

Answer 2–60.
a) 192.16.10.0

A mask of /27 is 255.255.255.224.

224 in the fourth octet means that every subnet address will be a multiple of 32.

All of the 255.255.255.224 subnets are listed below:

	128	64	32	16	8	4	2	1
224	1	1	1	0	0	0	0	0
0	0	0	0	0	0	0	0	0
32	0	0	1	0	0	0	0	0
64	0	1	0	0	0	0	0	0
96	0	1	1	0	0	0	0	0
128	1	0	0	0	0	0	0	0
160	1	0	1	0	0	0	0	0
192	1	1	0	0	0	0	0	0
224	1	1	1	0	0	0	0	0

Thirty two is the value of the least subnet bit. Therefore, as the chart above shows, every subnet is a multiple of 32.

To determine what subnet this host is attached to, ask yourself the question "What is the highest multiple of 32 that is less than 30?" The answer is 0. As a result, 192.16.10.30 is on the 192.16.10.0 subnet.

This presents us with a minor problem (or maybe a major problem). Not all networking devices recognize the "zero" subnet.

Cisco requires the "ip subnet-zero" command for the above address to be used.

Refer to the following example:

```
Router>en
Router#conf t
Enter configuration commands, one per line.  End with CNTL/Z.
Router(config)#int s0
Router(config-if)#ip address 192.16.10.30 255.255.255.224
Bad mask /27 for address 192.16.10.30

Router(config-if)#exit
Router(config)#ip subnet-zero
Router(config)#int s0
Router(config-if)#ip address 192.16.10.30 255.255.255.224
```

As a result of the "ip subnet-zero" command, there is no bad mask error.

Answer 2–61.
   b) ARPA

SNAP is the default encapsulation for a token ring interface;
NOVELL-ETHER is the default encapsulation for a IPX interface.

Answer 2–62.
   a) Major network address
   c) Subnet address
   d) Host address

Example:

192.10.10.9/30

192.10.10.0 is the major network portion.
192.10.10.8 is the subnet portion.
192.10.10.9 address a specific host.

Answer 2–63.
   d) The Network layer

Below is a capture of an ICMP echo request, which is the first part of a ping.

```
Ethernet Version II
    Address: 00-10-7B-15-BD-41 --->00-80-C7-CA-0A-8A
    Ethernet II Protocol Type: IP
Internet Protocol
    Version(MSB 4 bits): 4
    Header length(LSB 4 bits): 5 (32-bit word)
    Service type: Precd=Routine,Delay=Normal,Thrput=Normal,Reli=Normal
    Total length: 100 (Octets)
    Fragment ID: 20
    Flags: May be fragmented,Last fragment,Offset=0 (0x00)
    Time to live: 255 seconds/hops
    IP protocol type: ICMP (0x01)
    Checksum: 0xA57E
    IP address 10.1.1.2 ->10.1.1.3
    No option
IP Internet Control Message Protocol
    Type: Echo Request
    Code: 0
    Checksum: 0xF76D
    Identifier: 0
    Sequence Number: 6219
```

(This would be followed by an echo reply.)

```
⊟ 💷 Ethernet Version II
   │   📃 Address: 00-80-C7-CA-0A-8A --->00-10-7B-15-BD-41
   │   📃 Ethernet II Protocol Type: IP
⊟ 💡 Internet Protocol
   │   📃 Version(MSB 4 bits): 4
   │   📃 Header length(LSB 4 bits): 5 (32-bit word)
   ⊞ 📃 Service type: Precd=Routine,Delay=Normal,Thrput=Normal,Reli=Normal
   │   📃 Total length: 100 (Octets)
   │   📃 Fragment ID: 6144
   ⊞ 📃 Flags: May be fragmented,Last fragment,Offset=0 (0x00)
   │   📃 Time to live: 32 seconds/hops
   │   📃 IP protocol type: ICMP (0x01)
   │   📃 Checksum: 0x6C93
   │   📃 IP address 10.1.1.3 ->10.1.1.2
   │   📃 No option
⊟ 💷 IP Internet Control Message Protocol
       📃 Type: Echo Reply
       📃 Code: 0
       📃 Checksum: 0xFF6D
       📃 Identifier: 0
       📃 Sequence Number: 6219
```

Answer 2–64.
  b) **Routers broadcast their routing table at periodic intervals.**
  d) **Routers discover the best path to destination networks based on accumulated metrics from each neighbor.**

Answer 2–65.
  a) **Prevents bridging loops**
  c) **Cisco supported feature that can be used per VLAN**

Transparent bridging requires that only one way exists through the bridge circuit to prevent bridging loops. Also, Cisco switching supports spanning tree on a per-VLAN basis. This is done by placing selected ports in a blocking mode. Remember that a router either forwards a packet or filters a packet based on its MAC address.

Answer 2–66.
  a) **Command Group I above**

```
Router_f(config)#interface s0
Router_f(config-if)#encapsulation frame-relay ietf
Router_f(config-if)#frame-relay lmi-type ansi
Router_f(config-if)#ip address 172.16.1.6 255.255.255.0
Router_f(config-if)#frame-relay map ip 172.16.1.1 604
```

There are several configuration parameters that must be checked to answer these frame relay questions.

LMI
Does not have to match end-to-end. This is communication between the local router and the local frame relay switch.

Encapsulation
This parameter needs to match end-to-end.

Frame map statement
The ip address here needs to be the next hop address, and the DLCI number needs to be the local DLCI.

The local DLCI for Router F is 604.
The next hop address is Router A 172.16.1.1.
Encapsulation of Router A is IETF.
Encapsulation of all our choices is Cisco.

The local DLCI for Router F is 604.
The next hop address is Router A 172.16.1.1.
Encapsulation is IETF.
LMI does not have to match.

Answer 2–67.
a) If no configuration file can be found

A saved copy of the configuration file is normally stored in NVRAM. Since the active or running configuration is lost at power down, the router will check NVRAM for this backup file to load into RAM. If no valid configuration file is found in NVRAM, the system will enter a system configuration dialog. During this dialog you will manually enter configuration information.

Once this information is entered you must accept or reject the configuration. If you reject it, the process starts over again. If you accept it, the configuration is stored to NVRAM and becomes the default configuration to be loaded the next time the router is initialized.

Incidentally, this is the only time that the router will automatically write a backup copy of the configuration to NVRAM. For all other times you must manually enter the command "copy start run" from the privileged prompt. This is a good habit to get into when making changes to the running configuration.

Note: A configuration can also be loaded from an tftp server with the command "copy tftp run" from the privileged prompt.

The following is a result of a router booting up with no configuration file stored in NVRAM:

```
Notice: NVRAM invalid, possibly due to write erase.
        --- System Configuration Dialog ---

At any point you may enter a question mark '?' for help.
Use ctrl-c to abort configuration dialog at any prompt.
Default settings are in square brackets '[]'.
Would you like to enter the initial configuration dialog? [yes]: y

First, would you like to see the current interface summary? [yes]: y

Any interface listed with OK? value "NO" does not have a valid configuration
```

```
Interface              IP-Address         OK?    Method Status   Protocol
BRI0                   unassigned         NO     unset  up       down
BRI0:1                 unassigned         YES    unset  down     down
BRI0:2                 unassigned         YES    unset  down     down
Serial0                unassigned         NO     unset  up       down
Serial1                unassigned         NO     unset  down     down
Serial2                unassigned         NO     unset  down     down

Serial3                unassigned         NO     unset  down     down
TokenRing0             unassigned         NO     unset  reset    down
```

Configuring global parameters:

    Enter host name [Router]: Router_C

The enable secret is a one-way cryptographic secret used
instead of the enable password when it exists.

    Enter enable secret: joan

The enable password is used when there is no enable secret
and when using older software and some boot images.

    Enter enable password: sally
    Enter virtual terminal password: fred
    Configure SNMP Network Management? [yes]: n
    Configure LAT? [yes]: nn
    Configure AppleTalk? [no]: n
    Configure DECnet? [no]: n
    Configure IP? [yes]: y
    Configure IGRP routing? [yes]: y
 Your IGRP autonomous system number [1]: 500
    Configure CLNS? [no]: n
    Configure IPX? [no]: n
    Configure Vines? [no]: n
    Configure XNS? [no]: n
    Configure Apollo? [no]: n
    Configure bridging? [no]: n
    Enter ISDN BRI Switch Type [none]: n

Configuring interface parameters:

shutdown
no ip address
!
interface Serial3
shutdown
no ip address
!
interface TokenRing0
shutdown
no ip address
!
router igrp 500
```

```

```
redistribute connected
network 192.10.10.0
!
end

Use this configuration? [yes/no]: y
Building configuration...
Use the enabled mode 'configure' command to modify this configuration.
```

Answer 2–68.
c) Actual communication is between physical addresses.

For a host to communicate with another host a Layer 2 MAC address is required. (Refer to the following capture.)

```
⊟ Ethernet Version II
    ⊟ Address: 00-80-C7-CA-0A-8A --->00-60-09-C3-DF-60
    ☑ Ethernet II Protocol Type: IP
⊟ Internet Protocol
    ⊟ Version(MSB 4 bits): 4
    ⊟ Header length(LSB 4 bits): 5 (32-bit word)
    ⊞ Service type: Precd=Routine,Delay=Normal,Thrput=Normal,Reli=Normal
    ⊟ Total length: 44 (Octets)
    ⊟ Fragment ID: 17159
    ⊞ Flags: Do not fragment,Last fragment,Offset=0 (0x00)
    ⊟ Time to live: 32 seconds/hops
    ⊟ IP protocol type: TCP (0x06)
    ⊟ Checksum: 0xEF93
    ⊟ IP address 172.20.0.3 ->172.20.0.1
```

Answer 2–69.
c) show host
d) sh hosts

```
Router_A#sh hosts
Default domain is not set
Name/address lookup uses domain service
Name servers are 255.255.255.255

Host                     Flags        Age Type    Address(es)
router_B                 (perm, OK)   7    IP     210.7.93.2   65.62.245.1
router_C                 (perm, OK)   7    IP     65.62.245.2

Router_A#sh host
Default domain is not set
Name/address lookup uses domain service
Name servers are 255.255.255.255

Host                     Flags        Age Type    Address(es)
router_B                 (perm, OK)   7    IP     210.7.93.2   65.62.245.1
router_C                 (perm, OK)   7    IP     65.62.245.2
```

Answer 2–70.
   c) **Are usually assigned by the source host, and are typically some number greater than 1023.**

The source port in the following capture is 1074:

```
Ethernet Version II
    Address: 00-80-C7-CA-0A-8A --->00-60-09-C3-DF-60
    Ethernet II Protocol Type: IP
Internet Protocol
    Version(MSB 4 bits): 4
    Header length(LSB 4 bits): 5 (32-bit word)
    Service type: Prec=Routine,Delay=Normal,Thrput=Normal,Reli=Normal
    Total length: 40 (Octets)
    Fragment ID: 17415
    Flags: Do not fragment,Last fragment,Offset=0 (0x00)
    Time to live: 32 seconds/hops
    IP protocol type: TCP (0x06)
    Checksum: 0xBE9C
    IP address 172.20.0.3 --->172.20.0.1
    No option
IP Transmission Control Protocol
    Port 1074 ---> Telnet
    Sequence Number: 39635901
    Acknowledgement Number: 1891894734
    Header Length(MSB 4 bits): 5 (32-bit word)
    Reserved(LSB 4 bits): 0
    Code: ACK,
    Window: 8760
    Checksum: 0xEC7A
    Urgent Pointer: 0x0000
```

Answer 2–71.
   a) **Increases bandwidth available to nodes**
   b) **Controls broadcasts**
   d) **Reduces the number of collisions**

On a router each port is its own broadcast and collision domain.

Answer 2–72.
   b) **show fr ma**
   c) **show frame-relay lmi**
   e) **show interface serial 0/0**

The CCNA test can be very tricky. Keep in mind that a command can be truncated.

"sh fr ma" is short for "show frame-relay map".

Some examples of the show commands are shown below:

```
Router_A#sh frame map
Serial0/0 (up): ip 172.16.10.2 dlci 200(0xC8,0x3080), dynamic,
          broadcast,, status defined, active

Router_A#sh frame pvc

PVC Statistics for interface Serial0/0 (Frame Relay DTE)

DLCI = 200, DLCI USAGE = LOCAL, PVC STATUS = ACTIVE, INTERFACE = Serial0/0
```

```
     input pkts 337          output pkts 2355         in bytes 105250
     out bytes 217874        dropped pkts 0           in FECN pkts 0
     in BECN pkts 0          out FECN pkts 0          out BECN pkts 0
     in DE pkts 0            out DE pkts 0
     out bcast pkts 2355       out bcast bytes 217874
     pvc create time 05:36:44, last time pvc status changed 05:36:24

   Router_A#sh int s0/0
   Serial0/0 is up, line protocol is up
     Hardware is QUICC Serial
     Internet address is 172.16.10.1/24
     MTU 1500 bytes, BW 1544 Kbit, DLY 20000 usec, rely 255/255, load 1/255
     Encapsulation FRAME-RELAY, loopback not set, keepalive set (10 sec)
     LMI enq sent  2298, LMI stat recvd 2298, LMI upd recvd 0, DTE LMI up
     LMI enq recvd 0, LMI stat sent  0, LMI upd sent  0
     LMI DLCI 1023  LMI type is CISCO  frame relay DTE
     FR SVC disabled, LAPF state down
     Broadcast queue 0/64, broadcasts sent/dropped 2651/0, interface broadcasts
     227
0
     Last input 00:00:04, output 00:00:04, output hang never
     Last clearing of "show interface" counters never
     Input queue: 0/75/0 (size/max/drops); Total output drops: 0
     Queueing strategy: weighted fair
     Output queue: 0/64/0 (size/threshold/drops)
        Conversations  0/1 (active/max active)
        Reserved Conversations 0/0 (allocated/max allocated)
     5 minute input rate 0 bits/sec, 0 packets/sec
     5 minute output rate 0 bits/sec, 0 packets/sec
        2894 packets input, 165069 bytes, 0 no buffer
        Received 2298 broadcasts, 0 runts, 0 giants, 0 throttles
        2 input errors, 0 CRC, 2 frame, 0 overrun, 0 ignored, 0 abort
        4972 packets output, 276835 bytes, 0 underruns
        0 output errors, 0 collisions, 20 interface resets
        0 output buffer failures, 0 output buffers swapped out
        0 carrier transitions
        DCD=up  DSR=up  DTR=up  RTS=up  CTS=up

   Router_A#sh frame lmi

   LMI Statistics for interface Serial0/0 (Frame Relay DTE) LMI TYPE = CISCO
     Invalid Unnumbered info 0          Invalid Prot Disc 0
     Invalid dummy Call Ref 0           Invalid Msg Type 0
     Invalid Status Message 0           Invalid Lock Shift 0
     Invalid Information ID 0           Invalid Report IE Len 0
     Invalid Report Request 0           Invalid Keep IE Len 0
     Num Status Enq. Sent 2299          Num Status msgs Rcvd 2299
     Num Update Status Rcvd 0           Num Status Timeouts 0
```

Answer 2–73.
a) It is alternate one-way communication.

The other choices describe full duplex.

When my wife and I go the beach we take this narrow road. I have a full size Dodge pick-up, so when there is an on-coming car, to prevent a collision, I pull to the side of the road. This road, as far as I am concerned, is a half-duplex road. One way traffic and collisions are possible.

Answer 2–74.
    e) None of the above.

The address of 193.243.12.43/25 would be on the zero subnet and would be represented as 193.243.12.0

I have used the slash format to represent the mask. This means that the first 25 bits represent the address of the wire.

Answer 2–75.
    a) This is an IPX access list.
    d) All matches will be logged.

Information that will be logged includes:
- Source address
- Destination address
- Source socket
- Destination socket
- Protocol type
- Whether the packet was permitted or denied

Answer 2–76.
    a) Immediately

After the configuration command is issued, the change takes place immediately. There are times when the router needs to be bounced, but it is very rare.

Answer 2–77.
    a) E0

Answer 2–78.
    b) show protocol
    c) show run

Show ip protocol will show just the ip routing protocols that are currently configured. Show start may or may not show the current routed protocols.

Below is the output of show protocol

```
Router_B#show protocol
Global values:
  Internet Protocol routing is enabled
  Appletalk routing is enabled
BRI0 is administratively down, line protocol is down
```

```
BRIO:1 is administratively down, line protocol is down
BRIO:2 is administratively down, line protocol is down
Serial0 is administratively down, line protocol is down
Serial1 is administratively down, line protocol is down
Serial2 is administratively down, line protocol is down
Serial3 is administratively down, line protocol is down
TokenRing0 is administratively down, line protocol is down
```

Answer 2–79.
  b) show running-configuration file
  d) write terminal

Many who have some experience with older versions are familiar with the "show configuration" command and do not realize that this command shows the start-up configuration. Usually they have made a change to the running-configuration. Then they issue the show configuration command, and they think something is wrong with the router because the change doesn't show up. Since version 10.3 the command to show running-configuration will display the running configuration command. Prior to this version "write terminal" was the appropriate command. In general many of the 10.3 and later commands are intuitive, such as:

```
show run
show start
copy run start
copy start run
```

What may not be intuitive is that when a copy is made to the running-configuration this is not the same as a DOS-type copy. In other words the original running configuration is not lost the resulting running configuration file is a blending of the two files.

Answer 2–80.
  e) The number of octets that the sender is willing to accept

Answer 2–81.
  c) In ROM

Answer 2–82.
  d) 62

The above mask is using 6 bits to describe subnets. The formula used to determine the number of subnets is $2^n - 2$ where n is the number of subnet bits. This is the number to use when configuring a IP address with the setup dialog.

Answer 2–83.
  b) In RAM

Answer 2–84.
  b) Set a login password on the console terminal.

Refer to the following example.

```
Router_C#config t
Enter configuration commands, one per line. End with CNTL/Z.
Router_C(config)#line console 0
Router_C(config-line)#password ccieprep
```

Answer 2–85.
  c) show ip interface
  d) show interface

Examples of each of these commands are shown below:

```
Router_A#sh int e0/0
Ethernet0/0 is up, line protocol is up
  Hardware is AmdP2, address is 0010.7b15.bd41 (bia 0010.7b15.bd41)
  Internet address is 10.10.10.1/24
  MTU 1500 bytes, BW 10000 Kbit, DLY 1000 usec, rely 255/255, load 1/255
  Encapsulation ARPA, loopback not set, keepalive set (10 sec)
  ARP type: ARPA, ARP Timeout 04:00:00
  Last input never, output 00:00:06, output hang never
  Last clearing of "show interface" counters never
  Queueing strategy: fifo
  Output queue 0/40, 0 drops; input queue 0/75, 0 drops
  5 minute input rate 0 bits/sec, 0 packets/sec
  5 minute output rate 0 bits/sec, 0 packets/sec
     0 packets input, 0 bytes, 0 no buffer
     Received 0 broadcasts, 0 runts, 0 giants, 0 throttles
     0 input errors, 0 CRC, 0 frame, 0 overrun, 0 ignored, 0 abort
     0 input packets with dribble condition detected
     127 packets output, 11802 bytes, 0 underruns
     0 output errors, 0 collisions, 2 interface resets
     0 babbles, 0 late collision, 0 deferred
     0 lost carrier, 0 no carrier
     0 output buffer failures, 0 output buffers swapped out

Router_A#sh ip int e0/0
Ethernet0/0 is up, line protocol is up
  Internet address is 10.10.10.1/24
  Broadcast address is 255.255.255.255
  Address determined by non-volatile memory
  MTU is 1500 bytes
  Helper address is not set
  Directed broadcast forwarding is enabled
  Outgoing access list is not set
  Inbound access list is not set
  Proxy ARP is enabled
  Security level is default
  Split horizon is enabled
  ICMP redirects are always sent
  ICMP unreachables are always sent
  ICMP mask replies are never sent
  IP fast switching is enabled
  IP fast switching on the same interface is disabled
  IP multicast fast switching is enabled
```

2. Answers

```
Router Discovery is disabled
IP output packet accounting is disabled
IP access violation accounting is disabled
TCP/IP header compression is disabled
Probe proxy name replies are disabled
Gateway Discovery is disabled
Policy routing is disabled
Network address translation is disabled
```

Answer 2–86.
e) enable-password

Answer 2–87.
c) IPX

There are routing protocols and routed protocols. Some examples of routed protocols include IP, IPX, Appletalk and Decnet. A routed protocol travels through the network. Routing protocols such as OSPF, IP RIP, IPX RIP, IGRP and EIGRP represent the language that routers use to determine the best path through the network.

Answer 2–88.
e) To prevent IP datagrams that are caught in a routing loop from traversing the network forever.

Time to Live - how long a packet can survive on the network before it will be removed. Each host on the net should decrement the time TTL by one, usually 255 on an ethernet segment

Answer 2–89.
f) HDLC

The default encapsulation for a serial interface is HDLC.

Refer to the IPX routing table below:

```
Router_A#sh ipx route
%SYS-5-CONFIG_I: Configured from console by console
Codes: C - Connected primary network,
   c - Connected secondary network S - Static, F - Floating static,
   L - Local (internal), W - IPXWAN R - RIP, E - EIGRP,
   N - NLSP, X - External, A - Aggregate s - seconds, u - uses,
   U - Per-user static

4 Total IPX routes. Up to 1 parallel paths and 16 hops allowed.

No default route known.

C        BAD (NOVELL-ETHER),   Et0/0
C        CAD (HDLC),           Se0/0
R         AD [07/01] via       CAD.0007.7816.fe54,    89s, Se0/0
R        DAD [13/02] via       CAD.0007.7816.fe54,    89s, Se0/0
```

Answer 2–90.
 d) **EBC**

The Ethernet Bundling Controller (EBC) is responsible for Fast EtherChannel.

Answer 2–91.
 c) **show ip arp**

Example:

```
Router_A#sh ip arp
Protocol   Address       Age (min)    Hardware Addr   Type      Interface
Internet   1.1.1.2          -         0010.7b15.bd50  ARPA      FastEthernet1/0
Internet   10.10.10.1       -         0010.7b15.bd41  ARPA      Ethernet0/0
```

Answer 2–92.
 b) **The amount of memory and processing required**
 e) **The bandwidth consumed by the initial link state flood**

Answer 2–93.
 b) **The number of the packet expected next**

This number is the previous Sequence number +1.
Check out the sequence and the acknowledgement numbers below:

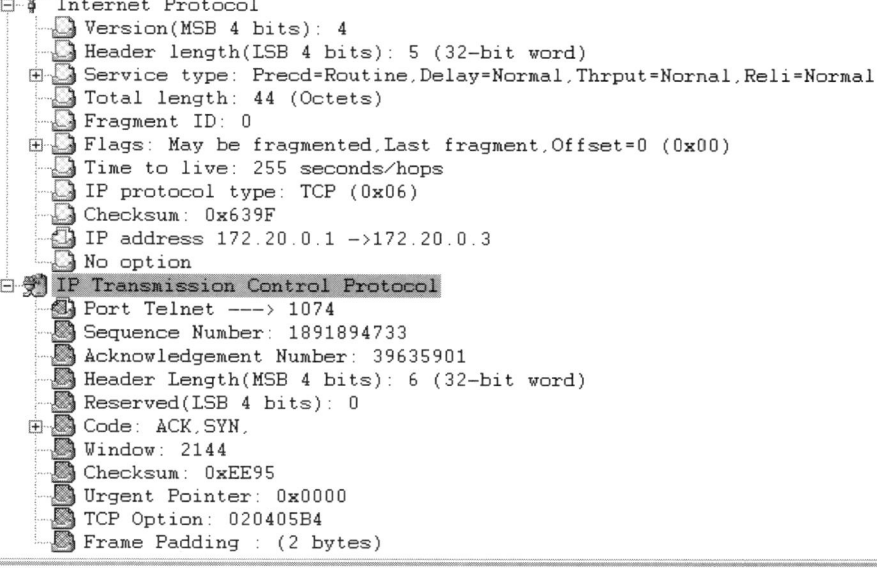

```
Internet Protocol
    Version(MSB 4 bits): 4
    Header length(LSB 4 bits): 5 (32-bit word)
    Service type: Precd=Routine,Delay=Normal,Thrput=Normal,Reli=Normal
    Total length: 44 (Octets)
    Fragment ID: 0
    Flags: May be fragmented,Last fragment,Offset=0 (0x00)
    Time to live: 255 seconds/hops
    IP protocol type: TCP (0x06)
    Checksum: 0x639F
    IP address 172.20.0.1 ->172.20.0.3
    No option
IP Transmission Control Protocol
    Port Telnet ---> 1074
    Sequence Number: 1891894733
    Acknowledgement Number: 39635901
    Header Length(MSB 4 bits): 6 (32-bit word)
    Reserved(LSB 4 bits): 0
    Code: ACK,SYN,
    Window: 2144
    Checksum: 0xEE95
    Urgent Pointer: 0x0000
    TCP Option: 020405B4
    Frame Padding : (2 bytes)
```

```
☐-▥ Ethernet Version II
│  ☐ Address: 00-80-C7-CA-0A-8A --->00-60-09-C3-DF-60
│  ☐ Ethernet II Protocol Type: IP
☐-▽ Internet Protocol
│  ☐ Version(MSB 4 bits): 4
│  ☐ Header length(LSB 4 bits): 5 (32-bit word)
│  ☐-☐ Service type: Precd=Routine,Delay=Normal,Thrput=Normal,Reli=Normal
│  ☐ Total length: 40 (Octets)
│  ☐ Fragment ID: 17415
│  ☐-☐ Flags: Do not fragment,Last fragment,Offset=0 (0x00)
│  ☐ Time to live: 32 seconds/hops
│  ☐ IP protocol type: TCP (0x06)
│  ☐ Checksum: 0xBE9C
│  ☐ IP address 172.20.0.3 ->172.20.0.1
│  ☐ No option
☐-☐ IP Transmission Control Protocol
   ☐ Port 1074 ---> Telnet
   ☐ Sequence Number: 39635901
   ☐ Acknowledgement Number: 1891894734
   ☐ Header Length(MSB 4 bits): 5 (32-bit word)
   ☐ Reserved(LSB 4 bits): 0
   ☐-☐ Code: ACK,
   ☐ Window: 8760
   ☐ Checksum: 0xEC7A
   ☐ Urgent Pointer: 0x0000
```

Answer 2–94.
e) 255.255.255.252

The 255.255.255.252 provides two host addresses. This is the exact number of host addresses we need for a serial connection. In the example below the two host addresses are shown in bold. The chart represents the fourth octet of a class C address. The mask is 255.255.255.252. The network number is 4. The broadcast address is 7.

	128	64	32	16	8	4	2	1
4	0	0	0	0	0	1	0	0
5	0	0	0	0	0	1	0	1
6	0	0	0	0	0	1	1	0
7	0	0	0	0	0	1	1	1

Answer 2–95.
d) 224.0.0.0 to 239.255.255.255

These are also called Class D addresses.

Answer 2–96.
d) The command will be executed and permit all traffic in and out.

There are two steps to use an access list:

1. Create the list
2. Place the access list on a interface

The analogy I use in class is:

Suppose you reside in a gated community. The community is not protected until you hire the guard and then place him at the gate. If you hire the guard and never place him at the gate all traffic will be permitted.

When there is no access list on an interface it is implicit permit any.
When an access list is placed on a interface it is implicit deny any.

Answer 2–97.
   a) IP is to TCP as IPX is to SPX.
   b) RTMP is to Appletalk as IP RIP is to IP.
   c) NLSP is to IPX as OSPF is to IP.

Answer 2–98.
   a) ARP is used to map an IP address to a MAC address.

Address Resolution Protocol (ARP) is independent of the MAC sublayer of the Data Link Layer, whether it's Ethernet, Token Ring or ARCnet. An ARP occurs when a host has a layer 3 address and needs to resolve a Layer 2 MAC address. Would the IPX protocol use an ARP? (Keep in mind what IPX uses for the node portion of the IPX address.)

The following is a ARP request. The ARP is sent as a broadcast to all stations on the subnet.

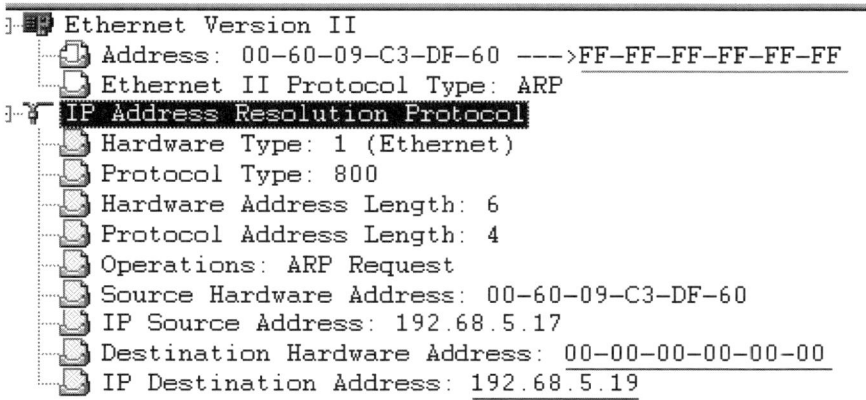

Answer 2–99.
  d) This is not a legal address.

First Octet Rules:

- If the first bit is 0, it's a Class A address
- If the first two bits are10, it's a Class B address.
- If the first three bits are 110 and the value is less than 224, it's a class C address.
- No address can have a value of zero (0) in the first octet
- The address of 127 will be reserved for loopback addresses
- Addresses with a value of 10 will be reserved for private use

The above rules provide us with the following ranges:

Class A   1 - 126
Class B   128 - 191
Class C   192 - 223

Refer to the following attempt to assign the above illegal address:

```
Router_C>en
Router_C#config t
Enter configuration commands, one per line.  End with CNTL/Z.
Router_C(config)#int e0

Router_C(config-if)#ip address 0.10.10.10 255.255.255.0
Not a valid host address - 0.10.10.10
Router_C(config-if)#
```

Answer 2–100.
c) IPX RIP, IGRP, RTMP

Appletalk's RTMP and Novell's IPX RIP are the default routing protocols.

Refer to the following routing tables of Router C:

```
Router_C#sh ip route
Codes: C - connected, S - static, I - IGRP, R - RIP, M - mobile,
  B - BGP, D - EIGRP, EX - EIGRP external, O - OSPF,
  IA - OSPF inter area, N1 - OSPF NSSA external type 1,
  N2 - OSPF NSSA external type 2, E1 - OSPF external type 1,
  E2 - OSPF external type 2, E - EGP, i - IS-IS,
  L1 - IS-IS level-1, L2 - IS-IS level-2,
  * - candidate default, U - per-user static route, o - ODR

Gateway of last resort is not set

I    10.0.0.0/8 [100/10576] via 172.17.1.1, 00:00:03, Serial0
     172.16.0.0/24 is subnetted, 1 subnets
C       172.16.1.0 is directly connected, Ethernet0
     172.17.0.0/16 is variably subnetted, 2 subnets, 2 masks
I       172.17.1.0/32 [100/8976] via 172.17.1.1, 00:00:03, Serial0
I       172.17.0.0/16 [100/8976] via 172.17.1.1, 00:00:03, Serial0
Router_C#sh app route
```

```
Codes: R - RTMP derived, E - EIGRP derived, C - connected, A - AURP
       S - static  P - proxy
4 routes in internet

The first zone listed for each entry is its default (primary) zone.

C Net 100-105 directly connected, Ethernet0, zone right
R Net 106-110 [2/G] via 120.125, 2 sec, Serial0, zone left
C Net 120-120 directly connected, Serial0, zone left
R Net 130-130 [1/G] via 120.125, 2 sec, Serial0, zone right
Router_C#sh ipx route
Codes: C - Connected primary network,
  c - Connected secondary network, S - Static,
  F - Floating static, L - Local (internal), W - IPXWAN,
  R - RIP, E - EIGRP, N - NLSP, X - External, A - Aggregate,
  s - seconds, u - uses

4 Total IPX routes. Up to 1 parallel paths and 16 hops allowed.

No default route known.

C         AD (HDLC),          Se0
C         DAD (NOVELL-ETHER),  Et0
R         BAD [13/02] via      AD.0007.7816.fe54,    28s, Se0
R         CAD [07/01] via      AD.0007.7816.fe54,    28s, Se0
```

Answer 2–101.
   a) DNS
   c) TFTP
   e) SNMP
   f) NFS

The following is a capture of a TFTP.

```
Ethernet version II
    Address: 00-60-09-C3-DF-60 --->00-80-C7-CA-0A-8A
    Ethernet II Protocol Type: IP
Internet Protocol
    Version(MSB 4 bits): 4
    Header length(LSB 4 bits): 5 (32-bit word)
    Service type: Precd=Routine,Delay=Normal,Thrput=Normal,Reli=Normal
    Total length: 46 (Octets)
    Fragment ID: 0
    Flags: May be fragmented,Last fragment,Offset=0 (0x00)
    Time to live: 255 seconds/hops
    IP protocol type: UDP (0x11)
    Checksum: 0x6392
    IP address 172.20.0.1 ->172.20.0.3
    No option
IP User Datagram Protocol
    Port 9412 ---> Trivial File Transfer
    Total length: 26 (Octets)
    Checksum: 0xF32E
TFTP Protocol
    OP Code: 1 - Read Request
    FileName: hosts.txt
    Mode: octet
```

Answer 2–102.
   a) An IP number can be used to identify a ring in a Token Ring network.
   b) An IP number can be used to identify a serial interface in a router.
   c) An IP number can be used to identify a logical Ethernet network.
   g) An IP number can be used to identify a Host on a remote logical network.

We might be getting a little tricky with this question.

An IP address has two parts: a network part, which describes the address of the wire and a host part, which describes the address of the host. The network part can describe a ring or an Ethernet wire. The host part can describe an interface of a router or any host residing locally or on a remote network. The IP address is always 32 bits in length. With a registered address you can not change the network bits, but obviously you can change the host bits.

Answer 2–103.
   c) "configure terminal" from the privileged prompt

Answer 2–104.
   c) At the router, it is the route used to direct frames for which the next hop has not been explicitly listed in the routing table.

The purpose of a default route is to route frames for which a next hop has not been explicitly listed in the routing table. To say it another way is to say that the default route points the way to go when there is no known path to follow. At a router, the default route is the address of the next hop if no other route is known or specified. Often the default route is set as a path to the Internet, where any unknown destination can hopefully be resolved.

Answer 2–105.
   d) Class A, B, and C addresses

Class D addresses are multicast addresses.
Class E addresses are experimental addresses

Answer 2–106.
   b) Store and forward

Store and forward mode receives the complete frame before forwarding takes place. After the destination and source addresses are read the cyclic redundancy check is performed, the frame is forwarded. Switch latency is dependent upon frame size.

Cut-through, on the other hand, starts forwarding the frame as soon as the destination address is read. This mode reduces latency in the switch.

Answer 2–107.
   e) All of the above.

Answer 2–108.
  c) **If Router_A receives a packet with a destination IP subnet address of 172.17.10.0, the packet will be sent to 172.16.10.1 (if there is no dynamic entry in the routing table).**
  e) **255 is the Administrative Distance (AD).**

There are three distinct components of this configuration statement.

- 172.17.10.0 identifies the destination subnet address
- 172.16.10.1 identifies the interface that the packet will be sent to (next hop address)
- 255 identifies the Administrative Distance (AD)

The administrator in this case only wanted this static route to be taken if a dynamic route to the destination is lost. The higher the AD the "less reliable" the information. 255 is as high as you can configure the AD.

Answer 2–109.
  d) **The process where a router will prioritize routing protocols so that, in the event two routing protocols have conflicting next hop addresses, the routing protocol with the lowest administrative distance will take priority.**

Cisco uses administrative distances (AD) to measure the reliability of the routing protocol. The lower the AD the more reliable the protocol.

```
Router_C#sh ip route
Codes: C - connected, S - static, I - IGRP, R - RIP, M - mobile, B - BGP
       D - EIGRP, EX - EIGRP external, O - OSPF, IA - OSPF inter area
       N1 - OSPF NSSA external type 1, N2 - OSPF NSSA external type 2
       E1 - OSPF external type 1, E2 - OSPF external type 2, E - EGP
       i - IS-IS, L1 - IS-IS level-1, L2 - IS-IS level-2, * - candidate default
       U - per-user static route, o - ODR

Gateway of last resort is not set

     172.16.0.0/24 is subnetted, 2 subnets
C       172.16.1.0 is directly connected, Serial1
C       172.16.2.0 is directly connected, Serial0
I    10.0.0.0/8 [100/8576] via 172.16.1.1, 00:00:09, Serial1
                [100/8576] via 172.16.2.1, 00:00:19, Serial0
The 100 in bold is the administrative distance for IGRP.
```

A partial list of administrative distances is included below:

Protocol	AD
EIGRP	90
IGRP	100
OSPF	110
RIP	120
BGP	180

If a router hears a IP RIP and a IGRP update for the same network, the router will discard the RIP information. IP RIP uses hop count as its metric, while IGRP uses a composite metric including bandwidth and load; speed is the primary consideration.

Answer 2–110.
   c) The serial 0 address of Router_C would be listed.
   d) No secondary IP address information would be listed.

"show cdp neighbor detail" will not list any secondary layer 3 addresses.

Answer 2–111.
   c) Used to provide congestion information in a Frame Relay environment

The following are definitions of each:

Backward Explicit Congestion Notification (BECN) - Bit set by a frame relay network in frames traveling in opposite direction of frames encountering a congested path. DTE receiving frames with the BECN bit set can request higher level protocols take flow control action.

Forward Explicit Congestion Notification (FECN) - Bit set by a frame relay network to inform DTE receiving frame that congestion was experienced in the path from source to destination.

Answer 2–112.
   d) Command Group IV above

```
Router_f(config)#interface s0
Router_f(config-if)#encapsulation frame-relay
Router_f(config-if)#frame-relay lmi-type ansi
Router_f(config-if)#ip address 172.16.1.6 255.255.255.0
Router_f(config-if)#frame-relay map ip 172.16.1.1 604
```

There are several configuration parameters that must be checked to answer these frame relay questions.

LMI
Does not have to match end-to-end. This is communication between the local router and the local frame relay switch

Encapsulation
This parameter needs to match end-to-end.

Frame map statement
The ip address here needs to be the next hop address and the DLCI number needs to be the local DLCI.

The local DLCI for Router F is 604.
The next hop address is Router A 172.16.1.1.
Encapsulation is Cisco, the default.

Answer 2–113.
  c) **Provides connectionless, best effort delivery routing of datagrams**

Answer 2–114.
  b) **Must be configured**

IPX load balances when configured. The command to use is "maximum paths". So if you have equal cost paths to a destination the default is that the router will choose the first path it receives, unlike Cisco's implementation of IP RIP that will use up to four equal cost paths.

Answer 2–115.
  b) **Can not be determined from configuration given.**
  d) **There is no DLCI configured, and this configuration will work.**

The local switch will announce its DLCI number, so it is not necessary to configure a DLCI. DLCI numbers are locally significant and thus do not have to match the remote side.

Review the following show commands:

```
Router_A#sh frame map
Serial0/0 (up): ip 172.16.10.2 dlci 200(0xC8,0x3080), dynamic,
             broadcast,, status defined, active

Router_A#sh frame pvc

PVC Statistics for interface Serial0/0 (Frame Relay DTE)

DLCI = 200, DLCI USAGE = LOCAL, PVC STATUS = ACTIVE, INTERFACE = Serial0/0

   input pkts 99          output pkts 98         in bytes 6656
   out bytes 6626         dropped pkts 0         in FECN pkts 0
   in BECN pkts 0         out FECN pkts 0        out BECN pkts 0
   in DE pkts 0           out DE pkts 0
   out bcast pkts 1        out bcast bytes 30
   pvc create time 01:37:23, last time pvc status changed 01:36:47

The local DLCI is 200
```

Answer 2–116.
  e) **<Esc><B>**

Answer 2–117.
  e) **None of the above.**

There are several configuration parameters that must be checked to answer these frame relay questions.

LMI
Does not have to match end-to-end. This is communication between the local router and the local frame relay switch.

2. Answers

Encapsulation
This parameter needs to match end-to-end.

Frame map statement
The ip address here needs to be the next hop address, and the DLCI number needs to be the local DLCI.

The local DLCI for Router F is 604.
The next hop address is Router A 172.16.1.1.
Encapsulation of Router A is IETF.
Encapsulation of all our choices is Cisco.

Answer 2–118.
e) Helps IP by providing control and messaging capabilities

ICMP is used for echo requests and echo replies. Here is a capture of a successful ping:

ICMP echo request:

```
Ethernet Version II
    Address: 00-10-7B-15-BD-41 --->00-80-C7-CA-0A-8A
    Ethernet II Protocol Type: IP
Internet Protocol
    Version(MSB 4 bits): 4
    Header length(LSB 4 bits): 5 (32-bit word)
    Service type: Precd=Routine,Delay=Normal,Thrput=Normal,Reli=Normal
    Total length: 100 (Octets)
    Fragment ID: 20
    Flags: May be fragmented,Last fragment,Offset=0 (0x00)
    Time to live: 255 seconds/hops
    IP protocol type: ICMP (0x01)
    Checksum: 0xA57E
    IP address 10.1.1.2 ->10.1.1.3
    No option
IP Internet Control Message Protocol
    Type: Echo Request
    Code: 0
    Checksum: 0xF76D
    Identifier: 0
    Sequence Number: 6219
```

ICMP echo reply:

```
Ethernet Version II
    Address: 00-80-C7-CA-0A-8A --->00-10-7B-15-BD-41
    Ethernet II Protocol Type: IP
Internet Protocol
    Version(MSB 4 bits): 4
    Header length(LSB 4 bits): 5 (32-bit word)
    Service type: Precd=Routine,Delay=Normal,Thrput=Normal,Reli=Normal
    Total length: 100 (Octets)
    Fragment ID: 6144
    Flags: May be fragmented,Last fragment,Offset=0 (0x00)
    Time to live: 32 seconds/hops
    IP protocol type: ICMP (0x01)
    Checksum: 0x6C93
    IP address 10.1.1.3 ->10.1.1.2
    No option
IP Internet Control Message Protocol
    Type: Echo Reply
    Code: 0
    Checksum: 0xFF6D
    Identifier: 0
    Sequence Number: 6219
```

2. Answers

Answer 2–119.
   e) **Router (config-if) #clock rate 56000**

Some versions may support clockrate as a single word command, but our goal here is to help you pass the exam.

The clock rate would be set on a DCE interface only.

```
Router_C(config-if)#clock rate ?
        Speed (bits per second)
1200
2400
4800
9600
19200
38400
56000
64000
72000
125000
148000
250000
500000
800000
1000000
1300000
2000000
4000000
  <300-8000000>
  Choose clockrate from list above
```

Answer 2–120.
   e) **All of the above.**

Every access list has an implicit deny all at the end. What would the need be to create a access list with just deny statements. Access-list are processed from the top down therefore the order of each statement could be critical, for instance suppose you created an access list and the first line was a permit any and the next line was a deny. Since it's top down processing a packet would be permitted to pass on the first line and the second line would never be executed. An extended list will give you a "match count" that will help in determining what the most efficient order should be.

Answer 2–121.
   b) **A triggered update is a new routing table that is sent to neighbor routers based upon some change.**
   c) **Triggered updates in conjunction with hold-down timers help prevent routing loops**

Below is an example of an IGRP triggered update.

```
Router_C(config)#int e0
```

```
Router_C(config-if)#shut
Router_C(config-if)#
IGRP: edition is now 5
IGRP: sending update to 255.255.255.255 via Serial0 (192.68.5.10)
      network 10.0.0.0, metric=-1
IGRP: Update contains 0 interior, 1 system, and 0 exterior routes.
IGRP: Total routes in update: 1
IGRP: broadcasting request on Serial0
IGRP: received update from 192.68.5.50 on Serial0
      subnet 192.68.5.48, metric 10476 (neighbor 8476)
IGRP: Update contains 1 interior, 0 system, and 0 exterior routes.
IGRP: Total routes in update: 1
%LINEPROTO-5-UPDOWN: Line protocol on Interface Ethernet0, changed state to
  down

%LINK-5-CHANGED: Interface Ethernet0, changed state to administratively down
Router_C(config-if)#

IGRP: sending update to 255.255.255.255 via Serial0 (192.68.5.10)
IGRP: Update contains 0 interior, 0 system, and 0 exterior routes.
IGRP: Total routes in update: 0 - suppressing null update
```

Answer 2–122.
   b) OSPF
   e) IS-IS

A link state routing protocol advertises, to its neighbors, the state of the link when the state of the link changes. A distance vector routing protocol advertises its routing table periodically.

Answer 2–123.
   e) Condition not possible.

Let's review all the possibilities:

Serial 0 down & line protocol down
Serial 0 administratively down and line protocol down
Serial 0 up and protocol down
Serial 0 up and protocol down (looped)
Serial 0 up and protocol up

Serial 0 up and protocol up is a fully working link, which means that both the interface and the line protocol have successfully initialized, and protocol keep alives are being received.

Serial 0 administratively down and line protocol down - This condition indicates that a shut command has been configured on this interface. To reverse this condition execute a no shut command.

Serial 0 up and protocol down (looped) - This condition indicates that this interface is receiving it's own keep alives, which is a result of putting a CSU/DSU in loop back mode.

Serial 0 down & line protocol down - This means that carrier detect signal (DCD) is not being received. You might want to make a call to your carrier to see if the local loop is up!

Serial 0 up and protocol down - This condition exists if an interface has detected a large number of errors during a keep alive period, possibly caused by a defective CSU/DSU.

Answer 2–124.
a) **Router Platform**
b) **All layer 3 addresses limited to one per protocol**
c) **IOS version**
d) **Incoming and outgoing port**
g) **Router Name**

I have configured the neighbor Router_C with a secondary address:

```
Router_C#sh
%SYS-5-CONFIG_I: Configured from console by console ip in sC
Serial0 is up, line protocol is up
  Internet address is 192.68.5.10/24
  Broadcast address is 255.255.255.255
  Address determined by setup command
  MTU is 1500 bytes
  Helper address is not set
  Directed broadcast forwarding is enabled
  Secondary address 12.12.12.1/24
  Outgoing access list is not set
  Inbound access list is not set
  Proxy ARP is enabled
  Security level is default
  Split horizon is enabled
  ICMP redirects are always sent
  ICMP unreachables are always sent
  ICMP mask replies are never sent
  IP fast switching is enabled
  IP fast switching on the same interface is enabled
  IP multicast fast switching is enabled
  Router Discovery is disabled
  IP output packet accounting is disabled
  IP access violation accounting is disabled
  TCP/IP header compression is disabled
  Probe proxy name replies are disabled
  Gateway Discovery is disabled
  Policy routing is disabled
  Network address translation is disabled
```

The result of the show cdp command:

```
Router_B#sh cdp
%SYS-5-CONFIG_I: Configured from console by consolenei det
-------------------------
Device ID: Router_C
Entry address(es):
```

```
   IP address: 192.68.5.10
Platform: cisco 2500,   Capabilities: Router
Interface: Serial0,   Port ID (outgoing port): Serial0
Holdtime : 169 sec

Version:
Cisco Internetwork Operating System Software
IOS (tm) 2500 Software (C2500-J-L), Version 11.2(3), RELEASE SOFTWARE (fc2)
Copyright (c) 1986-1996 by cisco Systems, Inc.
Compiled Mon 30-Dec-96 21:28 by ajchopra
```

Answer 2–125.
  b) Multiple stations listen for traffic and transmit at the same time.

Collisions is a term that is used in an ethernet environment. Ethernet can be described as a listen then transmit scenario. First a station will listen for traffic. If no traffic is sensed then a transmission will take place. If two stations transmit at the same time, collisions will occur. The first station to detect the collision sends out a jamming signal to alert all stations a collision has occurred. At this point these stations set up a random interval timer when the timer expires re-transmission will occur.

Token ring is a token-passing process a station can transmit only when it has the token. There never can be multiple tokens on the ring. Early token release allows up to two data frames to be transmitted on a token ring LAN at the same time. Collisions do not occur on a token ring.

Because of the point-to-point nature of serial links collisions do not occur.

Beaconing is a term used in a token passing environment.

Answer 2–126.
  b) Whenever the router is powered on
  c) Whenever the command "copy start run" is executed

Answer 2–127.
  e) Choice a and b

The type of mask used here is an inverse mask meaning that when the mask has a bit value of 0 the access list must match the corresponding bits. If the inverse mask has a value of 1 it's "don't care," meaning the access list does not care about the corresponding bit.

Since the inverse mask has a value of 0 in the first and second octet the access list must match the first 16 bits. Since the value of the fourth octet is 255 that means all the bits are ones, so the access list does not care about the value of the fourth octet.

10	1	8	0
0	0	7	255

The octet that is not so obvious is the third octet. The inverse mask of 7 gives us 0's for the most significant five bits and one's for the last three. Refer to the chart below.

Since the least three significant bits are 1's they can be anything, which gives us the subnets 8-15.

128	64	32	16	8	4	2	1	Value
0	0	0	0	1	0	0	0	8
0	0	0	0	0	1	1	1	7
0	0	0	0	1	0	0	0	8
0	0	0	0	1	0	0	1	9
0	0	0	0	1	0	1	0	10
0	0	0	0	1	0	1	1	11
0	0	0	0	1	1	0	0	12
0	0	0	0	1	1	0	1	13
0	0	0	0	1	1	1	0	14
0	0	0	0	1	1	1	1	15

Answer 2–128.
   c) **clear arp-cache**

If you have changed an IP address or a NIC card on a host, you might use this command to reset the cache.

Answer 2–129.
   c) **TCP**
   e) **TCP over IP**

This question is meant to be a little tricky. TCP is layer 4, which uses IP at layer 3.

Answer 2–130.
   a) **Expectational**

TCP uses expectational acknowledgements, meaning that the acknowledgement number refers to the packet which is expected next. For instance, assume that the sender had just sent segments 12, 13 and 14. If the receiver receives all three of these segments correctly, the receiver would ack 15. This means the receiver is acknowledging the correct receipt of segments 12, 13 and 14 and now expects to receive segment 15 next.

Refer to the captures following:

```
Internet Protocol
    Version(MSB 4 bits): 4
    Header length(LSB 4 bits): 5 (32-bit word)
    Service type: Precd=Routine,Delay=Normal,Thrput=Normal,Reli=Normal
    Total length: 44 (Octets)
    Fragment ID: 0
    Flags: May be fragmented,Last fragment,Offset=0 (0x00)
    Time to live: 255 seconds/hops
    IP protocol type: TCP (0x06)
    Checksum: 0x639F
    IP address 172.20.0.1 ->172.20.0.3
    No option
IP Transmission Control Protocol
    Port Telnet ---> 1074
    Sequence Number: 1891894733
    Acknowledgement Number: 39635901
    Header Length(MSB 4 bits): 6 (32-bit word)
    Reserved(LSB 4 bits): 0
    Code: ACK,SYN,
    Window: 2144
    Checksum: 0xEE95
    Urgent Pointer: 0x0000
    TCP Option: 020405B4
    Frame Padding : (2 bytes)
```

Based on the above capture the receiver of the above packet would ACK with 1891894734.

Refer to the next capture:

```
Ethernet Version II
    Address: 00-80-C7-CA-0A-8A --->00-60-09-C3-DF-60
    Ethernet II Protocol Type: IP
Internet Protocol
    Version(MSB 4 bits): 4
    Header length(LSB 4 bits): 5 (32-bit word)
    Service type: Precd=Routine,Delay=Normal,Thrput=Normal,Reli=Normal
    Total length: 40 (Octets)
    Fragment ID: 17415
    Flags: Do not fragment,Last fragment,Offset=0 (0x00)
    Time to live: 32 seconds/hops
    IP protocol type: TCP (0x06)
    Checksum: 0xBE9C
    IP address 172.20.0.3 ->172.20.0.1
    No option
IP Transmission Control Protocol
    Port 1074 ---> Telnet
    Sequence Number: 39635901
    Acknowledgement Number: 1891894734
    Header Length(MSB 4 bits): 5 (32-bit word)
    Reserved(LSB 4 bits): 0
    Code: ACK,
    Window: 8760
    Checksum: 0xEC7A
    Urgent Pointer: 0x0000
```

Answer 2–131.
a) ip address 1.1.1.1 255.255.255.0

If you are not in the configuration mode, the IP address can be set by using the setup mode.

```
Configuring interface Ethernet0/0:
```

```
Is this interface in use? [yes]:
Configure IP on this interface? [yes]:
  IP address for this interface [10.10.10.1]: 10.10.10.1
  Number of bits in subnet field [16]: 16
  Class A network is 10.0.0.0, 16 subnet bits; mask is /24
```

Take note when using the setup mode the mask is configured using the number of subnet bits.

Answer 2–132.
   c) **The startup-configuration file**
   d) **The running version of the Cisco IOS**

The startup-configuration file resides in NVRAM of Cisco Routers. The running version of Cisco IOS normally resides in RAM of a Cisco Router, unless the router is a 'Run from Flash" router. The Cisco 2500 and 3000 series routers are "Run from Flash". This allows more RAM for applications, routing tables, buffers, and logging if configured.

2. Answers

Chapter Three
Cisco Design Questions

This chapter contains questions modeled after those that appear on either of two different Cisco Design exams:

- Cisco Design Specialist (or Designing Cisco Networks) Exam: (exam #9E0-004)
- Cisco Internetwork Design Exam: (exam #640-025)

Each of these exams consist of 100 questions. There is a three-hour time limit for the Cisco Design Specialist (CDS) exam and a two-hour limit for the Cisco Internetwork Design (CID) exam. The minimum passing score for both exams is 70 percent.

You can find out more about the objectives of each of these exams by visiting http://www.cisco.com/warp/public/10/wwtraining/, and looking for references to these specific exams and the courses that help you prepare for them. Be prepared to dig around at the Cisco website for this information and keep in mind that Cisco updates it frequently.

The actual design exams will most likely contain a company scenario. You will use this scenario throughout the exam to answer questions concerning the fictional company's current situation and base your recommendations upon their needs.

The CDS exam is concerned more with SOHO (Small Office Home Office) situations. The CID exam covers design issues on a larger operational scale.

When using this Study Guide's CD-ROM to study and/or test your knowledge of the objectives addressed in Cisco Design Exams, you will need to select the "CCIE" option at the *select exam* window. You must then select *study session*, and select all questions with the certification code of "D".

There is a total universe of 40 model design questions in this reference. Each time you request a Design *study session* using the CD-ROM, the resulting questions will be selected randomly from this universe.

3. Design

Question 3–1. [CxDx] Which of the following is true of the Channel Interface Processor Card (CIP)?

    a) Emulates a 3172
    b) Emulates a 3745 gateway
    c) Supports Bus and Tag connection
    d) Supports ESCON connection
    e) Supports CLAW
    f) All of the above

Question 3–2. [xxDx] For which one of the following situations would a routing solution be recommended over a switching solution?

    a) High rate of Ethernet collisions
    b) Excessive number of late collisions
    c) High rate of intra-user group traffic
    d) High rate of inter user group traffic
    e) Several routed protocols advertising services

Question 3–3. [RIDx] With respect to "load balancing" which one of the following are true?

    a) IP RIP requires that parallel links have the same bandwidth.
    b) IGRP requires that parallel links have the same bandwidth.
    c) Enhanced IGRP requires that all parallel links have the same bandwidth.
    d) IP RIP, IGRP & EIGRP can load balance over parallel links of unequal bandwidth.
    e) None of the above.

Question 3–4. [RADx] How many Appletalk RTMP updates can be carried in a single update?

    a) 25
    b) 104
    c) 97
    d) 50
    e) 7

Question 3–5. [xxDx] As a general rule WAN links are considered saturated when utilization reaches:

    a) 10%
    b) 20%
    c) 30%
    d) 40%
    e) 50%
    f) 70%

3. Design

Question 3–6. [CxDx] Which two tasks would be included in identifying customer needs?

a) Characterize the existing network
b) Write a design document
c) Design the topologies
d) Extract new customer requirements
e) All of the above

Question 3–7. [xxDx] Which of the following is the Interface Description Block (IDB) limit of Cisco IOS release 11.1 and 11.2?

a) 12
b) 24
c) 48
d) 100
e) 300

Question 3–8. [RXDx] How many IPX SAP updates can be carried in a single update?

a) 25
b) 104
c) 97
d) 50
e) 7

Question 3–9. [RIDx] How many IP RIP routes can be carried in a single update?

a) 25
b) 104
c) 97
d) 50
e) 7

Question 3–10. [xxDx] Which of the following best describes traffic shaping?

a) The ability to send traffic through the internetwork as quickly as possible
b) The ability to provide error-free connection-oriented transport
c) The ability to control traffic on LAN links
d) The ability to throttle back traffic to downstream links from the source side
e) None of the above

Question 3–11. [xIDx] What does the MAC address 01:00:5e:01:00:00 identify?

a) Multicast
b) Local Broadcast
c) Unicast
d) Directed Broadcast
e) Can not be determined

3. Design

Question 3–12. [xIDx] Which protocol is used by multicast routers to keep track of group memberships?

    a) IGMP
    b) ICMP
    c) CGPM
    d) SNMP
    e) There is no such protocol.

Question 3–13. [AxDx] Private ATM addressing uses:

    a) NSAP (Network Service Access Point) addressing
    b) E.164 addressing
    c) Standard IP addressing format
    d) ANF (Account Number Format)
    e) None of the above

Question 3–14. [xxDx] Which of the following are true of "time to convergence"? (Choose two.)

    a) Dependent on the time it takes to detect a link failure
    b) Dependent on time it takes for link to fail
    c) Dependent on time it takes to propagate failure through out the network
    d) Independent of routing protocol being used
    e) All of the above

Question 3–15. [RxDx] In a hub and spoke environment with low bandwidth which routing method would you recommend?

    a) IGRP
    b) EIGRP
    c) IP RIP
    d) Static Routing
    e) Bridging

Question 3–16. [CxDx] Cisco supports two compression methods, STAC and Predictor. Which of the following are true?

    a) STAC requires more memory than Predictor.
    b) STAC requires more CPU cycles than Predictor.
    c) STAC tries to predict the next sequence of characters in the data stream.
    d) STAC and Predictor have been "tweaked" by Cisco engineers.
    e) Predictor is based on the Lempel-Ziv compression algorithm.

Question 3–17. [CxDx] Which is true of automatic redistribution of IP RIP and IP EIGRP?

a) Hop count is maintained.
b) Hop count is increased by 1.
c) Tick count is maintained.
d) Tick count is increased by 6.
e) There is no automatic redistribution of IP RIP and IP EIGRP.

Question 3–18. [CxDx] Which one of the following layers provides users and workgroups access to the network?

a) Core
b) Access
c) Distribution
d) Physical
e) None of the above

Question 3–19. [xxDx] The Cisco 1604 Router includes:

a) Ethernet port and a Frame Relay port
b) Token Ring port and a WAN slot
c) Ethernet port, WAN slot and a Token Ring port
d) Ethernet port, WAN slot and a ISDN BRI U
e) None of the above

Question 3–20. [CxDx] Cisco's Process Switching method for IPX can be best described as:

a) Destination-by-Destination
b) Packet-by-Packet
c) Frame Tagging
d) TAG identification
e) Frame Filtering

Question 3–21. [CxDx] Assuming all the defaults, which of the following would be true as they relate to the IPX routing table of Router_B? (Refer to the diagram below.)

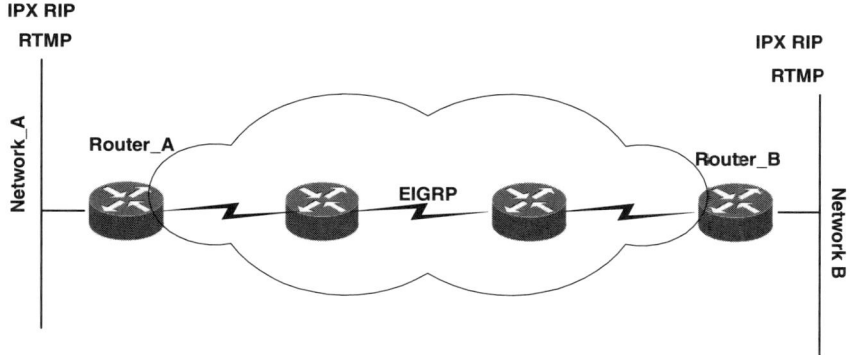

a)   Network_A is 1 hop and 1 tick away.
b)   Network_A is 2 hops and 1 tick away.
c)   Network_A is 3 hops and 19 ticks away.
d)   Network_A is 2 hops and 19 ticks away.
e)   It would depend on the default metric configured.

Question 3–22. [RxDx] Assume there are multiple best ways to get to a destination contained in a routing table. If one of these ways should be lost, which of the following are true of convergence time?

a)   Depends on the routing protocol configured
b)   Convergence time will be 0.
c)   Depends on the type of link
d)   Depends on the processing speed of the router
e)   All of the above

Question 3–23. [RADx] An AppleTalk extended network:

a)   Supports a maximum of 256 devices
b)   Extends the distant limitations of ethernet
c)   Allows assignment of cable ranges
d)   Eliminates the need for zone names
e)   Reduces broadcast traffic

Question 3–24. [CxDx] A feature of some Cisco routers that provides Layer 2 performance with Layer 3 routing is called:

a)   Frame Tagging
b)   Frame Filtering
c)   Process Switching
d)   Fast Switching
e)   Tag Switching

Question 3–25. [CxDx] Which one of the following Layers should provide optimal transport between sites?

a)   Core
b)   Access
c)   Distribution
d)   Physical
e)   None of the above

Question 3–26. [RXDx] How many IPX RIP updates can be carried in a single update?

a)   25
b)   104
c)   97
d)   50
e)   7

Question 3–27. [xxDx] Which of the following are true? (Choose four.)

a) Class I repeater has a latency of 0.7 microseconds or less.
b) Class II repeater allows only one repeater hop.
c) Class I repeater allows only one repeater hop.
d) Class II repeater has a latency of 0.7 microseconds or less.
e) Class II repeater allows one or two repeater hop.
f) Class II repeater has a latency of 0.46 microseconds or less.

Question 3–28. [CxDx] Which one of the following layers should provide policy-based connectivity?

a) Core
b) Access
c) Distribution
d) Physical
e) None of the above

Question 3–29. [CxDx] Assuming all the defaults, which of the following would be true as they relate to the Appletalk routing table of Router_B? (Refer to the diagram below.)

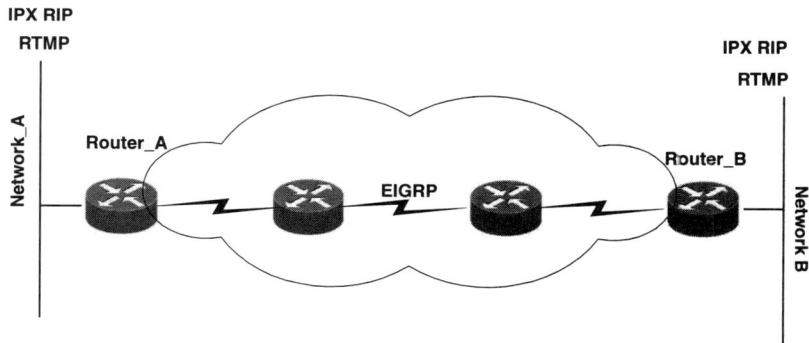

a) Network_A is 1 hop away.
b) Network_A is 2 hops away.
c) Network_A is 3 hops away.
d) Network_A is 4 hops away.
e) It would depend on the default metric configured.

Question 3–30. [AxDx] An ATM cell format contains a total of 53 bytes. How many bytes are contained in the header?

a) 1
b) 2
c) 3
d) 4
e) 5

Question 3–31. [CxDx] Which of the following is true of DLSw+?

a) Supports Explorer Firewalls
b) Is an IEEE standard
c) Has maximum Hop Count of 7
d) Can be used across different vendors
e) All of the above

Question 3–32. [AxDx] Public ATM addressing uses:

a) NSAP (Network Service Access Point) addressing
b) E.164 addressing
c) Standard IP addressing format
d) ANF (Account Number Format)
e) None of the above

Question 3–33. [RIDx] Which RFC deals with private IP addressing?

a) RFC 1600
b) RFC 1122
c) RFC 1123
d) RFC 1581
e) RFC 1597

Question 3–34. [NxDx] Which of the following ISDN devices takes the 2-wire local loop and converts to a 4-wire ISDN connection? (I,D)

a) TE1
b) TE2
c) Terminal Adapter
d) NT1
e) ISDN does not use a 4 wire connection

Question 3–35. [CxDx] Cisco has identified three different areas to be examined when considering whether to use a layer 2 or a layer 3 design solution. What are these three areas?

a) Protocol
b) Media
c) Transport
d) Physical
e) Session
f) Presentation

Question 3–36. [RxDx] When IP RIP is configured in a hierarchical design, the maximum number of hops any packet should take is:

a) 15
b) 16
c) 6
d) 8
e) Can not be determined

Question 3–37. [CxDx] Which of the following is true of EIGRP?

a) It keeps the active routing table of its adjacent neighbors.
b) It is a Link State routing protocol.
c) It communicates with routers within the AS
d) It is an "IP" only protocol.
e) All of the above.

Question 3–38. [RIDx] How many IP IGRP updates can be carried in a single update?

a) 25
b) 104
c) 97
d) 50
e) 7

Question 3–39. [CxDx] Which three of the following are the layers of the design Hierarchical Model?

a) Application Layer
b) Physical Layer
c) Core Layer
d) Access layer
e) Distribution layer

Question 3–40. [xxDx] What are the three layers of a classic "firewall system?"

a) Access Lists
b) Physical Security
c) An Isolation LAN
d) A router performing outside packet filtering
e) A router performing inside packet filtering

3. Design

Answer 3–1.
   f) All of the above

Answer 3–2.
   e) Several routed protocols advertising services

LAN protocols broadcast their services. A router interface defines a broadcast domain. In other words by default a router will "kill" a broadcast packet. A switch is used to define a collision domain NOT a broadcast domain.

Answer 3–3.
   d) IP RIP, IGRP & EIGRP can load balance over parallel links of unequal bandwidth.

IP RIP uses hop count for a metric. If the hop count is the same IP RIP will load balance regardless of the bandidth. IGRP and EIGRP use a composite metric of bandwidth, delay, load, reliability and Maximum Transmission Unit (MTU). Cisco's IGRP and EIGRP have a feature called "variance" will allow load balancing over multiple routes with unequal metrics.

Refer to the following diagram, show commands and configuration:

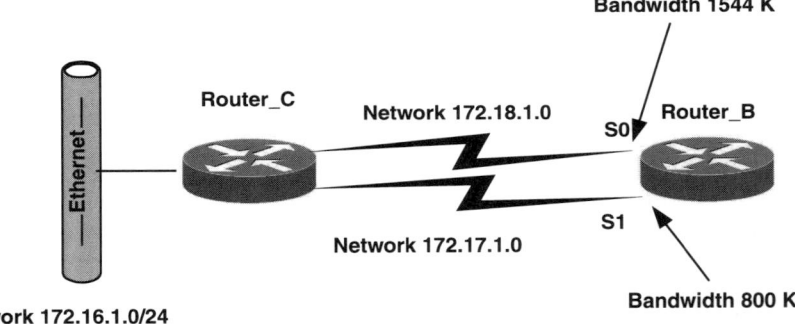

Before Variance is configured:

```
Router_B#sh ip route
Codes: C - connected, S - static, I - IGRP, R - RIP, M - mobile,
 B - BGP, D - EIGRP, EX - EIGRP external, O - OSPF,
 IA - OSPF inter area, N1 - OSPF NSSA external type 1,
 N2 - OSPF NSSA external type 2, E1 - OSPF external type 1,
 E2 - OSPF external type 2, E - EGP, i - IS-IS,
 L1 - IS-IS level-1, L2 - IS-IS level-2, * - candidate default
 U - per-user static route, o - ODR

Gateway of last resort is not set

     172.17.0.0/24 is subnetted, 1 subnets
C        172.17.1.0 is directly connected, Serial1
I     172.16.0.0/16 [100/8576] via 172.18.1.1, 00:00:56, Serial0
      172.18.0.0/24 is subnetted, 1 subnets
```

```
C       172.18.1.0 is directly connected, Serial0
```

After variance is configured:

```
Router_B#sh ip route
Codes: C - connected, S - static, I - IGRP, R - RIP, M - mobile,
 B - BGP, D - EIGRP, EX - EIGRP external, O - OSPF,
 IA - OSPF inter area, N1 - OSPF NSSA external type 1,
 N2 - OSPF NSSA external type 2, E1 - OSPF external type 1,
 E2 - OSPF external type 2, E - EGP, i - IS-IS,
 L1 - IS-IS level-1, L2 - IS-IS level-2, * - candidate default,
 U - per-user static route, o - ODR

Gateway of last resort is not set

     172.17.0.0/24 is subnetted, 1 subnets
C       172.17.1.0 is directly connected, Serial1
I    172.16.0.0/16 [100/8576] via 172.18.1.1, 00:00:13, Serial0
                   [100/14600] via 172.17.1.1, 00:00:13, Serial1
     172.18.0.0/24 is subnetted, 1 subnets
C       172.18.1.0 is directly connected, Serial0

Router_B#sh run
Building configuration...

Current configuration:
!
version 11.3
no service password-encryption
!
hostname Router_B
!
!
!
interface Serial0
 ip address 172.18.1.2 255.255.255.0
!
interface Serial1
 ip address 172.17.1.2 255.255.255.0
 no ip mroute-cache
 bandwidth 800
!
interface Serial2
 no ip address
 shutdown
!
interface Serial3
 no ip address
 shutdown
!
interface TokenRing0
 no ip address
 shutdown
```

```
!
interface BRI0
 no ip address
 shutdown
!
router igrp 100
 variance 2
 network 172.17.0.0
 network 172.18.0.0
!
ip classless
!
!
line con 0
line aux 0
line vty 0 4
 login
!
end

Router_B#sh ip prot
Routing Protocol is "igrp 100"
  Sending updates every 90 seconds, next due in 16 seconds
  Invalid after 270 seconds, hold down 280, flushed after 630
  Outgoing update filter list for all interfaces is not set
  Incoming update filter list for all interfaces is not set
  Default networks flagged in outgoing updates
  Default networks accepted from incoming updates
  IGRP metric weight K1=1, K2=0, K3=1, K4=0, K5=0
  IGRP maximum hopcount 100
  IGRP maximum metric variance 2
  Redistributing: igrp 100
  Routing for Networks:
    172.17.0.0
    172.18.0.0
  Routing Information Sources:
    Gateway          Distance        Last Update
    172.17.1.1            100        00:00:00
    172.18.1.1            100        00:00:00
  Distance: (default is 100)
```

Answer 3–4.
  c) **97**

IP RIP, IPX RIP, IPX SAP and Appletalk RTMP will all hit the middle buffers. You may find it necessary to increase the minimum and maximum number of buffers.

Take notice of IP IGRP. IGRP is much more efficient in that the packet size can be a maximum of 1488 bytes and it will not "bang away" at those middle buffers. IGRP will use the big buffers.

All sizes are in bytes.

```
Router_B>sh buffers
Buffer elements:
     500 in free list (500 max allowed)
     4650 hits, 0 misses, 0 created

Public buffer pools:
Small buffers, 104 bytes (total 50, permanent 50):
     49 in free list (20 min, 150 max allowed)
     1858 hits, 0 misses, 0 trims, 0 created
     0 failures (0 no memory)
Middle buffers, 600 bytes (total 25, permanent 25):
     25 in free list (10 min, 150 max allowed)
     69 hits, 0 misses, 0 trims, 0 created
     0 failures (0 no memory)
Big buffers, 1524 bytes (total 50, permanent 50):
     50 in free list (5 min, 150 max allowed)
     295 hits, 0 misses, 0 trims, 0 created
     0 failures (0 no memory)
VeryBig buffers, 4520 bytes (total 10, permanent 10):
     10 in free list (0 min, 100 max allowed)
     1 hits, 0 misses, 0 trims, 0 created
     0 failures (0 no memory)
Large buffers, 5024 bytes (total 0, permanent 0):
     0 in free list (0 min, 10 max allowed)
     0 hits, 0 misses, 0 trims, 0 created
     0 failures (0 no memory)
Huge buffers, 18024 bytes (total 0, permanent 0):
     0 in free list (0 min, 4 max allowed)
     0 hits, 0 misses, 0 trims, 0 created
     0 failures (0 no memory)

Router_B(config)#buffers middle ?
  initial     Temporary buffers allocated at system reload
  max-free    Maximum number of free buffers
  min-free    Minimum number of free buffers
  permanent   Number of permanent buffers
```

To change the minimum buffers:

```
Router_B(config)#buffers middle min-free ?
  <0-20480>  Number of buffers

Router_B(config)#buffers middle min-free 200
```

To change the maximum buffers:

```
Router_B(config)#buffers middle max-free 400
Router_B(config)#exit
```

Answer 3–5.
   f)   70%

Answer 3–6.
- a) **Characterize the existing network**
- d) **Extract new customer requirements**

Answer 3–7.
- e) **300**

Answer 3–8.
- e) **7.**

IP RIP, IPX RIP, IPX SAP and Appletalk RTMP will all hit the middle buffers. You may find it necessary to increase the minimum and maximum number of buffers.

Take notice of IP IGRP. IGRP is much more efficient in that the packet size can be a maximum of 1488 bytes and it will not "bang away" at those middle buffers. IGRP will use the big buffers.

All sizes are in bytes.

```
Router_B>sh buffers
Buffer elements:
    500 in free list (500 max allowed)
    4650 hits, 0 misses, 0 created

Public buffer pools:
Small buffers, 104 bytes (total 50, permanent 50):
    49 in free list (20 min, 150 max allowed)
    1858 hits, 0 misses, 0 trims, 0 created
    0 failures (0 no memory)
Middle buffers, 600 bytes (total 25, permanent 25):
    25 in free list (10 min, 150 max allowed)
    69 hits, 0 misses, 0 trims, 0 created
    0 failures (0 no memory)
Big buffers, 1524 bytes (total 50, permanent 50):
    50 in free list (5 min, 150 max allowed)
    295 hits, 0 misses, 0 trims, 0 created
    0 failures (0 no memory)
VeryBig buffers, 4520 bytes (total 10, permanent 10):
    10 in free list (0 min, 100 max allowed)
    1 hits, 0 misses, 0 trims, 0 created
    0 failures (0 no memory)
Large buffers, 5024 bytes (total 0, permanent 0):
    0 in free list (0 min, 10 max allowed)
    0 hits, 0 misses, 0 trims, 0 created
    0 failures (0 no memory)
Huge buffers, 18024 bytes (total 0, permanent 0):
    0 in free list (0 min, 4 max allowed)
    0 hits, 0 misses, 0 trims, 0 created
    0 failures (0 no memory)

Router_B(config)#buffers middle ?
```

```
initial     Temporary buffers allocated at system reload
max-free    Maximum number of free buffers
min-free    Minimum number of free buffers
permanent   Number of permanent buffers
```

To change the minimum buffers:

```
Router_B(config)#buffers middle min-free ?
  <0-20480>  Number of buffers

Router_B(config)#buffers middle min-free 200
```

To change the maximum buffers:

```
Router_B(config)#buffers middle max-free 400
Router_B(config)#exit
```

Answer 3–9.
   a) **25**

IP RIP, IPX RIP, IPX SAP and Appletalk RTMP will all hit the middle buffers. You may find it necessary to increase the minimum and maximum number of buffers.

Take notice of IP IGRP. IGRP is much more efficient in that the packet size can be a maximum of 1488 bytes and it will not "bang away" at those middle buffers. IGRP will use the big buffers.

All sizes are in bytes.

```
Router_B>sh buffers
Buffer elements:
     500 in free list (500 max allowed)
     4650 hits, 0 misses, 0 created

Public buffer pools:
Small buffers, 104 bytes (total 50, permanent 50):
     49 in free list (20 min, 150 max allowed)
     1858 hits, 0 misses, 0 trims, 0 created
     0 failures (0 no memory)
Middle buffers, 600 bytes (total 25, permanent 25):
     25 in free list (10 min, 150 max allowed)
     69 hits, 0 misses, 0 trims, 0 created
     0 failures (0 no memory)
Big buffers, 1524 bytes (total 50, permanent 50):
     50 in free list (5 min, 150 max allowed)
     295 hits, 0 misses, 0 trims, 0 created
     0 failures (0 no memory)
VeryBig buffers, 4520 bytes (total 10, permanent 10):
     10 in free list (0 min, 100 max allowed)
     1 hits, 0 misses, 0 trims, 0 created
     0 failures (0 no memory)
Large buffers, 5024 bytes (total 0, permanent 0):
```

3. Answers

```
      0 in free list (0 min, 10 max allowed)
      0 hits, 0 misses, 0 trims, 0 created
      0 failures (0 no memory)
 Huge buffers, 18024 bytes (total 0, permanent 0):
      0 in free list (0 min, 4 max allowed)
      0 hits, 0 misses, 0 trims, 0 created
      0 failures (0 no memory)

 Router_B(config)#buffers middle ?
   initial    Temporary buffers allocated at system reload
   max-free   Maximum number of free buffers
   min-free   Minimum number of free buffers
   permanent  Number of permanent buffers
```

To change the minimum buffers:

```
 Router_B(config)#buffers middle min-free ?
   <0-20480>  Number of buffers

 Router_B(config)#buffers middle min-free 200
```

To change the maximum buffers:

```
 Router_B(config)#buffers middle max-free 400
 Router_B(config)#exit
```

Answer 3–10.
    d) The ability to throttle back traffic to downstream links from the source side

Used when the downstream link can not handle the bit rate from the upstream host. The router can be configured to send at a lower bit rate than the interface bit rate.

Answer 3–11.
    a) Multicast

The IANA owns a block of ethernet addresses ranging from 00:00:5e:00:00:00 to 00:00:5e:ff:ff:ff. The first byte of an Ethernet address must be 01 to specify a IP multicast address.

Answer 3–12.
    a) IGMP

The Internet Group Management Protocol (IGMP) is used by multicast routers to manage and keep track of IP hosts group memberships. Cisco currently supports IGMP and a proprietary protocol for communication to Catalyst switches called Cisco Group Management Protocol (CGMP).

Answer 3–13.
    a) NSAP (Network Service Access Point) addressing

Answer 3–14.
   a)   **Dependent on the time it takes to detect a link failure**
   c)   **Dependent on time it takes to propagate failure through out the network**

Answer 3–15.
   d)   **Static Routing**

Sometimes we have to take the good with the bad. Static routing will reduce the traffic, but we do have to manually administer them.

Answer 3–16.
   b)   **STAC requires more CPU cycles than Predictor.**
   d)   **STAC and Predictor have been "tweaked" by Cisco engineers.**

Predictor, of course, attempts to predict the next sequence of characters. It uses a compression dictionary to do so, and thus uses more memory than STAC. Both algorithms have been tweaked by Cisco engineers.

Answer 3–17.
   e)   **There is no automatic redistribution of IP RIP and IP EIGRP.**

Answer 3–18.
   b)   **Access**

Answer 3–19.
   d)   **Ethernet port, WAN slot and a ISDN BRI U**

Answer 3–20.
   b)   **Packet-by-Packet**

Process switching for IPX differs from that for IP. IP process switching is destination-by-destination.

Answer 3–21.
   b)   **Network_A is 2 hops and 1 tick away.**

With IPX and EIGRP redistribution, the EIGRP cloud appears as 1 hop and 0 ticks.

Answer 3–22.
   b)   **Convergence time will be 0.**

Since there are multiple ways to get to the destination in the routing table, the router can immediately reach the destination over the remaining good paths.

Answer 3–23.
   c)   **Allows assignment of cable ranges**

The AppleTalk extended network allows up to 253 workstations and servers to be co-located on the same physical wire. Also, an administrator can configure multiple logical networks per

3. Answers

physical wire. This is accomplished by configuring cable ranges. Zone names are always required.

Answer 3–24.
　e)　Tag Switching

Tag switching inserts a tag between Layer 2 and Layer 3. Each router builds a database that has a port association based on the Tag. Instead of the router having to look at the destination Layer 3 address, it can just look at the TAG, thereby processing the packet much faster.

Answer 3–25.
　a)　Core

Answer 3–26.
　d)　50

Refer to the chart below:

Routing Protocol	Routing Entry Size	Overhead	Routes per Packet	Total Packet Size
IP RIP	20	32	25	532
IP IGRP	14	32	104	1488
RTMP	6	17	97	599
IPX SAP	64	32	7	480
IPX RIP	8	32	50	432

The importance of this question is related to the buffers that routing protocols will use.

IP RIP, IPX RIP, IPX SAP and Appletalk RTMP will all hit the middle buffers. You may find it necessary to increase the minimum and maximum number of buffers.

Take notice of IP IGRP. IGRP is much more efficient in that the packet size can be a maximum of 1488 bytes and it will not "bang away" at those middle buffers. IGRP will use the big buffers.

All sizes are in bytes.

```
Router_B>sh buffers
Buffer elements:
     500 in free list (500 max allowed)
     4650 hits, 0 misses, 0 created

Public buffer pools:
Small buffers, 104 bytes (total 50, permanent 50):
     49 in free list (20 min, 150 max allowed)
     1858 hits, 0 misses, 0 trims, 0 created
     0 failures (0 no memory)
Middle buffers, 600 bytes (total 25, permanent 25):
```

```
      25 in free list (10 min, 150 max allowed)
      69 hits, 0 misses, 0 trims, 0 created
      0 failures (0 no memory)
 Big buffers, 1524 bytes (total 50, permanent 50):
      50 in free list (5 min, 150 max allowed)
      295 hits, 0 misses, 0 trims, 0 created
      0 failures (0 no memory)
VeryBig buffers, 4520 bytes (total 10, permanent 10):
      10 in free list (0 min, 100 max allowed)
      1 hits, 0 misses, 0 trims, 0 created
      0 failures (0 no memory)
Large buffers, 5024 bytes (total 0, permanent 0):
      0 in free list (0 min, 10 max allowed)
      0 hits, 0 misses, 0 trims, 0 created
      0 failures (0 no memory)
Huge buffers, 18024 bytes (total 0, permanent 0):
      0 in free list (0 min, 4 max allowed)
      0 hits, 0 misses, 0 trims, 0 created
      0 failures (0 no memory)

Router_B(config)#buffers middle ?
  initial    Temporary buffers allocated at system reload
  max-free   Maximum number of free buffers
  min-free   Minimum number of free buffers
  permanent  Number of permanent buffers
```

To change the minimum buffers:

```
Router_B(config)#buffers middle min-free ?
  <0-20480>  Number of buffers

Router_B(config)#buffers middle min-free 200
```

To change the maximum buffers:

```
Router_B(config)#buffers middle max-free 400
Router_B(config)#exit
```

Answer 3–27.
   a) **Class I repeater has a latency of 0.7 microseconds or less.**
   c) **Class I repeater allows only one repeater hop.**
   e) **Class II repeater allows one or two repeater hop.**
   f) **Class II repeater has a latency of 0.46 microseconds or less.**

Answer 3–28.
   c) **Distribution**

Answer 3–29.
   a) **Network_A is 1 hop away.**

With Appletalk and EIGRP redistribution, the hop count is maintained across the EIGRP cloud.

Answer 3–30.
   e) 5

The following information is contained in the header of the ATM cell:

- Generic flow control
- Virtual Path ID (VPI)
- Virtual Channel ID (VCI)
- Payload type
- Cell loss priority
- Header Error Control

Answer 3–31.
   a) **Supports Explorer Firewalls**

Explorer Firewalls prevent a router from forwarding more than one explorer packet across the WAN. Once the destination MAC has been located, there is no need to send subsequent explorer packets for that destination.

Answer 3–32.
   b) **E.164 addressing**

Answer 3–33.
   e) **RFC 1597**

Answer 3–34.
   d) **NT1**

Answer 3–35.
   a) **Protocol**
   b) **Media**
   c) **Transport**

Answer 3–36.
   c) **6**

Refer to the following diagram:

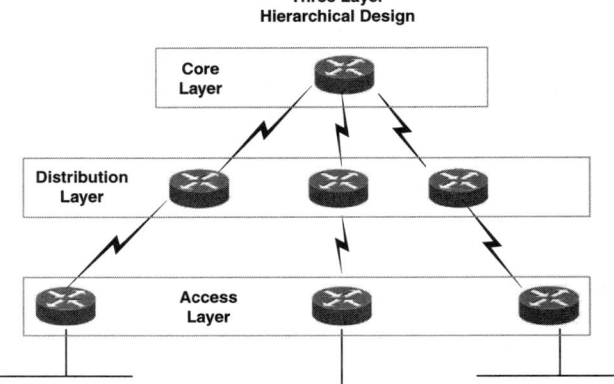

Answer 3–37.
   a)   **It keeps the active routing table of its adjacent neighbors.**

Answer 3–38.
   b)   **104**

IP RIP, IPX RIP, IPX SAP and Appletalk RTMP will all hit the middle buffers. You may find it necessary to increase the minimum and maximum number of buffers.

Take notice of IP IGRP. IGRP is much more efficient in that the packet size can be a maximum of 1488 bytes and it will not "bang away" at those middle buffers. IGRP will use the big buffers.

All sizes are in bytes.

```
Router_B>sh buffers
Buffer elements:
     500 in free list (500 max allowed)
     4650 hits, 0 misses, 0 created

Public buffer pools:
Small buffers, 104 bytes (total 50, permanent 50):
     49 in free list (20 min, 150 max allowed)
     1858 hits, 0 misses, 0 trims, 0 created
     0 failures (0 no memory)
Middle buffers, 600 bytes (total 25, permanent 25):
     25 in free list (10 min, 150 max allowed)
     69 hits, 0 misses, 0 trims, 0 created
     0 failures (0 no memory)
Big buffers, 1524 bytes (total 50, permanent 50):
     50 in free list (5 min, 150 max allowed)
     295 hits, 0 misses, 0 trims, 0 created
     0 failures (0 no memory)
VeryBig buffers, 4520 bytes (total 10, permanent 10):
     10 in free list (0 min, 100 max allowed)
     1 hits, 0 misses, 0 trims, 0 created
     0 failures (0 no memory)
Large buffers, 5024 bytes (total 0, permanent 0):
     0 in free list (0 min, 10 max allowed)
     0 hits, 0 misses, 0 trims, 0 created
     0 failures (0 no memory)
Huge buffers, 18024 bytes (total 0, permanent 0):
     0 in free list (0 min, 4 max allowed)
     0 hits, 0 misses, 0 trims, 0 created
     0 failures (0 no memory)

Router_B(config)#buffers middle ?
   initial     Temporary buffers allocated at system reload
   max-free    Maximum number of free buffers
   min-free    Minimum number of free buffers
   permanent   Number of permanent buffers
```

3. Answers

To change the minimum buffers:

```
Router_B(config)#buffers middle min-free ?
  <0-20480>  Number of buffers

Router_B(config)#buffers middle min-free 200
```

To change the maximum buffers:

```
Router_B(config)#buffers middle max-free 400
Router_B(config)#exit
```

Answer 3–39.
    c) **Core Layer**
    d) **Access layer**
    e) **Distribution layer**

Answer 3–40.
    c) **An Isolation LAN**
    d) **A router performing outside packet filtering**
    e) **A router performing inside packet filtering**

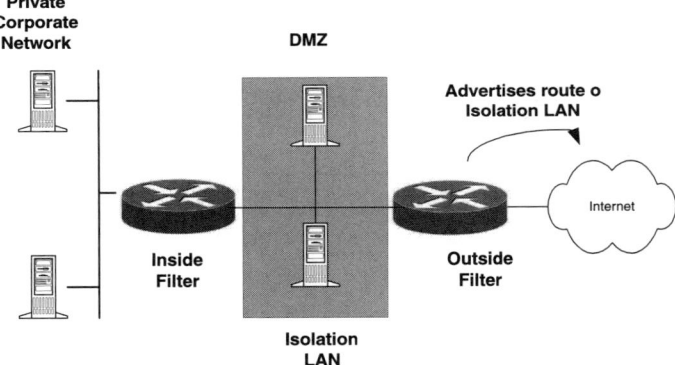

Chapter Four
Cisco Monitoring and Troubleshooting (CMTD) Questions

This chapter contains questions modeled after those that appear on the Cisco Monitoring and Troubleshooting (CMTD) exam (exam #640-405). Also presented are the answers and explanations for the model questions.

The actual exam consists of 64 questions. There is a 90-minute time limit for taking this exam and you must score at least 70 percent to pass. This is one of the few exams that will have fill-in-the-blank questions. The cost for taking the actual exam is $100.00 per attempt.

You can find out more about the objectives of this exam by visiting http://www.cisco.com/warp/public/10/wwtraining/, and looking for references to it. Remember, you need to dig around at the Cisco website for this information and keep in mind that Cisco updates it frequently.

When using this Study Guide's CD-ROM to study and/or test your knowledge of questions modeled after those you are likely to encounter on a CMTD exam, you will need to select "CMTD" at the *select exam* window and then select either the *study session* or *simulated exam* option. If you select the *study session* option, you'll be able to designate the number of CMTD questions you want presented during the *study session*.

When you select the *simulated exam*, the program will present you with a simulated CMTD exam containing 60 questions that address the objectives listed below. The program will automatically set a time limit of 85 minutes for you to complete the exam. When you've finished, or the time has elapsed, the program will calculate your score and help you evaluate your performance.

There is a total universe of 63 CMTD exam questions in this reference. Each time you request a CMTD *simulated exam* using the CD-ROM, the questions will be presented in a different sequence. The answer choices for each question will also be presented in different sequences than were used the last time the question was presented. This scrambling of question and answer choice sequences will help users continue to effectively test their CMTD knowledge using the same limited universe of questions.

4. CMTD

Question 4–1. [xLPx] Which of the following are features of the Cisco IOS-700 Release 4.0? (Choose all correct answers.)

a) Supports Appletalk
b) Can be configured with a graphical interface
c) Provides DHCP services
d) Port Address Translation (PAT)
e) All of the above

Question 4–2. [xLPx] Which of the following configures a modem for auto-discovery?

a) Modem inout
b) Transport auto
c) Modem discovery
d) Modem autoconfigure discovery
e) Modem autoconfigure all

Question 4–3. [xLPx] As it relates to Basic Telephone Service, what protocol is used for path setup?

a) Control (C)-plane
b) Management (M)-plane
c) User (U)-plane
d) Path (P)-plane
e) None of the above

Question 4–4. [NLPx] Which of the following is true of an S/T interface? (Choose all correct answers.)

a) Governed by ITU I.430
b) Governed by ITU Q.430
c) Governed by ITU E.430
d) Requires a NT1 device
e) Requires a Terminal Adapter (TA)

Question 4–5. [xLPx] Which of the following are conditions when DDR (Dial on Demand Routing) would be appropriate?

a) Low-volume periodic traffic
b) The Telecommuter
c) When WAN costs are a concern
d) When remote offices send their sales transactions to the home office
e) All of the above

Question 4–6. [xLPx] A device that converts analog signals to digital signals and vice versa is called a:

   a) Mux
   b) Flux capacitor
   c) DTE
   d) Modem
   e) Converter

Question 4–7. [xLPx] Which of the following commands will display the modem signal configured?

   a) show line
   b) show modem
   c) display modem
   d) show interface async
   e) show tty

Question 4–8. [xLPx] Cisco software releases 4.1 and later, for the Cisco 700 series routers, use which of the following as the default encapsulation type?

   a) HDLC
   b) PPP
   c) CHAP
   d) SNAP
   e) STAC

Question 4–9. [CLPx] Snapshot Routing is a Cisco feature for controlling which of the following distance-vector routing protocols? (Choose all that apply.)

   a) IP RIP
   b) IP IGRP
   c) IP EIGRP
   d) DECnet
   e) Banyan Vines RTP

Question 4–10. [xLPx] Which of the following are true of 56k modems?

   a) Eliminates one digital-to-analog signaling conversion.
   b) Service provider must have a direct digital link to the telco.
   c) FCC limits transmission speed to 53kbps.
   d) Download at 56kps upload at 33.6 kps
   e) All of the above

Question 4–11. [xLPx] Which of the following is true: (Refer to the following configuration.)

```
Current configuration:
!
version 11.3
no service password-encryption
!
hostname Router_B
!
interface Loopback0
 ip address 12.71.3.1 255.255.255.0
!
interface Serial0
 no ip address
 shutdown
!
interface Serial1
 no ip address
 shutdown
!
interface Serial2
 no ip address
 shutdown
!
interface Serial3
 no ip address
 shutdown
!
interface TokenRing0
 no ip address
 shutdown
!
interface BRI0
 ip address 10.100.2.2 255.255.255.0
dialer map ip 10.100.2.1 name Router_C 8505554444
 dialer-group 1
 isdn spid1 85055514410101
 isdn spid2 85055514420101
!
ip classless
dialer-list 1 protocol ip permit
!
line con 0
line aux 0
line vty 0 4
 login
!
end
```

a) Router_B would dial when any traffic hits the BRI 0 interface.
b) Router_B would dial when any IP traffic hits the BRI 0 interface.
c) Router_B would dial Router_C.
d) Router_B would dial 8505551441.
e) Router_B would dial 8505554444.

Question 4–12. [CLPx] Which of the following modes would be used if a catastrophic event occurred, such as loss of the IOS in flash memory?

 a) User EXEC mode
 b) SuperUser mode
 c) RX-BOOT mode
 d) Privileged EXEC mode
 e) Setup Mode

Question 4–13. [xLPx] Which of the following commands are used to configure a Virtual Private Data Network (VPDN) Gateway? (Choose all that apply.)

 a) vpdn enable
 b) username
 c) vpdn incoming
 d) vpdn outgoing
 e) set vpdn 700

Question 4–14. [CLPx] Which of the following are true of the command: "ppp authentication chap pap callin"?

 a) This is an illegal command.
 b) Authentication method used will be PAP or CHAP.
 c) Authentication process will take place in both directions.
 d) The router name calling in must be callin.
 e) The password used must be callin.

Question 4–15. [xLPx] What advantage does "spoofing" provide when configured on a DDR interface?

 a) Allows you to gain access without your own signature
 b) Allows the server to release a logged in user on the other side
 c) Allows the router to respond as a workstation
 d) There is no advantage.
 e) There is no such thing as spoofing.

Question 4–16. [CLPx] Which three of the following best describes a Cisco 2509 Access Server?

 a) 8 asynchronous ports
 b) 16 asynchronous ports
 c) 1 Ethernet interface
 d) 1 synchronous serial interface
 e) 2 synchronous serial interfaces
 f) 4 synchronous serial interfaces
 g) 2 Ethernet interfaces

4. CMTD

Question 4–17. [xLPx] Which of the following commands are used to configure an IP address on a 700 series router? (Select the best answer.)

```
------------------------------
```
I. Command Group I:
```
------------------------------
```

```
  set ip address 172.16.10.1 255.255.255.0
  set ip routing on
  set ip bridging off
```

```
------------------------------
```
II. Command Group II:
```
------------------------------
```

```
  set ip address 172.16.10.1/24
  set ip routing on
  set ip bridging off
```

```
------------------------------
```
III. Command Group III:
```
------------------------------
```

```
  set ip address 172.16.10.1
  set ip routing on
  set ip bridging off
```

```
------------------------------
```
IV. Command Group IV:
```
------------------------------
```

```
  set ip address 172.16.10.1
  set ip netmask 255.255.255.0
  set ip routing on
  set ip bridging off
```

a) Command Group I above
b) Command Group II above
c) Command Group III above
d) Command Group IV above

Question 4–18. [xLPx] Which of the following are true of ADSL? (Choose all the best answers)

a) Different speeds for upload and download
b) 1 pair wire and 18,000 feet limitation
c) 1 pair wire and 4500 feet limitation
d) Up to 52 Mbps downstream data rate
e) Up to 640 kbps upstream data rate

Question 4–19. [CLPx] Which of the following are advantages of Dialer Profiles over Legacy DDR?

   a) Dialer Profiles take less time to configure.
   b) Dialer Profiles provide for unique configuration parameters for each user group.
   c) Dialer Profiles use the same configuration parameters for each physical interface.
   d) Dialer Profiles provides for multiple calls to be made simultaneously.
   e) Dialer Profiles can be used on Serial interfaces and BRI interfaces where legacy DDR was restricted to BRI interfaces.

Question 4–20. [xLPx] Which of the following are true about Dial-on-Demand Routing?

   a) Only "interesting" traffic as defined by an access list will travel on the link.
   b) An "idle" period can be configured to disconnect the link.
   c) The DCE device must support V.25bis dialing.
   d) Static routes are typically specified so that routing updates are not exchanged.
   e) All of the above.

Question 4–21. [xLPx] Which one of the following is not an example of a packet-switched network?

   a) X.25
   b) ATM
   c) SMDS
   d) Frame Relay
   e) HDLC

Question 4–22. [xLPx] Which of the following are true:

   a) A Digital Signaling Zero (DS0) is a 64-kps channel.
   b) A T1 is 24 DS0s.
   c) A T3 is 28 T1s.
   d) In some cases a DS0 may only carry 56-kps.
   e) All of the above.

Question 4–23. [xLPx] Which of the following commands are used to reset the IP NAT translation table? (Choose the best answer.)

   a) clear ip nat *
   b) ip nat restart *
   c) restart ip nat
   d) ip nat clear
   e) nat clear *

4. CMTD

Question 4–24. [NLPx] Which of the following is true of a U interface? (Choose all correct answers.)

a) Governed by ITU I.431
b) Governed by ITU Q.431
c) Governed by ITU E.431
d) Requires a NT1 device
e) Requires a Terminal Adapter (TA)

Question 4–25. [PLPx] Which of the following are advantages of using PPP?

a) Security
b) Multiple protocol support
c) Supports Compression
d) Less overhead when compared with other Link-layer protocols
e) All of the above

Question 4–26. [xLPx] Which of the following are true of a Remote Control connection?

a) Only screens and keyboard information are transferred.
b) Needs a dedicated host
c) Provides good performance with Window applications
d) Provides good performance with older DOS applications
e) All of the above

Question 4–27. [NLPx] An ISDN PRI line consists of how many B channels?

a) 30
b) 24
c) 23
d) 31
e) 15

Question 4–28. [NLPx] Which one of the following describes the difference between OSPF external Type 1 and External Type 2 routes?

a) External Type 2 have a different Administrative Distance than Type 1.
b) External Type 2 will always have a higher cost than Type 1.
c) External Type 2 identify external cost only; Type 1 identifies internal and external costs.
d) All of the above.
e) None of the above.

Question 4–29. [xLPx] Which of the following Standard Modem commands is used to "Auto Answer"?

a) AT&F
b) ATS0=1
c) AT&D3
d) ATE0
e) ATQ1

Question 4–30. [xLPx] Which of the following command lines is used to execute a menu?

a) menu
b) autocommand menu
c) exec-menu
d) login menu
e) menu-execute

Question 4–31. [PLPx] Remote-Node services describe a single user accessing a LAN. Which of the following is the most commonly used Link-Layer protocol?

a) SLIP
b) PPP
c) ARAP
d) ARP
e) RARP

Question 4–32. [xLPx] The Cisco 700 series routers have three permanent profiles. What are they?

a) LAN
b) Standard
c) Internal
d) User
e) Privilege

Question 4–33. [xLPx] Which of the following are features of Network Address Translation (NAT)?

a) Address overloading
b) Static address translation
c) Dynamic source address translation
d) TCP load distribution
e) All of the above

Question 4–34. [xLPx] A null modem cable is required for:

a) DCE to DCE connection
b) DTE to DCE connection
c) DCE to DTE connection
d) DTE to DTE connection
e) No such device

Question 4–35. [xLPx] Which of the following commands changes IBM directives into dumb terminal commands?

a) ttyibm
b) keymap
c) ttycap
d) enable ANSI
e) None of the above

Question 4–36. [xLPx] Which of the following routers are designed for SOHO Internet connectivity?

a) Cisco 700 series
b) Cisco 1000 series
c) Cisco 1600 series
d) Cisco 200 series
e) Cisco 3620 series

Question 4–37. [xLPx] Which of the following are correct configuration statements to perform compression? (Choose two.)

a) compress
b) compress stac
c) compress predictor
d) compress stacker
e) predictor compress

Question 4–38. [CLPx] Which of the following events could be configured to start a chat script? (Choose all the best answers.)

a) Incoming traffic
b) Reverse Telnet
c) Async line reset
d) Dial-on Demand Routing (DDR)
e) All of the above

Question 4–39. [xLPx] Which of the following is the primary reason for employing the Asynchronous Callback feature?

a) Security
b) Simplification of configuration
c) Bill consolidation
d) Ease of use by end user
e) Tracking

Question 4–40. [xLPx] Which of the following devices takes the two-wire pair local loop and converts to ISDN four-wire pair connection?

a) TE1
b) TE2
c) NT1
d) TA
e) LE

Question 4–41. [xLPx] A DB-25 is a 25-pin connector that is used to connect a DTE device to a DCE device. Of these 25 pins how many are actually used?

a) 4
b) 5
c) 6
d) 7
e) 8

Question 4–42. [xLPx] Which of the following are true of a Remote Node connection?

a) Only screens and keyboard information are transferred.
b) Needs a dedicated host
c) Provides good performance with Window applications
d) Provides access to all network services
e) All of the above

Question 4–43. [xLPx] A call tear down involves which three messages?

a) Release
b) Sync
c) ACK
d) Released
e) Release complete

Question 4–44. [xLPx] A European channelized E1 line consists of how many B channels?

a) 30
b) 24
c) 23
d) 31
e) 15

Question 4–45. [xLPx] Which of the following commands are used to configure a Virtual Private Data Network (VPDN) NAS? (Choose all that apply.)

a) vpdn enable
b) username
c) vpdn incoming
d) vpdn outgoing
e) set vpdn 700

Question 4–46. [CLPx] Chat scripts could be configured to perform which of the following tasks? (Choose all the best answers.)

a) To trigger an access server start
b) To initialize an attached modem
c) To start a dialing sequence
d) To log in to a remote system
e) All of the above

Question 4–47. [CLPx] Which of the following are true of the "map-class" command?

a) It is used to simplify configurations.
b) It is required to configure DDR.
c) A dialer-idle timeout can be associated with a map class.
d) A dialer interface can be associated with a map class.
e) All of the above.

Question 4–48. [PLPx] Which of the following are advantages of Multi-link PPP(MPP)? (Choose all correct answers.)

a) Provides load balancing
b) Allows bundling of physical interfaces
c) Can improve throughput
d) Supported by Cisco series 700 routers
e) All of the above

Question 4–49. [CLPx] If there was contention on the BRI 0 interface, which of the following would be true? (Consider the configuration below.)

```
interface BRI0
 no ip address
 encapsulation ppp
 shutdown
 dialer pool-member 16 priority 200
 dialer pool-member 5 priority 255
 ppp authentication pap
!
interface Dialer1
 no ip address
 encapsulation ppp
 dialer remote-name ccna
 dialer string 5551212 class ccie
 dialer pool 16
!
interface Dialer2
 no ip address
 encapsulation ppp
 dialer remote-name cisco
 dialer string 5551213 class ccie
 dialer pool 5
```

a) 5551213 would be dialed first.
b) 5551212 would be dialed first.
c) Both numbers would be dialed at the same time.
d) Data would be load balanced over the BRI interface.
e) Not enough information is given.

Question 4–50. [xLPx] An RS-232 connector is used for a:

a) DCE to DCE connection
b) DTE to DCE connection
c) DCE to DTE connection
d) DTE to DTE connection
e) No such connector

Question 4–51. [CLPx] Which of the following can be used to eliminate regular routing updates over a dial-up link?

a) Static Routes
b) Snap Shot Routing
c) Quiet Routing
d) DDR
e) All of the above

Question 4–52. [xLPx] How many user profiles can be configured for the Cisco 700 series routers?

a) 2
b) 4
c) 8
d) 12
e) 16

Question 4–53. [xLPx] Which of the following are considerations concerning Network Address Translation (NAT)?

a) NAT does not scale well in large networks.
b) There may be times when the "real" identity of the host needs to be known.
c) Network design may be limited.
d) Degradation of performance
e) All of the above

Question 4–54. [xLPx] Which of the following best describes NAT address overloading?

a) When a single inside local address maps to multiple outside global addresses
b) When a single outside global address maps to a single inside global addresses
c) When multiple inside local addresses map to a single inside global address
d) When a single outside local address maps to multiple outside global addresses
e) When multiple inside local addresses map to a single outside global addresses

Question 4–55. [NLPx] Which of the following are true of PRI? (Choose all correct answers.)

a) Uses an NT1 device
b) D channel can be used for data
c) D channel is 23 in Europe
d) D channel is 15 in North America
e) None of the above

Question 4–56. [xLPx] Which of the following are advantages of Network Address Translation (NAT)?

a) Ability to connect to the internet with a private address
b) Provides additional security
c) Load sharing
d) Increase router performance
e) All of the above

Question 4–57. [xLPx] Some Cisco interfaces are switchable from Asynchronous to Synchronus. Which of the following commands is used to set an interface to asynchronus?

a) mode-type async
b) set async
c) layer1-async
d) physical-layer async
e) encap async

Question 4–58. [xLPx] Which of the following are compression methods supported by the Cisco IOS? (Choose two.)

a) Stacker
b) Predictor
c) Compress
d) PKZIP
e) Stuffit

Question 4–59. [NLPx] Which of the following would NOT be a PRI switch type for North America?

a) basic-net3
b) basic-5ess
c) basic-ni1
d) basic-dms100
e) All of the above switches can be used in North America.

Question 4–60. [xLPx] A Cisco Access Server provides which of the following services?

a) Remote-node services
b) Terminal Services
c) Protocol translation services
d) Dial-on Demand Routing services
e) All of the above

Question 4–61. [PLPx] Which one of the following is the main advantage of multilink PPP?

a) Improved throughput
b) Combining of multiple physical links into a logical link
c) Combining multiple bearer channels per physical port
d) Combining multiple physical ports across multiple chassis
e) None of the above

Question 4–62. [xLPx] The number of DS0 timeslots within a T1 circuit is which of the following?

a) 24
b) 32
c) 30
d) 21
e) Depends

Question 4–63. [xLPx] A signaling method in which bits are used from the user data channel for signaling is called? (Choose all that apply.)

a) Robbed bit signaling
b) NRIZ signaling
c) In-band signaling
d) Non-return to zero
e) Manchester

Answer 4–1.
  b) **Can be configured with a graphical interface**
  c) **Provides DHCP services**
  d) **Port Address Translation (PAT)**

PAT enables a single address to be assigned to an entire LAN thereby conserving addresses.

Answer 4–2.
  d) **Modem autoconfigure discovery**

Example:

```
Router(config-line)#mode autoconfigure ?
  discovery  Attempt to determine modem type automatically
  type       Specify modem type

Router(config-line)#mode autoconfigure discovery
```

Answer 4–3.
  b) **Management (M)-plane**

The path setup is done using the M-plane. A C-plane event begins when the called party picks up the telephone, this goes back to the local switch. The C-plane protocol will notify the calling phone that the path is available, at this point the user can begin to talk. The digitized voice takes place over the U-plane protocol

Answer 4–4.
  a) **Governed by ITU I.430**
  d) **Requires a NT1 device**

Don't be concerned about knowing the actual number the ITU set, it is the letter is that is important.

The "I" series refers to interfaces
The "Q" series refers to switching and signaling
The "E" series refers to addressing

An NT1 device converts BRI signals into a signal that can be used by the ISDN digital line. A Cisco 2521 has a BRI interface or an S/T interface, therefore an NT1 is required.

A TA is a device that would convert a serial signal like EIA/TIA-232 into a BRI signal. A Cisco 2514 has no BRI interface, just serial interfaces, so a TA device would be required. In reality you would purchase what the industry calls an ISDN "modem."

A U interface has a built-in TA and NT1, and no external devices are required. A Cisco 1604 is an example of a router with an ISDN U interface.

Answer 4–5.
   e) **All of the above**

Answer 4–6.
   d) **Modem**

A modem (MOdulator/DEModulator) is a Data Circuit-Terminating Equipment (DCE) device. A flux capacitor is obviously used for time travel.

Answer 4–7.
   a) **show line**

```
Router(config)#line 2
Router(config-line)#modem autoconfigure discovery

Router(config-line)#flowcontrol none

Router(config-line)#modem dialin

Router#show line

%SYS-5-CONFIG_I: Configured from console by console
   Tty Typ    Tx/Rx      A Modem  Roty AccO AccI  Uses    Noise   Overruns
*   0 CTY        -        -   -      -    -    -    0         1      0/0
*   2 TTY    1200/1200    - DialIn   -    -    -    0         0      0/0
    4 AUX    9600/9600    -   -      -    -    -    0         0      0/0
    5 VTY                 -   -      -    -    -    0         0      0/0
    6 VTY                 -   -      -    -    -    0         0      0/0
    7 VTY                 -   -      -    -    -    0         0      0/0
    8 VTY                 -   -      -    -    -    0         0      0/0
    9 VTY                 -   -      -    -    -    0         0      0/0

Line(s) not in async mode -or- with no hardware support:
1, 3
```

Answer 4–8.
   b) **PPP**

Answer 4–9.
   a) **IP RIP**
   b) **IP IGRP**
   e) **Banyan Vines RTP**

DECnet is not supported, and EIGRP does not use periodic updates. Therefore, there would be no benefit derived by using Snapshot Routing.

Answer 4–10.
   e) **All of the above**

Answer 4–11.
  b) Router_B would dial when any IP traffic hits the BRI 0 interface.
  c) Router_B would dial Router_C.
  d) Router_B would dial 8505551441.

The command dialer-list 1 protocol ip permit means that any IP traffic will be defined as interesting. The number will be dialed. The dialer map command tells the router which router to dial and the phone number of that router. 10.100.2.2 is the next hop address.

Answer 4–12.
  c) RX-BOOT mode

In the event that flash memory were erased, it would most likely be necessary for the router to use the backup copy of IOS that resides in ROM. When a router boots from this image, which is often called the boot-helper image, the router is said to be in RX-BOOT mode.

Answer 4–13.
  a) vpdn enable
  b) username
  c) vpdn incoming

Answer 4–14.
  b) Authentication method used will be PAP or CHAP.

The authentication procedure will only take place for calls coming in.

Answer 4–15.
  c) Allows the router to respond as a workstation

The advantage of spoofing is to allow the router to "act" as a workstation and respond to watchdog packets or SPX connections. When the router responds the dial-up link will not be brought up.

Answer 4–16.
  a) 8 asynchronous ports
  c) 1 Ethernet interface
  e) 2 synchronous serial interfaces

The eight asynchronous ports are provided through a 68-pin SCSI connector. A breakout cable of various configurations can be used to access each individual line. In our LAB we use a CAB-OCTAL-ASYNC cable, which has 8 RJ-45's.

Answer 4–17.
  d) Command Group IV above

```
set ip address 172.16.10.1
set ip netmask 255.255.255.0
set ip routing on
set ip bridging off
```

Answer 4–18.
a) **Different speeds for upload and download**
b) **1 pair wire and 18,000 feet limitation**
e) **Up to 640 kbps upstream data rate**

Answer 4–19.
b) **Dialer Profiles provide for unique configuration parameters for each user group.**

Dialer Profiles were introduced by Cisco in version 11.3

Answer 4–20.
b) **An "idle" period can be configured to disconnect the link.**
c) **The DCE device must support V.25bis dialing.**
d) **Static routes are typically specified so that routing updates are not exchanged.**

Very often students have a misunderstanding concerning interesting traffic. Once interesting traffic is seen on the link, and the call is made, all traffic can pass over the link.

Answer 4–21.
e) **HDLC**

Answer 4–22.
e) **All of the above.**

Answer 4–23.
a) **clear ip nat ***

Answer 4–24.
a) **Governed by ITU I.431**

Don't be concerned about knowing the actual number the ITU set, it is the letter is that is important.

The "I" series refers to interfaces
The "Q" series refers to switching and signaling
The "E" series refers to addressing

An NT1 device converts BRI signals into a signal that can be used by the ISDN digital line. A Cisco 2521 has a BRI interface or an S/T interface, so an NT1 is required.

A TA is a device that would convert a serial signal like EIA/TIA-232 into a BRI signal. A Cisco 2514 has no BRI interface, just serial interfaces, so a TA device would be required. In reality you would purchase what the industry calls an ISDN "modem."

A U interface has a built-in TA and NT1, and no external devices are required. A Cisco 1604 is an example of a router with an ISDN U interface.

Answer 4–25.
  e) **All of the above**

Answer 4–26.
  a) **Only screens and keyboard information are transferred.**
  b) **Needs a dedicated host**
  d) **Provides good performance with older DOS applications**

Remote control solution requires a host on the LAN that is dedicated to the remote control node.

Screens and keystrokes are transmitted across the wire but not applications and data files. This was a great solution several years ago to run DOS applications from a remote location.

The drawback is that a dedicated host is needed. I used a Cubix solution in the early nineties. We installed a Cubix card in the Netware server. This card had two 486 processors that were used for the remote control nodes.

Answer 4–27.
  c) **23**

Answer 4–28.
  c) **External Type 2 identify external cost only; Type 1 identifies internal and external costs.**

Answer 4–29.
  b) **ATS0=1**

Some other Standard Modem Commands:

AT&F - Loads factory default settings
AT&D3 - Hangs up
ATE0 - Echo off
ATQ1 - Codes off Quiet mode
ATS2=255 - Ignore in-band signaling

Answer 4–30.
  b) **autocommand menu**

Refer to the following configuration:

```
Router_B#sh run
Building configuration...
Current configuration:
!
version 11.3
no service password-encryption
!
hostname Router_B
```

```
!
enable secret 5 $1$F1L/$o6UBu.eE0dr0WGXR6ahPM0
enable password ccie
!
interface Serial0
 ip address 172.1.1.1 255.255.0.0
 no ip mroute-cache
 shutdown
!
interface Serial1
 no ip address
 shutdown
!
interface Serial2
 no ip address
 shutdown
!
interface Serial3
 no ip address
 shutdown
!
interface TokenRing0
 no ip address
 shutdown
!
interface BRI0
 no ip address
 shutdown
!
router igrp 10
 redistribute connected
 network 172.1.0.0
!
ip classless
!
menu ccie-lab title ^C

WELCOME TO THE CCIEprep.com LAB
^C
menu ccie-lab text 1 Configure 2514
menu ccie-lab text 2 Configure 2509
menu ccie-lab command 2 telnet r2509
menu ccie-lab text 3 Configure 3620
menu ccie-lab command 3 telnet r3620
menu ccie-lab text 4 Configure 2521
menu ccie-lab command 4 telnet r2521
menu ccie-lab text 5 Exit Menu
menu ccie-lab command 5 menu-exit
menu ccie-lab clear-screen
!
line con 0
 autocommand menu ccie-lab
line aux 0
line vty 0 4
```

```
 password ccnaprep
 login
 !
end
```

When a user enters the Router_B through Line 0 it results in the following:

```
WELCOME TO THE CCIEprep.com LAB

    1       Configure 2514

    2       Configure 2509

    3       Configure 3620

    4       Configure 2521

    5       Exit Menu
```

Answer 4–31.
  b) PPP

Answer 4–32.
  a) LAN
  b) Standard
  c) Internal

LAN - Determines how data is routed to the Ethernet connection
Standard - Used for ISDN incoming calls
Internal - Only used when routing is enabled and determines how data will flow from the bridge engine to the routing engine.

Answer 4–33.
  e) All of the above

Address Overloading
Allows the mapping of more than one internal inside address to a single inside global address.

Static Address Translation
A one-to-one mapping inside local address to global address

Dynamic Source Address Translation
A dynamic mapping of inside local addresses to global addresses.

TCP Load Distribution
A dynamic outside-to-inside translation, if a destination address (inside) matches an access list a address will be assigned from the pool.

Answer 4–34.
  d) **DTE to DTE connection**

Answer 4–35.
  c) **ttycap**

keymap - maps the keys of a non-3270 keyboard to a 3270 keyboard

Answer 4–36.
  a) **Cisco 700 series**
  b) **Cisco 1000 series**
  c) **Cisco 1600 series**

The Cisco 200 is a card and not a router.

Answer 4–37.
  b) **compress stac**
  c) **compress predictor**

Refer to the example below:

```
Router(config-if)#encap lapb
Router(config-if)#compress ?
  predictor  predictor compression type
  stac       stac compression algorithm
```

Answer 4–38.
  e) **All of the above**

Answer 4–39.
  c) **Bill consolidation**

Answer 4–40.
  c) **NT1**

- TE1 ISDN Terminal Equipment - an example would be Cisco's 1004 router
- TE2 Non-ISDN Terminal Equipment - an example would be Cisco's 2514. In this case the serial interface is used with an external Terminal Adapter.
- NT1 Network Termination terminates the local loop.
- TA Terminal Adapter performs protocol conversion V.35 or EIA/TIA-232 to ISDN.
- LE The Telco ISDN switch

Answer 4–41.
  e) **8**

The following is a description of each pin.

Data Transfer

DB-25 PIN #	Name	Description
2	TxD	The DTE transmits data to DCE
3	RxD	The DTE receives data
7	GRD	Ground

Hardware Flow Control

DB-25 PIN #	Name	Description
4	RTS	Request to Send, the DTE has free buffers to receive data from the DCE
5	CTS	Clear To Send, the DCE has free buffers to receive data from the DTE

Modem Control

DB-25 PIN #	Name	Description
20	DTR	Data Terminal Ready, the DTE is ready to receive a call
8	CD	Carrier Detect, the DCE has established a connection
6	DSR	Data Set Ready, the DCE is available

Answer 4–42.
c) **Provides good performance with Window applications**
d) **Provides access to all network services**

A remote node is a good name for this connection. Just think of it as being attached to the network even though it is in a remote location. Years ago I remember looking at a Citrix remote node solution that was very good and very expensive, so I went with PC Anywhere as a remote control solution.

Answer 4–43.
a) **Release**
d) **Released**
e) **Release complete**

Answer 4–44.
a) **30**

E1 consists of 31 total channels. Channel 15 is the D channel.

Answer 4–45.
a) **vpdn enable**
b) **username**
d) **vpdn outgoing**

The following example shows how to set up a VPDN:

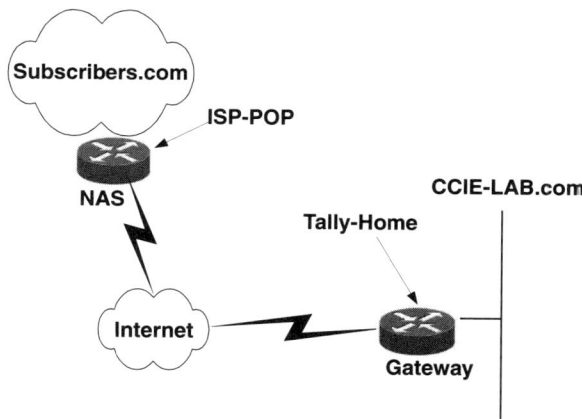

At the NAS

```
NAS(config)#vpdn enable
NAS(config)#username isp-pop password ccieprep
NAS(config)#username Tally-Home password ccieprep
NAS(config)#vpdn outgoing ccielab.com isp-pop ip 1.1.1.1
```

At the Gateway

```
Gateway(config)#vpdn enable
Gateway(config)#username subscriber password ccieprep
Gateway(config)#username Tally-Home password ccieprep
Gateway(config)#vpdn incoming isp-pop ccielab.com virtual-template 16

Gateway(config)#int virtual-template 16
Gateway(config-if)#ip unnumbered to0
Gateway(config-if)#ppp authentcation chap
```

Answer 4–46.
   b) **To initialize an attached modem**
   c) **To start a dialing sequence**
   d) **To log in to a remote system**

Answer 4–47.
   a) **It is used to simplify configurations.**
   c) **A dialer-idle timeout can be associated with a map class.**
   d) **A dialer interface can be associated with a map class.**

Refer to the following:

```
interface Dialer1
 no ip address
 dialer in-band
 dialer string 5551212 class ccie
 no cdp enable
```

```
!
interface Dialer2
 no ip address
 dialer in-band
 dialer string 5551213 class ccie
 no cdp enable
!
interface Dialer3
 no ip address
 dialer in-band
 dialer string 5551214 class ccie
 no cdp enable
!
ip classless
!
map-class dialer acct
!
map-class dialer ccie
 dialer idle-timeout 300
 dialer isdn speed 56
```

All the characteristics of the dialer class "ccie" can easily be associated with any dialer interface.

Answer 4–48.
  e) All of the above

Answer 4–49.
  a) 5551213 would be dialed first.

The number that follows the word priority signifies the order in which the dialer interfaces will be dialed. The higher the number, the higher the priority. 255 is the highest.

Answer 4–50.
  b) DTE to DCE connection
  c) DCE to DTE connection

Answer 4–51.
  a) Static Routes
  b) Snap Shot Routing

Snap shot routing is a CISCO IOS feature that was introduced in 11.2.

Answer 4–52.
  e) 16

These are very similar to Dialer Profiles in Cisco's 11.3 IOS.

A user profile can be set up with a customized set of dial up configuration parameters.

Answer 4–53.
  e) **All of the above**

Keep in mind that the router has extra work to do, which means CPU cycles devoted to address translation and not to moving user data.

You may have to dance around the design somewhat because you need the traffic to pass through the address translation.

Answer 4–54.
  c) **When multiple inside local addresses map to a single inside global address**

This is a feature that helps preserve inside addresses.

Answer 4–55.
  e) **None of the above**

PRI uses a CSU/DSU device. A PRI D channel can not be used for data, but a BRI D channel can be used for data. The D channel is 23 in North America, 0-22 are B channels for a total of 23 B channels. The European channelized E1 has the D channel on channel 15 and has 30 B channels.

Answer 4–56.
  a) **Ability to connect to the internet with a private address**
  b) **Provides additional security**
  c) **Load sharing**

Answer 4–57.
  d) **physical-layer async**

Example:

```
Router(config-if)#physical-layer ?
  async   Configure asynchronous physical layer on serial interface
  sync    Configure synchronous physical layer on serial interface

Router(config-if)#physical-layer async
```

Answer 4–58.
  a) **Stacker**
  b) **Predictor**

Stacker is more CPU intensive and less memory intensive. Predictor is more memory intensive and less CPU intensive.

Answer 4–59.
  a) **basic-net3**

Example:

```
Router(config)#isdn switch-type ?
  basic-1tr6     1TR6 switch type for Germany
  basic-5ess     AT&T 5ESS switch type for the U.S.
  basic-dms100   Northern DMS-100 switch type
  basic-net3     NET3 switch type for UK and Europe
  basic-ni1      National ISDN-1 switch type
  basic-nwnet3   NET3 switch type for Norway
  basic-nznet3   NET3 switch type for New Zealand
  basic-ts013    TS013 switch type for Australia
  ntt            NTT switch type for Japan
  vn2            VN2 switch type for France
  vn3            VN3 and VN4 switch types for France
```

Answer 4–60.
  e) **All of the above**

Answer 4–61.
  a) **Improved throughput**

Answer 4–62.
  a) **24**

These 24 channels transmit at 64 kbps for a total of 1536 kbps, but an additional 8 kbps is used for control and synchronization for the resulting bandwidth of 1.544 Mbps.

Answer 4–63.
  a) **Robbed bit signaling**
  c) **In-band signaling**

Chapter Five
Cisco LAN Switch (CLSC) Questions

This chapter contains questions modeled after those that appear on the Cisco LAN Switch (CLSC) exam (exam #640-404). Also presented are the answers and explanations for these model questions. This chapter will give you a taste of the questions you can expect to see.

The actual exam consists of 70 questions. There is a 60-minute time limit for taking this exam, and a score of at least 70 percent is necessary to pass. The cost for taking the actual exam is $100.00 per attempt.

You can find out more about the objectives of this exam by visiting http://www.cisco.com/warp/public/10/wwtraining/, and looking for references to it and the courses that help you prepare for it. Remember, you need to dig around at the Cisco website for this information and keep in mind that Cisco updates it frequently.

Understanding basic– as well as advanced–switching concepts is an important part of CLSC. Additionally, you must have a good handle on the configuration commands associated with the Catalyst series of switches. Lastly, the exam will cover some module-specific questions that could be hard without some hands-on experience.

When using this Study Guide's CD-ROM to study and/or test your knowledge of questions modeled after those you are likely to encounter on a CLSC exam, you will need to select "CLSC" at the *select exam* window and then select either the *study session* or *simulated exam* option. If you select the *study session* option, you'll be able to designate the number of CLSC questions you want presented during the *study session*.

When you select the *simulated exam*, the program will present you with a simulated CLSC exam containing 70 questions that address objectives of the test. The program will automatically set a time limit of 60 minutes for you to complete the exam. When you've finished, or the time has elapsed, the program will calculate your score and help you evaluate your performance.

There is a total universe of 113 model CLSC exam questions in this reference. Each time you request a CLSC *sample exam* using the CD-ROM, 70 questions will be chosen randomly from this universe.

Question 5–1. [SxPx] Which of the following devices can be used to control broadcasts?

a) Router
b) Switch
c) Bridge
d) Repeater
e) None of the above

Question 5–2. [SxPx] Which of the following is not a supported feature of a Catalyst 5000 or 5500 switch running 2.3 or above?

a) CGMP
b) NTP
c) DNS
d) TACACS+
e) IGRP
f) Broadcast suppression

Question 5–3. [SxPx] In which circumstances will a Catalyst 5000 or 5500 switch perform a BOOTP to resolve an IP address for interface sc0?

a) When the switch has an invalid IP address assigned to its interface sc0
b) When the IP address of the interface sc0 is 0.0.0.0
c) When the switch is using its default settings for the interface sc0
d) When the IP address of the interface sc0 is cleared
e) None of the above

Question 5–4. [SxPx] Which ASIC is responsible for operation of an Ethernet or Fast Ethernet port on a Catalyst 5500 and 5000 switch?

a) EARL
b) CBL
c) SAGE
d) LTL
e) SAINT

Question 5–5. [SxPx] Which of the following commands will configure an SC0 interface to be in VLAN 10 with an IP address of 172.16.0.2 and a subnet mask of 255.255.255.0?

a) set sc0 172.16.0.2 255.255.255.0 10
b) set sc0 interface 11 172.16.0.2.10
c) set interface sc0 172.16.0.2 255.255.255.0 10
d) set interface sc0 10 172.16.0.2 255.255.255.0
e) set interface sc0 10 172.16.0.2

Question 5–6. [SxPx] Assuming that LANE version 1.0 is being used, and the Simple Server Redundancy Protocol (SSRP) is not being used, how many Broadcast and Unknown Servers (BUS) will need to be configured?

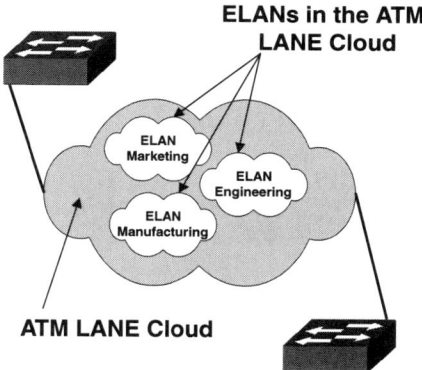

a) 1
b) 2
c) 3
d) 6
e) No Broadcast and Unknown Servers (BUS) are required..

Question 5–7. [SxPx] What is the required number of LAN Emulation Configuration Servers (LECS), assuming that LANE version 1.0 is being used? We are not using the Simple Server Redundancy Protocol.

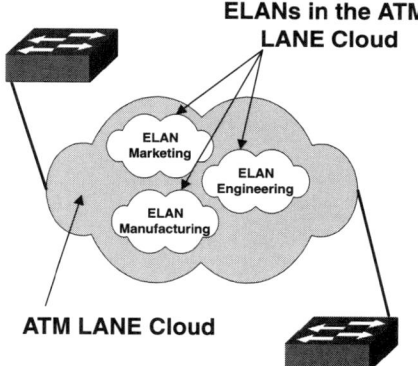

a) 1
b) 2
c) 5
d) 6
e) A LECS is not required in this configuration.

Question 5–8. [SxPx] Which of the following statements accurately define the purpose of VTP pruning?

    a) To keep the size of the spanning tree per VLAN down to a minimum
    b) To prevent unwanted VTP traffic from propagating across links
    c) To prevent VTP traffic from reaching certain devices
    d) To restrict VLAN traffic from traversing trunk lines to switches that have no ports in those VLANs
    e) None of the above

Question 5–9. [SxPx] Refer to the following diagram. Which of the following stations will have bi-directional connectivity to Host B, assuming proxy ARP is disabled? (Choose all that apply)

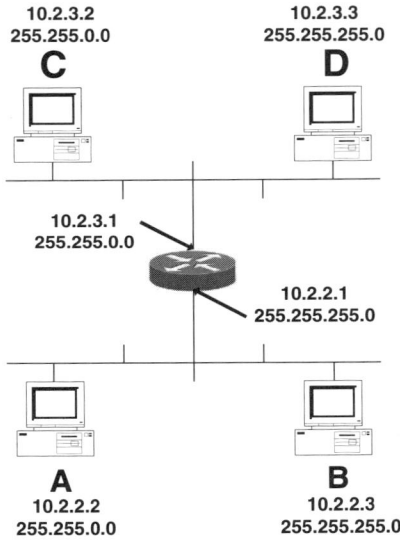

    a) A
    b) No one will have connectivity to B
    c) C
    d) D
    e) The IP addressing on the router is invalid.

Question 5–10. [SxPx] Which of the following is not a component of LANE?

    a) LAN Emulation Client (LEC)
    b) LAN Emulation Configuration Server (LECS)
    c) LAN Emulation Server (LES)
    d) LAN Emulation Gateway (LEG)
    e) Broadcast and Unknown Server (BUS)

Question 5–11. [SxPx] On the Catalyst 5000 and 5500 what commands will display the VLAN to port mappings? (Choose two that apply.)

a) show VLAN
b) show port
c) show port VLAN
d) show VLAN port
e) There is no way to view the VLAN to port mappings on a Catalyst 5000 and 5500.

Question 5–12. [SxPx] Which of the following statements are true of LAN Emulation (LANE)? (Choose all that apply.)

a) LANE is the process of making an ATM Cloud look like an Ethernet or Token Ring LAN.
b) LANE indicates the path the data will travel to and from certain destinations in NetFlow switching.
c) LANE is required to trunk across ATM.
d) ATM and LANE are the same process.
e) ATM uses LANE to distribute information about Virtual Circuits between ATM switches.

Question 5–13. [SxPx] Which of the following commands will set the VTP management domain name to "ARI" and the VTP mode to server?

a) set domain name ARI mode server
b) set domain mode server name ARI
c) set vtp domain name ARI mode server
d) set domain name ARI <return> set domain mode server
e) None of the above.

Question 5–14. [SxPx] What is the command to bring interface SC0 out of the administratively down state?

a) no shutdown interface SC0
b) interface SC0 no shutdown
c) set interface SC0 no shutdown
d) set no shutdown interface SC0
e) None of the above

Question 5–15. [SxPx] On Catalyst switches the ability to perform frame tagging provides which capability?

a) Prevents broadcasts from being propagated across switches
b) Increases available bandwidth
c) Allows for multicasts
d) Prevents erroneous traffic such as routing updates
e) Allows for VLANs to span across multiple switches

5. CLSC

Question 5–16. [SxPx] Which of the following is the backplane capacity of the Catalyst 5500 for Cell Switching?

    a) 533 MB
    b) 1.066 GB
    c) 1.2 GB
    d) 3.6 GB
    e) 5.0 GB

Question 5–17. [SxPx] Assuming no redundancy, what is the number of LAN Emulation Configuration Servers (LECS) that must be configured on an ATM cloud to configure LAN Emulation?

    a) 1
    b) 2
    c) 1 per Switch
    d) 1 per ELAN
    e) The LECS is optional.

Question 5–18. [SxPx] Which of the following commands will show all VLANs in the Management Domain?

    a) show vtp domain
    b) show vtp
    c) show vlan
    d) show vlan all
    e) There is no command to view all VLANs in the management domain.

Question 5–19. [SxPx] Assuming that LANE version 1.0 is being used and the Simple Server Redundancy Protocol (SSRP) is not being used, how many LAN Emulation Servers (LES) will need to be configured?

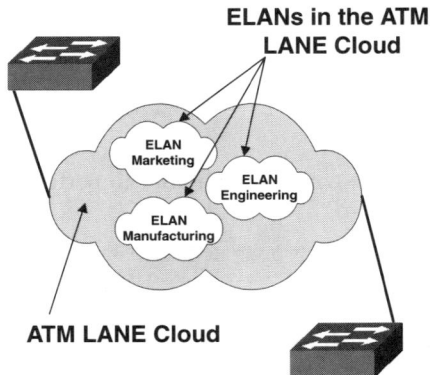

    a) 1
    b) 2
    c) 3
    d) 6
    e) No LAN Emulation Servers (LES) need to be configured.

Question 5–20. [SxPx] Which of the following is true of the operating system that runs the ATM LANE Module for the Catalyst 5000 and 5500?

a) The ATM LANE Module uses the Catalyst Operating System of the Supervisor Engine.
b) The ATM LANE Module uses its own proprietary operating system, yet is still configured from the supervisor engine.
c) The ATM LANE Module uses its own proprietary operating system and its own Command Line Interface.
d) The ATM LANE Module uses the Cisco Internetworking Operating System with its own Command Line Interface (CLI).
e) The ATM LANE Module uses the same Operating System as the Catalyst 3000 series switches.

Question 5–21. [SxPx] What is the controlling body for ATM?

a) ATM Group
b) IEEE
c) CCITT
d) ATM Forum
e) ISO

Question 5–22. [SxPx] By default, what is the default route of the SC0 interface?

a) 1.1.1.1
b) 0.0.0.0
c) 172.16.0.1
d) 10.0.0.1
e) There is no default route.

Question 5–23. [SxPx] What is the destination MAC address of a Cisco Discovery Protocol frame?

a) 0000.0cff.ffff
b) 0100.0cff.ffff
c) 0100.0ccc.cccc
d) 0000.0ccc.cccc
e) ffff.ffff.ffff

Question 5–24. [SxPx] What are the advantages of Cisco's Spanning Tree instance per VLAN?

a) Less processing required to recalculate the spanning tree when a change occurs
b) Decreases the time to recover from a change in the bridge topology
c) Reduces the administrative overhead
d) Allows for more efficient paths through the bridge network
e) All of the above

Question 5–25. [SxPx] The default speed, priority level, and duplex method of a 10/100 ethernet port on a Catalyst 5000 or 5500 will be which of the following choices?

	Speed	Priority Level	Duplex Method
I	10	normal	full
II	100	high	auto
III	auto	normal	auto
IV	auto	high	auto
V	100	normal	full

a) Line I above
b) Line II above
c) Line III above
d) Line IV above
e) Line V above

Question 5–26. [SxPx] What method(s) of remote management is (are) possible with the Catalyst 5000 and 5500 switch?

a) PPP to the Supervisor Engine's console port
b) Telnet to the Interface sc0
c) Dial in using CiscoWorks remote
d) Dial in using SLIP to a modem attached to the Supervisor Engine's console port
e) No remote management is supported on the Catalyst 5000 or 5500 switches.

Question 5–27. [SxPx] What is the purpose of the Virtual Trunking Protocol (VTP)?

a) To allow multiple VLAN traffic across trunk lines
b) To prevent unnecessary traffic to traverse trunk lines
c) To allow switches to maintain a consistent VLAN configuration across multiple switches
d) To allow switches to automatically configure ports to be trunks
e) None of the above

Question 5–28. [SxPx] Which of the following statements concerning the VLAN Trunking Protocol (VTP) are true?

a) A switch that is configured as a VTP server will receive updates and change its configuration based on those updates.
b) A switch that is configured as a VTP client will receive updates and change its configuration based on those updates.
c) A switch that is configured as a VTP transparent will receive updates and change its configuration based on those updates.
d) You can configure VLANs on a switch that is configured as a VTP client.
e) You can configure VLANs on a switch that is configured as a VTP transparent.

Question 5–29. [SxPx] Which of the following commands will assign ports 2/1-12 and ports 3/1-12 to VLAN 10 on a Catalyst 5000 and 5500 switch?

a) set port 2/1-12 vlan 10 <return> set port 3/1-12 vlan 10
b) set vlan 10 3/1-12, 2/1-12
c) set vlan 3/1-12,2/1-12 10
d) set vlan 3/1-12 10 <return> set vlan 2/1-12 10
e) None of the above

Question 5–30. [SxPx] Which of the following are benefits of creating VLANs?

a) Better control of broadcasts
b) Reduction in the number of collisions
c) Reduction in the amount of routing updates
d) More available bandwidth
e) Fewer users per physical segment

Question 5–31. [SxPx] What is the processor responsible for the command line interface, the spanning tree calculations and system configuration of a Catalyst 5500 and 5000?

a) MCP
b) LTL
c) CBL
d) NMP
e) SAMBA

Question 5–32. [SxPx] What is the Application Specific Integrated Circuit (ASIC) responsible for the bridging together of the three backplanes on the Supervisor Engine III?

a) SAINT
b) SAGE
c) SAMBA
d) EARL
e) PHOENIX

Question 5–33. [SxPx] What is the command to assign VLAN number 10 to a Cisco Router Fast Ethernet Sub-Interface?

a) encap sde 10
b) encap VLAN 10
c) encap LANE 10
d) encap 10
e) encap isl 10

5. CLSC

Question 5–34. [SxPx] How many times does a frame travel across the backplane of a Catalyst 5000 or 5500 switch?

a) 1
b) 2
c) 4
d) Depends on the type of frame
e) Frames do not travel across the backplane.

Question 5–35. [SxPx] The Layer 3 switching engine feature card of the Supervisor Engines II and III use which method of switching?

a) NetFlow Switching
b) Fast Switching
c) Super Switching
d) Optimum Switching
e) None of the above

Question 5–36. [SxPx] The Catalyst 5000 series switch supports which version of Spanning Tree on its Ethernet ports?

a) IEEE 802.1d
b) DEC
c) IBM
d) Proprietary
e) None of the above

Question 5–37. [SxPx] Which one of the following is NOT a requirement for Full-duplex Ethernet?

a) Full-duplex Ethernet controllers or a controller for each path
b) Collision detection disabled
c) Distance limitations are one-tenth of Half-duplex design.
d) Two data paths
e) All of the above are required.

Question 5–38. [SxPx] Which of the following are valid advantages of segmenting LANs with switches or bridges?

a) Increases bandwidth available to nodes
b) Controls broadcasts
c) Increases the size of the frames
d) Reduces the number of collisions
e) None of the above

5. CLSC

Question 5–39. [SxPx] How many LAN Emulation Servers (LES) are necessary to properly configure LAN Emulation?

    a) 1
    b) 2
    c) 1 per Switch
    d) 1 per ELAN
    e) The LES is optional.

Question 5–40. [SxPx] Which of the following is the correct command to enter the privileged mode on a Catalyst 5000 or 5500 switch?

    a) login
    b) set mode privileged
    c) enable
    d) <return>
    e) Privilege mode is for routers only, not switches.

Question 5–41. [SxPx] What is the default IP address assigned to the SC0 interface of a Catalyst switch?

    a) 1.1.1.1
    b) 0.0.0.0.
    c) 172.16.0.1
    d) 10.0.0.1
    e) 192.168.5
    f) There is no IP address.

Question 5–42. [SxPx] Which of the following may be required to configure ISDN? (Choose all that apply.)

    a) X.121 address
    b) ISDN Switch Type
    c) SPID number
    d) DLCI number
    e) LMI type

Question 5–43. [SxPx] What traffic will be seen by a protocol analyzer that is connected to a port on an Ethernet Hub?

    a) All broadcast traffic
    b) All data traffic and all broadcast traffic
    c) Only traffic that is destined for the protocol analyzer
    d) All broadcast traffic and traffic that is destined for the protocol analyzer
    e) All traffic

Question 5–44. [SxPx] What is the command to set the default gateway of the SC0 interface to 1.1.1.1?

  a) set interface sc0 default gateway 1.1.1.1
  b) set interface default gateway 1.1.1.1
  c) set default gateway 1.1.1.1
  d) set ip route default 1.1.1.1
  e) None of the above

Question 5–45. [SxPx] What is the purpose of the Network Time Protocol (NTP)?

  a) To automatically set the time of new devices coming into the network
  b) To keep switches informed of VLANs
  c) To keep a consistent time between routers only
  d) To synchronize timekeeping between all devices that support NTP
  e) To synchronize timekeeping between switches only

Question 5–46. [SxPx] A VLAN is the equivalent of _____? (Choose all that apply.)

  a) An IP Subnet
  b) A Logical Segment
  c) A Physical Segment
  d) A Broadcast Domain
  e) None of the above

Question 5–47. [SxPx] Which of the following commands will set ethernet port 2/1 to full-duplex mode?

  a) set port duplex 2/1 full
  b) set duplex 2/1 full
  c) set port duplex full 2/1
  d) set port full duplex 2/1
  e) set full 2/1

Question 5–48. [SxPx] Which of the following Virtual Channel Circuits (VCCs) is automatically configured between the LAN Emulation Configuration Server (LECS) and a LAN Emulation Client (LEC)?

  a) Channel Direct VCC
  b) Control Direct VCC
  c) Control Distribute VCC
  d) Configuration Direct VCC
  e) There is no VCC set up automatically between the LECS and a LEC.

Question 5–49. [SxPx] What are the two methods by which ports on a Catalyst switch may be assigned to a VLAN?

a) Static
b) Linear
c) Dynamic
d) Cut-through
e) Store-and-Forward

Question 5–50. [SxPx] Which of the following lines is the correct syntax for setting the password to get into privileged mode?

a) enable secret [password] <return>
b) enable password [password]
c) set enable password [password]
d) set enablepass [password]
e) set enablepass <return>

Question 5–51. [SxPx] The Cisco Catalyst 5000 and 5500 support which method(s) of switching? (Choose all that apply.)

a) Cut-through
b) Store and Forward
c) Pass-Trough
d) Fast Switching
e) Super Fast Switching.

Question 5–52. [SxPx] What is the size of the ISL Frame Header (not including the trailer)?

a) 24 bytes
b) 26 bytes
c) 30 bytes
d) 34 bytes
e) None of the above

Question 5–53. [SxPx] What is the ASIC responsible for forwarding decisions on the Catalyst 5500 and 5000?

a) SAINT
b) SAGE
c) SAMBA
d) EARL
e) PHOENIX

Question 5–54. [SxPx] Which of the following fields will be automatically set to the MAC address that has been assigned to the LANE device?

    a) Authority Format Identifier (AFI)
    b) Domain Specific Part (DSP)
    c) Data Country Code (DCC)
    d) High Order Part of Domain Specific Part (HO-DSP)
    e) End System Identifier (ESI)

Question 5–55. [SxPx] What is the proper command to enable port 1/2, which is assigned to VLAN 10, to forward while it is in the spanning-tree listening mode on a Catalyst 5000 and 5500 switch?

    a) set spantree 1/2 fast-forward enable.
    b) set spantree 10 1/2 disable
    c) set spantree portfast 1/2 disable
    d) set spantree portfast 1/2 enable
    e) It is not possible to forward while in listening mode on a Catalyst Switch.

Question 5–56. [SxPx] What is true of the Integrated Local Management Interface (ILMI)? (Choose all that apply.)

    a) ILMI is the process of making an ATM Cloud look like an Ethernet or Token Ring LAN.
    b) ILMI indicates the path in which data will travel to and from certain destinations in NetFlow switching.
    c) ILMI uses the SNMP protocol and Management Information Bases.
    d) ILMI and SNMP are the same process.
    e) LAN Emulation Clients can use ILMI to locate the LAN Emulation Configuration Sever.

Question 5–57. [SxPx] What is the maximum bandwidth possible on a Fast EtherChannel with each of its ports in Full-Duplex mode?

    a) 200 MB
    b) 400 MB
    c) 600 MB
    d) 800 MB
    e) 1000 MB

Question 5–58. [SxPx] Which command(s) would we have to use to upgrade our Catalyst Operating System?

    a) copy tftp running-configuration
    b) copy tftp flash
    c) copy flash tftp
    d) download [ip address] [file name]
    e) None of the above

Question 5–59. [SxPx] Which field in the IEEE 802.10 header is used to uniquely identify the VLAN number of the encapsulated frame on a FDDI trunk?

a) ISL field
b) VLAN field
c) HSA field
d) SAID field
e) You cannot trunk on an FDDI port.

Question 5–60. [SxPx] On the Catalyst 5000 and 5500 what is the command to display the VLAN the SC0 is in?

a) show interface SC0
b) show interface
c) show SC0
d) show vlan
e) show module

Question 5–61. [SxPx] What does a switch do with frames that have a destination MAC address that is not in its bridge table?

a) Buffer the frame until the switch learns where the destination is
b) Forward the frame to a router for learning
c) Discard the frame and force the sender to retransmit at a later time
d) Flood the frame out all ports in the VLAN
e) None of the above

Question 5–62. [SxPx] Refer to the diagram below. Which of the following stations will have bi-directional IP connectivity to Host B, assuming proxy ARP is disabled? (Choose all that apply.)

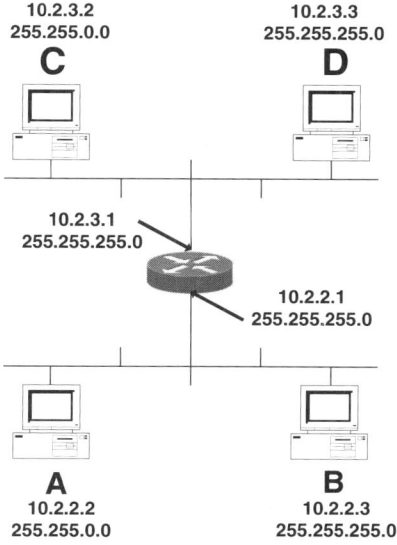

a) A
b) No one will have connectivity to B
c) C
d) D
e) None of the above

Question 5–63. [SxPx] Which of the following trunking methods will be used over FDDI connections on Catalyst switches?

a) IEEE 802.10
b) Cut-Through
c) Static
d) Inter-Switch Link (ISL)
e) LAN Emulation (LANE)

Question 5–64. [SxPx] Which of the following applications is optional in the CiscoWorks for Switched Internetworking (CWSI) Application Suite?

a) VLAN Director
b) ATM Director
c) CiscoView
d) Traffic Director
e) All of these applications are standard with CWSI.

Question 5–65. [SxPx] Which of the following commands will show the port to VLAN assignments?

a) show ports
b) show vlan
c) show port
d) show port vlan
e) None of the above

Question 5–66. [SxPx] What is the command to view the current status of all LAN Emulation Servers (LES) of an ATM LANE Cloud, assuming that you are at the CLI of the switch that is the LAN Emulation Configuration Server (LECS), and none of the LES reside on this switch?

a) show lane server
b) show lane client
c) show lane bus
d) show lane configuration
e) None of the above

Question 5–67. [SxPx] What are the default setting and values for SNMP on Catalyst 5000 series switches? (Refer to the following table.)

	Status	Read	Write	Read-WriteAll
a)	ENABLED	private	public	secret
b)	DISABLED	public	secret	private
c)	ENABLED	private	public	secret
d)	DISABLED	public	private	secret
e)	ENABLED	public	private	secret

a) ENABLED private public secret
b) DISABLED public secret private
c) ENABLED private public secret
d) DISABLED public private secret
e) ENABLED public private secret

Question 5–68. [SxPx] What is the Default password of a Catalyst switch?

a) cisco
b) san-fran.
c) password
d) <return>
e) There is no default password on a Catalyst switch.

Question 5–69. [SxPx] When using Cisco Catalyst switches running Catalyst software 2.3 - 3.x, what are the possible methods of assigning ports to a VLAN?

a) Manually assigning ports to VLANs
b) Manually assigning protocol addresses to VLANs
c) Automatically assigning VLANs to ports based on a configuration file on a tftp server
d) Automatically assigning VLANs to ports based on protocol address
e) None of the above

Question 5–70. [SxPx] What is the purpose of the Simple Server Redundancy Protocol (SSRP)?

a) SSRP is the protocol for Cisco Catalyst switches to exchange information about ELANs over an ATM Cloud.
b) SSRP is a standard protocol for fault tolerance communication between both Cisco and Non-Cisco ATM LANE products.
c) SSRP provides redundancy for the LAN Emulation Servers (LES) only.
d) SSRP is an IEEE standard protocol for tag switching.
e) None of the above

5. CLSC

Question 5–71. [SxPx] Which of the following commands will set the time of a Catalyst 5000 or 6600 switch?

    a) set time Thursday 08/24/98 15:34:00
    b) set clock Thursday 08/24/98 15:34:00
    c) clock set Thursday 08/24/98 15:34:00
    d) set time 15:34:00 August 24 1998
    e) set clock 15:34:00 August 24 1998

Question 5–72. [SxPx] To backup your configuration file to a tftp server on a Catalyst 5000 or 5500 switch, which of the following commands would you use?

    a) write network
    b) write tftp
    c) copy run start
    d) copy start tftp
    e) write [ip address of tftp server] [name of file to be saved]

Question 5–73. [SxPx] Which of the following commands will show the model number, serial number, and status of all modules in a Catalyst 5000 or 5500?

    a) show interface
    b) show modules all
    c) show modules
    d) show module
    e) None of the above

Question 5–74. [SxPx] Which of the following commands will configure Fast EtherChannel on ports 3/1-4 on a Catalyst 5000 or 5500?

    a) set fast EtherChannel 3/1-4
    b) set port fast 3/1-4
    c) set fast port 3/1-4
    d) set port 3/1-4 channel
    e) set port channel 3/1-4

Question 5–75. [SxPx] Using the ATM LANE Modules for the Catalyst 5000 and 5500 switch will produce what maximum bandwidth?

    a) 25 Mbps
    b) 155 Mbps
    c) 622 Mbps
    d) 2.4 Gbps
    e) None of the above

Question 5–76. [SxPx] Which of the following devices make forwarding decisions based on Layer 3 information?

   a) Switch
   b) Router
   c) Bridge
   d) Hub
   e) None of the above

Question 5–77. [SxPx] What requirements must be satisfied to configure Fast EtherChannel on a Catalyst 5000 or 5500 switch running 3.x software? (Choose all that apply.)

   a) All ports must be in the same VLAN.
   b) All ports must be set to trunk.
   c) All ports must not be set to trunk.
   d) All ports must have the same spanning-tree settings.
   e) There are no requirements on the ports.

Question 5–78. [SxPx] Which of the following trunking methods will be used over Fast Ethernet connections?

   a) IEEE 802.10
   b) Cut-Through
   c) Static
   d) Inter-Switch Link (ISL)
   e) LAN Emulation (LANE)

Question 5–79. [SxPx] Which of the following devices make decisions based on Layer 2 information? (Choose all that apply.)

   a) Switch
   b) Router
   c) Bridge
   d) Hub
   e) None of the above

Question 5–80. [SxPx] Which VTP mode is the default mode on Catalyst 5000 and 5500 switches running 2.4 or later?

   a) Transparent
   b) Server
   c) Client
   d) VTP is not enabled by default
   e) None of the above

5. CLSC

Question 5–81. [SxPx] What is the maximum distance of an FDDI Single Mode Fiber (SMF) connection between two Catalyst 5000 or 5500 switches?

a) 100 m
b) 1000 m
c) 2000 m
d) 10000 m
e) 32000 m

Question 5–82. [SxPx] Which of the following commands will create a FDDI VLAN named Marketing, numbered 7 with a SAID value of 100007?

a) set vlan 7
b) set vlan 7 name Marketing
c) set vlan 7 name Marketing type FDDI
d) set vlan number 7 name Marketing type FDDI said 7
e) None of the above

Question 5–83. [SxPx] Which of the following are true of Frame Filtering?

a) Can increase switch latency
b) Can degrade switch performance
c) Adds administration overhead
d) Used by the Catalyst 5000
e) Places an identifier in each frame

Question 5–84. [SxPx] What is the purpose of Automated Packet Recognition and Translation (APaRT) on a Catalyst switch?

a) To help route packets from Ethernet to FDDI and vice versa
b) To prevent unwanted FDDI frames from being translated into Ethernet frames
c) To prevent unwanted Ethernet frames from being translated into FDDI frames
d) To help the switch decide which Ethernet frame type to translate FDDI frames into
e) None of the above

Question 5–85. [SxPx] Which of the following trunking methods will be used over ATM connections on Catalyst switches?

a) IEEE 802.10
b) Cut-Through
c) Static
d) Inter-Switch Link (ISL)
e) LAN Emulation (LANE)

Question 5–86. [SxPx] Which of the following are valid Spanning Tree Protocol (STP) states for a port on a Catalyst Switch?

a) Blocking
b) Listening
c) Learning
d) Teaching
e) All of the above

Question 5–87. [SxPx] Which of the following is the proper command to create a LAN Emulation Client on a sub-interface that is a member of the Marketing ELAN and is being mapped to VLAN 100?

a) lane client Marketing 100
b) client Marketing 100
c) client 100 Marketing
d) lane client 100 Marketing
e) None of the above

Question 5–88. [SxPx] What is the size of an ATM Network Service Access Point (NSAP) address in bits?

a) 40
b) 100
c) 120
d) 160
e) None of the above

Question 5–89. [SxPx] The ISDN Basic Rate interface (BRI) provides:

a) 23 B channels and a 16-kps D channel
b) The same as a PRI in Europe
c) 23 B channels and a 64-kps D channel
d) Two 64-kps B channels and a 16-kps D channel
e) None of the above

Question 5–90. [SxPx] Which of the following are types of VTP messages?

a) Standard Advertisements
b) Summary Advertisements
c) Sub-Interface Advertisements
d) Subset Advertisements
e) Advertisement Requests

Question 5–91. [SxPx] Which of the follwing commands will set the port speed of the 2/1 port to 100MB?

    a)   set port level 2/1100
    b)   set speed 2/1 100
    c)   set port speed 2/1 100
    d)   set speed 100 2/1
    e)   set port speed 100 2/1

Question 5–92. [SxPx] Which of the following commands will set up broadcast suppression on port 3/4 of a Catalyst 5000 or 5500 such that no more than 70% of all traffic on the port is broadcast?

    a)   set port broadcast 3/4 70%
    b)   set port broadcast 3/4 70
    c)   set broadcast suppression 70%
    d)   set broadcast port suppression 70%
    e)   None of the above

Question 5–93. [SxPx] Which of the following is NOT true of the Inter-Switch Link (ISL) Tag?

    a)   The tagging is performed in a hardware ASIC.
    b)   ISL is proprietary to Cisco devices.
    c)   ISL is not dependent on Layer 3 protocols.
    d)   Cisco routers support ISL trunking.
    e)   ISL is the IEEE 802.1q standard.

Question 5–94. [SxPx] Which of the following is NOT a benefit of the VLAN Trunking Protocol (VTP)? (Choose all that apply.)

    a)   Keeps a consistent VLAN configuration throughout a Management Domain
    b)   Reduces administrative overhead
    c)   Used to exchange Layer 3 addressing information
    d)   Can be set up to route for IPX
    e)   Can be used to help keep unwanted traffic off trunk lines by pruning

Question 5–95. [SxPx] On the Catalyst 5000 and 5500, which processor is responsible for operation of a non-Ethernet, non-Fast Ethernet port?

    a)   SAINT
    b)   LTL
    c)   CBL
    d)   SAGE
    e)   EARL

Question 5–96. [SxPx] What is the Backplane Capacity for frames of the Catalyst 5500 with a Supervisor Engine III?

a) 533 MB
b) 1.066 GB
c) 1.2 GB
d) 3.6 GB
e) 5.0 GB

Question 5–97. [SxPx] When an ATM device needs to resolve an ATM Address from a MAC address what will it do?

a) Use the ATM Address Resolution Protocol (ATM-ARP) to resolve the ATM address
b) Use the LAN Emulation Address Resolution Protocol (LE-ARP) to resolve the ATM address
c) Use a text file that resides on the LAN Emulation Configuration Server (LECS).
d) Use the regular IP-ARP protocol.
e) None of the above

Question 5–98. [SxPx] What is the maximum number of active VLANs supported on a Catalyst 5000 or 5500 switch, where an active VLAN is defined as a VLAN with ports assigned to it?

a) 100
b) 150
c) 200
d) 250
e) 1000

Question 5–99. [SxPx] The Catalyst 5500 and 5000 use a Serial Management Bus running at 761Kbps, what processors are responsible for access to this bus?

a) MCP
b) LTL
c) CBL
d) LCP
e) SAMBA

Question 5–100. [SxPx] Assuming that there are three VLANs configured on the Ethernet ports of the two switches on either side of the ATM LANE cloud and the switches shown are the only devices connected into the cloud, how many LAN Emulation Clients (LEC) will most likely be configured?

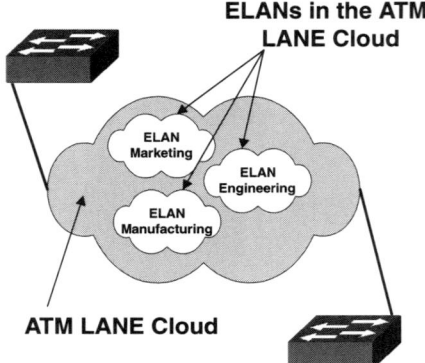

ELANs in the ATM LANE Cloud

ATM LANE Cloud

a) 1
b) 2
c) 5
d) 6
e) A LAN Emulation Client is not required.

Question 5–101. [SxPx] What will be the result of the "set system name CAT" command when typed on a Catalyst 5000 or 5500?

a) The system name when viewed with a SNMP management station will be "CAT"
b) The prompt will be changed to "CAT>"
c) The switch will be affectionately called CAT by its peers
d) The system name when viewed with a SNMP management station will be &quote;CAT&quote; and the prompt will be changed to "CAT>"
e) It is an invalid command on a Catalyst switch

Question 5–102. [SxPx] An ATM LANE Module for the Catalyst 5000 or 5500 can be configured as which of the following ATM LANE components? (Choose all that apply.)

a) LAN Emulation Client (LEC)
b) LAN Emulation Configuration Server (LECS)
c) LAN Emulation Server (LES)
d) LAN Emulation Gateway (LEG)
e) Broadcast and Unknown Server (BUS)

Question 5–103. [SxPx] Which of the following are automatically configured Virtual Channel Circuit (VCC) when a LAN Emulation Client joins an ATM LANE Cloud? (Choose all that apply.)

a) Channel Direct VCC
b) Control Direct VCC
c) Control Distribute VCC
d) Configuration Direct VCC
e) Data Direct VCC

Question 5–104. [SxPx] What is true of the interface assignments to LANE devices?

a) The LAN Emulation Configuration Server (LECS) is always assigned to the major interface.
b) The LAN Emulation Server (LES) and the LAN Emulation Client (LEC) are always assigned to the major interface.
c) The LES and LEC of two different ELANs can be assigned to the same sub-interface.
d) Two LESs can be assigned to the same sub-interface.
e) Two LECs can be assigned to the same sub-interface.

Question 5–105. [SxPx] What traffic will be seen by a protocol analyzer that is connected to a switch? (Choose all that apply.)

a) All broadcast traffic
b) All data traffic and all broadcast traffic
c) Only traffic that is destined for the protocol analyzer
d) All traffic

Question 5–106. [SxPx] What is the Backplane Capacity for frames of the Catalyst 5500 with a Supervisor Engine II?

a) 533 MB
b) 1.066 GB
c) 1.2 GB
d) 3.6 GB
e) 5.0 GB

Question 5–107. [SxPx] A broadcast is used in which of the following circumstances?

a) To resolve Layer 2 Mac Addresses
b) To send Distance Vector routing protocol updates
c) To validate routes on the network
d) To test connectivity between hosts
e) To find and advertise network services

Question 5–108. [SxPx] Which of the following commands will allow you to restore a backed up configuration from a tftp server?

a) copy tftp running-configuration
b) copy tftp config
c) restore configuration
d) configure network
e) None of the above

Question 5–109. [SxPx] Which of the following commands will enable RMON on a Catalyst 5000 or 5500 switch?

a)　enable rmon
b)　set enable rmon
c)　set snmp enable
d)　set snmp rmon enable
e)　None of the above

Question 5–110. [SxPx] Which of the following commands will enable port mirroring from port 3/4 to port 3/5 of a Catalyst 5000 or 5500 switch?

a)　set port span enable 3/4 3/5
b)　set port span enable 3/5 3/4
c)　set span enable 3/4 3/5
d)　set span enable 3/5 3/4
e)　None of the above

Question 5–111. [SxPx] The Dual PHY ATM Line Module for the Catalyst 5000 and 5500 has two physical ports for what purpose?

a)　To provide either redundant connections to the same ATM cloud or connections to two different ATM clouds
b)　To provide connectivity to two different ATM clouds only
c)　To provide redundant connections to the same ATM cloud only
d)　To provide ATM and Ethernet connectivity
e)　None of the above

Question 5–112. [SxPx] Which one of the following devices can not be made redundant on the Catalyst 5500?

a)　Clocking Module
b)　Supervisor Engine
c)　Power Supply
d)　Backplane
e)　ATM LANE cards

Question 5–113. [SxPx] Which command(s) will show the entire configuration file of a Catalyst 5000 or 5500 switch?

a)　show config
b)　show runnning-configuration
c)　show startup-configuration
d)　write terminal
e)　None of the above

Answer 5–1.
   a)   **Router**
   b)   **Switch**

A router controls broadcasts by not forwarding them. A bridge forwards broadcast frames by default and thus can do nothing to control broadcast traffic. A switch behaves like a bridge and forwards broadcasts but can control broadcasts with VLANS. A VLAN is a group of switch ports that will send and receive broadcasts. If a switch has two ports on different VLANS it will not provide any connectivity between the ports, including broadcasts.

Answer 5–2.
   e)   **IGRP**

The Catalyst 5000 and 5500 support all of these features except IGRP. It is a switch, not a router, therefore, it does not need to run a routing protocol.

Answer 5–3.
   b)   **When the IP address of the interface sc0 is 0.0.0.0**
   c)   **When the switch is using its default settings for the interface sc0**

The switch will perform a BOOTP request when the IP address of interface sc0 is set to 0.0.0.0, which is also the default setting. To determine the MAC address that will be used, simply take the first MAC address listed in the range of MAC addresses on module 1 of the "show module" command.

```
CAT> (enable) show module
Mod Module-Name  Ports Module-Type          Model     Serial-Num Status
--- ----------- ----- -------------------- --------- ---------- ------
1   Supervisor    2    100BaseTX Supervisor WS-X5009 002650014  ok
2   Management    24   10BaseT Ethernet     WS-X5010 002475046  ok

Mod MAC-Address(es)                              Hw    Fw    Sw
--- -------------------------------------------- ----  ----  ----
1   00-40-cb-ca-80-00 thru 00-40-cb-ca-83-ff 1.6   1.4   2.1
2   00-40-fb-e4-92-58 thru 00-40-fb-e4-92-6f 1.0   1.4   2.1
```

Answer 5–4.
   e)   **SAINT**

The Synergy Advanced Interface and Network Termination (SAINT) ASIC is responsible for operation of an Ethernet of Fast Ethernet port on a Catalyst 5500 and 5000. The SAINT gives an Ethernet or Fast Ethernet port such capabilities as trunking and half or full duplex.

Answer 5–5.
   d)   **set interface sc0 10 172.16.0.2 255.255.255.0**

Refer to the following output:

```
CAT> (enable) set interface sc0 10 172.16.0.2 255.255.255.0
Interface sc0 IP address and netmask set.
```

```
CAT> (enable) sh int
sl0:  flags=51<UP,POINTOPOINT,RUNNING>
         slip 0.0.0.0 dest 0.0.0.0
sc0:  flags=63<UP,BROADCAST,RUNNING>
         vlan 10 inet 172.16.0.2 netmask 255.255.255.0 broadcast 172.16.100.255
CAT> (enable)
```

Answer 5–6.
   c)   3

In LANE, a Broadcast and Unknown Server (BUS) needs to be configured for every LAN Emulation Server (LES) that is created. The diagram calls for three LES and therefore requires three BUS.

Answer 5–7.
   a)   1

In the graphic depicted there is one ATM LANE cloud with three ELANs. There only needs to be one LAN Emulation Configuration Server (LECS) per ATM LANE Cloud.

Answer 5–8.
   d)   To restrict VLAN traffic from traversing trunk lines to switches that have no ports in those VLANs

VTP pruning is not used to restrict VTP traffic in any way. VTP pruning is used to keep VLAN traffic from propagating onto switches that do not have ports in those VLANs, thus reducing the amount of unwanted traffic.

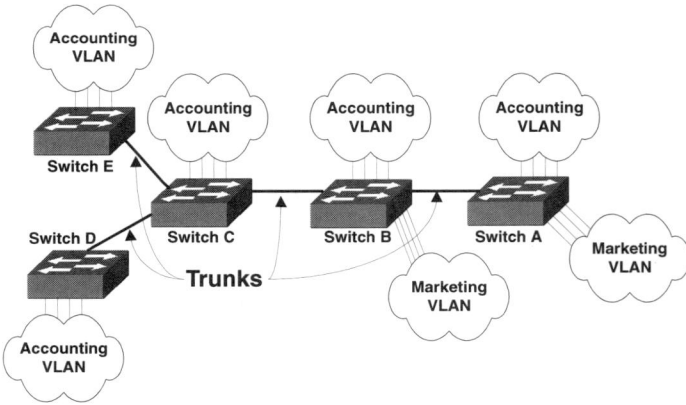

All of the above switches have trunks to one another. However, only Switch A and Switch B actually have ports that are in the Marketing VLAN. Traffic coming from ports in the Marketing VLAN of switches A and B will be transmitted to switches C, D, and E over the trunk lines. This is unnecessary traffic. VTP pruning, when enabled, will stop only the Marketing traffic from propagating across the trunk lines between Switch B and C. Therefore, switches C, D, and E will never see this unwanted traffic.

If any of Switches C, D, and E were to have ports assigned to the Marketing VLAN, VTP would start forwarding that traffic appropriately.

Answer 5–9.
  b) **No one will have connectivity to B**
  e) **The IP addressing on the router is invalid.**

The two interfaces of the router are in the same address space and are invalid unless Variable Length Subnet Masking has been enabled.

Host A was a little tricky. Host A thinks that Host B is on the local network, which indeed it is. Therefore, A will ARP for B and B will receive the ARP request. The question clearly called for bi-directional connectivity, meaning that B must be able to communicate with A. When B goes to respond to A, B will not ARP for A, it will ARP for the default gateway. This is because A appears to be on a different network from B.

Answer 5–10.
  d) **LAN Emulation Gateway (LEG)**

LAN Emulation uses only four components:

LAN Emulation Client (LEC)
LAN Emulation Configuration Server (LECS)
LAN Emulation Server (LES)
Broadcast and Unknown Server (BUS)

Answer 5–11.
  a) **show VLAN**
  b) **show port**

Answer 5–12.
  a) **LANE is the process of making an ATM Cloud look like an Ethernet or Token Ring LAN.**
  c) **LANE is required to trunk across ATM.**

ATM LAN Emulation is the process of making an ATM cloud look like an Ethernet or Token Ring segment to other LANs. This process is necessary for trunking over ATM.

Answer 5–13.
  c) **set vtp domain name ARI mode server**

The management domain name and mode can be set using the "set vtp" command. See below.

```
CAT> (enable) set vtp domain ARI mode server
VTP: domain ARI modified
CAT> (enable)
```

Answer 5–14.
  e) **None of the above**

The correct command is "set interface sc0 up".

```
CAT> (enable) set interface sc0 up <Enter>
Interface sc0 administratively up
CAT> (enable)
```

Answer 5–15.
  e) **Allows for VLANs to span across multiple switches**

Frame tagging allows Catalyst switches to propagate frames across special lines called trunks and remain in their respective VLAN. This capability has been adopted by the IEEE 802.1q committee. Cisco at this point uses a proprietary frame tagging method.

Answer 5–16.
  e) **5.0 GB**

The Catalyst 5500 can switch cells across a 5 GB backplane that connects to the bottom 5 slots. An ATM switch processor must be purchased and placed in slot 13 for the 5500 to have this capability.

Answer 5–17.
  a) **1**

In LAN Emulation, you need only configure one LECS. It manages the entire ATM cloud, including all of the configured ELANs. When redundancy is required you must use either LANE version 2.0, which is not currently supported (August 1998), or Cisco's proprietary Simple Server Redundancy Protocol (SSRP).

Answer 5–18.
  c) **show vlan**

The "show vlan" command will display all VLANs that are configured in the management domain regardless of whether or not interfaces are participating. Below is an example of the output from the "show vlan" command on a switch with version 3.2.1a:

```
CAT> (enable) sh vlan
VLAN Name                             Status    Mod/Ports, Vlans
---- -------------------------------- --------- ----------------------------
1    default                          active    1/2
                                                4/1,4/3,4/5-7,4/9-12

11   Accounting                       active
110  Finance                          active
120  Marketing                        active
130  Brokers                          active
140  Engineering                      active
150  IS                               active
160  Manufacturing                    active
```

```
170   Production                          active
180   Management                          active
1002  fddi-default                        active
1003  token-ring-default                  active
1004  fddinet-default                     active
1005  trnet-default                       active
```

VLAN	Type	SAID	MTU	Parent	RingNo	BrdgNo	Stp	BrdgMode	Trans1	Trans2
1	enet	100001	1500	-	-	-	-	-	0	0
11	enet	100011	1500	-	-	-	-	-	0	0
110	enet	100110	1500	-	-	-	-	-	0	0
120	enet	100120	1500	-	-	-	-	-	0	0
130	enet	100130	1500	-	-	-	-	-	0	0
140	enet	100140	1500	-	-	-	-	-	0	0
150	enet	100150	1500	-	-	-	-	-	0	0
160	enet	100160	1500	-	-	-	-	-	0	0
170	enet	100170	1500	-	-	-	-	-	0	0
180	enet	100180	1500	-						
1002	fddi	101002	1500	-	0x0	-	-	-	0	0
1003	trcrf	101003	1500	0	0x0	-	-	-	0	0
1004	fdnet	101004	1500	-	-	0x0	ieee	-	0	0
1005	trbrf	101005	1500	-	-	0x0	ibm	-	0	0

VLAN	AREHops	STEHops	Backup CRF
1003	0	0	off

Answer 5–19.
  c)   3

LAN Emulation requires that a single LAN Emulation Server (LES) be created for every ELAN. Therefore, we will require three LES, one per ELAN. If LANE version 2.0 or the Simple Server Redundancy Protocol (SSRP) were configured, it would be possible to have two or more LES per ELAN.

Answer 5–20.
  d)   **The ATM LANE Module uses the Cisco Internetworking Operating System with its own Command Line Interface (CLI).**

The ATM LANE module for the Catalyst 5000 and 5500 switch uses its own operating system that resides in flash memory of the module. This operating system is the Cisco IOS with the familiar CLI.

Answer 5–21.
  d)   **ATM Forum**

The ATM forum is the body currently developing the standards that most vendors use today. It currently has over 2000 members, including Cisco Systems.

Answer 5–22.
    e) **There is no default route.**

Answer 5–23.
    c) **0100.0ccc.cccc**

CDP uses the Layer 2 Multicast address 0100.0CCC.CCCC. See the NetXray trace following:

```
  7 cisco 7EDB5B  cisco 7EDA65  LOOPB 00-00-0C-7E-DB-5B ==> 00-00-0C-7E-DB-
  8 cisco 7EDA65  cisco 7EDA65  LOOPB 00-00-0C-7E-DA-65 ==> 00-00-0C-7E-DA-
  9 cisco 7EDB01  01000CCCCCCC  LLC   Sap 0xAA ---> 0xAA (Command)
 10 cisco 7EDB01  Atalk_Broadca  ARTMP Response
 11 151.204.200.20 BROADCAST     RIP   2 (Response), Ver=1
 12 cisco 13D931   Atalk_Broadca  ARTMP Response
```

Answer 5–24.
    e) **All of the above**

By running a different instance of the spanning tree protocol per VLAN, the size of the spanning tree is reduced.
The processing time is also reduced.
The time required by the switch to calculate or recalculate the spanning tree is reduced.
All of these benefits of reduced processing time will decrease the time to recover from a change and allow for more efficient paths through the bridged network.

We have to remember that a bridged network will have a single path through it, which may not be the most efficient, especially as the spanning tree gets larger.

Answer 5–25.
    c) **Line III above**

	Speed	Priority Level	Duplex Method
III	auto	normal	auto

By default all 10/100 ethernet ports will be set to auto speed and duplex and normal priority level. In contrast the 10MB ports and 100MB ports will be set to half duplex.

Answer 5–26.
    b) **Telnet to the Interface sc0**
    d) **Dial in using SLIP to a modem attached to the Supervisor Engine's console port**

The Catalyst 5000 and 5500 switches support SLIP on the Supervisor Engines console port. To configure you must use the "slip attach" command. You can also use the telnet application to access the logical management interface, sc0.

Answer 5–27.
    c) **To allow switches to maintain a consistent VLAN configuration across multiple switches**

5. Answers

The virtual trunking protocol is used by Catalyst switches to maintain a consistent VLAN configuration across a management domain.

Answer 5–28.
   a) **A switch that is configured as a VTP server will receive updates and change its configuration based on those updates.**
   b) **A switch that is configured as a VTP client will receive updates and change its configuration based on those updates.**
   e) **You can configure VLANs on a switch that is configured as a VTP transparent.**

There are three VTP modes that a switch can be configured in:

1. Server - A switch will send updates, receive updates, listen to those updates.
2. Client - A switch will send updates, receive updates, listen to those updates.
3. Transparent - A switch will send updates, receive updates, and NOT listen to those updates. It will only propagate those updates out other trunk ports.

It is important to remember that the only difference between a Client and a Server is that a Client cannot have VLANs configured on its CLI. It can only receive updates from another VTP node.

Answer 5–29.
   b) **set vlan 10 3/1-12, 2/1-12**

To assign ports to a vlan use the command "set vlan".

```
set vlan [vlan_num] [mod/ports]
```

Also note that a range of ports can be specified. You do not need to type in a separate line for ports on two different modules; simply use the comma.

Answer 5–30.
   a) **Better control of broadcasts**

Switches themselves will provide more physical segments and thus have fewer users per segment, more available bandwidth per node, and fewer collisions; however, this has nothing to do with VLANs. VLANs are going to help control broadcast traffic. A VLAN will allow broadcasts to be propagated only on ports that have been assigned to that VLAN. This is unlike a switch with no VLANs configured, which will propagate broadcasts out all ports.

Answer 5–31.
   d) **NMP**

The Network Management Processor (NMP) is responsible for all the management and spanning tree calculations. This is a separate processor, freeing the EARL from any management, and thus giving it more processing time to make forwarding decisions.

5. Answers

Answer 5–32.
   e)   PHOENIX

The Supervisor Engine III uses ASICs called Phoenix to bridge together the three backplanes, creating an aggregate backplane bandwidth of 3.6GB.

The Supervisor Engine II uses a repeater chip that simply repeats all traffic over all backplanes, creating a single backplane of 1.2GB.

Answer 5–33.
   e)   encap isl 10

To route between VLANs you must use a router. To create a trunk to the router, you must use sub-interfaces as shown below.

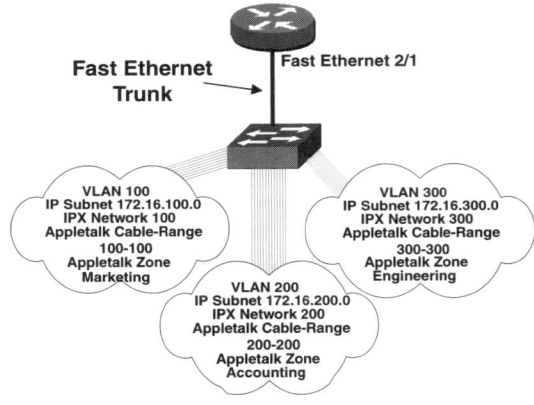

```
interface FastEthernet 2/1.1
ip address 172.16.100.1 255.255.255.0
ipx network 100
appletalk cable-range 100-100
appletalk zone Marketing
encap isl 100
!
interface FastEthernet 2/1.2
ip address 172.16.200.1 255.255.255.0
ipx network 200
appletalk cable-range 200-200
appletalk zone Accounting
encap isl 200
!
interface FastEthernet 2/1.3
ip address 172.16.300.1 255.255.255.0
ipx network 300
appletalk cable-range 300-300
appletalk zone Engineering
encap isl 300
```

Answer 5–34.
  a)   1

The Catalyst 5000 and 5500 send all frames to all interfaces while the Embedded Address Recognition Logic (EARL) makes forwarding decisions. The EARL will then decide which ports will actually forward the frame.

Answer 5–35.
  a)   **NetFlow Switching**

The Layer 3 Switching feature card uses NetFlow Switching. NetFlow Switching forwards frames based on the Layer 3 flow of traffic.

The first frame will be switched by a Router. Every subsequent frame will be forwarded by the L3 feature card on the Supervisor Engine II or III.

Answer 5–36.
  a)   **IEEE 802.1d**

The Catalyst 5000 series switch supports only the IEEE version of Spanning Tree, which can be a problem in a multi-vendor switch environment. Check to verify that the proper version of Spanning Tree is in use.

Answer 5–37.
  a)   **Full-duplex Ethernet controllers or a controller for each path**
  b)   **Collision detection disabled**
  d)   **Two data paths**

Answer 5–38.
  a)   **Increases bandwidth available to nodes**
  d)   **Reduces the number of collisions**

Segmenting LANs with switches and bridges reduces the number of hosts per wire, which reduces the number of collisions and gives more available bandwidth per node. On a switch or a bridge, each port is its own collision domain.

Answer 5–39.
  d)   **1 per ELAN**

In ATM LAN Emulation we will break our cloud into ELANs, which are basically VLANs for ATM. For the Catalyst 5000 and 5500 to trunk, create an ELAN for every VLAN that needs to be trunked across the ATM Cloud. For every ELAN there must be a LAN Emulation Server, one per ELAN.

5. Answers

Answer 5–40.
  c) **enable**

The Catalyst Operating System used by the 5000 and 5500 has two modes, User and Privileged, similar to the Cisco IOS. To move from user mode to privileged mode, the command is the same, "enable".

Answer 5–41.
  b) **0.0.0.0.**

By default, the SC0 interface sends a bootp request, and, if there is no reply, keeps the address 0.0.0.0 with a matching subnet mask and broadcast address.

Answer 5–42.
  b) **ISDN Switch Type**
  c) **SPID number**

Currently these parameters are required, during the next year we will probably be able to go "SPIDLESS" and the switch type will not be required.

Refer to the sample configuration below:

```
show run
Building configuration...
Current configuration:
!
version 11.0
!
hostname Router_A
!
enable secret 5 $1$HaL/$Ej1F78CuSx1cohZJQ4VSW/
!
username Router_B password 7 07032E4F45031812
isdn switch-type basic-ni1
!
interface Ethernet0
 ip address 10.10.2.1 255.255.255.0
!
interface Serial0
 ip address 10.30.1.2 255.255.255.0
 no fair-queue
 clockrate 64000
!
interface Serial1
ip address 20.20.2.1 255.255.255.0
!
interface BRI0
 ip address 15.150.1.2 255.255.255.0
 encapsulation ppp
 isdn spid1 21255524231010
 isdn spid2 21255524241010
```

```
 dialer map ip 150.150.1.1 name north 5551000
 dialer load-threshold 50 either
 dialer-group 1
 no fair-queue
ppp authentication chap
 !
ip route 0.0.0.0 0.0.0.0 15.150.1.1
dialer-list 1 protocol ip permit
 !
line con 0
line aux 0
line vty 0 4
login
end
```

Answer 5–43.
   e)   All traffic

A hub is merely a repeater; all traffic that comes into any one of its ports is sent out to all the other ports. A protocol analyzer that is plugged into a hub will see all traffic on that hub. This can be a security issue if too many individuals have access to open hub ports. All they need to do is plug a protocol analyzer in the hub port, and they now have access to all traffic on that hub.

Answer 5–44.
   d)   set ip route default 1.1.1.1

The switch management interface is treated as any other IP node and needs an IP address.

```
CAT> (enable) set ip route default 1.1.1.1 <Enter>
Route added.
CAT> (enable)
```

Now use the command "show ip route" to check that the route has been properly added to our routing table.

```
CAT> (enable) show ip route <Enter>
Fragmentation   Redirect   Unreachable
-------------   --------   -----------
enabled         enabled    enabled

Destination        Gateway            Flags   Use          Interface
---------------    ---------------    ------  ----------   --------
default            1.1.1.1            UG               0   sc0
1.1.1.0            1.1.1.10           U                0   sc0
default            default            UH               0   sl0
CAT> (enable)
```

Answer 5–45.
   d)   To synchronize timekeeping between all devices that support NTP

Answer 5–46.
- a) **An IP Subnet**
- d) **A Broadcast Domain**

Answer 5–47.
- a) **set port duplex 2/1 full**

The following is the result of using the "set port duplex 2/1 full" command.

```
CAT> (enable) set port duplex 2/1 full
Port 2/1 set to full-duplex.
```

Answer 5–48.
- d) **Configuration Direct VCC**

When a LAN Emulation Client (LEC) joins a LANE cloud, it first contacts the LECS. Once the ATM Address has been discovered via ILMI, preconfigured address, or a well-known ATM address, the Configuration Direct VCC is set up.

Answer 5–49.
- a) **Static**
- c) **Dynamic**

Ports can be manually assigned to a VLAN through the command line interface (static) or dynamically assigned based on the source MAC address of incoming frames (dynamic).

Answer 5–50.
- e) **set enablepass <return>**

The command for setting the password to enter privileged mode is "set enablepass <return>", after which you will be prompted for the old password and then the new password twice, to be sure it was typed correctly. See the following:

```
CAT> (enable) en
CAT> (enable) set enablepass
Enter old password:<return>
Enter new password: cisco <return>
Retype new password: cisco <return>
Password changed.
CAT> (enable)
```

Answer 5–51.
- b) **Store and Forward**

The Catalyst 5000 and 5500 switches architecture does not support Cut-Through switching currently.

Answer 5–52.
   b) **26 bytes**

The ISL header consists of the following fields totaling 26 bytes.

Destination Address -	This is a Multicast destination address used by ISL	(5 bytes)
Type -	Describes the type of encapsulated frame	(1/2 byte)
User -	Varies based on Type	(1/2 byte)
Source Address -	The MAC address of the transmitting switch	(6 bytes)
Length-	The length of the entire frame minus the DA, SA, LEN, and CRC fields.	(2 bytes)
802.2 LLC header-	This field is always AAAA03	(3 bytes)
HSA or OUI-	The 3 byte header used in a company's MAC address	(3 bytes)
VLAN-	The VLAN number, currently only 10 of the 15 bits are used	(1 15/16 bytes)
BPDU-	The Bridge Packet Data Unit identifier	(1/16 byte)
Index-	To identify the transmitting port	(2 bytes)
Reserved-	Reserved for additional information such as FDDI FC field	(2 bytes)
	Total Bytes	**(26 bytes)**

Answer 5–53.
   d) **EARL**

The Embedded Address Recognition Logic (EARL) ASIC is responsible for forwarding decisions in the Catalyst 5500 and 5000.

Answer 5–54.
   e) **End System Identifier (ESI)**

The ATM address will come from the ATM switches that make up the cloud. However, the last two fields of the address will be the End System Identifier (ESI) and the Selector Byte (SEL). These two fields will come from the switch, not from the ATM cloud. The ESI will come from the MAC address assigned to the ATM device.

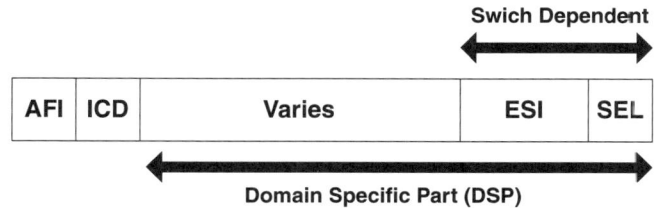

The MAC address will come from a pool of addresses that is assigned to the ATM LANE card by Cisco Systems. The First MAC address will be assigned to the LAN Emulation Clients (LEC) assigned to that interface; the second to all LAN Emulation Servers (LES); the third to all Broadcast and Unknown Servers (BUS); and the fourth to the LAN Emulation Configuration Server (LECS) if configured.

Answer 5–55.
    d) set spantree portfast 1/2 enable

Portfast will allow a port to forward while in the listening mode.

```
CAT> (enable) set spantree portfast 1/2 enable
Warning: Spantree port fast start should only be enabled on ports connected to
   a single host. Connecting hubs, concentrators, switches, bridges, etc.. to a
   fast start port can cause temporary spanning tree loops. Use with caution.
Spantree port 1/2 fast start enabled.
```

Answer 5–56.
    c) ILMI uses the SNMP protocol and Management Information Bases.
    e) LAN Emulation Clients can use ILMI to locate the LAN Emulation Configuration Sever.

ILMI is used by any ATM device to exchange whatever information is necessary, including the location of the LAN Emulation Configuration Server. This information is exchanged using the Simple Network Management (SNMP) protocol and its Management Information Bases (MIB).

Answer 5–57.
    d) 800 MB

The maximum number of interfaces possible in a Fast EtherChannel is four 100 MB ports. When all four are set to full-duplex, this will give an aggregate bandwidth of 800 MB.

Answer 5–58.
    b) copy tftp flash
    c) copy flash tftp

The Cisco IOS command "copy tftp flash" will have the same effect as the "download" command except you will be prompted to enter the parameters, unlike the download command where you must enter them on the same line. See the following.

```
CAT> (enable) download 1.1.1.2 sup2-311.img
Download image sup2-311.img from 1.1.1.2 to module 1 FLASH (y/n) [n]? y
Done. Finished Network Download. (2203505 bytes)
```

Answer 5–59.
    d) SAID field

The SAID field inside the 802.10 header identifies which VLAN the encapsulated frame is in. This field is 32 bits in length and resides in the clear portion of the 802.10 header.

Answer 5–60.
   a) **show interface SC0**

The only way to view the status of the SC0 interface is with the show interface SC0 command.

Answer 5–61.
   d) **Flood the frame out all ports in the VLAN**

When a switch receives a frame, and the destination address is unknown, the frame is forwarded out all ports in the VLAN that is assigned to the port where the frame was received.

Answer 5–62.
   d) **D**

B and D both have a 24-bit subnet mask, as well as the router interfaces. The addresses match the assigned subnetworks, therefore there will be connectivity between B and D through the router.

Host C has an incorrect subnet mask. Rather than communicating through its default gateway, it will ARP for Host B. Since Host B is not on the local segment and the router is not configured to proxy ARP there will be no response and no connectivity.

Host A was a little tricky. Host A thinks that Host B is on the local network, which indeed it is. Therefore A will ARP for B and B will receive the ARP request. The question clearly called for bi-directional connectivity, meaning that B must be able to communicate with A. When B goes to respond to A, B will not ARP for A, it will ARP for the default gateway. This is because A appears to be on a different network from B.

Answer 5–63.
   a) **IEEE 802.10**

When frames traverse a FDDI trunk line, the IEEE 802.10 header is used to identify the VLAN that a frame belongs to.

Answer 5–64.
   b) **ATM Director**

Answer 5–65.
   b) **show vlan**
   c) **show port**

Notice that both the "show vlan" and "show port" will show us the vlan to port assignments.

```
Catalyst> (enable) show vlan <Enter>
VLAN Name                              Status    Mod/Ports
---- --------------------------     --------  ----------------
1    default                           active    1/1-2
                                                 2/1-12
                                                 3/1-2
```

```
1002 fddi-default                active
1003 token-ring-default          active
1004 fddinet-default             active
1005 trnet-default               active
...
Catalyst> (enable)
```

and

```
Catalyst> (enable) show port <Enter>
Port Name            Status     Vlan  Level  Duplex Speed Type
---- ------------    ---------- ----- ------ ------ ----- ------------
1/1                  notconnect 1     normal half   100   100BaseTX
1/2                  notconnect 1     normal half   100   100BaseTX
2/1                  notconnect 1     normal half   100   FDDI
2/2                  notconnect 1     normal half   100   FDDI
3/1                  notconnect 1     normal auto   auto  10/100BaseTX
3/2                  notconnect 1     normal auto   auto  10/100BaseTX
3/3                  notconnect 1     normal auto   auto  10/100BaseTX
3/4                  notconnect 1     normal auto   auto  10/100BaseTX
3/5                  notconnect 1     normal auto   auto  10/100BaseTX
3/6                  notconnect 1     normal auto   auto  10/100BaseTX
3/7                  notconnect 1     normal auto   auto  10/100BaseTX
3/8                  notconnect 1     normal auto   auto  10/100BaseTX
3/9                  notconnect 1     normal auto   auto  10/100BaseTX
3/10                 notconnect 1     normal auto   auto  10/100BaseTX
3/11                 notconnect 1     normal auto   auto  10/100BaseTX
3/12                 notconnect 1     normal auto   auto  10/100BaseTX
                 [remaining text omitted]
```

Answer 5–66.
d) show lane configuration

The resulting display gives not only the status of the LAN Emulation Configuration Server (LECS) but also the status of the LAN Emulation Servers (LES) that this LECS is managing.

```
ATM#sh lane config
LE Config Server ATM0 config table: nfl
Admin: up  State: operational
LECS Mastership State: active master
list of global LECS addresses (38 seconds to update):
47.00918100000000905FF4A001.00905FF49C43.00  <-------- me
ATM Address of this LECS: 47.00918100000000905FF4A001.00905FF49C43.00 (auto)
 vcd  rxCnt  txCnt  callingParty
2732     5      5  47.00918100000000905FF4A001.00905FF49C41.01    LES
  Marketing   0 active
2744     4      4  47.00918100000000905FF4A001.00905FF49C41.0A    LES
  Engineering 0 active
cumulative total number of unrecognized packets received so far: 0
cumulative total number of config requests received so far: 23940
cumulative total number of config failures so far: 14413
    cause of last failure: no configuration
    culprit for the last failure: 47.00918100000000905FF4A001.00905FF49C40.B4
```

Notice the "active" to the right of the entries for the LESs.

Answer 5–67.
  e) **ENABLED** **public** **private** **secret**

By default SNMP is enabled with the string values of public, private, and secret for read, read-write, and read-write all, respectively. This can be a serious security issue for a Catalyst Switch. Anything that can be done from the command line interface can be done from a SNMP management station. In other words, anyone who knows the default strings can make changes to the configuration. Changing of the default settings is highly recommended.

Answer 5–68.
  d) **<return>**

Answer 5–69.
  a) **Manually assigning ports to VLANs**
  c) **Automatically assigning VLANs to ports based on a configuration file on a tftp server**

Catalyst switch ports can be assigned to one, and only one, VLAN currently. That port-to-VLAN assignment can occur one of three ways:

  1. The port is never manually configured and therefore remains in the default VLAN of 1.

  2. The port is manually assigned to a VLAN via the CLI or SNMP.

  3. The port is put into what's called Dynamic Mode, where the port will look at the source MAC address of frames coming into the port and compare it to a text file residing on a tftp server. In the text file will be a MAC to VLAN mapping controlling which VLAN the port is assigned to.

Answer 5–70.
  e) **None of the above**

The Simple Server Redundancy Protocol (SSRP) is a proprietary protocol for Cisco Catalyst Switches to provide redundant LECS, LES, and BUS for an ATM Cloud. There will be no load balancing between the redundant devices. The redundant devices will be used only in the event the primary fails.

Answer 5–71.
  a) **set time Thursday 08/24/98 15:34:00**

On the switch we use the "set time" command; unlike the routers, where we use the "clock set" command.

Answer 5–72.

    a)   write network

    e)   write [ip address of tftp server] [name of file to be saved]

Either of the commands will backup your configuration to a tftp server as shown by the following:

```
CAT> (enable) write network
IP address or name of host? 1.1.1.2
Name of configuration file to write? CATCFG.txt
Upload configuration to system5.cfg on VFR (y/n) [y]? y
.........................................
Done. Finished Network Upload. (9003 bytes)
 CAT> (enable)
```

or

```
CAT> (enable) write 1.1.1.2 CATCFG.txt
Upload configuration to system5.cfg on VFR (y/n) [y]? y
.........................................
Done. Finished Network Upload. (9003 bytes)
CAT> (enable)
```

Answer 5–73.

    e)   None of the above

The "show module" command will show the module name, number of ports on each, module type, model number, serial number, and status. See the following:

```
CAT> (enable) show module
Mod Module-Name  Ports Module-Type         Model    Serial-Num Status
--- ----------   ----- ------------------- -------- ---------- ------
1   Supervisor   2     100BaseTX Supervisor WS-X5009 002650014 ok
2   Management   24    10BaseT Ethernet    WS-X5010 002475046 ok

Mod MAC-Address(es)                        Hw     Fw     Sw
--- -------------------------------------- ------ ------ ------
1   00-40-cb-ca-80-00 thru 00-40-cb-ca-83-ff 1.6    1.4    2.1
2   00-40-fb-e4-92-58 thru 00-40-fb-e4-92-6f 1.0    1.4    2.1
```

Answer 5–74.

    e)   set port channel 3/1-4

To configure a Fast EtherChannel you must use the command "set port channel [port number]" as shown following.

```
CAT> (enable) set port channel 3/1-4 <Enter>
Port(s) 3/1-4 channel mode set to on.
CAT> (enable)
```

Answer 5–75.
   c) **622 Mbps**

As of this writing, the only ATM LANE Module that can be purchased supports speeds of up to OC-12, which has a bandwidth of 622 Mbps. Note that in the future Cisco will likely support OC-48, which will support a bandwidth of 2.4 Gbps.

Answer 5–76.
   b) **Router**

Answer 5–77.
   a) **All ports must be in the same VLAN.**
   c) **All ports must not be set to trunk.**
   d) **All ports must have the same spanning-tree settings.**

Answer 5–78.
   d) **Inter-Switch Link (ISL)**

Trunking over Fast Ethernet connections uses a frame-tagging method called Inter-Switch Link (ISL), the method is proprietary to Cisco. The ISL tag identifies which VLAN the frame belongs to as it travels across the trunk lines.

Answer 5–79.
   a) **Switch**
   c) **Bridge**

Answer 5–80.
   b) **Server**

Answer 5–81.
   e) **32000 m**

The distance limitations are as follows for Catlayst 5000 and 5500 FDDI modules:

Module	Maximum Distance
CDDI Module (UTP)	100 m
FDDI Module (MMF)	1000 m
FDDI Module (SMF)	32000 m

Answer 5–82.
   c) **set vlan 7 name Marketing type FDDI**

You do not need to specify the SAID value. It will default to 100000 plus the VLAN number.

```
CAT> (enable) set vlan 7 name Marketing type FDDI
VLAN 7 Added
CAT> (enable)
```

Answer 5–83.
   a)   **Can increase switch latency**
   b)   **Can degrade switch performance**
   c)   **Adds administration overhead**

Frame filtering is a scheme by which a switch can identify a frame by using user-defined parameters.
Parameters can be Mac station addresses, layer 3 protocol type or application types.

The Catalyst 5000 and the Catalyst 3000 use the Frame Tagging scheme. The Frame Tagging scheme places an ID in the header of each frame. This ID is understood by each switch as the frame passes from switch to switch. The switch will remove this ID as it exits to a non-trunk link.

Answer 5–84.
   d)   **To help the switch decide which Ethernet frame type to translate FDDI frames into**

FDDI servers that communicate with Ethernet clients through a Catalyst switch do not know that they are communicating across a translational bridge. It is up to the bridge to translate the FDDI frames into Ethernet frames. The problem lies in the fact that Novell and Appletalk have several different frame types for Ethernet. APaRT caches the MAC address and frame types of Ethernet workstations so that when frames are destined to the Ethernet segments from the FDDI, the switch knows the appropriate Ethernet frame type.

Answer 5–85.
   e)   **LAN Emulation (LANE)**

ATM connections are always trunk lines and use LAN Emulation (LANE) to identify which VLAN a frame is in.

Answer 5–86.
   a)   **Blocking**
   b)   **Listening**
   c)   **Learning**

The Catalyst switch can have ports in the following STP states:

Listening-The initial state of a port. The port listens to determine if there is a possible redundant link. While listening the port will not forward frames.

Learning-The state a port is in while it is learning addresses.

Forwarding- If Spanning Tree determines there is no bridge loop, the port will go into the forwarding state.

Blocking-If Spanning Tree determines there is a bridge loop, the port will go into the blocking state to prevent a bridge loop.

Disabled-The port will be disabled if it is disabled in the command line interface or through a SNMP management server.

Answer 5–87.
   d) **lane client 100 Marketing**

To trunk the VLAN numbered 100 across an ATM interface, that interface must be a Client of the Marketing ELAN. The command "lane client 100 Marketing" indicates that this interface is a client of Marketing. All traffic it receives on this sub-interface is to be sent to the VLAN 100 ports.

Answer 5–88.
   d) **160**

The Asynchronous Transfer Mode (ATM) address is defined by the OSI and is based on the Network Service Access Point model, which is 160 bits or 20 bytes in length. In contrast, an IP address has 32 bits. (And you thought IP addressing was difficult!)

Answer 5–89.
   d) **Two 64-kps B channels and a 16-kps D channel**

Answer 5–90.
   b) **Summary Advertisements**
   c) **Sub-Interface Advertisements**
   e) **Advertisement Requests**

These advertisements contain information pertaining to VLANs. Updates are sent at 5-minute intervals, except for Advertisement Requests, which will trigger a flash update.

Answer 5–91.
   c) **set port speed 2/1 100**

The "set port speed [port] [speed]" will change the speed of a 10/100 port. If you have 10 only or 100 only ports this command will have no effect.

```
CAT> (enable) set port speed 2/1 100
Port 2/1 speed set to 100 Mbps.
CAT> (enable)
```

Answer 5–92.
   a) **set port broadcast 3/4 70%**

Answer 5–93.
   e) **ISL is the IEEE 802.1q standard.**

The IEEE 802.1q standard is not ISL. Cisco now supports the new standard in various Ethernet modules. Trunking is done in hardware, the hardware must support 802.1q as well as the software. Be sure to verify that the line module you are purchasing supports this trunking method.

Answer 5–94.
   c) **Used to exchange Layer 3 addressing information**

VTP can only exchange information about VLANs. In no way can it understand any Layer 3 address information.

Answer 5–95.
   d) **SAGE**

The Synergy Advanced Gate-array Engine (SAGE) is responsible for the operation of a non-Ethernet or non-Fast Ethernet ports such as ATM or FDDI ports. The SAGE has the same responsibilities as the SAINT except it is used on non-Ethernet or Fast Ethernet ports.

Answer 5–96.
   d) **3.6 GB**

The Catalyst 5500 with a Supervisor Engine III has an aggregate backplane capacity of 3.6GB; however it is the combination of three 1.2 GB backplanes that gives us the 3.6 GB backplane bandwidth. The slot you place your line module in will determine which of the three backplanes your card will use. The backplanes are then bridged together using the Supervisor Engine III.

Answer 5–97.
   b) **Use the LAN Emulation Address Resolution Protocol (LE-ARP) to resolve the ATM address**

The LAN Emulation ARP (LE-ARP) is used to resolve an ATM address from a MAC address.

Answer 5–98.
   d) **250**

Remember that there are a maximum of 1000 VLAN numbers but only 250 VLANs can actually be assigned to ports on any one switch.

Answer 5–99.
   a) **MCP**
   d) **LCP**

The Master Communications Processor (MCP) and Line Communications Processor (LCP) are responsible for access to the management bus of the Catalyst 5000 and 5500. The bus is used for such tasks as helping the forwarding decision, local diagnostics, downloading run-time code.

Answer 5–100.
   d) **6**

If we have three ELANs and assume that each of the two switches needs to have connectivity to all three ELANs, we are forced to create a LEC per ELAN per Switch for a total of six.

Answer 5–101.
a)   **The system name when viewed with a SNMP management station will be "CAT"**

When the system name is set, the switch will be identified to a SNMP management station as the text value. It will not change the prompt like the Cisco IOS. To change the prompt, the "set prompt [prompt]" command must be used.

```
Console> (enable) set system name CAT <Enter>
System name set.
Console> (enable)
```

Notice that after entering the command the prompt does not change.

Answer 5–102.
a)   **LAN Emulation Client (LEC)**
b)   **LAN Emulation Configuration Server (LECS)**
c)   **LAN Emulation Server (LES)**
e)   **Broadcast and Unknown Server (BUS)**

The ATM LANE Board can be any of the LAN Emulation components necessary.

Answer 5–103.
b)   **Control Direct VCC**
c)   **Control Distribute VCC**
d)   **Configuration Direct VCC**

A LAN Emulation Client (LEC) will first configure a bi-directional circuit between itself and the LAN Emulation Configuration Server (LECS) called the Configuration Direct VCC. It will then configure the Control Direct VCC and the Control Distribute VCC between itself and the LAN Emulation Server (LES). The last two VCCs, the Mulicast Send and Multicast Forward VCCs, are between the LEC and the Broadcast and Unknown Server (BUS).

Answer 5–104.
a)   **The LAN Emulation Configuration Server (LECS) is always assigned to the major interface.**

The LAN Emulation Configuration Server must always be assigned to the major interface. The LAN Emulation Server (LES), Broadcast and Unknown Server (BUS), and LAN Emulation Client (LEC) will always be assigned to a sub-interface. The only other requirement is that no sub-interface contain devices that are a part of different ELANs. A sub-interface can contain the LES, BUS, and LEC of the same ELAN, but you cannot mix and match devices of different ELANs.

Answer 5–105.
   a)   **All broadcast traffic**
   c)   **Only traffic that is destined for the protocol analyzer**

On a switch there are two types of traffic that will be seen on its ports, frames that are destined for the MAC address that have been learned on that port and all layer 2 broadcast traffic. A switch gives us a little better security than a hub.

Answer 5–106.
   c)   **1.2 GB**

The Catalyst 5500 with a Supervisor Engine II has a Backplane Capacity of 1.2 GB.

The Catalyst 5500 with a Supervisor Engine III has an aggregate backplane capacity of 3.6GB. However, the 3.6 is the combination of three 1.2 GB backplanes. That gives us the 3.6 GB backplane bandwidth. The slot you place your line module in will determine which of the three backplanes your card will use. The backplanes are then bridged together using the Supervisor Engine III.

Answer 5–107.
   a)   **To resolve Layer 2 Mac Addresses**
   b)   **To send Distance Vector routing protocol updates**
   e)   **To find and advertise network services**

Broadcasts are typically used with IP ARP, a protocol used to resolve layer 2 addresses from layer 3 IP addresses. They are also used with distance vector routing protocols when sending updates, you will notice the destination address is always a local network broadcast. Novell is famous for its use of the Service Advertising Protocol to advertise services to its clients. This advertisement is also a broadcast address

Answer 5–108.
   d)   **configure network**

We could also use the command configure [ip address of tftp server] [file name] as shown following.

```
CAT> (enable) configure 1.1.1.2 CATCFG.txt
Configure using system5.cfg from cres (y/n) [n]? y
/
Done. Finished Network Download. (1463 bytes)
```

Answer 5–109.
   d)   **set snmp rmon enable**

RMON is not enabled by default, unlike SNMP. To allow Remote Monitoring (RMON), the command "set snmp rmon enable" must be used. Remember that a RMON license must be purchased before you can legally enable RMON.

```
CAT> (enable) set snmp rmon enable
SNMP RMON support enabled.
CAT> show snmp
RMON: Enabled
```

Answer 5–110.
    d) set span enable 3/5 3/4

Answer 5–111.
    c) To provide redundant connections to the same ATM cloud only

The Dual PHY indicates that there are two physical connections on the card. Both of these connections must go to the same ATM cloud. They are for redundancy only! It works very similar to Dual Homing in FDDI. There is no load balancing; the secondary connection is dormant until the primary fails.

Answer 5–112.
    d) Backplane

The Catalyst 5500 has no redundant feature, however the backplane is passive and is very unlikely to fail.

Answer 5–113.
    a) show config
    d) write terminal

Either of these commands will allow you to view the configuration file.

5. Answers

5. Answers

Chapter Six
CCIE

The questions in this chapter are modeled after those that appear on the Cisco Certified Internetwork Expert (CCIE) R/S exam (exam #350-001). The actual exam will contain some questions modeled after those presented in the previous five chapters of this Study Guide, but the vast majority of the questions you'll encounter will be similar in structure and content to the questions presented in this chapter.

The CCIE R/S exam consists of 100 questions. There is a two-hour time limit for taking this exam, and a score of at least 65 percent is necessary to pass (Cisco employees taking this test must score at least 70 percent to pass.). The cost for taking the actual exam is $200.00 per attempt.

When using this Study Guide's CD-ROM to study and/or test your knowledge of questions modeled after those you are likely to encounter on a CCIE exam, you will need to select "CCIE" at the *select exam* window and then select either the *study session* or *simulated exam* option.

If you select the *study session* option, you'll be able to designate the category and protocol of the questions you want to review. You will also be able to choose the number of questions you want presented during the *study session*.

When you select the *simulated exam*, the program will present you with a simulated CCIE exam containing 100 questions. The program will automatically set a time limit of 120 minutes for you to complete the exam. When you've finished, or the time has elapsed, the program will calculate your score and help you evaluate your performance within the specific categories and protocols covered by the exam. You can then set up *study sessions* in those protocols and categories in which you did not score well.

There are a total universe of 600 model CCIE exam questions in this reference.

In addition to appearing on the CCIE R/S exam, this chapter contains questions modeled after those that appear on three other Cisco exams:

Foundation Routing and Switching (FRS) Exam: (exam #640-409) - One hundred and thirty two questions; 165-minute time limit; passing score of 60 percent; cost to take exam is $200.00.

Advanced Cisco Router Configuration (ACRC 11.3) Exam: (exam #640-403)- Seventy-two questions; 90 minute time limit; passing score is 60 percent; cost to take exam is $100.00.

Cisco Internetwork Troubleshooting (CIT) Exam: (exam #640-406)- Sixty nine questions; 60 minute time limit; passing score of 60 percent; cost to take exam is $100.00.

More information regarding each of these exams can be found at the Cisco website.

Question 6–1. [RNPx] Which of the following are features of NLSP that are not features of IPX RIP?

    a) NLSP has a Hop count limitation of 15.
    b) NLSP is not limited by the use of the IPX addressing scheme.
    c) NLSP is a quieter protocol.
    d) NLSP also supports IP.
    e) All of the above.

Question 6–2. [TxPx] In a Token Ring MAC frame, the RIF route descriptor field contains the following information: (Choose all that apply.)

    a) Mac Address
    b) Ring number
    c) Explorer type
    d) Length of RIF
    e) Direction in which the RIF should be read
    f) Largest frame size
    g) Bridge number

Question 6–3. [RIPx] Assume the routing table below:

```
172.16.0.0/24 is subnetted, 2 subnets
C       172.16.1.0 is directly connected, Serial1
C       172.16.2.0 is directly connected, Serial0
D       10.0.0.0/8 [90/2195456] via 172.16.1.1, 00:03:32, Serial0
D       10.1.0.0/16 [90/2195456] via 172.16.1.1, 00:03:32, Serial1
D       10.1.3.0/24 [90/2195456] via 172.16.2.1, 00:03:32, Serial2
D       100.1.3.5/32 [90/2195456] via 172.16.1.1, 00:03:32, Serial3
D       10.0.3.5/32 [90/2195456] via 172.16.2.1, 00:03:32, Serial4
```

Which Serial connection would this router take to get to 10.1.3.5?

    a) Serial 0
    b) Serial 1
    c) Serial 2
    d) Serial 3
    e) Serial 4

Question 6–4. [PxPx] On a Cisco router which of the following are features of PPP and NOT features of HDLC? (Choose all that apply.)

    a) CHAP
    b) PAP
    c) Can be used to connect to other vendors
    d) Caller Identification
    e) The default serial encapsulation method
    f) All of the above

6. CCIE

Question 6–5. [TxPx] Which of the following are true of Source Route Translational Bridging?

    a)   Mac addresses will appear the same on both a Token Ring and an Ethernet Link.
    b)   Ethernet links will "bit swap" the MAC addresses of a Token Ring link.
    c)   Ethernet and Token Ring use opposite "bit ordering" in relation to each other.
    d)   None of the above.

Question 6–6. [CxPx] Which of the following is not a configurable option when using the extended IP ping?

    a)   Frame Size
    b)   Source IP address
    c)   Data Pattern
    d)   Source interface
    e)   Time To Live Field

Question 6–7. [CIPx] Refer to the following access list. Which of the following are true:

```
L1: deny icmp host 172.16.10.5 host 172.18.1.1 echo (4 matches)
L2: deny icmp host 172.16.10.5 host 172.19.10.2 echo
L3: deny udp host 172.16.10.5 host 172.19.10.2 eq snmp
L4: deny udp host 172.16.10.5 host 172.19.18.1 eq snmp
L5: permit ip host 172.16.10.5 host 172.19.10.2
L6: permit tcp any any eq telnet (6 matches)
L7: permit udp any any eq tftp
```

    a)   Host 172.16.10.5 has had 4 successful pings to 172.18.1.1.
    b)   Host 172.16.10.5 will not be able to ping 172.18.1.1.
    c)   Host 172.16.10.5 has not attempted to ping 172.19.10.2.
    d)   Host 172.16.10.5 will not be able to ping 172.19.10.2.
    e)   Host 172.16.10.5 will not be able to respond to a ping from 172.19.10.2.

Question 6–8. [CxPx] What is the purpose of the 1 after the following command?

```
snmp-server community myrouter RW 1
```

    a)   This allows only one snmp session at a time.
    b)   This tells the router how many RW packets to send.
    c)   It associates an IP access list to the RW community string.
    d)   It identifies myrouter as the first router in the string.
    e)   None of the above.

Question 6–9. [IxPx] Which of the following is (are) true of FDDI?

    a)   It is very expensive in relation to other medias.
    b)   It is very inexpensive in relation to other media.
    c)   FDDI uses copper wire.
    d)   It uses CSMA/CD.
    e)   It uses a token passing method similar to token ring.

6. CCIE

f) It operates at 100MB.
g) It operates at 10MB.
h) It operates at 16MB.
i) FDDI can quickly be translated into ethernet.

Question 6–10. [RXPx] Assuming all defaults what does the address of 0007.7816.fe54 represent? (Answer all that apply.) (Refer to the following diagram and configurations.)

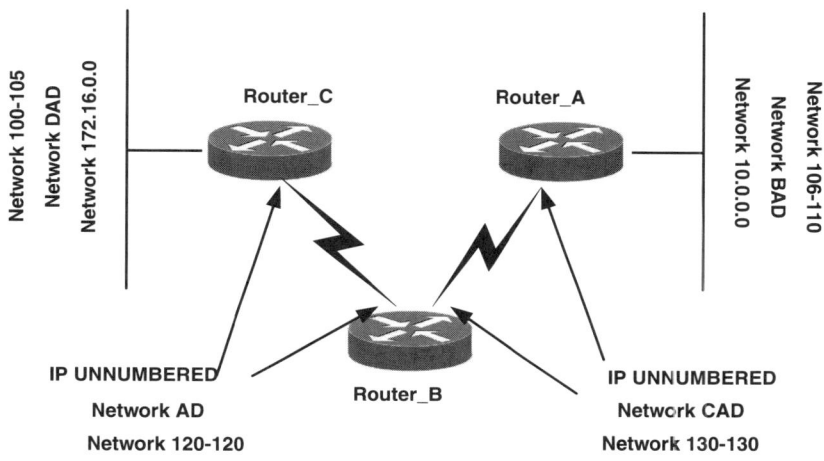

```
Router_C#sh run
Building configuration...

Current configuration:
!
version 11.2
!
hostname Router_C
!
!
appletalk routing
ipx routing 0060.09c3.df60
!
interface Ethernet0
 ip address 172.16.1.1 255.255.255.0
 appletalk cable-range 100-105 103.243
 appletalk zone right
 ipx network DAD
!
interface Ethernet1
 no ip address
 shutdown
!
interface Serial0
 ip unnumbered Ethernet0
 appletalk cable-range 120-120 120.17
```

```
 appletalk zone left
 ipx network AD
 clockrate 56000
!
interface Serial1
 no ip address
 shutdown
!
router igrp 100
 network 172.16.0.0
!
no ip classless
!!
line con 0
line aux 0
line vty 0 4
 login
!
end

Router_B#sh run
Building configuration...

Current configuration:
!
version 11.3
no service password-encryption
!
hostname Router_B
!
!
appletalk routing
ipx routing 0007.7816.fe54
!
interface Loopback0
 ip address 172.17.1.1 255.255.255.0
!
interface Serial0
 ip unnumbered Loopback0
 no ip mroute-cache
 appletalk cable-range 130-130 130.81
 appletalk zone right
 ipx network CAD
 no fair-queue
!
interface Serial1
 ip unnumbered Loopback0
 appletalk cable-range 120-120 120.125
 appletalk zone left
 ipx network AD
!
interface Serial2
 no ip address
 shutdown
```

6. CCIE

```
!
interface Serial3
 no ip address
 shutdown
!
interface TokenRing0
 no ip address
 shutdown
!
interface BRI0
 no ip address
 shutdown
!
router igrp 100
 network 172.17.0.0
!
ip classless
!
!
!
!
line con 0
line aux 0
line vty 0 4
 login
!
end

Router_A#sh run
Building configuration...

Current configuration:
!
version 11.3
no service password-encryption
!
hostname Router_A
!
!
appletalk routing
ipx routing 0010.7b15.bd41
!
interface Ethernet0/0
 ip address 10.1.1.1 255.255.255.0
 appletalk cable-range 106-110 106.17
 appletalk zone left
 ipx network BAD
!
interface Serial0/0
 ip unnumbered Ethernet0/0
 no ip mroute-cache
 appletalk cable-range 130-130 130.37
 appletalk zone right
```

6. CCIE

```
 ipx network CAD
 clockrate 56000
!
interface TokenRing0/0
 no ip address
 shutdown
 ring-speed 16
!
interface FastEthernet1/0
 no ip address
 shutdown
!
router igrp 100
 network 10.0.0.0
!
ip classless
!!
line con 0
line aux 0
line vty 0 4
 login
!
end
```

   a) A random number assigned by the IOS to identify the IPX routing process
   b) The IPX node number of all the serial interfaces on Router_B
   c) The IPX node number of the Serial 0 interface of Router_B
   d) The Token Ring 0 interface of Router_B
   e) None of the above

Question 6–11. [CIPx] Refer to the following access list. Which line permits host 172.16.10.5 to reply to a ping from 172.19.10.2?

```
L1: deny icmp host 172.16.10.5 host 172.18.1.1 echo (4 matches)
L2: deny icmp host 172.16.10.5 host 172.19.10.2 echo
L3: deny udp host 172.16.10.5 host 172.19.10.2 eq snmp
L4: deny udp host 172.16.10.5 host 172.19.18.1 eq snmp
L5: permit ip host 172.16.10.5 host 172.19.10.2
L6: permit tcp any any eq telnet (6 matches)
L7: permit udp any any eq tftp
```

   a) L1
   b) L2
   c) L3
   d) L4
   e) L5
   f) L6
   g) L7
   h) None of the above

Question 6–12. [CxPx] Which three of the following best describes a Cisco 2511 Access Server?

a) 8 asynchronous ports
b) 16 asynchronous ports
c) 1 Ethernet interface
d) 1 synchronous serial interface
e) 2 synchronous serial interfaces
f) 4 synchronous serial interfaces
g) 2 Ethernet interfaces

Question 6–13. [RIPx] Which of the following protocols would be used to route within an autonomous system?

a) BGP4
b) Exterior Gateway Protocol (EGP)
c) ABR
d) RIP
e) None of the above

Question 6–14. [TxPx] Under which condition(s) will a Token Ring interface go down and down?

a) When "no keepalives" is configured
b) When the cable is not plugged into the router
c) When the cable is not plugged into the MAU
d) When Ring Speed is not set
e) A token ring interface will never be in the down and down state.

Question 6–15. [CxPx] What is the effect of using the "logging ari_server" command?

a) Logs messages to a syslog server named ari_server.
b) Logs messages to the console named ari_server.
c) Logs messages to the buffer of the ari_server console.
d) Logs messages to a virtual terminal line called ari_server.

Question 6–16. [ROPx] Which of the following commands would be used to configure a "totally stubby" area on a internal router?

a) Area 3 stub
b) Area 3 totally stubby
c) Area 3 stub no-summary
d) Area 3
e) No such thing as totally stubby.

Question 6–17. [RIPx] Assuming IGRP is the routing protocol used for all networks on all routers: (Refer to the following diagram.)

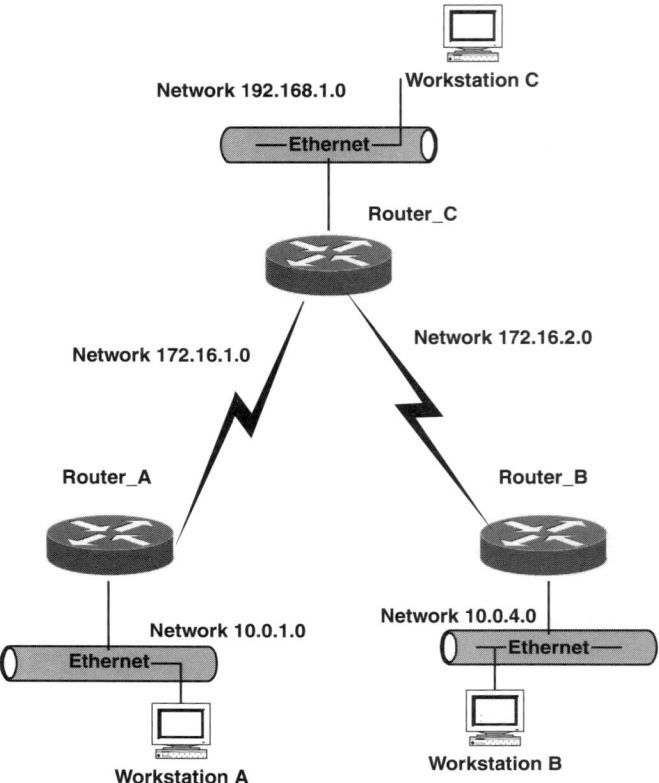

a) Router_C would ping Workstation B with a 100% success rate
b) Router_C would ping Workstation B with a 50% success rate
c) Router_C would ping Workstation B with a 0% success rate
d) Router_C would ping Workstation A with a 100% success rate
e) Router_C would ping Workstation A with a 0% success rate

Question 6–18. [CxPx] Given the following routing table, what is the administrative distance of EIGRP?

```
172.17.0.0/16 is variably subnetted, 2 subnets, 2 masks
C       172.17.1.0/24 is directly connected, Serial0
D       172.17.0.0/16 is a summary, 00:00:03, Null0
R    172.16.0.0/16 [120/1] via 172.17.1.1, 00:00:03, Serial0
D    172.19.0.0/16 [110/2195456] via 172.18.1.1, 00:00:03, Serial1
     172.18.0.0/16 is variably subnetted, 2 subnets, 2 masks
D       172.18.0.0/16 is a summary, 00:00:03, Null0
C       172.18.1.0/24 is directly connected, Serial1
```

a) 90
b) 170
c) 120
d) 110
e) 2195456

Question 6–19. [RAPx] Which one of the following is true pertaining to Appletalk RTMP and Load Balancing?

a) The parallel paths must have the same hop count.
b) The parallel paths must have the same bandwidth.
c) The parallel paths must have the same clock rate.
d) The parallel paths must have the same tick count and the same hop count.
e) None of the above.

Question 6–20. [CxPx] What would be the effect of the following commands? (Refer to the following configuration.)

```
Router_B#sh run
Building configuration...

Current configuration:
!
version 11.3
no service password-encryption
!
hostname Router_B
!
enable secret 5 $1$4Rzs$i9EC6.trjXdJe0pO6dpZm0
enable password Secret
!
ip host toronto 196.60.26.1
!
interface Serial0
 ip address 192.168.5.1 255.255.255.0
!
interface Serial1
 ip address 192.168.10.2 255.255.255.0
!
interface Serial2
 no ip address
 shutdown
!
interface Serial3
 no ip address
 shutdown
!
interface TokenRing0
 no ip address
 shutdown
!
```

```
interface BRI0
 no ip address
 shutdown
!
router rip
 network 196.60.26.0
!
ip classless
!
!
line con 0
 password notset
line aux 0
line vty 0 4
 password nologin
 login
!
end

line vty 0 4
no password login
```

   a) Would have no effect since the password was no login
   b) Would prevent any telnet sessions
   c) Would allow users to access a telnet session with no password
   d) An error message would be received.
   e) None of the above.

Question 6–21. [RIPx] What is the purpose of the "ip route 172.16.0.0 255.255.0.0 null 0" command? (Choose all that apply.)

   a) All traffic destined for the network 172.16.0.0 will be dropped.
   b) All traffic sourced from the network 172.16.0.0 will be dropped.
   c) Will save on CPU cycles when compared to access lists.
   d) Will not work unless the null 0 interface physically exists.
   e) All of the above.

Question 6–22. [BxPx] Which of the following is NOT true? Refer to the following diagram.

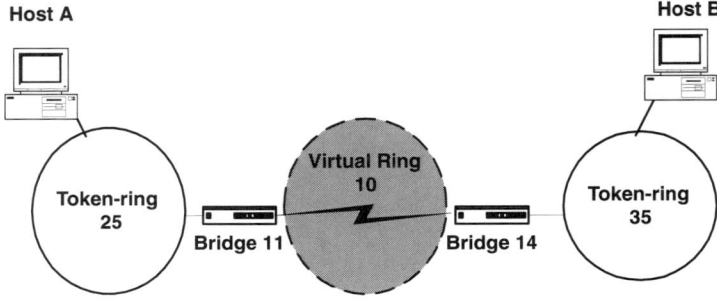

a) The RIF contains Bridge information.
b) The RIF contains Ring information.
c) The RIF contains Packet Type information.
d) The RIF contains MAC address information.
e) The RIF indicates what direction the RIF should be read.

Question 6–23. [RXPx] Assume that IPXWAN between Router_A and Router_B carries a tick count of 18. What would the tick count be from IPX network DAD to IPX network BAD? (Refer to the following diagram and configurations.)

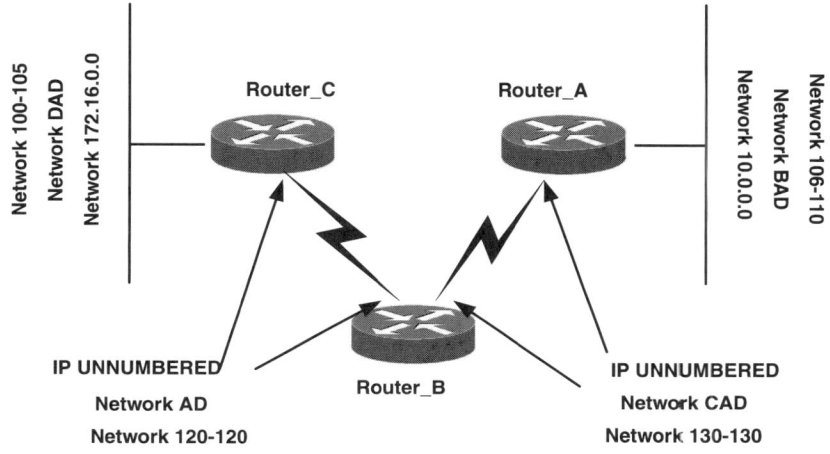

```
Router_C#sh run
Building configuration...

Current configuration:
!
version 11.2
!
hostname Router_C
!
!
appletalk routing
ipx routing 0060.09c3.df60
!
interface Ethernet0
 ip address 172.16.1.1 255.255.255.0
 appletalk cable-range 100-105 103.243
 appletalk zone right
 ipx network DAD
!
interface Ethernet1
 no ip address
 shutdown
!
interface Serial0
```

```
 ip unnumbered Ethernet0
 appletalk cable-range 120-120 120.17
 appletalk zone left
 ipx network AD
 clockrate 56000
!
interface Serial1
 no ip address
 shutdown
!
router igrp 100
 network 172.16.0.0
!
no ip classless
!!
line con 0
line aux 0
line vty 0 4
 login
!
end

Router_B#sh run
Building configuration...

Current configuration:
!
version 11.3
no service password-encryption
!
hostname Router_B
!
!
appletalk routing
ipx routing 0007.7816.fe54
!
interface Loopback0
 ip address 172.17.1.1 255.255.255.0
!
interface Serial0
 ip unnumbered Loopback0
 no ip mroute-cache
 appletalk cable-range 130-130 130.81
 appletalk zone right
 ipx network CAD
 no fair-queue
!
interface Serial1
 ip unnumbered Loopback0
 appletalk cable-range 120-120 120.125
 appletalk zone left
 ipx network AD
!
interface Serial2
```

```
 no ip address
 shutdown
!
interface Serial3
 no ip address
 shutdown
!
interface TokenRing0
 no ip address
 shutdown
!
interface BRI0
 no ip address
 shutdown
!
router igrp 100
 network 172.17.0.0
!
ip classless
!
!
!
!
!
line con 0
line aux 0
line vty 0 4
 login
!
end

Router_A#sh run
Building configuration...

Current configuration:
!
version 11.3
no service password-encryption
!
hostname Router_A
!
!
appletalk routing
ipx routing 0010.7b15.bd41
!
interface Ethernet0/0
 ip address 10.1.1.1 255.255.255.0
 appletalk cable-range 106-110 106.17
 appletalk zone left
 ipx network BAD
!
interface Serial0/0
 ip unnumbered Ethernet0/0
 no ip mroute-cache
```

```
 appletalk cable-range 130-130 130.37
 appletalk zone right
 ipx network CAD
 clockrate 56000
!
interface TokenRing0/0
 no ip address
 shutdown
 ring-speed 16
!
interface FastEthernet1/0
 no ip address
 shutdown
!
router igrp 100
 network 10.0.0.0
!
ip classless
!!
line con 0
line aux 0
line vty 0 4
 login
!
end
```

   a) 100
   b) 20
   c) 32
   d) 24
   e) 19
   f) 25

Question 6–24. [CxPx] A "floating static route" can be best described as:

   a) A static route where the administrator has changed the metric
   b) A static route used for oceanic links
   c) A static route that will be listed first in the routing table
   d) A static route where the administrator has changed the Administrative Distance
   e) None of the above

Question 6–25. [CxPx] The number of custom queue lists that a user can create is:

   a) 3
   b) 4
   c) 10
   d) 16
   e) 17

Question 6–26. [CxPx] What is the password for a telnet session to be granted? (Refer to the following configuration.)

```
Router_B#sh run
Building configuration...

Current configuration:
!
version 11.3
no service password-encryption
!
hostname Router_B
!
enable secret 5 $1$4Rzs$i9EC6.trjXdJe0pO6dpZm0
enable password Secret
!
ip host toronto 196.60.26.1
!
interface Serial0
 ip address 192.168.5.1 255.255.255.0
!
interface Serial1
 ip address 192.168.10.2 255.255.255.0
!
interface Serial2
 no ip address
 shutdown
!
interface Serial3
 no ip address
 shutdown
!
interface TokenRing0
 no ip address
 shutdown
!
interface BRI0
 no ip address
 shutdown
!
router rip
 network 196.60.26.0
!
ip classless
!
!
line con 0
 password notset
line aux 0
line vty 0 4
 password nologin
 login
!
end
```

a) No password has been set.
b) No login will be permitted.
c) Secret
d) Secret 5
e) nologin
f) not set
g) Can not be determined.

Question 6–27. [RIPx] Assuming you are at the "router(config)#" prompt, which of the following is the command to enable compatibility with the Classless Inter-network Domain Routing (CIDR)?

a) ip routing classless
b) ip routing cidr
c) no ip classes
d) ip classless
e) Cisco routers are not compatible with CIDR.

Question 6–28. [IxPx] Which of the following describe a FDDI Dual attachment station (DAS)?

a) A station that has two FDDI NICs installed
b) A station that is connected to two separate dual attachment connectors (DACs)
c) A station that is connected to the primary ring twice
d) A station the is connected to both the primary and the secondary ring
e) None of the above

Question 6–29. [ROPx] Which of the following routers would be defined as an Area Border Router? (Refer to the following diagram.)

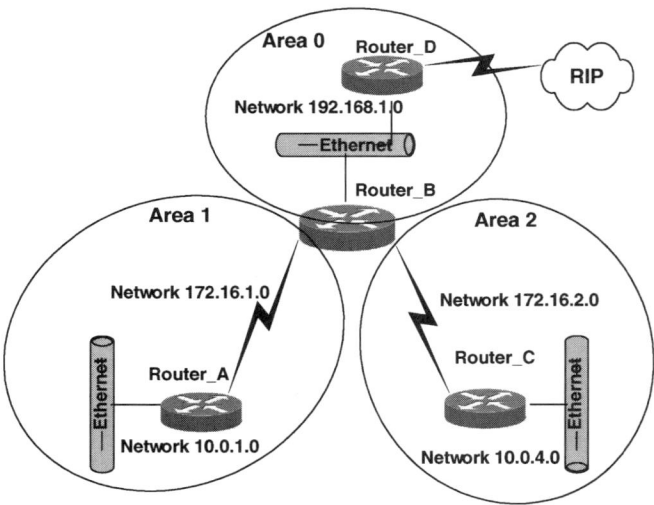

a) Router_A
b) Router_B
c) Router_C
d) Router_D
e) None of the above

Question 6–30. [BxPx] Given the router configuration that follows, if the command "no ip routing" were not configured then:

```
version 11.1
service udp-small-servers
service tcp-small-servers
!
hostname Router_C
!
no ip routing
appletalk routing
ipx routing 0060.09c3.df60
ipx internal-network C1
!
interface Ethernet0
 ip address 10.1.1.1 255.255.255.0
 no ip mroute-cache
 no ip route-cache
 appletalk cable-range 111-115 112.170
 appletalk zone bottom-ether
 ipx network CAD
 bridge-group 1
!
interface Ethernet1
 ip address 10.1.2.1 255.255.255.0
 no ip mroute-cache
 no ip route-cache
 appletalk cable-range 95-99 97.221
 appletalk zone left-ether
 ipx network FAD
 bridge-group 1
!
interface Serial0
 ip address 10.1.3.1 255.255.255.0
 no ip mroute-cache
 no ip route-cache
 appletalk cable-range 100-105 100.190
 appletalk zone leftserial
 ipx ipxwan 0 unnumbered Router_C
 clockrate 1200
 bridge-group 1
!
interface Serial1
 no ip address
 no ip mroute-cache
 no ip route-cache
 shutdown
```

```
  clockrate 4000000
!
no ip classless
!
ipx router nlsp
!
bridge 1 protocol dec
bridge 1 priority 1
!
line con 0
line aux 0
 transport input all
line vty 0 4
 login
!
end
```

   a)   IP RIP would be configured by default.
   b)   IGRP would be configured by default.
   c)   EIGRP would be configured by default.
   d)   No bridging of IP could take place.
   e)   None of the above.

Question 6–31. [TxPx] Which type of bridge has the ability to remove a RIF from a frame?

   a)   Transparent Bridge (TB)
   b)   Source Route Bridge (SRB)
   c)   Source Route Transparent Bridge (SRT)
   d)   Source Route Translational Bridge (SR/TLB)
   e)   No bridge will remove a RIF.

Question 6–32. [ExPx] If every Ethernet frame was being sent at the MTU, approximately how may packets per second would be transmitted?

   a)   200
   b)   500
   c)   800
   d)   1000
   e)   10000

Question 6–33. [BxPx] Based upon the following output, which statements are true:

```
Router_B#sh bridge group
Bridge Group 1 is running the DEC compatible Spanning Tree protocol
   Port 6 (Serial0) of bridge group 1 is forwarding
   Port 7 (Serial1) of bridge group 1 is blocking
```

   a)   Router_B will NEVER use Serial 1.
   b)   Router_B currently will not send frames out Serial 1.
   c)   Router_B currently will not allow frames to be received on Serial 1.
   d)   Router_B belongs to bridge group 1.
   e)   Router_B can only use DEC as the Spanning Tree protocol.

Question 6–34. [CxPx] What is the password required to change the configuration if the IOS was 9.x? (Refer to the following configuration.)

```
Router_B#sh run
Building configuration...

Current configuration:
!
version 11.3
no service password-encryption
!
hostname Router_B
!
enable secret 5 $1$4Rzs$i9EC6.trjXdJe0pO6dpZm0
enable password Secret
!
ip host toronto 196.60.26.1
!
interface Serial0
 ip address 192.168.5.1 255.255.255.0
!
interface Serial1
 ip address 192.168.10.2 255.255.255.0
!
interface Serial2
 no ip address
 shutdown
!
interface Serial3
 no ip address
 shutdown
!
interface TokenRing0
 no ip address
 shutdown
!
interface BRI0
 no ip address
 shutdown
!
router rip
 network 196.60.26.0
!
ip classless
!
!
line con 0
 password notset
line aux 0
line vty 0 4
 password nologin
 login
!
end
```

a)   No password has been set.
b)   No login will be permitted.
c)   Secret
d)   Secret 5
e)   nologin
f)   not set
g)   Can not be determined.

Question 6–35. [ROPx] If all possible totally stubby areas were defined, and assuming all Cisco defaults, what type of networks could an internal router see?

a)   External Type 1
b)   External Type 2
c)   Default routes
d)   Intra area routes
e)   Inter area routes

Question 6–36. [CxPx] The interface(s) that will be configured as part of the bridge group are: (Refer to the diagram below.)

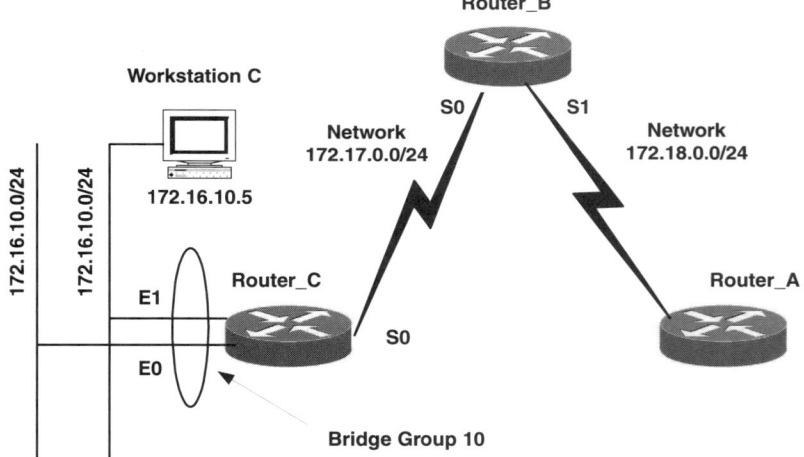

a)   E0 of Router_C
b)   S0 of Router_B
c)   E1 of Router_C
d)   All interfaces of all routers
e)   E0 & E1 of Router_C

Question 6–37. [RxPx] The main difference between OSPF and RIP is:

a) Both are IGP's, but the RIP convergence time is much shorter than that of OSPF.
b) RIP is a distance vector protocol, whereas OSPF is a link state protocol.
c) There is no difference between the two, other than RIP is used for IP, and OSPF is used for OSI.
d) OSPF allows for a lower hop count than RIP.
e) RIP works better in large internetworks than OSPF.

Question 6–38. [CxPx] In the following diagram, if Workstation C pings the S0 of Router_B, the destination MAC address as the packet exits Workstation C will be: (Choose the best answer.)

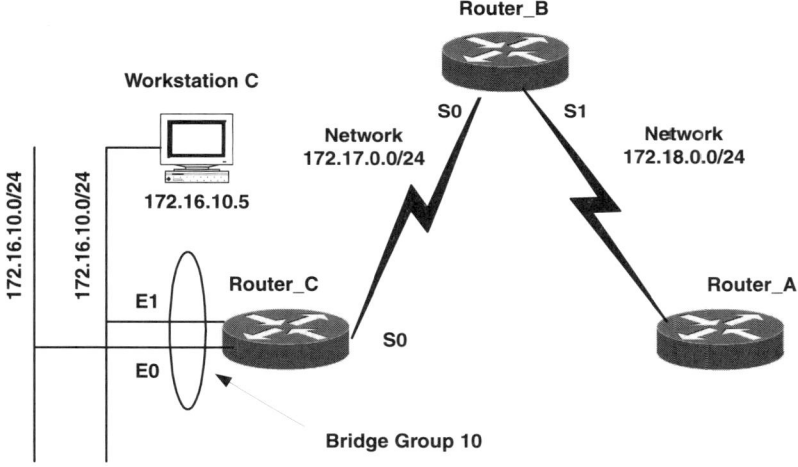

a) The E0 of Router_C
b) The E1 of Router_C
c) The BVI
d) The S0 of Router_B
e) The S0 of Router_C

Question 6–39. [TxPx] If DLSW is configured at both routers, which of the following could represent a RIF? (Choose all correct answers.)

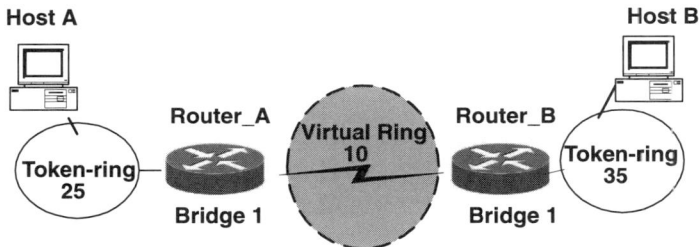

a) 0830.0191.00a1.0230
b) 0630.0191.00a0
c) 0830.0191.00a1.0231
d) 0630.00a1.0230
e) 0830.0251.0101.0350

Question 6–40. [RIPx] Which of the following best describes the purpose of the "ip classless" command?

a) This command is used with Bay Routers.
b) This command is required when using OSPF.
c) This command is required when using a distance vector routing protocol.
d) This command allows the IOS to forward to the best supernet route.
e) None of the above.

Question 6–41. [CxPx] Assuming proper configuration of IP and IRB in the diagram, Workstation C could successfully ping the: (Refer to the diagram below.)

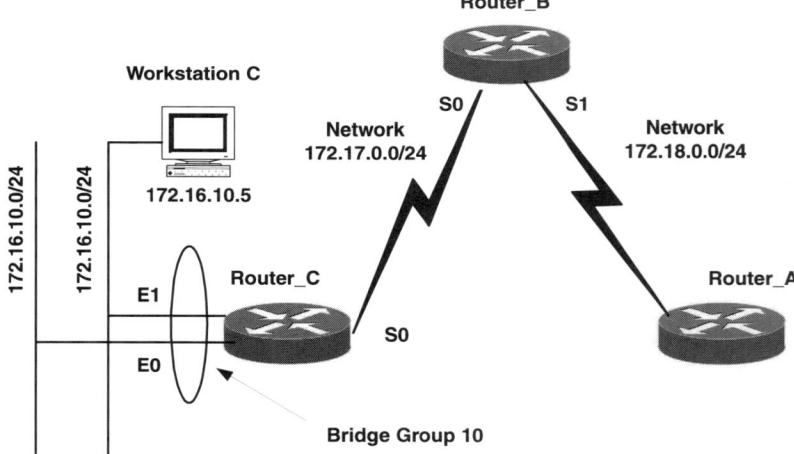

a) E0 of Router_C
b) E1 of Router_C
c) BVI
d) a and b
e) a, b and c

Question 6–42. [TxPx] Assume Transparent Bridging is configured on both Routers. Which of the following would be the value of the RIF on Host B's Token Ring segment.

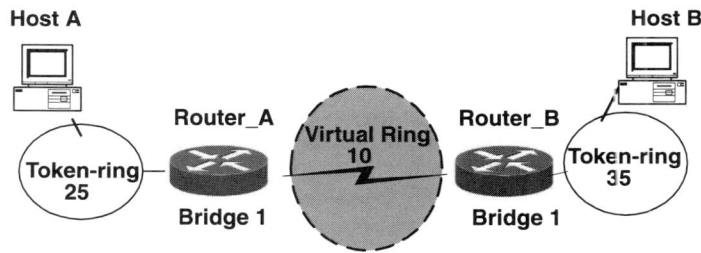

a)   0830.0191.00a1.0230
b)   0630.0191.00a1.0230
c)   0830.0191.00a1.0231
d)   0630.0191.00a1
e)   None of the above

Question 6–43. [RIPx] Refer to the diagram below. When Host A transmits to Host B, which device will handle reassembling of the fragmented IP packets coming over the serial link?

a)   Host A
b)   Router A
c)   Host B
d)   Router B
e)   The Token

Question 6–44. [TxPx] Assume Data Link Switching (DLSw) is configured on both routers. Which of the following are true:

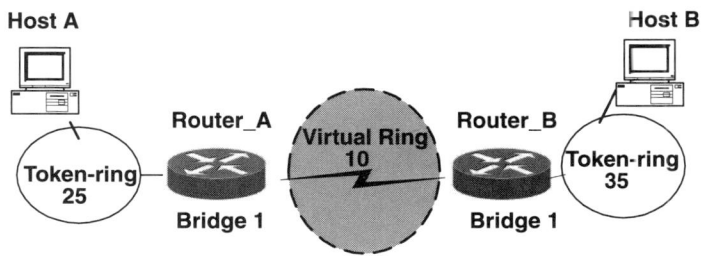

a)   The virtual ring numbers can be different on both bridges.
b)   Virtual Ring numbers must be the same on both bridges.
c)   When Host A communicates to Host B, the RIF will contain the entire path.
d)   The Route Description (RD) field will change based on the direction the frame travels.
e)   The Route Control (RC) field will change based on the direction the frame travels.

Question 6–45. [CxPx] Which of the following are true if the configuration register is 0x2100?

   a) The Cisco IOS will be read from flash if a flash exists.
   b) The Cisco IOS will be read from ROM.
   c) This causes the router to enter the ROM monitor mode.
   d) The configuration file will be read from flash.
   e) The configuration file will be read from ROM.
   f) The configuration file will be read from NVRAM.
   g) The configuration file will NOT be read from NVRAM.
   h) The baud rate will be set at 9600.
   i) The baud rate will be set at 4800.

Question 6–46. [CxPx] Which of the following represents configuration lines that need to be configured on Router_C? (Choose the best answers.)

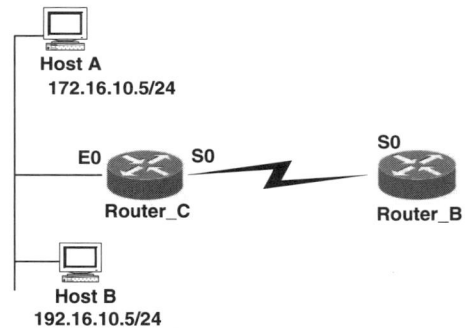

I. Command Group I:

```
config terminal
int e0
ip address 192.16.10.1 /24
ip address 172.16.10.1 /24 secondary
```

II. Command Group II:

```
config terminal
int e0
ip address 192.16.10.0 255.255.255.0
ip address 172.16.10.0 255.255.255.0 secondary
```

III. Command Group III:

```
config terminal
int e0
ip address 172.16.10.1 255.255.255.0
ip address 192.16.10.1 255.255.255.0 secondary
```

```
------------------------------
```
IV. Command Group IV:
```
------------------------------
```

```
config terminal
int e0
ip address 192.16.10.1 255.255.255.0 secondary
ip address 172.16.10.1 255.255.255.0
```

```
------------------------------
```
V. Command Group V:
```
------------------------------
```

```
config terminal
int e0
ip address 192.16.10.1 255.255.255.0
ip address 172.16.10.1 255.255.255.0
```

   a) Command Group I above
   b) Command Group II above
   c) Command Group III above
   d) Command Group IV above
   e) Command Group V above

Question 6–47. [CIPx] Given the following configuration statements, which of the following are true:

```
Router_B(config)#access-list 50 permit host 172.16.15.4
Router_B(config)#line vty 0 4
Router_B(config-line)#access-class 50 in
```

   a) Only 172.16.15.4 would be able to telnet to Router_B.
   b) Any address other than 172.16.15.4 would be denied to telnet through Router_B.
   c) Any host will be able to telnet to 172.16.15.4.
   d) Any host on the subnet 172.16.5.0 will be permitted to telnet to Router_B.
   e) Any interface of Router_B will be permitted to telnet to 172.16.15.4.

Question 6–48. [TxPx] Which of the following is true of the source MAC address as the frame passes from Ring 25 to Ring 35? (Choose all that apply.) (Refer to the diagram below.)

   a) MAC addresses never change.
   b) Only source MAC address will change as the frame traverses the network.
   c) Only destination MAC address will change as the frame traverses the network.
   d) Both the source and destination MAC address will change as the frame traverses the network.
   e) Token Ring does not use MAC addresses.

Question 6–49. [CxPx] Which is true of automatic redistribution of IGRP and EIGRP within the same AS?

a) Hop count is maintained.
b) Hop count is increased by 1.
c) A default metric must be set.
d) The metric is maintained because IGRP and EIGRP use the same metric.
e) There is no automatic redistribution of IGRP and EIGRP.

Question 6–50. [RIPx] Assuming IP OSPF is the routing protocol used for all networks on all routers. (Answer all that apply.) (Refer to the following diagram.)

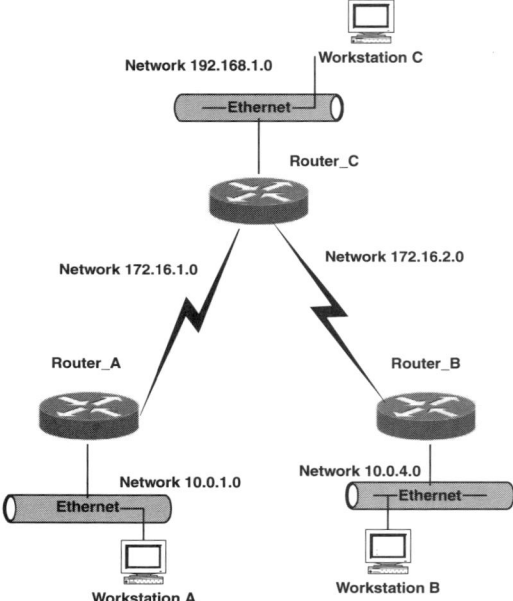

a) Workstation A could not successfully ping both serial interfaces of Router_C.
b) Workstation A could successfully ping the ethernet interface of Router_B.
c) Workstation A could not successfully ping the ethernet interface of Router_C.
d) Workstation A could successfully ping Workstation B.
e) Workstation A could not successfully ping Workstation B.

Question 6–51. [TxPx] Which is true of early token release?

a) Allows multiple tokens and a single data frame
b) Allows multiple data frames and a single token
c) Was introduced as the first version of token ring
d) Allows only a single token and data frame to exist on the ring
e) Tokens are not used.

Question 6–52. [xxPx] Workstation A sends a frame to Workstation B. The devices shown are repeaters. Which of the following are true? (Choose all that apply.) (Refer to the diagram below.)

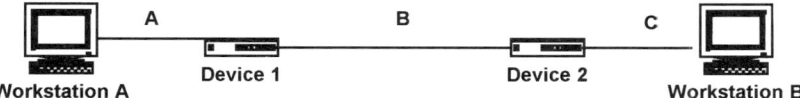

a) MAC addresses never change.
b) Only source MAC address will change as the frame traverses the network.
c) Only destination MAC address will change as the frame traverses the network.
d) Both the source and destination MAC address will change as the frame traverses the network.
e) Not enough information given.

Question 6–53. [TxPx] When Host A sends a frame to Host B what is the destination MAC address on Host A's Token Ring segment?

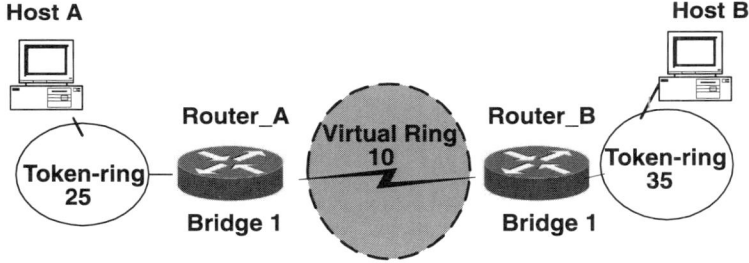

a) MAC of Host A
b) MAC of Host B
c) Serial MAC of Router A
d) Token Ring MAC of Router B
e) Token Ring MAC of Router A

Question 6–54. [CxPx] What is the password required to view passwords? (Refer to the following configuration.)

```
Router_B#sh run
Building configuration...

Current configuration:
!
version 11.3
no service password-encryption
!
hostname Router_B
!
enable secret 5 $1$4Rzs$i9EC6.trjXdJe0pO6dpZm0
enable password Secret
!
ip host toronto 196.60.26.1
```

```
!
interface Serial0
 ip address 192.168.5.1 255.255.255.0
!
interface Serial1
 ip address 192.168.10.2 255.255.255.0
!
interface Serial2
 no ip address
 shutdown
!
interface Serial3
 no ip address
 shutdown
!
interface TokenRing0
 no ip address
 shutdown
!
interface BRI0
 no ip address
 shutdown
!
router rip
 network 196.60.26.0
!
ip classless
!
!
line con 0
 password notset
line aux 0
line vty 0 4
 password nologin
 login
!
end
```

a) No password has been set.
b) No login will be permitted.
c) Secret
d) Secret 5
e) nologin
f) not set
g) Can not be determined.

Question 6–55. [CIPx] An IGRP header includes which one of the following?

    a) Hop count, Tick count
    b) Bandwidth, Delay Load, Reliability, MTU and Hop count
    c) Bandwidth, Delay
    d) Bandwidth, Delay, Load, Reliability and MTU
    e) Cost factor

Question 6–56. [RNPx] The IPX routing protocol used on the Serial links is:
(Refer to the following diagram and routing table.)

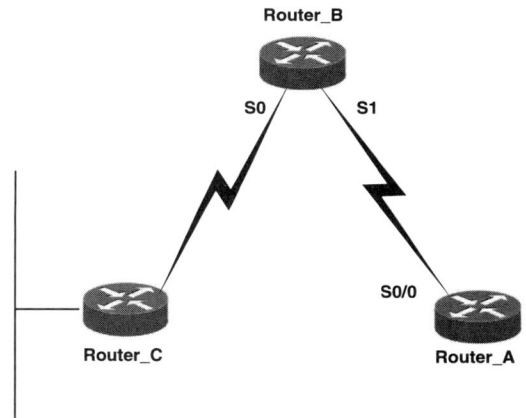

```
Router_B#sh ipx route
Codes: C - Connected primary network,
   c - Connected secondary network, S - Static,
   F - Floating static, L - Local (internal), W - IPXWAN
   R - RIP, E - EIGRP, N - NLSP, X - External, A - Aggregate
   s - seconds, u - uses, U - Per-user static

5 Total IPX routes. Up to 2 parallel paths and 16 hops allowed.

No default route known.

L          B1 is the internal network
R          A1 [07/01] via         0.0000.00a1.0000,     3s, Se1
R          C1 [07/01] via         0.0000.00a1.0000,     3s, Se0
R          CAD [07/01] via        0.0000.00a1.0000,     4s, Se1
                       via        0.0000.00a1.0000,     3s, Se0
R          FAD [07/01] via        0.0000.00a1.0000,     3s, Se0
```

    a) IPX RIP
    b) IPX EIGRP
    c) NLSP
    d) RTMP
    e) NLSPX

Question 6–57. [CxPx] What is the BIA of the Bridged Virtual Interface?

a) Will be assigned by the administrator
b) Will be the MAC address of a routed interface
c) Will be the MAC of a Bridged interface
d) Will be randomly chosen by the IOS
e) There is no BIA of the BVI.

Question 6–58. [CxPx] A Cisco feature that permits a packet received on a routed interface and to leave out a bridged interface and visa versa is called:

a) Integrated Routing and Bridging (IRB)
b) Concurrent Routing and Bridging (CRB)
c) Translational Bridging and Routing (TRB)
d) Cisco Bridging and Routing (CBR)
e) No such feature exists.

Question 6–59. [TxPx] Which of the following represents the contents of the RIF? (Refer to the diagram below.)

a) 0830.019b.01ee.0231
b) 0630.2511.3014.3500
c) 0830.019b.01ee.0230
d) 0630.0053.00b1
e) 0830.2519.3014.3500

Question 6–60. [RxPx] Workstation A sends a frame to Workstation B. The devices shown are routers. Which of the following are true? (Choose all that apply.) (Refer to the diagram below.)

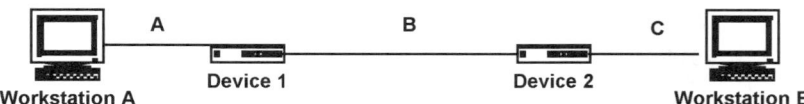

a) MAC addresses never change.
b) Only source MAC address will change as the frame traverses the network.
c) Only destination MAC address will change as the frame traverses the network.
d) Both the source and destination MAC address will change as the frame traverses the network
e) Routers are never concerned with MAC addresses.

Question 6–61. [CxPx] Which statement is true of the following command line? (Choose one.)

```
access-list 150 deny igrp any 255.255.255.255 0.0.0.0
```

a) Would deny igrp traffic from any source to any destination
b) Would deny igrp traffic from any source to any destination host with an address of 0.0.0.0
c) Would deny igrp updates from any source
d) All of the above
e) None of the above

Question 6–62. [ROPx] Which of the following routers would have to be configured to identify Area 1 and Area 2 as a stub area? (Refer to the following diagram.)

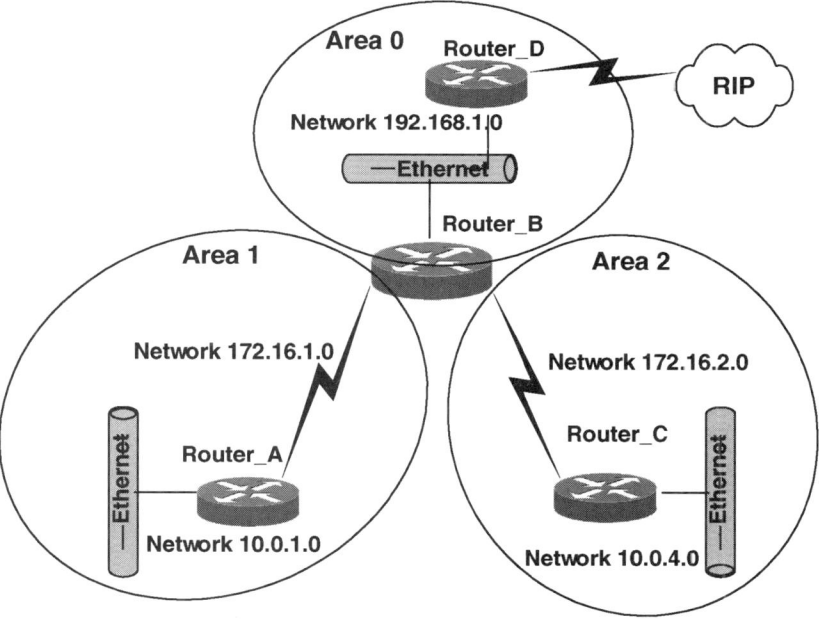

a) Router_A
b) Router_B
c) Router_C
d) Router_D
e) None of the above

Question 6–63. [CxPx] Given the following networks and their respective subnet masks, choose the proper group of commands (from Groups I through V below) to summarize these networks to the fewest number of routes possible.

```
172.16.24.0 255.255.248.0
172.16.32.0 255.255.248.0
```

6. CCIE

```
172.16.40.0 255.255.248.0
172.16.48.0 255.255.248.0
172.16.56.0 255.255.248.0
```

I. Command Group I:

```
router(config)#router ospf 69
router(config-router)#area 0 range 172.16.24.0 255.255.224.0
```

II. Command Group II:

```
router(config)#router ospf 69
router(config-router)#area 0 range 172.16.24.0 255.255.248.0
router(config-router)#area 0 range 172.16.32.0 255.255.255.0
router(config-router)#area 0 range 172.16.40.0 255.255.224.0
```

III. Command Group III:

```
router(config)#router ospf 69
router(config-router)#area 0 range 172.16.24.0 255.255.255.248
router(config-router)#area 0 range 172.16.32.0 255.255.255.224
```

IV. Command Group IV:

```
router(config)#router ospf 69
router(config-router)#area 0 range 172.16.24.0 255.255.224.0
router(config-router)#area 0 range 172.16.32.0 255.255.255.0
```

V. Command Group V:

```
router(config)#router ospf 69
router(config-router)#area 0 range 172.16.24.0 255.255.248.0
router(config-router)#area 0 range 172.16.32.0 255.255.224.0
```

Select from the following:

   a)   Command Group I above
   b)   Command Group II above
   c)   Command Group III above
   d)   Command Group IV above

e) Command Group V above

Question 6–64. [RAPx] What is the E0 appletalk network number of Router_C? (Refer to the following diagram and configurations.)

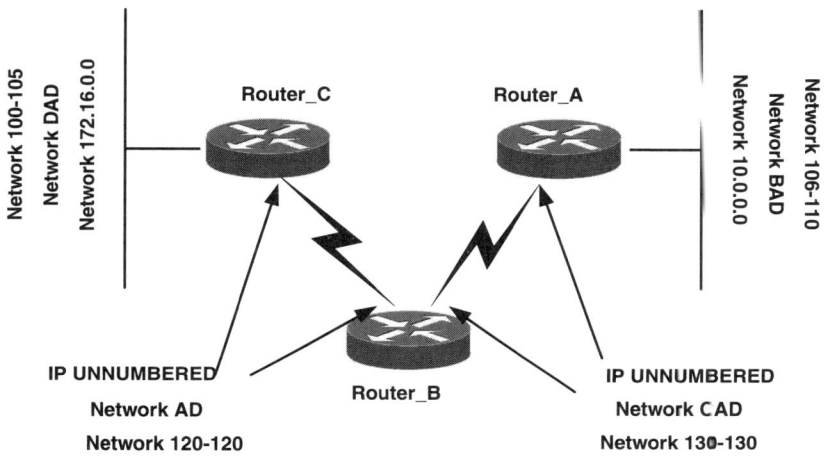

```
Router_C#sh run
Building configuration...

Current configuration:
!
version 11.2
!
hostname Router_C
!
!
appletalk routing
ipx routing 0060.09c3.df60
!
interface Ethernet0
 ip address 172.16.1.1 255.255.255.0
 appletalk cable-range 100-105 103.243
 appletalk zone right
 ipx network DAD
!
interface Ethernet1
 no ip address
 shutdown
!
interface Serial0
 ip unnumbered Ethernet0
 appletalk cable-range 120-120 120.17
 appletalk zone left
 ipx network AD
 clockrate 56000
!
```

```
interface Serial1
 no ip address
 shutdown
!
router igrp 100
 network 172.16.0.0
!
no ip classless
!!
line con 0
line aux 0
line vty 0 4
 login
!
end

Router_B#sh run
Building configuration...

Current configuration:
!
version 11.3
no service password-encryption
!
hostname Router_B
!
!
appletalk routing
ipx routing 0007.7816.fe54
!
interface Loopback0
 ip address 172.17.1.1 255.255.255.0
!
interface Serial0
 ip unnumbered Loopback0
 no ip mroute-cache
 appletalk cable-range 130-130 130.81
 appletalk zone right
 ipx network CAD
 no fair-queue
!
interface Serial1
 ip unnumbered Loopback0
 appletalk cable-range 120-120 120.125
 appletalk zone left
 ipx network AD
!
interface Serial2
 no ip address
 shutdown
!
interface Serial3
 no ip address
 shutdown
```

```
!
interface TokenRing0
 no ip address
 shutdown
!
interface BRI0
 no ip address
 shutdown
!
router igrp 100
 network 172.17.0.0
!
ip classless
!
!
!
!
!
line con 0
line aux 0
line vty 0 4
 login
!
end

Router_A#sh run
Building configuration...

Current configuration:
!
version 11.3
no service password-encryption
!
hostname Router_A
!
!
appletalk routing
ipx routing 0010.7b15.bd41
!
interface Ethernet0/0
 ip address 10.1.1.1 255.255.255.0
 appletalk cable-range 106-110 106.17
 appletalk zone left
 ipx network BAD
!
interface Serial0/0
 ip unnumbered Ethernet0/0
 no ip mroute-cache
 appletalk cable-range 130-130 130.37
 appletalk zone right
 ipx network CAD
 clockrate 56000
!
interface TokenRing0/0
```

```
 no ip address
 shutdown
 ring-speed 16
!
interface FastEthernet1/0
 no ip address
 shutdown
!
router igrp 100
 network 10.0.0.0
!
ip classless
!!
line con 0
line aux 0
line vty 0 4
 login
!
end
```

   a) 243
   b) 100-105
   c) 103
   d) Can not be determined
   e) 100

Question 6–65. [RXPx] The IPX routing protocol configured is: (Choose one.) (Refer to the following configuration.)

```
Router_C#sh run
Building configuration...

Current configuration:
!
version 11.2
!
hostname Router_C
!
!
ipx routing 0060.09c3.df60
!
interface Ethernet0
 ip address 10.3.0.3 255.255.0.0
 ipx network DAD
!
interface Ethernet1
 ip address 10.1.0.3 255.255.0.0
 ip policy route-map takeserial
 ipx network BAD
!
interface Serial0
 ip address 10.2.0.1 255.255.0.0
 clockrate 38400
```

```
!
interface Serial1
 no ip address
 shutdown
!
router ospf 100
 network 10.0.0.0 0.255.255.255 area 0
!
no ip classless
access-list 1 permit 10.1.0.5
route-map takeserial permit 10
 match ip address 1
 set interface Serial0
 set ip default next-hop 10.2.0.2
!
ipx router eigrp 1
 network BAD
 network DAD
!
line con 0
 password go
 login
line aux 0
line vty 0 4
 login
!
end
```

a) IPX RIP
b) RIP
c) EIGRP
d) IPX RIP & EIGRP
e) None of the above.

Question 6–66. [TxPx] Which of the following describes a difference between DLSw and bridging? (Choose all that apply.)

a) DLSw will provide a reliable transport.
b) DLSw will not terminate the data-link control.
c) DLSw is Cisco proprietary.
d) DLSw will reduce traffic.
e) None of the above.

Question 6–67. [CxPx] Which of the following commands will stop routing updates going out an interface but allow that interface to receive and process updates?

a) router#no send updates s0
b) router#no update s0
c) router(config)#passive interface s0
d) router(config-router)#passive interface s0
e) none of the above

6. CCIE

Question 6–68. [TxPx] Which of the following are true of Token Ring? (Choose all that apply.)

  a) Enabling of keepalives is necessary to keep an active ring.
  b) Keepalives are unnecessary due to a built-in reliability feature of Token Ring, and therefore can be disabled.
  c) Keepalive failure usually means that the interface has already failed.
  d) Failure detection is immediate.
  e) When Token Ring protocol failure occurs, the interface will go into transition state.

Question 6–69. [RXPx] The internal network of Router_C is: (Select best answer.)
(Refer to the following diagram and routing table.)

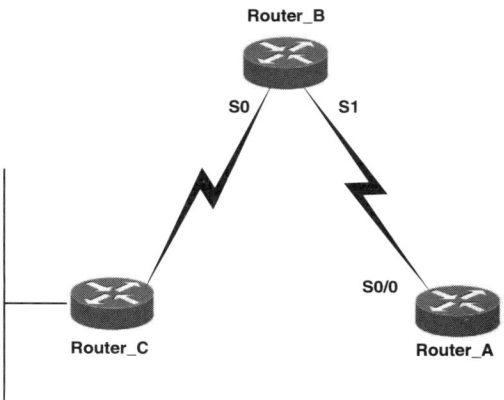

```
Router_B#sh ipx route
Codes: C - Connected primary network,
  c - Connected secondary network, S - Static,
  F - Floating static, L - Local (internal), W - IPXWAN
  R - RIP, E - EIGRP, N - NLSP, X - External, A - Aggregate
  s - seconds, u - uses, U - Per-user static

5 Total IPX routes. Up to 2 parallel paths and 16 hops allowed.

No default route known.

L         B1 is the internal network
R         A1 [07/01] via          0.0000.00a1.0000,     3s, Se1
R         C1 [07/01] via          0.0000.00a1.0000,     3s, Se0
R         CAD [07/01] via         0.0000.00a1.0000,     4s, Se1
                      via         0.0000.00a1.0000,     3s, Se0
R         FAD [07/01] via         0.0000.00a1.0000,     3s, Se0
```

  a) A1
  b) B1
  c) C1
  d) There is no internal network configured on Router_C.

e) Can not be determined.

Question 6–70. [RXPx] The internal network of Router_B is:
(Refer to the following diagram and routing table.)

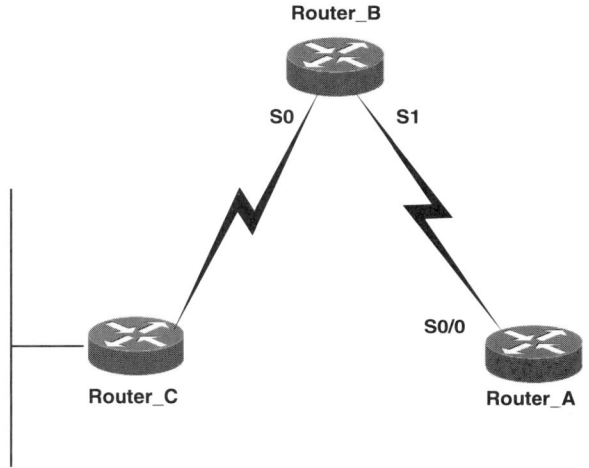

```
Router_B#sh ipx route
Codes: C - Connected primary network,
  c - Connected secondary network, S - Static,
  F - Floating static, L - Local (internal), W - IPXWAN
  R - RIP, E - EIGRP, N - NLSP, X - External, A - Aggregate
  s - seconds, u - uses, U - Per-user static

5 Total IPX routes. Up to 2 parallel paths and 16 hops allowed.

No default route known.

L         B1 is the internal network
R         A1 [07/01] via       0.0000.00a1.0000,   3s, Se1
R         C1 [07/01] via       0.0000.00a1.0000,   3s, Se0
R         CAD [07/01] via      0.0000.00a1.0000,   4s, Se1
                       via       0.0000.00a1.0000,   3s, Se0
R         FAD [07/01] via      0.0000.00a1.0000,   3s, Se0
```

a) A1
b) B1
c) C1
d) There is no internal network configured on Router_C.
e) Can not be determined.

Question 6–71. [RIPx] Will Router_C be able to ping the primary address (172.16.11.1) of the Token Ring interface of Router_B?

Assume that IP RIP is configured for all networks, and the Token Ring interface of Router_B has been configured with a secondary address of 20.20.20.1.

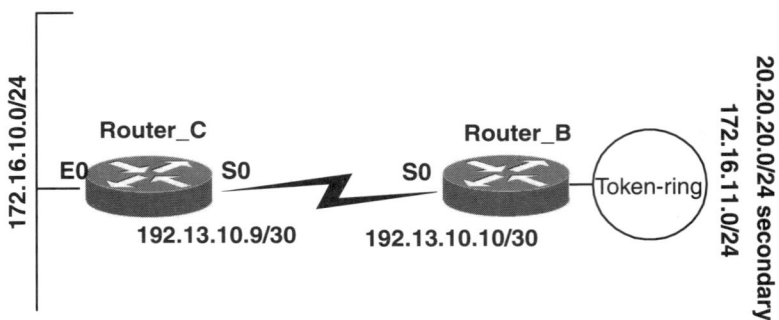

a) Yes
b) Yes 50% of the time
c) No
d) Not enough information given

Question 6–72. [XIPx] Select the appropriate X.25 configuration for Router_C. (Refer to the following diagram and the five suggested configurations.)

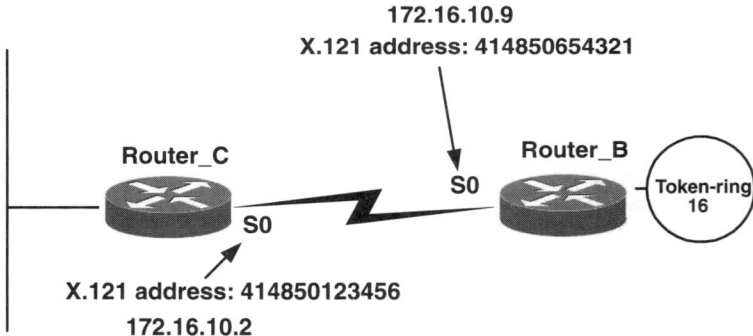

1. Configuration 1:
interface serial 0
encapsulaion x25
x25 address 414850123456
ip address 172.16.10.2 255.255.255.0
x25 map ip 172.16.10.9 414850654321

2. Configuration 2:
interface serial 0
encapsulaion x25
x25 address 414850123456
ip address 172.16.10.9 255.255.255.0

x25 map ip 172.16.10.2 414850654321

3. Configuration 3:
interface serial 0
encapsulaion x25
x25 address 414850123456
ip address 172.16.10.2 255.255.255.0
x25 map ip 172.16.10.9 414850123456

4. Configuration 4:
interface serial 0
encapsulaion x25
x25 address 414850123456
ip address 172.16.10.2 255.255.255.0
x25 map ip 172.16.10.2 414850654321

    a) Configuration 1 above
    b) Configuration 2 above
    c) Configuration 3 above
    d) Configuration 4 above

Question 6–73. [TxPx] Assume Remote Source Route Bridging (RSRB) is configured on both routers. Which of the following are true:

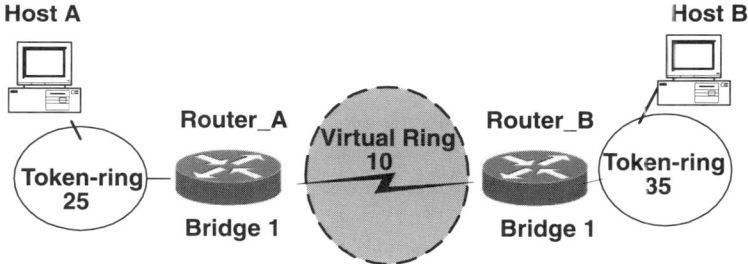

    a) The Virtual Ring numbers can be different on both bridges.
    b) Virtual Ring numbers must be the same on both bridges.
    c) When Host A communicates to Host B, the RIF will contain the entire path.
    d) The Route Description (RD) field will change based on the direction the frame travels.
    e) The Route Control (RC) field will change based on the direction the frame travels.

Question 6–74. [TxPx] Which one of the following is NOT a Translational Bridge challenge?

    a) MTU differences
    b) Bit ordering
    c) Multicast Addressing
    d) Embedded MAC addresses

e) Media Access Method

Question 6–75. [ROPx] Which of the following routers would be defined as Internal Routers? (Refer to the following diagram.)

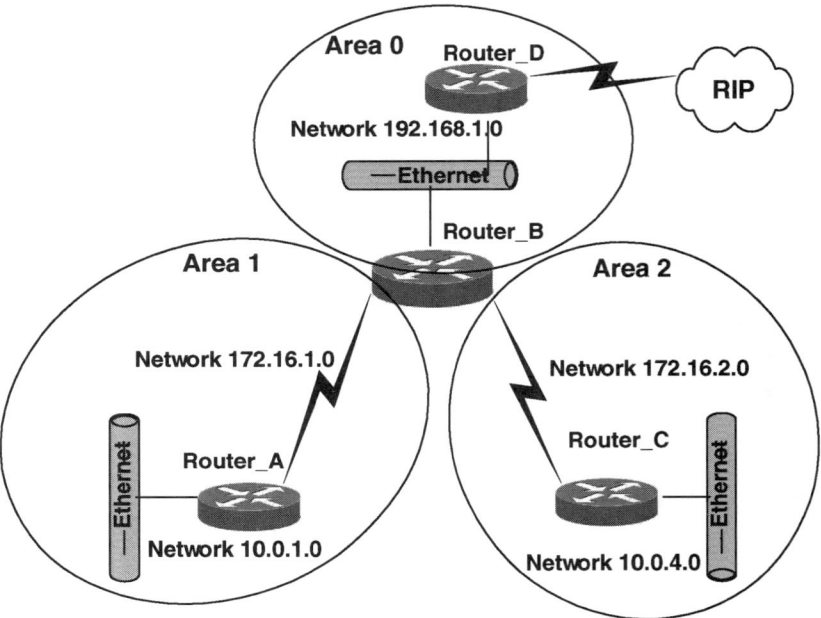

a) Router_A
b) Router_B
c) Router_C
d) Router_D
e) None of the above

Question 6–76. [CxPx] Which of the following commands would allow a router to bridge the routed protocol IP across a SRB network?

a) multi-route ip
b) bridge-route ip
c) multiring ip
d) muti-ring ip
e) bridge route ip

Question 6–77. [ROPx] Which of the following are true statements?

a) A stub area receives LSAs for all inter-area networks.
b) A totally stubby area receives LSAs for all intra-area networks.
c) A totally stubby area is Cisco proprietary.
d) Area 0 is not required when there is only a single area configured.

e) All of the above.

Question 6–78. [CXPx] If IPX were to be configured on Serial 0/0 the node number would be: (Refer to the following configuration.)

```
version 11.3
no service password-encryption
!
hostname Router_A
!
appletalk routing
ipx routing 0010.7b15.bd41
!
interface Ethernet0/0
 no ip address
 appletalk cable-range 100-150 128.85
 appletalk zone ccieprep
 ipx network DAD
!
interface Serial0/0
 no ip address
 no ip mroute-cache
 shutdown
 no fair-queue
!
interface TokenRing0/0
 no ip address
 shutdown
 ring-speed 16
!
interface FastEthernet1/0
 no ip address
 shutdown
!
ip classless
line con 0
line aux 0
line vty 0 4
 login
!
end
```

a) Dynamically determined by the interface
b) Assigned by the administrator
c) Would be the same as E0/0
d) Would be the MAC address of E0/0
e) IPX can not be configured on a serial interface.

Question 6–79. [CxPx] Which is true of automatic redistribution of IGRP and EIGRP between different AS?

a) Hop count is maintained.
b) Hop count is increased by 1.
c) Bandwidth for the additional link will be added.

d) The metric is maintained because IGRP and EIGRP use the same metric.

e) There is no automatic redistribution of IGRP and EIGRP between different AS.

Question 6–80. [ROPx] Which of the following routers would be defined as Autonomous System Boundary Routers? (Refer to the following diagram.)

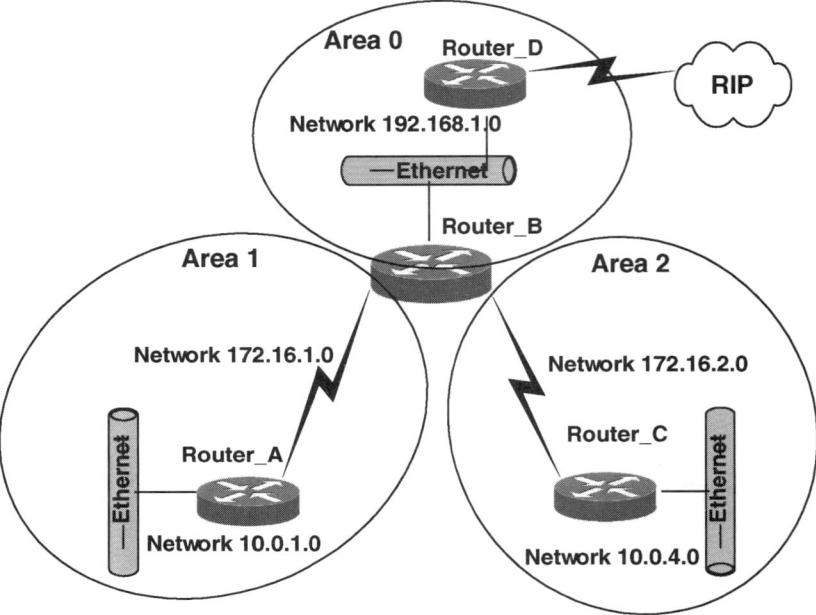

a) Router_A
b) Router_B
c) Router_C
d) Router_D
e) None of the above

Question 6–81. [CIPx] Which of the routing protocols would support the discontiguous addressing scheme used in the above topology? (Refer to the following graphic.) (Choose all that apply.)

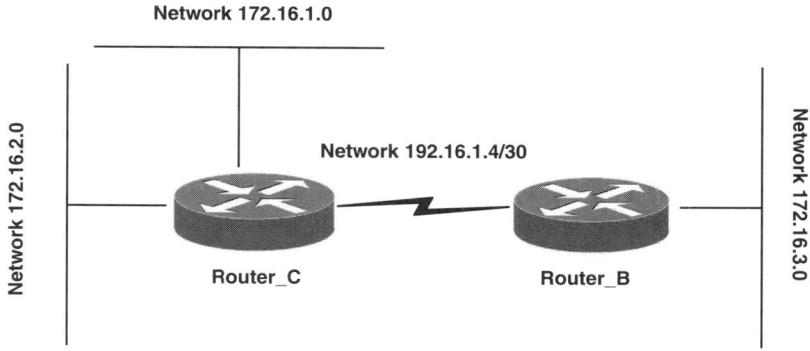

a) IGRP
b) EIGRP
c) IP RIP
d) OSPF
e) IP RIPv2

Question 6–82. [CxPx] Which of the following are true if the configuration register is 0x2142?

a) The Cisco IOS will be read from flash if a flash exists.
b) The Cisco IOS will be read from ROM.
c) The Cisco IOS will be read from NVRAM.
d) The configuration file will be read from flash.
e) The configuration file will be read from ROM.
f) The configuration file will be read from NVRAM.
g) The configuration file will NOT be read from NVRAM.
h) The baud rate will be set at 9600.
i) The baud rate will be set at 4800.

Question 6–83. [BxPx] Certain protocols such as SNA, Netbios and LAT are not routable and therefore must be bridged or encapsulated because:

a) Native IBM protocols do not conform to the OSI RM stack.
b) SNA and Netbios cannot be routed but LAT can.
c) They would be too CPU intensive.
d) They only run in "batch mode" processes where routing is not an issue.
e) These protocols have no explicit network address.

Question 6–84. [RAPx] How many different zones are used in the following network topology?

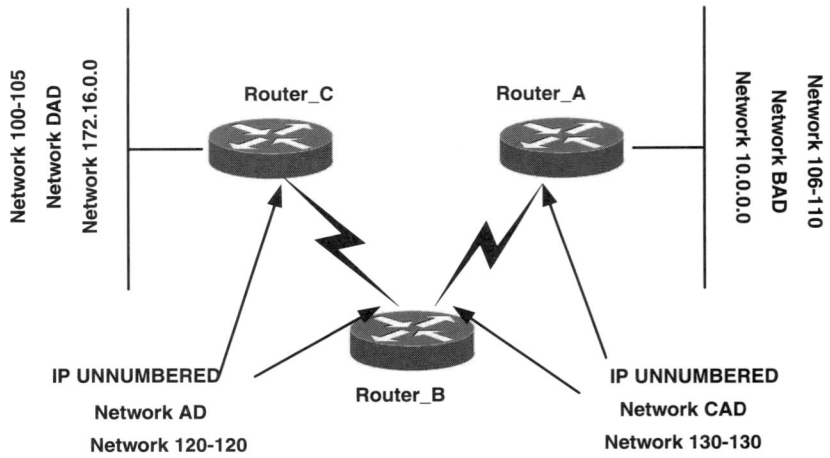

```
Router_C#sh run
Building configuration...

Current configuration:
!
version 11.2
!
hostname Router_C
!
!
appletalk routing
ipx routing 0060.09c3.df60
!
interface Ethernet0
 ip address 172.16.1.1 255.255.255.0
 appletalk cable-range 100-105 103.243
 appletalk zone right
 ipx network DAD
!
interface Ethernet1
 no ip address
 shutdown
!
interface Serial0
 ip unnumbered Ethernet0
 appletalk cable-range 120-120 120.17
 appletalk zone left
 ipx network AD
 clockrate 56000
!
interface Serial1
 no ip address
 shutdown
!
router igrp 100
```

```
 network 172.16.0.0
!
no ip classless
!!
line con 0
line aux 0
line vty 0 4
 login
!
end

Router_B#sh run
Building configuration...

Current configuration:
!
version 11.3
no service password-encryption
!
hostname Router_B
!
!
appletalk routing
ipx routing 0007.7816.fe54
!
interface Loopback0
 ip address 172.17.1.1 255.255.255.0
!
interface Serial0
 ip unnumbered Loopback0
 no ip mroute-cache
 appletalk cable-range 130-130 130.81
 appletalk zone right
 ipx network CAD
 no fair-queue
!
interface Serial1
 ip unnumbered Loopback0
 appletalk cable-range 120-120 120.125
 appletalk zone left
 ipx network AD
!
interface Serial2
 no ip address
 shutdown
!
interface Serial3
 no ip address
 shutdown
!
interface TokenRing0
 no ip address
 shutdown
!
```

6. CCIE

```
interface BRI0
 no ip address
 shutdown
!
router igrp 100
 network 172.17.0.0
!
ip classless
!
!
!
!
!
line con 0
line aux 0
line vty 0 4
 login
!
end

Router_A#sh run
Building configuration...

Current configuration:
!
version 11.3
no service password-encryption
!
hostname Router_A
!
!
appletalk routing
ipx routing 0010.7b15.bd41
!
interface Ethernet0/0
 ip address 10.1.1.1 255.255.255.0
 appletalk cable-range 106-110 106.17
 appletalk zone left
 ipx network BAD
!
interface Serial0/0
 ip unnumbered Ethernet0/0
 no ip mroute-cache
 appletalk cable-range 130-130 130.37
 appletalk zone right
 ipx network CAD
 clockrate 56000
!
interface TokenRing0/0
 no ip address
 shutdown
 ring-speed 16
!
interface FastEthernet1/0
```

```
 no ip address
 shutdown
!
router igrp 100
 network 10.0.0.0
!
ip classless
!!
line con 0
line aux 0
line vty 0 4
 login
!
end
```

    a) 1
    b) 2
    c) 3
    d) 4
    e) 5

Question 6–85. [IxPx] Which of the following are true of FDDI?

    a) Keepalives in most cases should be enabled.
    b) Enabling keepalives can cause unnecessary traffic.
    c) Failure detection time is immediate.
    d) A dual homed and a dual attached station (DAS) are connected to the ring in the same manner.
    e) The use of an optical bypass switch can prevent a ring from wrapping when a DAS fails.

Question 6–86. [RXPx] What is the IPX network not shown in the diagram?
(Refer to the following diagram and routing table.)

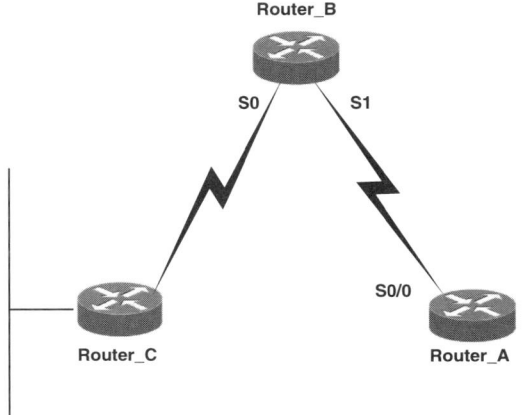

```
Router_B#sh ipx route
Codes: C - Connected primary network,
```

```
   c - Connected secondary network, S - Static,
   F - Floating static, L - Local (internal), W - IPXWAN
   R - RIP, E - EIGRP, N - NLSP, X - External, A - Aggregate
   s - seconds, u - uses, U - Per-user static

5 Total IPX routes. Up to 2 parallel paths and 16 hops allowed.

No default route known.

L         B1 is the internal network
R         A1 [07/01] via        0.0000.00a1.0000,    3s, Se1
R         C1 [07/01] via        0.0000.00a1.0000,    3s, Se0
R        CAD [07/01] via        0.0000.00a1.0000,    4s, Se1
                     via        0.0000.00a1.0000,    3s, Se0
R        FAD [07/01] via        0.0000.00a1.0000,    3s, Se0
```

a) FAD
b) CAD
c) DAD
d) BAD
e) The network is unnumbered.

Question 6–87. [FIPx] Host A and Host B are running the TCP/IP protocol, Router A and Router B are connected together using a Frame Relay serial connection. When Host A transmits to Host B a frame is lost during transmission across the Frame Relay serial connection. Who will be responsible for retransmission? (Refer to the following diagram.)

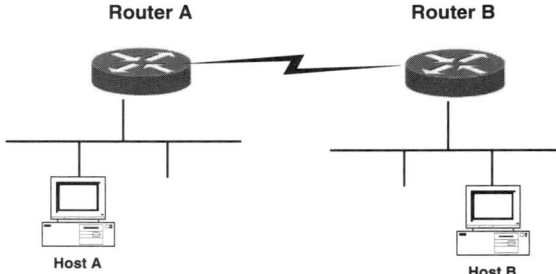

a) Router B
b) Router A
c) Host B
d) It depends on the configuration of Router B.
e) None of the above

Question 6–88. [ExPx] Which of the following is true of Ethernet?

a) Ethernet uses CSMA/CD.
b) Ethernet operates at 10 MB.
c) Ethernet operates at 100MB.
d) Ethernet operates at 1000MB.

e) All of the above.

Question 6–89. [RXPx] When using IPXWAN, what is the default tick count assigned to the interface?

a) 1
b) 6
c) 10
d) bandwidth/clockrate
e) There is no default tick count.

Question 6–90. [CxPx] Assuming that the s0 interface is on the outside of a Network Address Translation (NAT) router, select the proper command to enable NAT on this interface.

a) ip nat enable
b) ip enable nat
c) ip enable nat outside
d) ip nat outside
e) ip nat enable outside

Question 6–91. [RNPx] Which of the following is true about Novell's NLSP?

a) NLSP is a Link State Routing Protocol.
b) IPX network numbers are required on serial interfaces.
c) IPXWAN can be used with NLSP, in which case no IPX network number should be configured on a serial interface.
d) NLSP will converge more rapidly than IPX RIP.
e) All of the above.

Question 6–92. [CxPx] Which of the following best describes the use of no auto-summary?

a) Used by all distance vector routing protocols
b) Used by all Link State routing protocols
c) Used only by Cisco proprietary protocols
d) Used by Cisco's IGRP
e) Used by Cisco's Enhanced IGRP

Question 6–93. [XxPx] Which of the following may be required to configure X.25? (Choose all that apply.)

a) X.121 address
b) X.25 Switch Type
c) SPID number
d) DLCI number
e) LMI type

Question 6–94. [RXPx] A link is missing from the diagram. Where should it be placed? (Refer to the following diagram and routing table.)

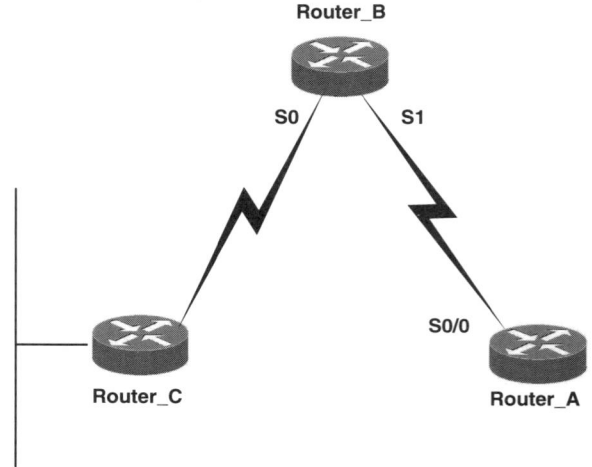

```
Router_B#sh ipx route
Codes: C - Connected primary network,
  c - Connected secondary network, S - Static,
  F - Floating static, L - Local (internal), W - IPXWAN
  R - RIP, E - EIGRP, N - NLSP, X - External, A - Aggregate
  s - seconds, u - uses, U - Per-user static

5 Total IPX routes. Up to 2 parallel paths and 16 hops allowed.

No default route known.

L       B1 is the internal network
R       A1 [07/01] via          0.0000.00a1.0000,     3s, Se1
R       C1 [07/01] via          0.0000.00a1.0000,     3s, Se0
R      CAD [07/01] via          0.0000.00a1.0000,     4s, Se1
                   via          0.0000.00a1.0000,     3s, Se0
R      FAD [07/01] via          0.0000.00a1.0000,     3s, Se0
```

    a)   Between Router_A and Router_B
    b)   Between Router_B and Router_C
    c)   An Ethernet link off of Router_B
    d)   There is no Link missing
    e)   A link between Router_A and Router_C

Question 6–95. [BxPx] If the command "bridge-group 1 path-cost" is not used what will be the result?

    a)   The cost of an ethernet link will always be 10.
    b)   The cost of a serial link will always be 6.
    c)   The cost of a 10 meg ethernet link will always be 100.
    d)   No cost will be used.
    e)   None of the above.

Question 6–96. [RIPx] Which field does the "trace" command manipulate inside an IP header to calculate the path that was taken from source to destination?

a) Source Port
b) Destination Port
c) Source IP address
d) Destination IP address
e) None of the above

Question 6–97. [RIPx] Which of the following lists the correct values of the ICMP type field of an Echo Request and Echo Reply?

a) Echo Request: 3, Echo Reply: 0
b) Echo Request: 8, Echo Reply: 3
c) Echo Request: 0, Echo Reply: 3
d) Echo Request: 4, Echo Reply: 0
e) Echo Request: 8, Echo Reply: 0

Question 6–98. [TxPx] If RSRB is configured at both routers, which of the following could represent a RIF? (Refer to the following diagram.) (Choose the best answer)

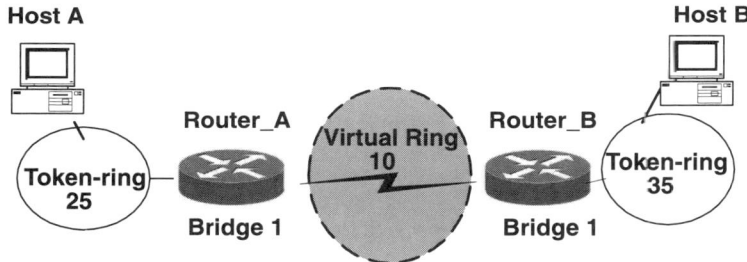

a) 0830.0191.00a1.0230
b) 0630.0191.00a1.0230
c) 0830.0191.00a1.0231
d) 0630.0191.00a1
e) 0830.0251.0101.0350

Question 6–99. [RIPx] Assuming IGRP is the routing protocol used for all networks on all routers: (Refer to the following diagram.)

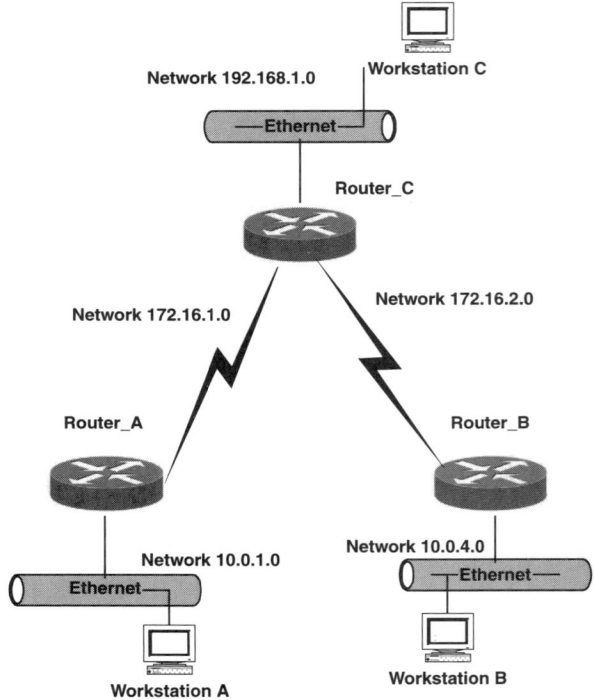

a) Workstation A could not successfully ping both serial interfaces of Router_C.
b) Workstation A could successfully ping the ethernet interface of Router_B.
c) Workstation A could not successfully ping the ethernet interface of Router_C.
d) Workstation A could successfully ping Workstation B.
e) Workstation A could not successfully ping Workstation B.

Question 6–100. [xxPx] Which of the following describes a Bus topology? (Choose all best answers.)

a) There is a central distribution point.
b) A linear transmission media
c) Easier to trouble shoot than star topolgy
d) All nodes are directly attached to the media.
e) Requires more cabling than other topologies

Question 6–101. [CIPx] Which of the following is true of the configuration line below?

```
access-list 10 permit 153.19.0.128 0.0.255.127
```

a)   The source address less than 153.19.10.126 would be permitted.
b)   The destination address less then 153.19.0.129 would be denied.
c)   The source address greater than 153.19.100.129 would be permitted.
d)   The destination address less than 153.19.129.12 would be permitted.
e)   Configuration statement shown is illegal.

Question 6–102. [xIPx] What does the term "IP spoofing" generally refer to?

a)   When an IP host scares another IP host. (NO, that's IP spooking)
b)   When an IP host runs the same applications as another host.
c)   When an IP host uses an IP address that belongs to another device on purpose.
d)   When an IP host uses a MAC address that is assigned to another device.
e)   None of the above

Question 6–103. [TxPx] When will Source Route Bridging (SRB) block ports?

a)   When more than one path exists to a destination
b)   When the bridging algorithm determines a better metric
c)   When the cost of a link becomes too high
d)   When a bridge is the Root Bridge
e)   None of the above

Question 6–104. [TxPx] If communication was to go from Host B to Host A, assuming RSRB, what would be the value of the Route Descriptor Field? Refer to the following diagram.

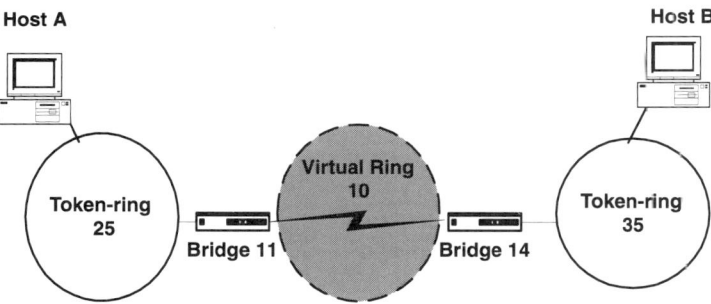

a)   019b.00ae.0230
b)   2511.1014.3500
c)   3514.1011.2500
d)   023e.ooab.1900
e)   None of the above

Question 6–105. [CxPx] The Cisco feature that allows a protocol to come in a bridged interface and exit a routed interface and visa versa is called:

a)   IRB
b)   CRB
c)   SRB
d)   T B
e)   SRTB

Question 6–106. [RxPx] Which of the following is a component used to determine time to convergence?

a)   Metric
b)   Administrative distance
c)   Time to detect link failure
d)   Timers
e)   All of the above.

Question 6–107. [BxPx] A bridge that tunnels frames across a WAN or FDDI link is a:

a)   Transparent bridge
b)   SRB
c)   S R T
d)   Translational bridge
e)   Encapsulating bridge.

Question 6–108. [RxPx] Workstation A sends a frame to Workstation B. The devices shown are routers. Which of the following are true of the Layer 3 addresses? (Choose all that apply.) (Refer to the diagram below.)

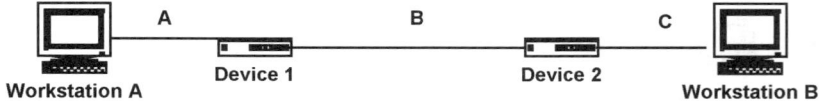

a)   Layer 3 addresses never change.
b)   Only source Layer 3 address will change as the frame traverses the network.
c)   Only destination Layer 3 address will change as the frame traverses the network.
d)   Both the source and destination Layer 3 addresses will change as the frame traverses the network.
e)   Routers do not use a Layer 3 address to determine destination.

Question 6–109. [XIPx] Host A and Host B are running the TCP/IP protocol, Router A and Router B are connected together using a X.25 serial connection. When Host A transmits to Host B a frame is lost during transmission across the X.25 serial connection. Who will be responsible for retransmission? (Refer to the following diagram.)

Router A   Router B

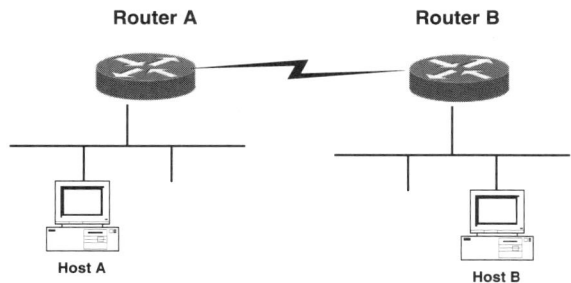

Host A

Host B

a)   Router B
b)   Router A
c)   Host B
d)   It depends on the configuration of Router A.
e)   It depends on the configuration of Router B.

Question 6–110. [CxPx] The Cisco feature that allows a protocol to be bridged among bridged interfaces and another protocol to be routed among routed interfaces within the same router would be called:

a)   IRB
b)   CRB
c)   SRB
d)   T B
e)   S R T B

Question 6–111. [TxPx] In a Token Ring MAC frame, the RIF route control field contains the following information: (Choose all that apply.)

a)   Mac Address
b)   Ring number
c)   Explorer type
d)   Length of RIF
e)   Direction in which the RIF should be read
f)   Largest frame size
g)   Bridge number

Question 6–112. [RAPx] The total number of bits in an appletalk address is:

a)   8
b)   16
c)   24
d)   32
e)   40

Question 6–113. [CxPx] Refer to the following configuration. What is the tunnel encapsulation method?

```
Current configuration:
!
version 11.3
no service password-encryption
!
hostname Router_A
!
enable secret 5 $1$.s1R$iaEqZxLnYJo2QlZi8UNaO0
enable password ccnaprep
!
ipx routing 0010.7b15.bd41
!
interface Tunnel0
 no ip address
 ipx network FAD
 tunnel source Serial0/0
 tunnel destination 65.62.245.2
!
interface Ethernet0/0
 ip address 172.17.10.1 255.255.255.0
 no ip mroute-cache
 ipx network BAD
 no cdp enable
!
interface Serial0/0
 ip address 65.62.245.1 255.255.255.0
 encapsulation frame-relay
 no ip mroute-cache
 frame-relay lmi-type cisco
!
interface TokenRing0/0
 no ip address
 no ip mroute-cache
 shutdown
 ring-speed 16
 no cdp enable
!
interface FastEthernet1/0
 no ip address
 no ip mroute-cache
 shutdown
 no cdp enable
!
ip classless
no cdp run
!
line con 0
 exec-timeout 0 0
line aux 0
line vty 0 4
```

```
 password ccieprep
 login
end
```

a) ipip
b) gre
c) iptalk
d) nos
e) dvmrp

Question 6–114. [RIPx] Which one of the following is true about the IP checksum?

a) It checks the header only.
b) It checks the header and the data.
c) It checks the data only.
d) If an error is detected it will retransmit.
e) ICMP, IGMP, UDP and TCP use a different checksum algorithm.

Question 6–115. [CAPx] Which two of the following are true of the appletalk protocol command?

a) It is a global configuration command.
b) It is required to route appletalk.
c) It would be used to select EIGRP as the routing protocol.
d) There is no such command the proper command is appletalk routing.
e) It would be used to select AURP as the routing protocol.

Question 6–116. [ROPx] Which of the following routers would the switch no-summary be configured to define totally stubby areas? (Refer to the following diagram.)

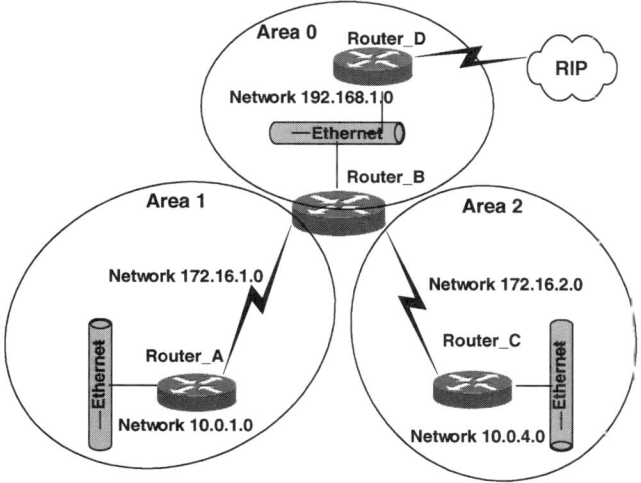

a) Router_A
b) Router_B
c) Router_C
d) Router_D
e) None of the above

Question 6–117. [RXPx] The IPX network number of Serial link S0 is:
(Refer to the following diagram and routing table.)

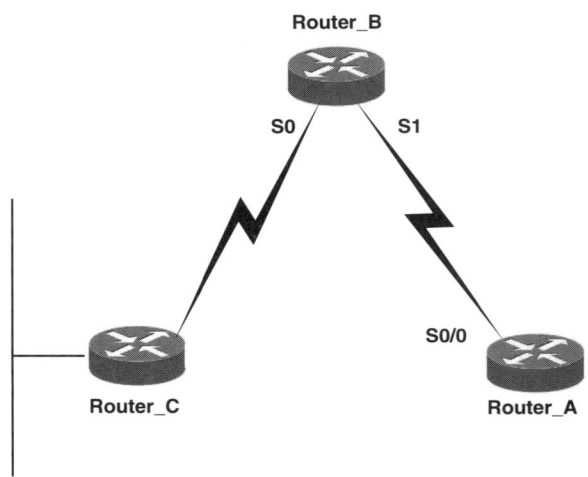

```
Router_B#sh ipx route
Codes: C - Connected primary network,
  c - Connected secondary network, S - Static,
  F - Floating static, L - Local (internal), W - IPXWAN
  R - RIP, E - EIGRP, N - NLSP, X - External, A - Aggregate
  s - seconds, u - uses, U - Per-user static

5 Total IPX routes. Up to 2 parallel paths and 16 hops allowed.

No default route known.

L         B1 is the internal network
R         A1 [07/01] via        0.0000.00a1.0000,    3s, Se1
R         C1 [07/01] via        0.0000.00a1.0000,    3s, Se0
R         CAD [07/01] via       0.0000.00a1.0000,    4s, Se1
                      via       0.0000.00a1.0000,    3s, Se0
R         FAD [07/01] via       0.0000.00a1.0000,    3s, Se0
```

a) CAD
b) FAD
c) DAD
d) Can not be determined.
e) There is no IPX network number configured on Serial 0.

Question 6–118. [CxPx] Which of the following commands will configure your router to use the neighbor 150.100.10.72 as the gateway of last resort?

a) ip route 255.255.255.255 150.100.10.72.
b) ip route 0.0.0.0 150.100.10.72
c) ip route 0.0.0.0 0.0.0.0 150.100.10.72
d) ip route 255.255.255.255 0.0.0.0 150.100.10.72.
e) ip route default 150.100.10.72

Question 6–119. [RAPx] Which one of the following is a feature unique to Appletalk Phase 2?

a) Allows no more than 127 hosts
b) Allows discontinuous zones
c) Allows a single network number per wire
d) Allows up to 253 nodes
e) Allows for dynamic address assignment

Question 6–120. [RXPx] The IPX network number of Serial link S1 is:
(Refer to the following diagram and routing table.)

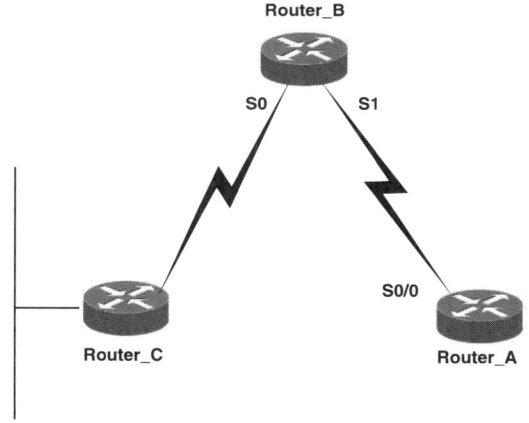

```
Router_B#sh ipx route
Codes: C - Connected primary network,
    c - Connected secondary network, S - Static,
    F - Floating static, L - Local (internal), W - IPXWAN
    R - RIP, E - EIGRP, N - NLSP, X - External, A - Aggregate
    s - seconds, u - uses, U - Per-user static

5 Total IPX routes. Up to 2 parallel paths and 16 hops allowed.

No default route known.

L        B1 is the internal network
R        A1 [07/01] via        0.0000.00a1.0000,    3s, Se1
R        C1 [07/01] via        0.0000.00a1.0000,    3s, Se0
R        CAD [07/01] via       0.0000.00a1.0000,    4s, Se1
                    via        0.0000.00a1.0000,    3s, Se0
R        FAD [07/01] via       0.0000.00a1.0000,    3s, Se0
```

a)   CAD
b)   FAD
c)   DAD
d)   Can not be determined.
e)   There is no IPX network number configured on Serial 0.

Question 6–121. [RIPx] Host A and Host B are running the TCP/IP protocol, Router A and Router B are connected together using a X25 serial connection. When Host A transmits to Host B, what will be the destination address in the frame header when Host A encapsulates on the ethernet segment ? (Refer to the following diagram.)

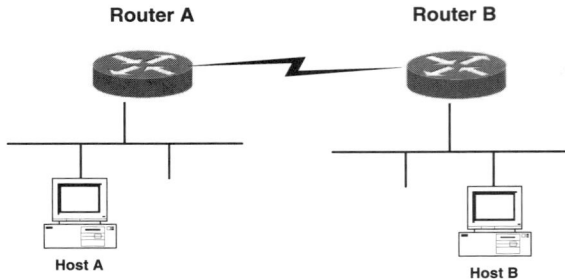

a)   Router B
b)   Router A
c)   Host B
d)   Because it's using X25 there will be no frame header.
e)   None of the above.

Question 6–122. [TxPx] Which of the following best describes the relationship between ring speed and the IGRP metric? (Choose the best answer.)

a)   The IGRP metric is completely based on the ring speed.
b)   The IGRP metric is partially based on ring Speed.
c)   The IGRP metric is completely based on Bandwidth, which is based on ring speed.
d)   The IGRP metric is partially based on Bandwidth, which is based on ring speed.
e)   The IGRP metric is partially based on Bandwidth, which is based on ring speed, but can be overridden by manually configuring bandwidth on the interface.

Question 6–123. [CxPx] Given the following configuration which one of the following is true of Interface Serial 0?

```
Router_B#sh run
Building configuration...

Current configuration:
!
version 11.3
no service password-encryption
!
hostname Router_B
!
```

```
interface Serial0
 ip address 172.18.1.2 255.255.255.0
!
[OUTPUT OMMITTED]
router igrp 100
 variance 2
 network 172.17.0.0
 network 172.18.0.0
!
ip classless
!
line con 0
line aux 0
line vty 0 4
 login
!
end
```

a) Serial 0 is configured as DCE interface
b) Serial 0 is configured as a DTE interface
c) Serial 0 is configured with a bandwidth of 800Kbit
d) Serial 0 is configured with a bandwidth of 1544Kbit
e) The configuration provided does not provide us with any information about S0

Question 6–124. [RIPx] Assuming IP RIP is the routing protocol used for all networks on all routers: (Refer to the following diagram.)

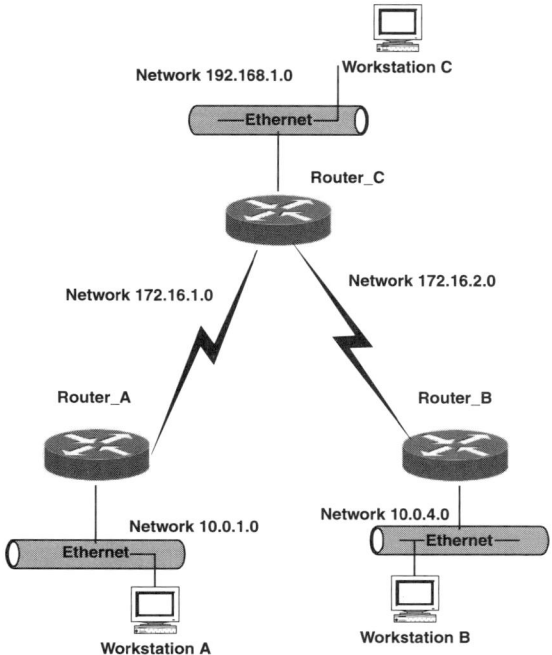

    a)   Workstation A could not successfully ping both serial interfaces of Router_C.
    b)   Workstation A could successfully ping the ethernet interface of Router_B.
    c)   Workstation A could not successfully ping the ethernet interface of Router_C.
    d)   Workstation A could successfully ping Workstation B.
    e)   Workstation A could not successfully ping Workstation B.

Question 6–125. [TxPx] Which of the following is true of Source Route Transparent Bridging? (Choose all that apply.)

    a)   Allows communication between Ethernet and Token Ring hosts
    b)   Will insert a RIF when communicating to a Source Route Bridge
    c)   Will remove a RIF when communicating to a Transparent Bridge
    d)   Frames that don't have a RIF never gain a RIF, frames that have a RIF never loose a RIF.
    e)   When the RII bit is set to 1 frames will be transparently bridged

Question 6–126. [CxPx] Given the following configuration, which two statements are true about telnet?

```
Current configuration:
!
version 11.3
no service password-encryption
!
hostname Router_B

no ip routing
appletalk routing
appletalk maximum-paths 2
ipx routing 0007.7816.fe54
ipx internal-network B1
!
interface Serial0
 ip address 10.1.3.2 255.255.255.0
no fair-queue
 bridge-group 1
!
interface Serial1
 ip address 10.1.4.1 255.255.255.0
clockrate 4000000
 bridge-group 1
!
interface Serial2
 no ip address
 no ip route-cache
 shutdown
!
interface Serial3
 no ip address
 no ip route-cache
 shutdown
!
interface TokenRing0
```

```
 no ip address
 no ip route-cache
 shutdown
!
interface BRI0
 no ip address
 no ip route-cache
 shutdown
!
ip classless

!
ipx router nlsp
bridge 1 protocol dec
!
line con 0
line aux 0
line vty 0 4
 no login
!
end
```

a) No user would be permitted to telnet to Router_B.
b) All users will be able to telnet to Router_B.
c) No user would be able to access the privilege mode of Router_B.
d) All users would be able to access the privilege mode of Router_B.
e) Can not be determined.

Question 6–127. [RIPx] Refer to the diagram below. When Host A transmits to Host B, which device will handle the IP fragmentation when going from the Token Ring to the Serial line?

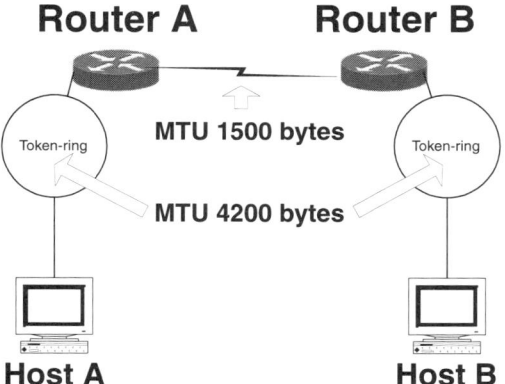

a) Host A
b) Router A
c) Host B
d) Router B
e) The Token

Question 6–128. [CxPx] What are advantages of using Asynchronous as opposed to Synchronous interfaces?

    a)   Supports CSU/DSU connectivity
    b)   Supports ATM services
    c)   Cost effective, non-dedicated connectivity
    d)   Supports ISDN services
    e)   All of the above

Question 6–129. [IxPx] The failure of a Single Attached Station (SAS) will cause which of the following to occur? (Choose the best answer.)

    a)   The ring will wrap.
    b)   The primary ring will fail.
    c)   If an optical bypass switch is used, network communication will continue with no interruption.
    d)   Network communication will continue with no interruption.
    e)   None of the above.

Question 6–130. [CxPx] EIGRP:

    a)   Is a link state routing protocol
    b)   Does not allow discontinuous networks to be configured
    c)   Can only be used to route between registered Autonomous Systems
    d)   Supports VLSM
    e)   All of the above

Question 6–131. [ROPx] Given the fact there are two OSPF areas, how many Designated Routers (DR) will there be?

    a)   2
    b)   1
    c)   1 for each internal Autonomous System (AS) network
    d)   1 for each AS
    e)   Can not be determined

Question 6–132. [CxPx] The BVI should be configured as:

    a)   A routed interface
    b)   A bridged port
    c)   Part of the bridge group
    d)   With MAC address
    e)   None of the above

Question 6–133. [CxPx] What is the password required to change a password? (Refer to the following configuration.)

```
Router_B#sh run
```

```
Building configuration...

Current configuration:
!
version 11.3
no service password-encryption
!
hostname Router_B
!
enable secret 5 $1$4Rzs$i9EC6.trjXdJe0pO6dpZm0
enable password Secret
!
ip host toronto 196.60.26.1
!
interface Serial0
 ip address 192.168.5.1 255.255.255.0
!
interface Serial1
 ip address 192.168.10.2 255.255.255.0
!
interface Serial2
 no ip address
 shutdown
!
interface Serial3
 no ip address
 shutdown
!
interface TokenRing0
 no ip address
 shutdown
!
interface BRI0
 no ip address
 shutdown
!
router rip
 network 196.60.26.0
!
ip classless
!
!
line con 0
 password notset
line aux 0
line vty 0 4
 password nologin
 login
!
end
```

6. CCIE

a) No password has been set.
b) No login will be permitted.
c) Secret
d) Secret 5
e) nologin
f) not set
g) Can not be determined.

Question 6–134. [CxPx] Which of the following are true as they pertain to EIGRP and route summarization?

a) Summarization is automatic to the subnet boundary.
b) There is no Auto Summarization.
c) Summarization is automatic to the Class boundaries.
d) Use the command no auto-summary to turn off summarization.
e) To change the EIGRP defaults use the command ip summary-address eigrp on an interface.

Question 6–135. [BxPx] A transparent bridge constructs its bridging table by:

a) Listening to all traffic and associating the layer 3 address with an interface
b) Listening to the destination host and recording its host address
c) Listening to the source host and recording its host address
d) Listening to the source host and associating its MAC address to a port
e) All of the above

Question 6–136. [TxPx] What are two major problems with bridging between two dissimilar media (e.g., bridging between Token Ring and Ethernet or FDDI and Ethernet?

a) Bit-ordering
b) MTU
c) Media contention
d) Ring speed
e) Broadcast

Question 6–137. [ExPx] A Ethernet LAN to Ethernet LAN file transfer has been initiated, and you have determined that it is proceeding at 10,000 error free PPS, what do you do?

a) Call a Cisco tech immediately.
b) Do nothing.
c) Your router needs to be slowed down.
d) Investigate your file transfer application.
e) Your router should be replaced.

Question 6–138. [TxPx] Which of the following is true as it relates to DLSw?

a) DLSw does not provide connection-oriented service.
b) DLSw provides end-to-end connectivity at the data-link control level.
c) DLSw operates as Remote Source Route Bridging.
d) DLSw will terminate the data-link control for connection-oriented data.
e) DLSw is Cisco proprietary.

Question 6–139. [RIPx] Will Router_C be able to ping the secondary address (20.20.20.1) of the Token Ring interface of Router_B?

Assume that IP RIP is configured for all networks, and the Token Ring interface of Router_B has been configured with a secondary address of 20.20.20.1.

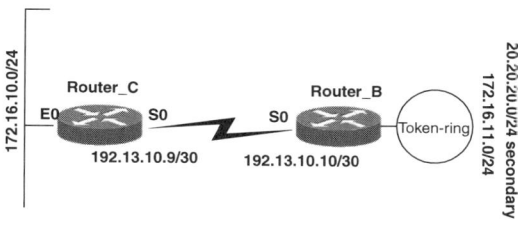

a) Yes
b) Yes 50% of the time
c) No
d) Not enough information given.

Question 6–140. [XxPx] CCITT X.21 is defined at which layer?

a) Physical Layer 1
b) Data-Link Layer 2
c) Network Layer 3
d) Transport Layer 4

Question 6–141. [CxPx] When configuring two tunnels on the same router, which of the following is false?

a) Each tunnel may not have the same source and destination address.
b) A loopback interface may be configured to provide unique addressing.
c) The tunnel will always be configured with a Layer 3 protocol address.
d) Tunneling in all cases provides additional overhead.
e) All of the above are false.

Question 6–142. [RIPx] If Workstation A were to ping a host on network 10.4.0.0, Router_C would send the packet out: (Refer to the following diagram and configuration.)

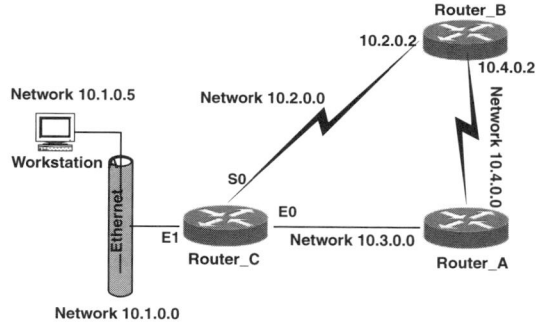

```
Current configuration:
!
version 11.2
!
hostname Router_C
!
interface Ethernet0
 ip address 10.3.0.3 255.255.0.0
!
interface Ethernet1
 ip address 10.1.0.3 255.255.0.0
 ip policy route-map thisway
!
interface Serial0
 ip address 10.2.0.1 255.255.0.0
 clockrate 38400
!
interface Serial1
 no ip address
 shutdown
!
router ospf 100
 network 10.0.0.0 0.255.255.255 area 0
!
no ip classless
access-list 1 permit 10.1.0.5
route-map thisway permit 10
 match ip address 1
 set interface Serial0
!
line con 0
line aux 0
line vty 0 4
 login
!
end

Router_C#sh ip route
Codes: C - connected, S - static, I - IGRP, R - RIP, M - mobile, B - BGP
       D - EIGRP, EX - EIGRP external, O - OSPF, IA - OSPF inter area
       N1 - OSPF NSSA external type 1, N2 - OSPF NSSA external type 2
       E1 - OSPF external type 1, E2 - OSPF external type 2, E - EGP
       i - IS-IS, L1 - IS-IS level-1, L2 - IS-IS level-2, * - candidate default
       U - per-user static route, o - ODR

Gateway of last resort is not set

     10.0.0.0/16 is subnetted, 3 subnets
C       10.2.0.0 is directly connected, Serial0
C       10.3.0.0 is directly connected, Ethernet0
O       10.4.0.0 [110/74] via 10.3.0.1, 00:00:13, Ethernet0
```

a) E0
b) E1
c) S0
d) E0 or S0
e) Can't be determined.

Question 6–143. [CIPx] Assuming EIGRP is the routing protocol the "no auto-summary" command will have to be configured on: (Refer to the following diagram.)

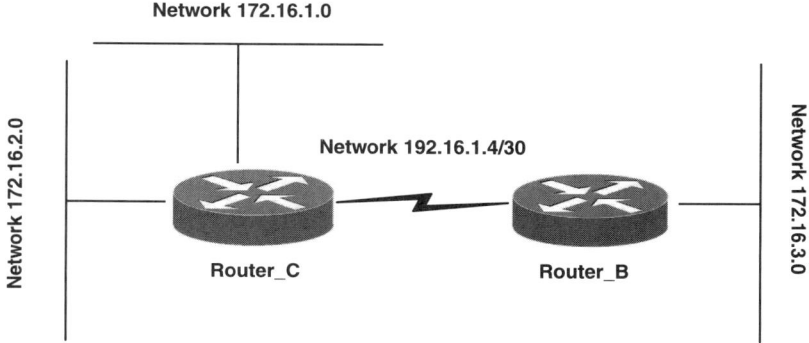

Network 172.16.1.0

Network 172.16.2.0

Network 192.16.1.4/30

Network 172.16.3.0

Router_C

Router_B

a) Router_C
b) Router_B
c) Router_C & Router_B
d) "no auto-summary" is not an EIGRP command.
e) It would not be necessary to configure "no-auto-summary."

Question 6–144. [BxPx] Digital Equipment Corporation developed transparent bridges in the early 80s. IEEE incorporated Digital's work into which one of the following standards:

a) 802.3
b) 802.2
c) 802.1q
d) 802.2d
e) 802.1d

Question 6–145. [CxPx] The routing protocols currently configured on Router_A are: (Refer to the following configuration.)

```
version 11.3
no service password-encryption
!
hostname Router_A
!
appletalk routing
ipx routing 0010.7b15.bd41
!
interface Ethernet0/0
```

```
 no ip address
 appletalk cable-range 100-150 128.85
 appletalk zone ccieprep
 ipx network DAD
!
interface Serial0/0
 no ip address
 no ip mroute-cache
 shutdown
 no fair-queue
!
interface TokenRing0/0
 no ip address
 shutdown
 ring-speed 16
!
interface FastEthernet1/0
 no ip address
 shutdown
!
ip classless
line con 0
line aux 0
line vty 0 4
 login
!
end
```

   a)   IP RIP, IPX RIP and AURP
   b)   IPX RIP and RTMP
   c)   No routing protocols have been configured
   d)   IP, IPX RIP, RTMP
   e)   IP and RTMP

Question 6–146. [XxPx] Which encapsulation type is the default layer 2 protocol for X.25?

   a)   sdlc
   b)   hdlc
   c)   PPP
   d)   PAP
   e)   LAPB

Question 6–147. [CxPx] What effect would the command "bridge 1 priority 1" have? (Choose all that apply.)

   a)   Would assign the bridge (Router) to the bridge group priority 1
   b)   Would mean that most likely the bridge (Router) will become the "Root Bridge"
   c)   Would force the bridge (Router) to forward on all ports
   d)   Would disqualify the bridge (Router) from being a "route bridge"
   e)   Would force the bridge (Router) to use 1 as the MAC address

Question 6–148. [RxPx] Workstation A sends a frame to Workstation B. The devices shown are routers. Which of the following are true of the Layer 3 addresses at reference point A? (Choose all that apply.) (Refer to the diagram below.)

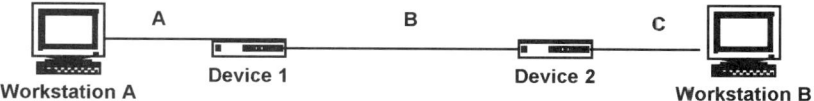

a) The destination address will be that of Workstation B.
b) The source address will be that of Workstation A.
c) The source address will be the outbound interface of Device 2.
d) Routers never change the Layer 3 address.
e) The destination address will be the inbound interface of device 1.

Question 6–149. [CxPx] Which of the following is true of the "ip host" command?

a) A dynamic host table will be built.
b) A static mapping will be made between Host names and IP addresses.
c) Only one IP address is allowed per host name.
d) A ping will only use the first address configured.
e) A telnet will only use the first address configured.

Question 6–150. [CxPx] The MAC address of the BVI: (Refer to the diagram below.)

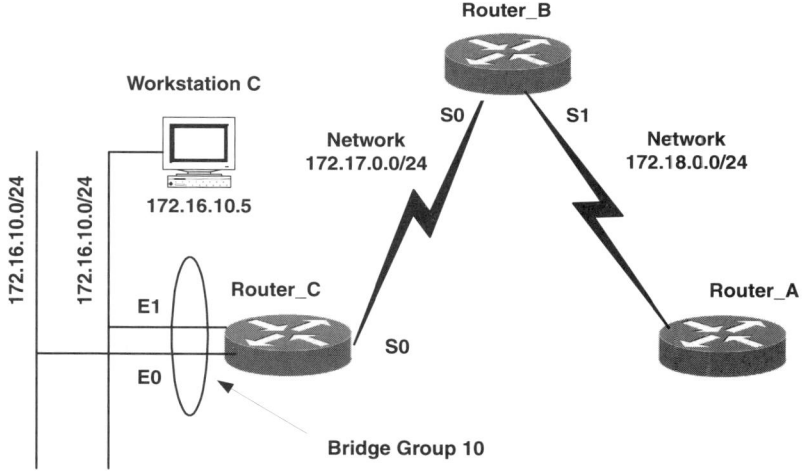

a) Will be assigned by the administrator
b) Will be the MAC address of S0
c) Will be the MAC address of E0
d) Will be randomly chosen by the IOS
e) There is no MAC address of the BVI.

Question 6–151. [ROPx] When would an OSPF virtual link be used?

a) When there are two discontinuous Autonomous Systems
b) When there is only one area
c) When an area does not have a link to area 0
d) To connect two external areas
e) To connect two internal networks

Question 6–152. [RAPx] Which one of the following is true about Appletalk Zones?

a) Zones are used to limit the range of routing updates.
b) Zones are used to limit NBP requests.
c) Zones must be contiguous.
d) Zones must not overlap.
e) Zones must be configured on an Appletalk client.

Question 6–153. [TxPx] What is the purpose of the "source-bridge proxy-explorer" command?

a) Enables a Token Ring interface to send explorer packets
b) Enables a Token Ring interface to participate in Spanning-Tree
c) Enables SRB in a Transparent Bridge environment
d) Allows an interface to convert explorer packets to specifically routed frames
e) None of the above

Question 6–154. [TxPx] Assume Source Route Bridging (SRB) is configured, and Host A sends a frame to Host B. Which of the following would best describes the contents of the RIF at Host B? Refer to the following diagram.

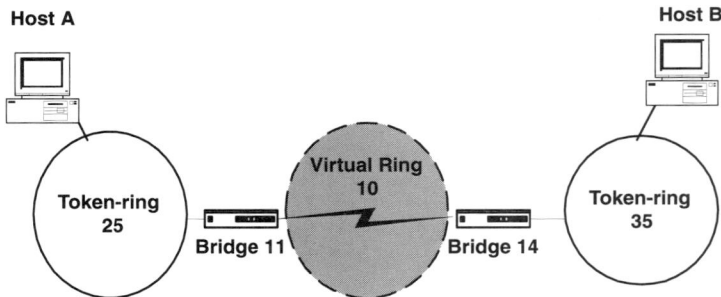

a) 0630.019b.00ae.0230
b) 2511.1014.3500
c) 0830.2511.1014.3500
d) 0830.019b.00ae.0230
e) None of the above

Question 6–155. [RAPx] Which of the following is true as it pertains to Appletalk?

   a)   All appletalk devices can be in discovery mode.
   b)   Appletalk will advertise its routes every 30 seconds.
   c)   There should be at least one Appletalk seed router.
   d)   Cable-Range of 0-0 should only be used on serial interfaces.
   e)   All of the above.

Question 6–156. [CIPx] An access list that would deny Router_B to telnet to hosts on network 192.16.5.0, should be placed on:
(Refer to the following diagram.)

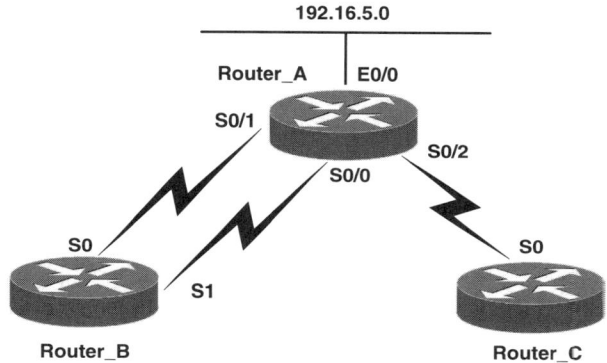

   a)   S0/0 and S0/1 of Router_A
   b)   S0 and S1of Router_B
   c)   S1 of Router_B
   d)   S0 of Router B
   e)   Choice a or choice b would work.

Question 6–157. [BxPx] Given the following router configuration, which of the following protocols would be bridged?

```
version 11.1
service udp-small-servers
service tcp-small-servers
!
hostname Router_C
!
no ip routing
appletalk routing
ipx routing 0060.09c3.df60
ipx internal-network C1
!
interface Ethernet0
 ip address 10.1.1.1 255.255.255.0
 no ip mroute-cache
 no ip route-cache
```

```
 appletalk cable-range 111-115 112.170
 appletalk zone bottom-ether
 ipx network CAD
 bridge-group 1
!
interface Ethernet1
 ip address 10.1.2.1 255.255.255.0
 no ip mroute-cache
 no ip route-cache
 appletalk cable-range 95-99 97.221
 appletalk zone left-ether
 ipx network FAD
 bridge-group 1
!
interface Serial0
 ip address 10.1.3.1 255.255.255.0
 no ip mroute-cache
 no ip route-cache
 appletalk cable-range 100-105 100.190
 appletalk zone leftserial
 ipx ipxwan 0 unnumbered Router_C
 clockrate 1200
 bridge-group 1
!
interface Serial1
 no ip address
 no ip mroute-cache
 no ip route-cache
 shutdown
 clockrate 4000000
!
no ip classless
!
ipx router nlsp
!
bridge 1 protocol dec
bridge 1 priority 1
!
line con 0
line aux 0
 transport input all
line vty 0 4
 login
!
end
```

a)   IP, IPX, Appletalk
b)   IPX, IP
c)   IP, Banyan, DECnet
d)   Appletalk, IPX
e)   No bridging will take place because routing is configured.

Question 6–158. [CxPx] Which of the following are true if the configuration register is 0x2102?

    a)   The Cisco IOS will be read from flash if a flash exists.
    b)   The Cisco IOS will be read from ROM.
    c)   The Cisco IOS will be read from NVRAM.
    d)   The configuration file will be read from flash.
    e)   The configuration file will be read from ROM.
    f)   The configuration file will be read from NVRAM.
    g)   The configuration file will NOT be read.
    h)   The baud rate will be set at 9600.
    i)   The baud rate will be set at 4800.

Question 6–159. [RIPx] On which router(s) would it be most possible to configure load balancing?

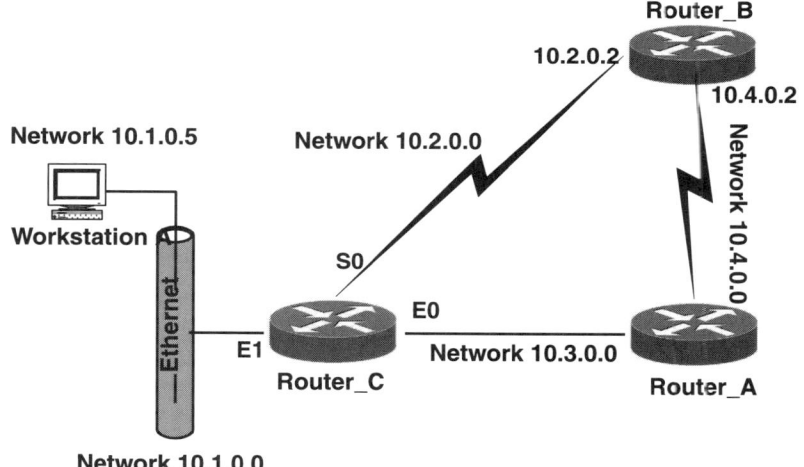

```
Current configuration:
!
version 11.2
!
hostname Router_C
!
interface Ethernet0
 ip address 10.3.0.3 255.255.0.0
!
interface Ethernet1
 ip address 10.1.0.3 255.255.0.0
 ip policy route-map thisway
!
interface Serial0
 ip address 10.2.0.1 255.255.0.0
 clockrate 38400
!
```

```
interface Serial1
 no ip address
 shutdown
!
router ospf 100
 network 10.0.0.0 0.255.255.255 area 0
!
no ip classless
access-list 1 permit 10.1.0.5
route-map thisway permit 10
 match ip address 1
 set interface Serial0
!
line con 0
line aux 0
line vty 0 4
 login
!
end


Router_C#sh ip route
Codes: C - connected, S - static, I - IGRP, R - RIP, M - mobile, B - BGP
       D - EIGRP, EX - EIGRP external, O - OSPF, IA - OSPF inter area
       N1 - OSPF NSSA external type 1, N2 - OSPF NSSA external type 2
       E1 - OSPF external type 1, E2 - OSPF external type 2, E - EGP
       i - IS-IS, L1 - IS-IS level-1, L2 - IS-IS level-2, * - candidate default
       U - per-user static route, o - ODR

Gateway of last resort is not set

     10.0.0.0/16 is subnetted, 3 subnets
C       10.2.0.0 is directly connected, Serial0
C       10.3.0.0 is directly connected, Ethernet0
O       10.4.0.0 [110/74] via 10.3.0.1, 00:00:13, Ethernet0
```

a) Router_A
b) Router_B
c) Router_C
d) All of the above
e) None of the above

Question 6–160. [CxPx] Assume the following access-list is used to define interesting traffic on a DDR link. Which of the following is true?

```
access-list 101 permit tcp 172.16.10.0 0.0.0.255 any eq 25
```

a) Only SMTP traffic from the subnet 172.16.10.0 will pass on the link.
b) Only SMTP traffic going to the subnet 172.16.10.0 will pass on the link.
c) Only SMTP traffic from the subnet 172.16.10.0 going to 0.0.0.0 will pass on the link.
d) All traffic that hits the link will be pass on the link, if the link is up.
e) None of the above.

Question 6–161. [CxPx] Which of the following commands would be proper to set a default route on Router_C? (Refer to the diagram below.) (Choose the best answer.)

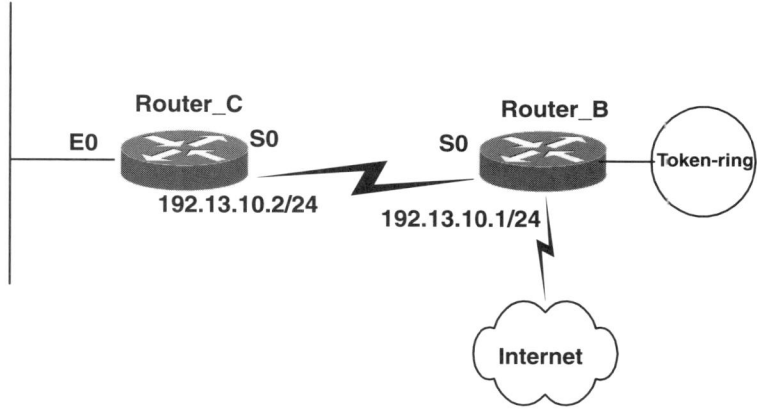

   a)   ip route 192.13.10.1 255.255.255.255 192.13.10.2
   b)   ip route 0.0.0.0 255.255.255.255 192.13.10.1
   c)   ip route 0.0.0.0 0.0.0.0 192.13.10.1 220
   d)   ip route 192.13.10.1 255.255.255.255 192.13.10.1
   e)   ip route 0.0.0.0 255.255.255.255 192.13.10.2

Answer 6–1.
   c)   **NLSP is a quieter protocol.**

NLSP is Novell's Link State Routing Protocol, which is based on IS-IS. A link state routing protocol is much quieter than a distance vector routing protocol such as IPX RIP.

Answer 6–2.
   b)   **Ring number**
   g)   **Bridge number**

The route descriptor field is made up of ring and bridge numbers only.

Answer 6–3.
   c)   **Serial 2**

The router will look for the longest match. For that reason the router will not use Serial 0 or Serial 1.

Answer 6–4.
   a)   **CHAP**
   b)   **PAP**
   c)   **Can be used to connect to other vendors**

Cisco proprietary HDLC is the default encapsulation type on a serial interface. HDLC has no authentication methods other than caller ID, which is the ability to identify the calling number.

Answer 6–5.
   b)   **Ethernet links will "bit swap" the MAC addresses of a Token Ring link.**
   c)   **Ethernet and Token Ring use opposite "bit ordering" in relation to each other.**

A MAC address on the Token Ring link will not appear the same on the Ethernet link due to "bit swapping".

Answer 6–6.
   e)   **Time To Live Field**

The Time to Live (TTL) field is not a configurable option in an IP extended ping. Refer to the following example:

```
Router_B#ping
%SYS-5-CONFIG_I: Configured from console by console
Protocol [ip]:
Target IP address: 2.2.2.2
Repeat count [5]:
Datagram size [100]:
Timeout in seconds [2]:
Extended commands [n]: y
Source address or interface: 1.1.1.1
Type of service [0]:
Set DF bit in IP header? [no]:
```

```
Validate reply data? [no]:
Data pattern [0xABCD]:
Loose, Strict, Record, Timestamp, Verbose[none]:
Sweep range of sizes [n]:
Type escape sequence to abort.
Sending 5, 100-byte ICMP Echos to 2.2.2.2, timeout is 2 seconds:
```

Answer 6–7.
   b) **Host 172.16.10.5 will not be able to ping 172.18.1.1.**
   c) **Host 172.16.10.5 has not attempted to ping 172.19.10.2.**
   d) **Host 172.16.10.5 will not be able to ping 172.19.10.2.**

Four matches have been recorded of 172.16.10.5 unsuccessfully attempting to ping 172.18.1.1.
Echo reply is not denied. As a result 172.19.10.2 would be able to ping 172.16.10.5.

Answer 6–8.
   c) **It associates an IP access list to the RW community string.**

This associates an IP access list to the RW community string. thereby allowing only those IP
hosts that are permitted in the list to have Read-Write capability to the router.

Answer 6–9.
   a) **It is very expensive in relation to other medias.**
   e) **It uses a token passing method similar to token ring.**
   f) **It operates at 100MB.**

FDDI is a token passing fiber based media that is very expensive to implement.

On Cisco Catalyst switches:
Translational bridging between ethernet and FDDI usually produces about 85,000 pps
throughput. Ethernet to Fast Ethernet switching usually produces numbers in the millions of
packets per second.

Answer 6–10.
   b) **The IPX node number of all the serial interfaces on Router_B**
   d) **The Token Ring 0 interface of Router_B**

IPX uses the MAC address of an interface as the node portion of the IPX address. Due to the
fact that there is no MAC address assigned to a Serial interface, Cisco has built in to their IOS
that the MAC address of a LAN interface will serve as the IPX node portion of all Serial
interfaces. Router_B is a 2521 and has only one LAN interface Token Ring 0.

Answer 6–11.
   e) **L5**

Answer 6–12.
   b) **16 asynchronous ports**
   c) **1 Ethernet interface**
   e) **2 synchronous serial interfaces**

6. Answers

The 16 asynchronous ports are provided through two 68-pin SCSI connectors. A breakout cable of various configurations can be used to access each individual line. In our LAB we use a CAB-OCTAL-ASYNC cable which has 8 RJ-45's.

Answer 6–13.
   d)   RIP

ABR is a router that is used to communicate within an autonomous system. EGP and BGP4 are protocols used to communicate from one AS to another.

Answer 6–14.
   b)   When the cable is not plugged into the router
   c)   When the cable is not plugged into the MAU

If there is no ring speed set on a Token Ring interface, you can not perform a no shut.

Example:

```
Router_B[Config]#int to0
Router_B[Config-if]#no ring
Interface must be shutdown to remove the ring speed.
```

If the cable is not plugged into the Token Ring interface or the MAU, the following condition will result:

Example:

```
Router_B#
%TR-3-WIREFAULT: Unit 0, wire fault: check the lobe cable MAU connection.
Router_B#
%LINEPROTO-5-UPDOWN: Line protocol on Interface TokenRing0, changed state to
   down
Router_B#^Z
Router_B#
%LINK-3-UPDOWN: Interface TokenRing0, changed state to down
Router_B#sh int to0
TokenRing0 is down, line protocol is down
Hardware is TMS380, address is 0007.7816.fe54 (bia 0007.7816.fe54)
Internet address is 172.16.10.10/24
 MTU 4464 bytes, BW 4000000 Kbit, DLY 630 usec, rely 255/255, load 1/255
Encapsulation SNAP, loopback not set, keepalive not set
ARP type: SNAP, ARP Timeout 04:00:00
Ring speed: 16 Mbps
Single ring node, Source Route Transparent Bridge capable
Source bridging enabled, srn 16 bn 1 trn 10 [Ring group)
 proxy explorers disabled, spanning explorer disabled, NetBIOS cache disable
```

Answer 6–15.
   a)   Logs messages to a syslog server named ari_server.

Answer 6–16.
   a) Area 3 stub

The "area 3 stub no-summary" command is used on an area border router (ABR).

In the following example Router_C is the ABR, and Router B is an internal router.

```
Router_C (config)#router ospf 100
Router_C (config-router)#area 2 stub no-summary
```

When an area is identified as a totally stubby area all inter area routes and external routes are hidden. The ABR will feed a default gateway into the stub area. Refer to the following example:

```
Router_B>sh ip route
Codes: C - connected, S - static, I - IGRP, R - RIP, M - mobile, B - BGP
   D - EIGRP, EX - EIGRP external, O - OSPF, IA - OSPF inter area
   N1 - OSPF NSSA external type 1, N2 - OSPF NSSA external type 2
   E1 - OSPF external type 1, E2 - OSPF external type 2, E - EGP
   i - IS-IS, L1 - IS-IS level-1, L2 - IS-IS level-2, * - candidate default
   U - per-user static route, o - ODR

Gateway of last resort is 172.16.2.1 to network 0.0.0.0

     172.16.0.0/24 is subnetted, 1 subnets
C        172.16.2.0 is directly connected, Serial0
O*IA 0.0.0.0/0 [110/65] via 172.16.2.1, 00:02:36, Serial0
```

Answer 6–17.
   b) Router_C would ping Workstation B with a 50% success rate

Classful routing protocols only use the set prefixes of 8 bits for a Class A, 16 bits for a Class B and 24 bits for a Class C address. IGRP is a classful routing protocol and does not communicate the subnet across different major networks as a result Router_C hears routing updates relating to network 10.0.0.0 from Router_A and Router_B. These updates are sent with the same metric. Therefore Router_C assumes that it can reach the 10 network by going out S0 or S1. When a ping is initiated from Router_C or Workstation C, Router_C will load balance the packets.

Refer to the routing table of Router_C below:

```
Gateway of last resort is not set

     172.16.0.0/24 is subnetted, 2 subnets
C        172.16.1.0 is directly connected, Serial1
C        172.16.2.0 is directly connected, Serial0
I     10.0.0.0/8 [100/8576] via 172.16.1.1, 00:00:09, Serial1
                 [100/8576] via 172.16.2.1, 00:00:19, Serial0
```

Two pings are shown below:

```
Router_C#ping 10.0.4.1
```

6. Answers

```
Type escape sequence to abort.
Sending 5, 100-byte ICMP Echos to 10.0.4.1, timeout is 2 seconds:
U!.!U
Success rate is 40 percent (2/5), round-trip min/avg/max = 4/4/4 ms
Router_C#ping 10.0.4.1

Type escape sequence to abort.
Sending 5, 100-byte ICMP Echos to 10.0.4.1, timeout is 2 seconds:
!U!.!
Success rate is 60 percent (3/5), round-trip min/avg/max = 4/4/4 ms
```

Ten ping probes were successful five times or 50%.

Answer 6–18.
   d) 110

The following example illustrates how to change the AD of EIGRP

```
Router_B(config)#router eigrp 16
Router_B(config-router)#distance eigrp 110 180
```

The 110 is the AD for internal EIGRP and the 180 is the AD for external EIGRP

Answer 6–19.
   a) The parallel paths must have the same hop count.

Answer 6–20.
   b) Would prevent any telnet sessions

The fact that the no password command was executed is enough to remove a password. The no password command does not have to match the set password. Following is a sample that will illustrate the results:

```
Router_B(config)#line vty 0 4
Router_B(config-line)#no password login
Router_B(config-line)#^Z
Router_B#sh run
%SYS-5-CONFIG_I: Configured from console by vty0 (192.168.5.2)
Building configuration...
Current configuration:
!
version 11.3
no service password-encryption
!
hostname Router_B

<output omitted>

line vty 0 4
 login
```

```
 !
 end
```

Notice the telnet password is no longer configured.

The following message will occur when a telnet session is requested.

```
 Password required, but none set

 [Connection to 192.168.5.1 closed by foreign host]
```

Answer 6–21.
  a) **All traffic destined for the network 172.16.0.0 will be dropped.**
  c) **Will save on CPU cycles when compared to access lists.**

If you want to filter all traffic destined for a particular location the null interface can save on CPU cycles when compared to access lists. The null interface is a virtual interface. Traffic destined for the null interface will be dropped.

Answer 6–22.
  d) **The RIF contains MAC address information.**

The RIF is made up of two fields the RD and the RC.

The RD contains Ring and Bridge identifiers.

The following is a sample of a RC:

15	14	13	12	11	10	9	8	7	6	5	4	3	2	1	0
0	0	0	0	1	0	0	0	0	0	1	1				
	0				8				3				0		

The Bits 15-13 (first three) bits describe type of packet:

0xx Specific Route
10x All rings, all routes
11x Spanning Route

The Bits 12-8 (next five) bits describe the total length of the RIF represented in bytes.

The total length of the RIF is 8 bytes.

Bit 7 describes the direction the RIF should be read.

0 - from left to right
1 - from right to left

Bits 6-4 is a code for the largest frame accepted on route to the destination.

Answer 6–23.
   f)   25

Refer to the IPX routing table:

```
Router_C>en
Router_C#sh ipx route
Codes: C - Connected primary network,
  c - Connected secondary network, S - Static,
  F - Floating static, L - Local (internal), W - IPXWAN, - RIP,
  E - EIGRP, N - NLSP, X - External, A - Aggregate - seconds,
  u - uses

5 Total IPX routes. Up to 1 parallel paths and 16 hops allowed.

No default route known.

C          AD (HDLC),         Se0
C          DAD (NOVELL-ETHER), Et0
R          BAD [25/02] via     AD.0007.7816.fe54,   58s, Se0
R          CAD [07/01] via     AD.0007.7816.fe54,   59s, Se0
R          EAD [25/02] via     AD.0007.7816.fe54,   59s, Se0

Each LAN network is 1 tick ( Router_A to Network BAD)
Each Serial interface defaults to 6 tick  (Router_C to Router_B)
IPXWAN measured 18 ticks ( Router_B to Router_A)
```

Answer 6–24.
   d)   A static route where the administrator has changed the Administrative Distance

Assume that the router knows the path of a particular destination because it was discovered through a routing protocol. If the administrator defines a static route to the same destination but raises the Administrative Distance (AD), this would prevent the static route from being used unless the dynamic path was lost.

Example:

```
Router(config)#ip route 172.16.10.0 255.255.255.0 192.12.1.6 170
```

In the above example the AD for this static route is 170.

Answer 6–25.
   d)   16

Answer 6–26.
   e)   nologin

The telnet password is set under the vty 0 4 line. By default a login is required to establish a virtual terminal session.

Answer 6–27.
 d) **ip classless**

Classless routing protocols allow the mask to be defined at any length. A Classfull routing protocol defines the mask at a length of 8, 16 or 24 bits. Examples of routing protocols that support CIDR are EIGRP, OSPF, RIPv2 and IS-IS.

Answer 6–28.
 d) **A station the is connected to both the primary and the secondary ring**

Answer 6–29.
 b) **Router_B**

Internal routers - routers that have all their interfaces in the same area
Backbone routers - routers that have at least one interface connected to area 0
Area Border Routers (ABR) - routers that have interfaces attached to multiple areas
Autonomous System Boundary Routers (ASBR) - routers that have interfaces connected to external network (non-OSPF environment or another AS).

Keep in mind that a router can be defined in more than one category. For instance, in our diagram Router_B is an ABR and a Backbone router.

Answer 6–30.
 d) **No bridging of IP could take place.**

By default, the router will always attempt to route IP. If there is no IP routing protocol enabled, no routing will take place. Unfortunately, IP bridging will not take place unless the command "no ip routing" is configured. Since bridging has been configured, IP will be bridged.

Answer 6–31.
 d) **Source Route Translational Bridge (SR/TLB)**

The function of a translational bridge is to take a frame from an Ethernet environment and to convert it for transmission to a Token Ring environment and visa-versa. Insertion and removal of a RIF is required to perform this function.

Answer 6–32.
 c) **800**

Answer 6–33.
 b) **Router_B currently will not send frames out Serial 1.**
 c) **Router_B currently will not allow frames to be received on Serial 1.**

Router_B could use Serial 1 in the future if the bridging topology changes. Router_B doesn't belong to Bridge Group 1. Interfaces Serial 0 and Serial 1 belong to Bridge Group 1. Other interfaces of Router_B could belong to another bridge group. And, if another bridge group were configured, it could use the IEEE Spanning Tree Protocol.

6. Answers

Chapter 6. CCIE

Answer 6–34.

    c) **Secret**

There are two enable passwords that are stored in the configuration file:

1. The non-encrypted for earlier versions of IOS that did not recognize the encrypted version.
2. The encrypted version that was introduced in a more recent version of the IOS.

If the above configuration was loaded into a router with a earlier version IOS, the enable secret would not be understood, and the enable password would be used.

Answer 6–35.

    c) **Default routes**
    d) **Intra area routes**

Totally Stubby is a Cisco proprietary configuration that hides external networks. The inter area routes will also be hidden from the internal routers, thus reducing the routing table. The routing table of a router in a totally stubby area would contain intra area routes and a default gateway that points to the way out of the totally stubby area.

Example:

```
Router_B (config)#router ospf 100
Router_B (config-router)#area 2 stub no-summary
Router_C>sh ip route
Codes: C - connected, S - static, I - IGRP, R - RIP, M - mobile, B - BGP, D -
   EIGRP, EX - EIGRP external, O - OSPF, IA - OSPF inter area, N1 - OSPF NSSA
   external type 1, N2 - OSPF NSSA external type 2, E1 - OSPF external type 1,
   E2 - OSPF external type 2, E - EGP, i - IS-IS, L1 - IS-IS level-1, L2 - IS-IS
   level-2, * - candidate default, U - per-user static route, o - ODR
Gateway of last resort is 172.16.2.1 to network 0.0.0.0
       172.16.0.0/24 is subnetted, 1 subnets
C      172.16.2.0 is directly connected, Serial0
O*IA   0.0.0.0/0 [110/65] via 172.16.2.1, 00:02:36, Serial0
```

Answer 6–36.

    e) **E0 & E1 of Router_C**

Refer to the following show command:

```
hostname Router_C
!
interface Ethernet0
 no ip address
 no ip route-cache
 no ip mroute-cache
 bridge-group 10
!
interface Ethernet1
 no ip address
 no ip route-cache
 no ip mroute-cache
 bridge-group 10
```

Answer 6–37.
b) RIP is a distance vector protocol, whereas OSPF is a link state protocol.

To distinguish between Distance Vector and Link State, students should answer the following three questions:

1) What does the routing protocol talk?
2) When does the routing protocol talk?
3) Who does the routing protocol talk?

Distance Vector talks the entire routing table to directly connected neighbors (less split horizon) periodically!

Link State talks the state of the link to all neighbors when the state of the link changes.

What protocol are you using if your mother calls you every night to let you know that everyone in the family is alive?

Suppose you make an agreement with your mother to call you just when there is a death in the family?

Suppose Mom dies?
That's what hello packets are used for!

Answer 6–38.
c) The BVI

It is also true that the address is the MAC of E0, but BVI is the best answer. Refer to the following capture:

```
⊟ ▣ Ethernet Version II
    ▢ Address: 00-80-C7-CA-0A-8A --->00-60-09-C3-DF-60
    ▢ Ethernet II Protocol Type: IP
⊟ ▾ Internet Protocol
    ▢ Version(MSB 4 bits): 4
    ▢ Header length(LSB 4 bits): 5 (32-bit word)
  ⊞ ▢ Service type: Precd=Routine,Delay=Normal,Thrput=Normal,Reli=Normal
    ▢ Total length: 60 (Octets)
    ▢ Fragment ID: 6371
  ⊞ ▢ Flags: May be fragmented,Last fragment,Offset=0 (0x00)
    ▢ Time to live: 32 seconds/hops
    ▢ IP protocol type: ICMP (0x01)
    ▢ Checksum: 0x15B8
    ▢ IP address 172.16.10.5 ->172.16.10.1
    ▢ No option
⊟ ▣ IP Internet Control Message Protocol
    ▣ Type: Echo Request
```

Answer 6–39.
b) 0630.0191.00a0
d) 0630.00a1.0230

DLSw terminates the RIF. The answers are the RIF as they would be represented on each side.

Answer 6–40.
    d) **This command allows the IOS to forward to the best supernet route.**

Answer 6–41.
    c) **BVI**

Answer 6–42.
    e) **None of the above**

Transparent Bridging and a RIF? -- I don't think so!

Answer 6–43.
    c) **Host B**

The destination is always responsible for reassembly of fragmented IP packets.

Answer 6–44.
    a) **The virtual ring numbers can be different on both bridges.**
    e) **The Route Control (RC) field will change based on the direction the frame travels.**

Since DLSw terminates the RIF it is of no consequence that the virtual ring numbers of the bridges are different.

Answer 6–45.
    c) **This causes the router to enter the ROM monitor mode.**
    f) **The configuration file will be read from NVRAM.**
    h) **The baud rate will be set at 9600.**

```
Router_C(config)#config-reg 0x2100
Router_C#reload
Proceed with reload? [confirm]
```

Results of the commands above:

```
%SYS-5-RELOAD: Reload requested
System Bootstrap, Version 5.2(8a), RELEASE SOFTWARE
Copyright (c) 1986-1995 by cisco Systems
2500 processor with 16384 Kbytes of main memory
>
```

The greater than prompt above represents the ROM monitor mode.

```
>e/s2000002
```

The previous command examines the location where the configuration register is stored.

It OUTPUTs the value of the register:

```
2000002: 2100

>o/r 0x2102
```

The above command changes the configuration register.

```
>i
```

The previous command re-initializes the router.

The router will forward a packet based upon the destination Layer 3 address. The MAC addresses will change as the packet is forwarded to reflect the next Network Interface Card. The Layer 3 addresses will never change.

```
Router_C>sh int e1
Ethernet1 is up, line protocol is up
  Hardware is Lance, address is 0060.09c3.df61 (bia 0060.09c3.df61)
  Internet address is 10.1.16.1/24
```

The following is a protocol analyzer capture of a ping to the ip address of 172.16.1.2

```
Ethernet Version II
  Address: 00-80-C7-CA-0A-8A ---->00-60-09-C3-DF-61
  Ethernet II Protocol Type: IP
Internet Protocol
  Version(MSB 4 bits): 4
  Header length(LSB 4 bits): 5 (32-bit word)
  Service type: Precd=Routine,Delay=Normal,Thrput=Normal,Reli=Normal
  Total length: 60 (Octets)
  Fragment ID: 11008
  Flags: May be fragmented,Last fragment,Offset=0 (0x00)
  Time to live: 32 seconds/hops
  IP protocol type: ICMP (0x01)
  Checksum: 0xA8A9
  IP address 10.1.16.5 ->172.16.1.2
  No option
IP Internet Control Message Protocol
  Type: Echo Request
```

Notice in the screen capture above that the destination MAC address is the e1 interface of Router _C but the destination IP address is that of the ultimate destination.

Answer 6–46.
- c) **Command Group III above**
- d) **Command Group IV above**

III. Command Group III:

```
config terminal
int e0
ip address 172.16.10.1 255.255.255.0
ip address 192.16.10.1 255.255.255.0 secondary
```

IV. Command Group IV:

```
config terminal
int e0
ip address 192.16.10.1 255.255.255.0 secondary
ip address 172.16.10.1 255.255.255.0
```

Answer 6–47.
   a) Only 172.16.15.4 would be able to telnet to Router_B.

Answer 6–48.
   a) MAC addresses never change.

In a bridged environment MAC addresses are never changed. The main function of the Source Route Bridge (SRB) is to add the bridge identifier to the RIF. The SRB is the "dumbest" device in a SRB environment.

Answer 6–49.
   d) The metric is maintained because IGRP and EIGRP use the same metric.

Answer 6–50.
   b) Workstation A could successfully ping the ethernet interface of Router_B.
   d) Workstation A could successfully ping Workstation B.

A classless routing protocol can set the prefix at any length. OSPF is a classless routing protocol and does communicate the subnet across different major networks therefore Router_A can distinguish between subnets 10.0.1.0 and 10.0.4.0. Below is the routing table of Router_A

```
     172.16.0.0/24 is subnetted, 2 subnets
C        172.16.1.0 is directly connected, Serial0/0
O        172.16.2.0 [110/128] via 172.16.1.2, 00:01:06, Serial0/0
     10.0.0.0/24 is subnetted, 2 subnets
C        10.0.1.0 is directly connected, Ethernet0/0
10.0.4.0 [110/138] via 172.16.1.2, 00:01:06, Serial0/0
Any packet with a destination address of 10.0.4.x will be sent out the
  Serial0/0 interface.
```

Answer 6–51.
   b) Allows multiple data frames and a single token

Only one token is ever permitted to be on a ring at one time. Early token release will allow more than one data frame.

Answer 6–52.

a) **MAC addresses never change.**

A repeater is an active device that allows expansion by linking two segments together. The repeater amplifies and regenerates the signal. A repeater has nothing to do with addressing.

Answer 6–53.

b) **MAC of Host B**

Answer 6–54.

g) **Can not be determined.**

The password required to view the configuration file is by default the enable secret. The enable secret is, of course, encrypted.

Answer 6–55.

b) **Bandwidth, Delay Load, Reliability, MTU and Hop count**

IGRP does not use Hop count for the metric, but it still keeps track of it for maximum hop count purposes.

Refer to the capture below:

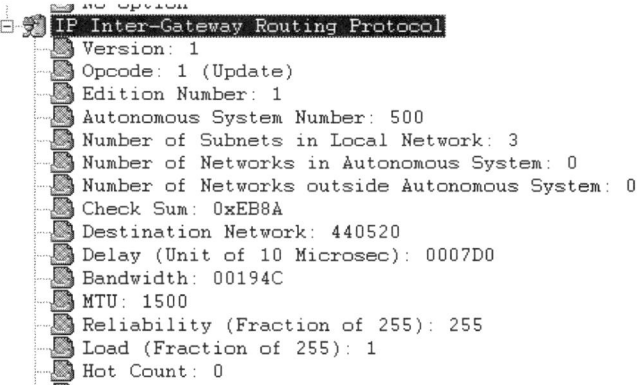

Answer 6–56.

c) **NLSP**

IPX RIP and IPX EIGRP would require that a IPX network number be used on the serial links. NLSP requires that there NOT be an IPX network number, IPX unnumbered.

Answer 6–57.

e) **There is no BIA of the BVI.**

The BVI does not have a BIA, but it does have a MAC.

Refer to the following show command:

```
Router_C# sh int bvi10
BVI10 is up, line protocol is up
Hardware is BVI, address is 0060.09c3.df60 (bia 0000.0000.0000)
Internet address is 172.16.10.1/24
MTU 1500 bytes, BW 10000 Kbit, DLY 5000 usec, rely 255/255, load 1/255
Encapsulation ARPA, loopback not set, keepalive set (10 sec)
 ARP type: ARPA, ARP Timeout 04:00:00
Last input never, output never, output hang never
Last clearing of "show interface" counters never
Queueing strategy: fifo
Output queue 0/0, 0 drops; input queue 0/75, 0 drops
5 minute input rate 0 bits/sec, 0 packets/sec
5 minute output rate 0 bits/sec, 0 packets/sec
45 packets input, 5848 bytes, 0 no buffer
Received 0 broadcasts, 0 runts, 0 giants, 0 throttles
 0 input errors, 0 CRC, 0 frame, 0 overrun, 0 ignored, 0 abort
 212 packets output, 456 bytes, 0 underruns
 0 output errors, 0 collisions, 0 interface resets
 0 output buffer failures, 0 output buffers swapped out
```

Answer 6–58.
    a) Integrated Routing and Bridging (IRB)

Concurrent Routing and Bridging (CRB) is coming in on a bridged interface and leaving on a bridge interface. Coming in on a routed interface and leaving on a routed interface.

Integrated Routing and Bridging is a feature that was introduced in Version 11.2. (Because IRB may be in the two-day practical we will provide a Lab Scenario using IRB in a future issue.)

Answer 6–59.
    c) 0830.019b.01ee.0230

The RIF is represented in HEX. If the ring and bridge numbers are given to you in decimal you will have to convert. Ring numbers are represented by 3 HEX digits. Bridge numbers are represented by 1 HEX digit. A RIF will always end with Bridge 0. The first four HEX digits are called the Routing Control field. The RC field describes type of packet, length of RIF and direction. The 8 in the RC field describes a RIF with a total length of 8 bytes.

Answer 6–60.
    d) Both the source and destination MAC address will change as the frame traverses the network

The router will forward a packet based upon the destination Layer 3 address. The MAC addresses will change as the packet is forwarded to reflect the next Network Interface Card. The Layer 3 addresses will never change.

```
Router_C>sh int e1
Ethernet1 is up, line protocol is up
  Hardware is Lance, address is 0060.09c3.df61 (bia 0060.09c3.df61)
    Internet address is 10.1.16.1/24
```

The following is a protocol analyzer capture of a ping to the ip address of 172.16.1.2

```
Ethernet Version II
  Address: 00-80-C7-CA-0A-8A ---->00-60-09-C3-DF-61
  Ethernet II Protocol Type: IP
Internet Protocol
  Version(MSB 4 bits): 4
  Header length(LSB 4 bits): 5 (32-bit word)
  Service type: Precd=Routine,Delay=Normal,Thrput=Normal,Reli=Normal
  Total length: 60 (Octets)
  Fragment ID: 11008
  Flags: May be fragmented,Last fragment,Offset=0 (0x00)
  Time to live: 32 seconds/hops
  IP protocol type: ICMP (0x01)
  Checksum: 0xA8A9
  IP address 10.1.16.5 ->172.16.1.2
  No option
IP Internet Control Message Protocol
  Type: Echo Request
```

Notice in the screen capture above that the destination MAC address is the e1 interface of Router _C but the destination IP address is that of the ultimate destination.

Answer 6–61.
   c) **Would deny igrp updates from any source**

The inverse mask is set to all 0s, therefore the address of 255.255.255.255 will be matched. This address is a broadcast address and, of course, no host would have that address. All routing updates are sent as a broadcast.

Answer 6–62.
   a) **Router_A**
   b) **Router_B**
   c) **Router_C**

Stub areas will not "see" external networks, thereby reducing the size of their routing table. The ABRs and the internal routers must carry the configuration command area x stub where x is the area to be defined as stub.

Example:

```
Router_C (config)#router ospf 100
Router_C (config-router)#area 2
```

Answer 6–63.
   e) **Command Group V above**

```
router(config)#router ospf 69
router(config-router)#area 0 range 172.16.24.0 255.255.248.0
router(config-router)#area 0 range 172.16.32.0 255.255.224.0
```

6. Answers

There is no way we can manipulate the first two octets. These 16 bits uniquely describe our network. Let's examine the third octet below. A mask of 248 means DO NOT change the bit pattern of the most significant 5 bits. This implies we can do what we want with the remaining 3 bits. The chart below lists all the possibilities, also included is the 36 address to show how the bit pattern will change.

THIRD OCTET

	128	64	32	16	8	4	2	1
248	1	1	1	1	1	0	0	0
24	0	0	0	1	1	0	0	0
25	0	0	0	1	1	0	0	1
26	0	0	0	1	1	0	1	0
27	0	0	0	1	1	0	1	1
28	0	0	0	1	1	1	0	0
29	0	0	0	1	1	1	0	1
30	0	0	0	1	1	1	1	0
31	0	0	0	1	1	1	1	1
32	0	0	1	0	0	0	0	0

The command area 0 range 172.16.24.0 255.255.248.0 will include the networks 24-31.

The command area 0 range 172.16.32.0 255.255.224.0 will include the networks 32-63.

THIRD OCTET

	128	64	32	16	8	4	2	1
224	1	1	1	0	0	0	0	0
32	0	0	1	0	0	0	0	0
40	0	0	1	0	1	0	0	0
48	0	0	1	1	0	0	0	0
56	0	0	1	1	1	0	0	0
64	0	1	0	0	0	0	0	0

Notice again how we have maintained the bit pattern of the first 3 bits up to a value of 64.

Answer 6–64.
   c) **103**

The network number can be any value within the cable-range. The node number (243) is dynamically chosen. The node number can range from 1 to 252.

Answer 6–65.
   d) **IPX RIP & EIGRP**

By default IPX RIP will run when the ipx routing command is executed. Therefore you must use the no network BAD command to turn off IPX RIP.

The following is output from debug ipx routing:

```
Router_C#debug IPX routing activity
IPX routing debugging is on
Router_C#debug IPX routing events
IPX routing events debugging is on
Router_C#
IPXRIP: positing full update to DAD.ffff.ffff.ffff via Ethernet0 (broadcast)
IPXRIP: src=DAD.0060.09c3.df60, dst=DAD.ffff.ffff.ffff, packet sent
    network BAD, hops 1,  delay 2
IPXRIP: positing full update to BAD.ffff.ffff.ffff via Ethernet1 (broadcast)
IPXRIP: src=BAD.0060.09c3.df61, dst=BAD.ffff.ffff.ffff, packet sent
    network DAD, hops 1,  delay 2
```

Answer 6–66.
   a) **DLSw will provide a reliable transport.**
   b) **DLSw will not terminate the data-link control.**

Answer 6–67.
   e) **none of the above**

This is a router command. The proper form of this command is "passive-interface serial 0" or, in the case of a modular router such as the 3620, we must include the slot number as shown below.

```
Router_A#config t
Enter configuration commands, one per line.  End with CNTL/Z.
Router_A(config)#router rip
Router_A(config-router)#passive serial 0/0
Router_A(config-router)#exit
Router_A(config)#
```

The effect of this command is that the interface will listen but not speak out the assigned interface. This command is commonly used when you are using more than one routing protocol for the same network.

Answer 6–68.
   b) **Keepalives are unnecessary due to a built-in reliability feature of Token Ring, and therefore can be disabled.**
   c) **Keepalive failure usually means that the interface has already failed.**
   d) **Failure detection is immediate.**
   e) **When Token Ring protocol failure occurs, the interface will go into transition state.**

6. Answers

Answer 6–69.
   c)   **C1**

Router_B learns of C1 over serial 0.

Answer 6–70.
   b)   **B1**

Router_B learns of A1 over Serial 1.

Answer 6–71.
   c)   **No**

Due to the fact that Router_C is directly connected to Network 172.16.0.0, it will send all packets destined for that major network address out its Ethernet 0 interface.

Keep in mind we are dealing with a classful routing protocol. Classful routing protocols do not communicate subnets across different major networks.

```
Router_C#ping 172.16.11.1

Type escape sequence to abort.
Sending 5, 100-byte ICMP Echos to 172.16.11.1, timeout is 2 seconds:
.....
Success rate is 0 percent (0/5)
```

Answer 6–72.
   a)   **Configuration 1 above**

Answer 6–73.
   b)   **Virtual Ring numbers must be the same on both bridges.**
   c)   **When Host A communicates to Host B, the RIF will contain the entire path.**
   e)   **The Route Control (RC) field will change based on the direction the frame travels.**

RSRB is not scalable because the entire path is maintained in the RIF and there is a limitation of 7 bridges. Because the RIF is maintained end-to-end, the virtual ring numbers of both bridges must match.

One of the advantages of DLSw is that the RIF is terminated. DLSw is scalable because of this fact.

One of the bits of the RC is direction which tells the bridge in what direction the RIF should be read. The Route Descriptor field does not change.

Answer 6–74.
   e)   **Media Access Method**

Answer 6–75.
   a)   **Router_A**
   c)   **Router_C**

Internal routers - routers that have all their interfaces in the same area
Backbone routers - routers that have at least one interface connected to area 0
Area Border Routers (ABR) - routers that have interfaces attached to multiple areas
Autonomous System Boundary Routers (ASBR) - routers that have interfaces connected to
external network (non-OSPF environment or another AS).

Keep in mind that a router can be defined in more than one category. For instance, in our
diagram Router_B is an ABR and a Backbone router.

Answer 6–76.
   c)   **multiring ip**

Answer 6–77.
   e)   **All of the above.**

Answer 6–78.
   c)   **Would be the same as E0/0**

There is no MAC address assigned to a serial interface. Cisco's solution is to use the MAC
address of the E0/0 interface. This does not present a problem because the network number
would be different for each interface.

Some show commands are included here for clarity:

```
Router_A#show int e0/0
Ethernet0/0 is up, line protocol is up
  Hardware is AmdP2, address is 0010.7b15.bd41 (bia 0010.7b15.bd41)
  Internet address is 10.1.1.1/24

Router_A#sh ipx int
Ethernet0/0 is up, line protocol is up
  IPX address is DAD.0010.7b15.bd41, NOVELL-ETHER [up]
  Delay of this IPX network, in ticks is 1 throughput 0 link delay 0
  IPXWAN processing not enabled on this interface.
  IPX SAP update interval is 60 seconds
  IPX type 20 propagation packet forwarding is disabled
  Incoming access list is not set
  Outgoing access list is not set
  IPX helper access list is not set

     [output omited]

Serial0/0 is down, line protocol is down
  IPX address is BAD.0010.7b15.bd41 [up]
  Delay of this IPX network, in ticks is 6 throughput 0 link delay 0
  IPXWAN processing not enabled on this interface.
```

6. Answers

Answer 6–79.
   e)   **There is no automatic redistribution of IGRP and EIGRP between different AS.**

Answer 6–80.
   d)   **Router_D**

Internal routers - routers that have all their interfaces in the same area
Backbone routers - routers that have at least one interface connected to area 0
Area Border Routers (ABR) - routers that have interfaces attached to multiple areas
Autonomous System Boundary Routers (ASBR - routers that have interfaces connected to external network (non-OSPF environment or another AS).

Keep in mind that a router can be defined in more than one category. For instance, in our diagram Router_B is an ABR and a Backbone router.

Answer 6–81.
   b)   **EIGRP**
   d)   **OSPF**
   e)   **IP RIPv2**

The above topology is an example of discontiguous addressing. Classless routing protocols are the only routing protocols that would support such a topology. A classless routing protocol has the ability to advertise subnets.

Answer 6–82.
   a)   **The Cisco IOS will be read from flash if a flash exists.**
   g)   **The configuration file will NOT be read from NVRAM.**
   h)   **The baud rate will be set at 9600.**

The results of a configuration register of 0x2142

At any point you may enter a question mark "?" for help.
Use ctrl-c to abort configuration dialog at any prompt.
Default settings are in square brackets "[ ]."
Would you like to enter the initial configuration dialog? [yes]:

Even though we have saved the configuration file above when the value of bit 6 is 1, the router upon a reload will ignore the configuration file stored in NVRAM.

You have not lost the configuration file; it has just been bypassed.

The router will forward a packet based upon the destination Layer 3 address. The MAC addresses will change as the packet is forwarded to reflect the next Network Interface Card. The Layer 3 addresses will never change.

```
Router_C>sh int e1
Ethernet1 is up, line protocol is up
  Hardware is Lance, address is 0060.09c3.df61 (bia 0060.09c3.df61)
  Internet address is 10.1.16.1/24
```

The following is a protocol analyzer capture of a ping to the ip address of 172.16.1.2:

```
Ethernet Version II
   Address: 00-80-C7-CA-0A-8A --->00-60-09-C3-DF-61
   Ethernet II Protocol Type: IP
Internet Protocol
   Version(MSB 4 bits): 4
   Header length(LSB 4 bits): 5 (32-bit word)
   Service type: Precd=Routine,Delay=Normal,Thrput=Normal,Reli=Normal
   Total length: 60 (Octets)
   Fragment ID: 11008
   Flags: May be fragmented,Last fragment,Offset=0 (0x00)
   Time to live: 32 seconds/hops
   IP protocol type: ICMP (0x01)
   Checksum: 0xA8A9
   IP address 10.1.16.5 ->172.16.1.2
   No option
IP Internet Control Message Protocol
   Type: Echo Request
```

Notice in the screen capture above that the destination MAC address is the e1 interface of Router _C but the destination IP address is that of the ultimate destination.

Answer 6–83.
   e)   These protocols have no explicit network address.

Routing requires a layer 3 address. IP, IPX, and Appletalk all have a layer 3 or logical address, therefore they can be routed.

Answer 6–84.
   b)   2

The left and the right zones are configured.

Answer 6–85.
   b)   Enabling keepalives can cause unnecessary traffic.
   c)   Failure detection time is immediate.
   e)   The use of an optical bypass switch can prevent a ring from wrapping when a DAS fails.

If the DAS goes down, the optical bypass switch will pass light through itself by using a set of internal mirrors. Thus, the ring is maintained and there is no need for wrapping. Keep in mind that FDDI provides fault tolerance for a single failure. If two failures occur, the ring will segment into multiple rings that can not communicate with each other. Hence the optical bypass will keep the ring from wrapping, and therefore more than one failure could occur, and the ring will remain up.

Answer 6–86.
   b)   CAD

The routing table of Router_B shows that it learned about four different networks. Two of these networks are C1 and A1, which are just the internal networks of Router_C and Router_A

respectively. The other two networks are FAD and CAD. Notice that there are two best ways to get to network CAD over serial 0 or serial 1. Since IPX RIP does not load balance unless the tick count is identical, we can only assume the link is placed between Router_C and Router_A.

Answer 6–87.
　e)　**None of the above**

Answer 6–88.
　e)　**All of the above.**

Ethernet uses Carrier Sense Multiple Access with Collision Detection that basically says that if no one is transmitting on the wire, then transmit; however, if someone is transmitting, then wait. What if two stations both listen on the wire and see that no one is transmitting, and both start to transmit at the same time? This is called a collision. Ethernet network interface cards have built-in collision detection that allows them to realize they have produced a collision and recover from it. This is done by first generating a jamming signal, which tells all other stations on the wire that there has been a collision and that they should wait to transmit. After the jam signal is transmitted both stations set a random timer. Whichever stations' timer expires first will be the first station to transmit.

Ethernet has improved over the years. The original specifications called for a bandwidth of 2MB but was quickly replaced with a second version conveniently called Ethernet Version 2 that had a bandwidth of 10MB. In the early nineties it was decided that 10MB was not enough and that 100MB would be necessary. This produced Fast Ethernet, adopted by the IEEE and assigned the 802.3u designation number. It was also recently upgraded to 1GB and is referred to as Gigabit Ethernet.

Answer 6–89.
　e)　**There is no default tick count.**

IPXWAN was developed by Novell to standardize how IPX treats serial links. The TICK count will be negotiated between the IPXWAN interfaces. There is no default. There is a default TICK count of 6 if IPXWAN is NOT used.

Answer 6–90.
　d)　**ip nat outside**

Please refer to the NAT Translation Lab Scenario for complete details.

Answer 6–91.
　e)　**All of the above.**

Answer 6–92.
　e)　**Used by Cisco's Enhanced IGRP**

Answer 6–93.
　a)　**X.121 address**

The first four digits of the International Data Number (IDN) are called the Data Network Identification Code (DNIC). The National Terminal Number (NTN) contains up to 10 digits.

Answer 6–94.
   e)   **A link between Router_A and Router_C**

The routing table of Router_B shows that it learned about four different networks. Two of these networks are C1 and A1, which are just the internal networks of Router_C and Router_A respectively. The other two networks are FAD and CAD. Notice that there are two best ways to get to network CAD over serial 0 or serial 1. Since IPX RIP does not load balance unless the tick count is identical, we can only assume the link is placed between Router_C and Router_A.

Answer 6–95.
   c)   **The cost of a 10 meg ethernet link will always be 100.**

By default the cost of a path is 1000Mbps/data rate

Answer 6–96.
   e)   **None of the above**

The Time to Live (TTL) field is manipulated such that an ICMP TTL exceeded message is generated on each router from the source to the destination. The trace application records the source IP address of each of the ICMP TTL exceeded messages to trace the path that an IP packet might take through the internetwork.

Answer 6–97.
   e)   **Echo Request: 8, Echo Reply: 0**

8 is the type number for an Echo Request, and 0 is the type number for an Echo Reply.

Some common ICMP type numbers...

ICMP Message Type	Type Field
Echo Reply	0
Echo Request	8
Destination Unreachable	3
Redirect	5
Time Exceeded for a Datagram	11

Answer 6–98.
   a)   **0830.0191.00a1.0230**

Keep in mind the RIF is represented in HEX. The virtual ring value used is 10 or 0xa.

Answer 6–99.
   e)   **Workstation A could not successfully ping Workstation B.**

6. Answers

Since Router_A is directly connected to network 10.0.0.0. Router_A will ignore the updates received from Router_C pertaining to 10.0.0.0 because the metric is higher. Classful routing protocols only use the set prefixes of 8 bits for a Class A, 16 bits for a Class B and 24 bits for a Class C address. IGRP is a classful routing protocol and does not communicate the subnet across different major networks. As a result there is no way Router_A can distinguish between the subnets 10.0.1.0 and 10.0.4.0.

When Workstation A pings the 10 address of Workstation B or Router_B, the ICMP echo request will remain on the subnet 10.0.1.0.

Answer 6–100.
    b) A linear transmission media
    d) All nodes are directly attached to the media.

Answer 6–101.
    c) The source address greater than 153.19.100.129 would be permitted.

The 0.0.255.127 portion of this configuration line is the wild card mask.

A 0 means to match the corresponding bit of the address.
A 1 means "I don't care" what the value is.

The first two octets must match the address 153.19.
The third octet can have any value.
The fourth octet must be greater than 128.

Let's examine the fourth octet.

128	64	32	16	8	4	2	1	Value
1	0	0	0	0	0	0	0	128
0	1	1	1	1	1	1	1	127

The only bit that has to match is the 128 bit, therefore the remaining bits may have any value, which gives us the range of 128-255.

Answer 6–102.
    c) When an IP host uses an IP address that belongs to another device on purpose.

IP spoofing is where an IP host, usually a hacker, will emulate another IP Host to get around a firewall restriction.

Answer 6–103.
    e) None of the above

SRB does not block ports like the Spanning Tree algorithm of Transparent Bridging (TB). Multiple paths to the destination can exist in a SRB environment.

Answer 6–104.
a) 019b.00ae.0230

The RD does not change when the frame flows in the opposite direction. The only bit that changes is the direction bit. The direction bit is part of the Route Control Field (RC).

Answer 6–105.
a) IRB

Integrated Routing and Bridging is a Cisco IOS 11.2 feature

Answer 6–106.
e) All of the above.

Answer 6–107.
e) Encapsulating bridge.

Answer 6–108.
a) Layer 3 addresses never change.

The router will forward a packet based upon the destination Layer 3 address. The MAC addresses will change as the packet is forwarded to reflect the next Network Interface Card. The Layer 3 addresses will never change.

```
Router_C>sh int e1
Ethernet1 is up, line protocol is up
   Hardware is Lance, address is 0060.09c3.df61 (bia 0060.09c3.df61)
   Internet address is 10.1.16.1/24
```

The following is a protocol analyzer capture of a ping to the ip address of 172.16.1.2:

```
Ethernet Version II
 Address: 00-80-C7-CA-0A-8A --->00-60-09-C3-DF-61
 Ethernet II Protocol Type: IP
Internet Protocol
 Version(MSB 4 bits): 4
 Header length(LSB 4 bits): 5 (32-bit word)
 Service type: Precd=Routine,Delay=Normal,Thrput=Normal,Reli=Normal
 Total length: 60 (Octets)
 Fragment ID: 11008
 Flags: May be fragmented,Last fragment,Offset=0 (0x00)
 Time to live: 32 seconds/hops
 IP protocol type: ICMP (0x01)
 Checksum: 0xA8A9
 IP address 10.1.16.5 ->172.16.1.2
 No option
IP Internet Control Message Protocol
 Type: Echo Request
```

Notice in the screen capture above that the destination MAC address is the e1 interface of Router _C but the destination IP address is that of the ultimate destination.

6. Answers

Answer 6–109.
   b)   Router A

X.25 uses LAPB as the layer 2 protocol. LAPB is connection oriented and will retransmit. Therefore Router A will do the retransmission. X.25 was developed when analog lines were predominate. Analog lines had a reliability rate of approximately 77%. With lines that were so unreliable, X.25 did all the retransmission.

Answer 6–110.
   b)   CRB

Concurrent Routing and Bridging (CRB) is an older IOS feature.

Answer 6–111.
   c)   Explorer type
   d)   Length of RIF
   e)   Direction in which the RIF should be read
   f)   Largest frame size

The first 2 bytes of a RIF is the Route Control field.

Answer 6–112.
   c)   24

The appletalk address is made up of a network portion (cable range) and a host potion. The network portion contains 16 bits. The host portion contains 8 bits. When an appletalk host comes up it will dynamically acquire an address between 1-252.

Answer 6–113.
   b)   gre

GRE IP is the default tunnel encapsulation method.

```
Router_C(config-if)#tunnel mode ?
  aurp    AURP TunnelTalk AppleTalk encapsulation
  cayman  Cayman TunnelTalk AppleTalk encapsulation
  dvmrp   DVMRP multicast tunnel
  eon     EON compatible CLNS tunnel
  gre     generic route encapsulation protocol
  ipip    IP over IP encapsulation
  iptalk  Apple IPTalk encapsulation
  nos     IP over IP encapsulation (KA9Q/NOS compatible)

show int tu0
Tunnel0 is up, line protocol is up
  Hardware is Tunnel
  MTU 1500 bytes, BW 9 Kbit, DLY 500000 usec, rely 255/255, load 1/255
  Encapsulation TUNNEL, loopback not set, keepalive set (10 sec)
  Tunnel source 172.16.10.1 (Serial0/0), destination 172.16.10.2
  Tunnel protocol/transport GRE/IP, key disabled, sequencing disabled
  Checksumming of packets disabled,  fast tunneling enabled
```

Answer 6–114.
a) **It checks the header only.**

ICMP, IGMP, UDP and TCP all have a checksum of their own. The algorithm used is the same as the IP header checksum.

Answer 6–115.
c) **It would be used to select EIGRP as the routing protocol.**
e) **It would be used to select AURP as the routing protocol.**

Answer 6–116.
b) **Router_B**

Totally Stubby is a Cisco proprietary configuration that hides external networks. The inter area routes will also be hidden from the internal routers, thus reducing the routing table. The recommendation is to create Totally Stubby areas whenever possible. The routing table of a router in a totally stubby area would contain intra area routes and a default gateway that points to the way out of the totally stubby area.

Example:

```
Router_B (config)#router ospf 100
Router_B (config-router)#area 2 stub no-summary
Router_C>sh ip route
Codes: C - connected, S - static, I - IGRP, R - RIP, M - mobile, B - BGP, D -
   EIGRP, EX - EIGRP external, O - OSPF, IA - OSPF inter area N1 - OSPF NSSA
   external type 1, N2 - OSPF NSSA external type 2, E1 - OSPF external type 1,
   E2 - OSPF external type 2, E - EGP, i - IS-IS, L1 - IS-IS level-1, L2 - IS-IS
   level-2, * - candidate default, U - per-user static route, o - ODR
Gateway of last resort is 172.16.2.1 to network 0.0.0.0
       172.16.0.0/24 is subnetted, 1 subnets
C      172.16.2.0 is directly connected, Serial0
O*IA   0.0.0.0/0 [110/65] via 172.16.2.1, 00:02:36, Serial0
```

Answer 6–117.
e) **There is no IPX network number configured on Serial 0.**

If there was an IPX network number configured on the serial links, the routing table would reflect that fact.

Refer to the example below:

```
Router_C>sh ipx route
Codes: C - Connected primary network,
   c - Connected secondary network, S - Static,
   F - Floating static, L - Local (internal), W - IPXWAN
   R - RIP, E - EIGRP, N - NLSP, X - External, A - Aggregate
   s - seconds, u - uses
```

6. Answers

```
5 Total IPX routes. Up to 1 parallel paths and 16 hops allowed.

No default route known.

L       C1 is the internal network
C       CAD (NOVELL-ETHER),   Et0
C       FAD (NOVELL-ETHER),   Et1
R       A1 [02/01] via        CAD.0010.7b15.bd41,    22s, Et0
R       B1 [07/01] via         0.0000.00b1.0000,     18s, Se0
```

Answer 6–118.
c)   ip route 0.0.0.0 0.0.0.0 150.100.10.72

By entering the ip route command as shown in choice c we get the following result. The route appears as the gateway of last resort and as a static route.

```
ISPsRouter#sh ip route
Codes: C - connected, S - static, I - IGRP, R - RIP, M - mobile, B - BGP
       D - EIGRP, EX - EIGRP external, O - OSPF, IA - OSPF inter area
       N1 - OSPF NSSA external type 1, N2 - OSPF NSSA external type 2
       E1 - OSPF external type 1, E2 - OSPF external type 2, E - EGP
       i - IS-IS, L1 - IS-IS level-1, L2 - IS-IS level-2, * - candidate default
       U - per-user static route, o - ODR

Gateway of last resort is 150.100.10.72 to network 0.0.0.0

S    200.200.200.0/24 [1/0] via 150.100.10.72
     150.100.0.0/24 is subnetted, 1 subnets
C       150.100.10.0 is directly connected, Serial1
S*   0.0.0.0/0 [1/0] via 150.100.10.72
```

Answer 6–119.
d)   Allows up to 253 nodes

Both Phase 1 and Phase 2 allowed for discontinuous zones and dynamic address resolution Phase 1 allowed no more than 127 hosts and 127 servers. Phase 1 also allowed only a single network number per wire.

Phase 2 extended addressing, in addition to allowing up to 253 nodes with no restriction as to hosts and servers, allows for a range of network numbers per wire. Refer to the following example:

```
Router_C(config-if)#appletalk cable-range 100-150

Router_C#sh app int e0
Ethernet0 is up, line protocol is up
  AppleTalk cable range is 100-150
  AppleTalk address is 128.20, Valid
  AppleTalk zone is "ccieprep"
  AppleTalk port configuration provided by 124.249
  AppleTalk discovery mode is enabled
  AppleTalk address gleaning is disabled
  AppleTalk route cache is enabled
```

Answer 6–120.
   e) **There is no IPX network number configured on Serial 0.**

If there was an IPX network number configured on the serial links, the routing table would reflect that fact.

Refer to the example below:

```
Router_C>sh ipx route
Codes: C - Connected primary network,
  c - Connected secondary network, S - Static,
  F - Floating static, L - Local (internal), W - IPXWAN
  R - RIP, E - EIGRP, N - NLSP, X - External, A - Aggregate
  s - seconds, u - uses

5 Total IPX routes. Up to 1 parallel paths and 16 hops allowed.

No default route known.

L       C1 is the internal network
C       CAD (NOVELL-ETHER),   Et0
C       FAD (NOVELL-ETHER),   Et1
R       A1 [02/01] via        CAD.0010.7b15.bd41,   22s, Et0
R       B1 [07/01] via         0.0000.00b1.0000,   18s, Se0
```

Answer 6–121.
   b) **Router A**

When Host A communicates to Host B the frame will first be sent to the ethernet interface of router A. As the frame passes through the network the layer 2 address will change to the next destination interface. Keep in mind that the layer 3 address will remain in tact from the source to the final destination. If we were to look at the frame after Router B sends to Host B the source layer 2 address will be the ethernet of Router B, and the destination MAC address will be that of Host B.

Answer 6–122.
   e) **The IGRP metric is partially based on Bandwidth, which is based on ring speed, but can be overridden by manually configuring bandwidth on the interface.**

IGRP by default uses Bandwidth and Load as components of its metrics.
Bandwidth is configurable by the administrator and is not related to "real life".
When a Ring Speed is configured on a Token Ring interface the bandwidth will reflect the ring speed.

At any time, the administrator can override the default bandwidth and change it to another value.

Example 1

In this first example, we have set the Ring Speed of the Token Ring interface to 16.

6. Answers

```
TokenRing0 is up, line protocol is up
   Hardware is TMS380, address is 0007.7816.fe54 (bia 0007.7816.fe54)
   Internet address is 172.16.10.10/24
   MTU 4464 bytes, BW 16000 Kbit, DLY 630 usec, rely 255/255, load 1/255
   Encapsulation SNAP, loopback not set, keepalive set (10 sec)
   ARP type: SNAP, ARP Timeout 04:00:00
   Ring speed: 16 Mbps
   Single ring node, Source Route Transparent Bridge capable
   Source bridging enabled, srn 16 bn 1 trn 10 [Ring group)
     proxy explorers disabled, spanning explorer disabled, NetBIOS cache disable
```

Example 2

In this example, we have left the Ring Speed at 16 and configured the bandwidth of the TO0
interface to 4000000.

```
Router_B[Config-if)#bandwidth 4000000
Router_B[Config-if)#^Z
Router_B#sh int to0
%SYS-5-CONFIG_I: Configured from console by console
TokenRing0 is up, line protocol is up
   Hardware is TMS380, address is 0007.7816.fe54 (bia 0007.7816.fe54)
   Internet address is 172.16.10.10/24
   MTU 4464 bytes, BW 4000000 Kbit, DLY 630 usec, rely 255/255, load 1/255
   Encapsulation SNAP, loopback not set, keepalive set (10 sec)
   ARP type: SNAP, ARP Timeout 04:00:00
   Ring speed: 16 Mbps
   Single ring node, Source Route Transparent Bridge capable
   Source bridging enabled, srn 16 bn 1 trn 10 [Ring group)
     proxy explorers disabled, spanning explorer disabled, NetBIOS cache disable
```

Answer 6–123.
   b) Serial 0 is configured as a DTE interface
   d) Serial 0 is configured with a bandwidth of 1544Kbit

The default bandwidth on a serial interface is 1544Kbit, refer to the following show command.
Also by default a serial interface is DTE configured.

```
Router_B>sh int s0
 Serial0 is up, line protocol is up
   Hardware is HD64570
   Internet address is 172.18.1.2/24
   MTU 1500 bytes, BW 1544 Kbit, DLY 20000 usec, rely 255/255, load 1/255
   Encapsulation HDLC, loopback not set, keepalive set (10 sec)
   Last input 00:00:01, output 00:00:05, output hang never
   Last clearing of "show interface" counters never
   Input queue: 0/75/0 (size/max/drops); Total output drops: 0
   Queueing strategy: weighted fair
   Output queue: 0/64/0 (size/threshold/drops)
      Conversations  0/1 (active/max active)
      Reserved Conversations 0/0 (allocated/max allocated)
   5 minute input rate 0 bits/sec, 0 packets/sec
```

```
5 minute output rate 0 bits/sec, 0 packets/sec
   400 packets input, 24192 bytes, 0 no buffer
   Received 400 broadcasts, 0 runts, 0 giants, 0 throttles
   0 input errors, 0 CRC, 0 frame, 0 overrun, 0 ignored, 0 abort
   391 packets output, 23257 bytes, 0 underruns
   0 output errors, 0 collisions, 3 interface resets
   0 output buffer failures, 0 output buffers swapped out
   0 carrier transitions
   DCD=up  DSR=up  DTR=up  RTS=up  CTS=up
```

Answer 6–124.
    e) Workstation A could not successfully ping Workstation B.

Since Router_A is directly connected to network 10.0.0.0, Router_A will ignore the updates received from Router_C that say's network 10.0.0.0 is 1 hop away. Classful routing protocols only use the set prefixes of 8 bits for a Class A, 16 bits for a Class B and 24 bits for a Class C address.

IP RIP is a classful routing protocol and does not communicate the subnet across different major networks. As a result there is no way Router_A can distinguish between the subnets 10.0.1.0 and 10.0.4.0.

When Workstation A pings the 10 address of Workstation B or Router_B the ICMP echo request will remain on the subnet 10.0.1.0.

Answer 6–125.
    d) Frames that don't have a RIF never gain a RIF, frames that have a RIF never loose a RIF.

Answer 6–126.
    b) All users will be able to telnet to Router_B.
    c) No user would be able to access the privilege mode of Router_B.

Refer to the example below:

```
Router_A#telnet 10.1.4.1
Trying 10.1.4.1 ... Open

Router_B>en
% No password set
```

Answer 6–127.
    d) Router B

Router A will be responsible for fragmenting the frames as they are re-encapsulated into serial frames.

Answer 6–128.
    c) Cost effective, non-dedicated connectivity
    d) Supports ISDN services

6. Answers

Answer 6–129.
   d) **Network communication will continue with no interruption.**

The SAS attaches to the primary ring through a concentrator. Therefore, if the SAS goes down, there is no need for the ring to wrap.

Answer 6–130.
   d) **Supports VLSM**

Cisco defines EIGRP as a advanced distance vector routing protocol. Mask information is communicated between hosts and therefore allows discontinuous networks to be defined.

The command "no auto-summary" is required to support discontinuous networks.

EIGRP is a internal routing protocol, which means it is used to route within a autonomous system. BGP4 is an example of a exterior routing protocol.
EIGRP also allows Variable Length Subnet Masking (VLSM) which means you can have different masks for the same major network number.

Answer 6–131.
   e) **Can not be determined**

Answer 6–132.
   a) **A routed interface**

Treat the BVI interface as you would any other routed interface.

Refer to the following show commands:

```
Router_C[Config]#int bvi10
Router_C[Config-if]#ip address 172.16.10.1 255.255.255.0

Router_C#sh int
BVI10 is up, line protocol is up
  Hardware is BVI, address is 0060.09c3.df60 (bia 0000.0000.0000)
  Internet address is 172.16.10.1/24
  MTU 1500 bytes, BW 10000 Kbit, DLY 5000 usec, rely 255/255, load 1/255
  Encapsulation ARPA, loopback not set, keepalive set (10 sec)
  ARP type: ARPA, ARP Timeout 04:00:00
  Last input never, output never, output hang never
  Last clearing of "show interface" counters never
  Queueing strategy: fifo
  Output queue 0/0, 0 drops; input queue 0/75, 0 drops
  5 minute input rate 0 bits/sec, 0 packets/sec
  5 minute output rate 0 bits/sec, 0 packets/sec
     44 packets input, 5598 bytes, 0 no buffer
     Received 0 broadcasts, 0 runts, 0 giants, 0 throttles
     0 input errors, 0 CRC, 0 frame, 0 overrun, 0 ignored, 0 abort
     191 packets output, 456 bytes, 0 underruns
     0 output errors, 0 collisions, 0 interface resets
     0 output buffer failures, 0 output buffers swapped out
```

Answer 6–133.
   g)   **Can not be determined.**

The password required to enter the configuration mode is the enable secret, which is encrypted.

Answer 6–134.
   c)   **Summarization is automatic to the Class boundaries.**
   d)   **Use the command no auto-summary to turn off summarization.**
   e)   **To change the EIGRP defaults use the command ip summary-address eigrp on an interface.**

Answer 6–135.
   d)   **Listening to the source host and associating its MAC address to a port**

A bridge is a promiscuous device. It listens to all traffic and records the MAC address of the source and the port it "heard" it on.

Answer 6–136.
   a)   **Bit-ordering**
   b)   **MTU**

Answer 6–137.
   d)   **Investigate your file transfer application.**

To understand this question we need to look at a couple of different factors:

What is the maximum frame length of this particular LAN segment? If we assume that this is ethernet, the maximum transmission unit (MTU) is 1500 bytes.

We also need to look at the transmission speed of the link. Let us further assume it is a 10 mega bits per second link.

If we were lucky enough to have an FTP application that supported the 1530 MTU, when we perform the following math

$1000000/8 = 1,250,000$ bytes/sec

$1,250,000/1530 = 817$ packets/sec

we can see that 817 would be the ideal number of packets to transmit on an ethernet segment. The answer to this question is to investigate the application because it appears as though it is using a very small transmission unit (approximately 84 bytes), which is very inefficient. Keep in mind there is no difference in the header that carries a small payload or a large payload!

Answer 6–138.
   d)   **DLSw will terminate the data-link control for connection-oriented data.**

6. Answers

HINT: DO NOT attempt the CCIE written exam until you thoroughly understand how to read a RIF and know the difference between DLSw and Remote Source Route Bridging.

Answer 6–139.
   a) Yes

It is true that this is a discontiguous network design, and we are using a classful routing protocol, but the fact still remains that Router_C does see network 20.0.0.0 across its serial interface. Refer to the routing table and ping below:

```
Router_C#sh ip rou
%SYS-5-CONFIG_I: Configured from console by consolete
Codes: C - connected, S - static, I - IGRP, R - RIP, M - mobile, B - BGP
       D - EIGRP, EX - EIGRP external, O - OSPF, IA - OSPF inter area
       N1 - OSPF NSSA external type 1, N2 - OSPF NSSA external type 2
       E1 - OSPF external type 1, E2 - OSPF external type 2, E - EGP
       i - IS-IS, L1 - IS-IS level-1, L2 - IS-IS level-2, * - candidate default
       U - per-user static route, o - ODR

Gateway of last resort is not set

R    20.0.0.0/8 [120/1] via 192.13.10.10, 00:00:00, Serial0
     172.16.0.0/24 is subnetted, 1 subnets
C       172.16.10.0 is directly connected, Ethernet0
     192.13.10.0/30 is subnetted, 1 subnets
C       192.13.10.8 is directly connected, Serial0
R    192.13.20.0/24 [120/1] via 192.13.10.10, 00:00:01, Serial0

Router_C#ping 20.20.20.1

Type escape sequence to abort.
Sending 5, 100-byte ICMP Echos to 20.20.20.1, timeout is 2 seconds:
!!!!!
Success rate is 100 percent (5/5), round-trip min/avg/max = 4/4/4 ms
```

Answer 6–140.
   a) Physical Layer 1

Answer 6–141.
   c) The tunnel will always be configured with a Layer 3 protocol address.

Cayman encapsulation with AppleTalk requires that no AppleTalk be configured on the interface.

Answer 6–142.
   c) S0

The route-map "thisway" sets up policy routing. The policy simply states that all traffic from 10.1.0.5 will be routed out s0.

Now we will ping 10.4.0.2 from Workstaton A:

```
Router_C#debug ip policy
Policy routing debugging is on
Router_C#
IP: s=10.1.0.5 (Ethernet1), d=10.4.0.2, len 74, policy match
IP: route map takeserial, item 10, permit
IP: s=10.1.0.5 (Ethernet1), d=10.4.0.2 (Serial0), len 74, policy routed
IP: Ethernet1 to Serial0 10.4.0.2
IP: s=10.1.0.5 (Ethernet1), d=10.4.0.2, len 74, policy match
IP: route map takeserial, item 10, permit
IP: s=10.1.0.5 (Ethernet1), d=10.4.0.2 (Serial0), len 74, policy routed
IP: Ethernet1 to Serial0 10.4.0.2
IP: s=10.1.0.5 (Ethernet1), d=10.4.0.2, len 74, policy match
IP: route map takeserial, item 10, permit
IP: s=10.1.0.5 (Ethernet1), d=10.4.0.2 (Serial0), len 74, policy routed
IP: Ethernet1 to Serial0 10.4.0.2
IP: s=10.1.0.5 (Ethernet1), d=10.4.0.2, len 74, policy match
IP: route map takeserial, item 10, permit
IP: s=10.1.0.5 (Ethernet1), d=10.4.0.2 (Serial0), len 74, policy routed
IP: Ethernet1 to Serial0 10.4.0.2
```

Answer 6–143.
   e)   It would not be necessary to configure "no-auto-summary."

If we do not configure no auto-summary on Router_C, Router_B would have no way of knowing the subnets of Network 172.16.0.0 and would send all traffic destined to network 172.16.0.0 to its serial interface with the exception of traffic to network 172.16.3.0 which is directly connected. The topology that is presented it is actually not necessary to configure no auto-summary since the best path to get to both subnets of 172.16.0.0 would be the Serial connection of Router_B.

EIGRP "knows" that 172.16.3.0 is directly connected and, of course, would use its ethernet interface to reach a destination on that network.

Refer to the following routing table:

```
Router_B#sh ip route
Codes: C - connected, S - static, I - IGRP, R - RIP, M - mobile,
 B - BGP, D - EIGRP, EX - EIGRP external, O - OSPF,
 IA - OSPF inter area, N1 - OSPF NSSA external type 1,
 N2 - OSPF NSSA external type 2, E1 - OSPF external type 1,
 E2 - OSPF external type 2, E - EGP, i - IS-IS,
 L1 - IS-IS level-1, L2 - IS-IS level-2, * - candidate default
 U - per-user static route, o - ODR

Gateway of last resort is not set

     172.16.0.0/16 is variably subnetted, 2 subnets, 2 masks
D       172.16.0.0/16 [90/2195456] via 192.16.1.5, 00:00:07, Serial0/0
C       172.16.3.0/24 is directly connected, Ethernet0/0
     192.16.1.0/30 is subnetted, 1 subnets
C       192.16.1.4 is directly connected, Serial0/0
```

The problem would be if additional 172.16.0.0 subnets were to be located at different sites. You should configure no auto-summary! After no auto-summary is configured on Router_C the routing table of Router_B is as follows:

```
Router_B#sh ip route
Codes: C - connected, S - static, I - IGRP, R - RIP, M - mobile,
 B - BGP, D - EIGRP, EX - EIGRP external, O - OSPF,
 IA - OSPF inter area, N1 - OSPF NSSA external type 1,
 N2 - OSPF NSSA external type 2, E1 - OSPF external type 1,
 E2 - OSPF external type 2, E - EGP, i - IS-IS,
 L1 - IS-IS level-1, L2 - IS-IS level-2, * - candidate default
 U - per-user static route, o - ODR
```

Gateway of last resort is not set

```
       172.16.0.0/16 is variably subnetted, 3 subnets, 2 masks
D         172.16.1.0/24 [90/2195456] via 192.16.1.5, 00:00:02, Serial0/0
D         172.16.2.0/24 [90/2195456] via 192.16.1.5, 00:00:02, Serial0/0
C         172.16.3.0/24 is directly connected, Ethernet0/0
       192.16.1.0/30 is subnetted, 1 subnets
C         192.16.1.4 is directly connected, Serial0/0
```

Answer 6–144.
   e)   802.1d

Radia Perlman was working for Digital at that time, and she developed the Spanning Tree Algorithm. Later on, while still working for Digital, she was a major force behind the development of IS-IS. In the early nineties Novell hired her to rework IS-IS into NLSP. In 1997, Oracle gave her a multi-million dollar signing bonus. Wow! When is the last time you heard of anyone getting a signing bonus who could not hit a baseball or throw a football?

Perlman has written several books, I recommend: "Interconnections: Bridges and Routers."

Answer 6–145.
   b)   IPX RIP and RTMP

The default routing protocols for IPX and Appletalk are IPX RIP and RTMP respectively. There is no IP routing protocol configured. IP is a routed protocol.

The following commands are an example of how to configure IP RIP.

```
Router_A(config-router)#int e0/0
Router_A(config-if)#ip address 10.1.1.1 255.255.255.0

Router_A(config-if)#router rip
Router_A(config-router)#network 10.0.0.0
```

Answer 6–146.
   e)   LAPB

Answer 6–147.
   b)   **Would mean that most likely the bridge (Router) will become the "Root Bridge"**
   c)   **Would force the bridge (Router) to forward on all ports**

The lower the priority number, the more likely the router will become the root bridge. The root bridge will always forward on all ports. Refer to the example following:

```
Router_C(config)#bridge 1 priority 1

Router_C#sh span

Bridge Group 1 is executing the DEC compatible Spanning Tree protocol
   Bridge Identifier has priority 1, address 0060.09c3.df60
   Configured hello time 1, max age 15, forward delay 30
   We are the root of the spanning tree
   Topology change flag not set, detected flag not set
   Times:  hold 1, topology change 30, notification 30
           hello 1, max age 15, forward delay 30, aging 300
   Timers: hello 1, topology change 0, notification 0

Router_C#sh bridge group

Bridge Group 1 is running the DEC compatible Spanning Tree protocol

   Port 2 (Ethernet0) of bridge group 1 is forwarding
   Port 3 (Ethernet1) of bridge group 1 is forwarding
   Port 4 (Serial0) of bridge group 1 is forwarding
```

Answer 6–148.
   a)   **The destination address will be that of Workstation B.**
   b)   **The source address will be that of Workstation A.**
   d)   **Routers never change the Layer 3 address.**

The router will forward a packet based upon the destination Layer 3 address. The MAC addresses will change as the packet is forwarded to reflect the next Network Interface Card. The Layer 3 addresses will never change.

```
Router_C>sh int e1
Ethernet1 is up, line protocol is up
   Hardware is Lance, address is 0060.09c3.df61 (bia 0060.09c3.df61)
   Internet address is 10.1.16.1/24
```

The following is a protocol analyzer capture of a ping to the ip address of 172.16.1.2:

Notice in the screen capture following that the destination MAC address is the e1 interface of Router _C but the destination IP address is that of the ultimate destination.

6. Answers

```
Ethernet Version II
  Address: 00-80-C7-CA-0A-8A --->00-60-09-C3-DF-61
  Ethernet II Protocol Type: IP
Internet Protocol
  Version(MSB 4 bits): 4
  Header length(LSB 4 bits): 5 (32-bit word)
  Service type: Precd=Routine,Delay=Normal,Thrput=Normal,Reli=Normal
  Total length: 60 (Octets)
  Fragment ID: 11008
  Flags: May be fragmented,Last fragment,Offset=0 (0x00)
  Time to live: 32 seconds/hops
  IP protocol type: ICMP (0x01)
  Checksum: 0xA8A9
  IP address 10.1.16.5 ->172.16.1.2
  No option
IP Internet Control Message Protocol
  Type: Echo Request
```

Answer 6–149.

    b) **A static mapping will be made between Host names and IP addresses.**

    d) **A ping will only use the first address configured.**

Answer 6–150.

    c) **Will be the MAC address of E0**

The BVI in our case will use the MAC of E0. Refer to the following show command:

```
Router_C#sh int bvi10
BVI10 is up, line protocol is up
  Hardware is BVI, address is 0060.09c3.df60 (bia 0000.0000.0000)
  Internet address is 172.16.10.1/24
  MTU 1500 bytes, BW 10000 Kbit, DLY 5000 usec, rely 255/255, load 1/255
  Encapsulation ARPA, loopback not set, keepalive set (10 sec)
  ARP type: ARPA, ARP Timeout 04:00:00
  Last input never, output never, output hang never
  Last clearing of "show interface" counters never
  Queueing strategy: fifo
  Output queue 0/0, 0 drops; input queue 0/75, 0 drops
  5 minute input rate 0 bits/sec, 0 packets/sec
  5 minute output rate 0 bits/sec, 0 packets/sec
     45 packets input, 5848 bytes, 0 no buffer
     Received 0 broadcasts, 0 runts, 0 giants, 0 throttles
     0 input errors, 0 CRC, 0 frame, 0 overrun, 0 ignored, 0 abort
     212 packets output, 456 bytes, 0 underruns
     0 output errors, 0 collisions, 0 interface resets
     0 output buffer failures, 0 output buffers swapped out
```

Answer 6–151.

    c) **When an area does not have a link to area 0**

Answer 6–152.

    b) **Zones are used to limit NBP requests.**

Zones do not have to be configured on an appletalk client.

Refer to the following example:

The interface has been configured for discovery mode. Then the client probes for the zone name. After the zone name has been "discovered" the interface is enabled.

```
Router_C(config-if)#appletalk cable-range 100-150
Router_C(config-if)#appletalk discovery

Router_C#sh app int e0
Ethernet0 is up, line protocol is up
  AppleTalk node down, Probing for node address
  AppleTalk cable range is 100-150
  AppleTalk address is 128.20, Probing
  AppleTalk zone is not set.
  AppleTalk discovery mode is enabled
  AppleTalk address gleaning is disabled
  AppleTalk route cache is not initialized

Router_C#
%AT-6-CONFIGOK: Ethernet0: AppleTalk port enabled; verified by 124.249

Router_C#sh app int e0
Ethernet0 is up, line protocol is up
  AppleTalk cable range is 100-150
  AppleTalk address is 128.20, Valid
  AppleTalk zone is "ccieprep"
  AppleTalk port configuration provided by 124.249
  AppleTalk discovery mode is enabled
  AppleTalk address gleaning is disabled
  AppleTalk route cache is enabled
```

Answer 6–153.
   d) Allows an interface to convert explorer packets to specifically routed frames

A bridge may receive an explorer packet looking for a destination MAC. If the bridge has RIF information for that destination MAC, the bridge will change the explorer packet to a specifically routed frame thereby reducing traffic.

Answer 6–154.
   d) 0830.019b.00ae.0230

The RIF is represented in HEX. If the ring and bridge numbers are given to you in decimal you will have to convert. The RIF is made up of two fields, the RD and the RC.

019b.00ae.0230 represents the Route Description Field (RD).
0830 represents the Route Control Field (RC).

The RD contains Ring and Bridge identifiers.

Ring numbers are 12 bits in length or 3 HEX digits

Bridge numbers are 4 bits in length or 1 HEX digit

HINT: The RD ALWAYS ends in 0. If you see a choice on your exam and the RD does not end in 0, eliminate it as a possible answer. There is no way the RD can describe a path to a bridge as a final destination.

The RC:

15	14	13	12	11	10	9	8	7	6	5	4	3	2	1	0
0	0	0	0	1	0	0	0	0	0	1	1				

      0   8   3   0

The Bits 15-13 (first three) bits describe type of packet:

0xx Specific Route
10x All rings, all routes
11x Spanning Route

The Bits 12-8 (next five) bits describe the total length of the RIF represented in bytes.

The total length of the RIF is 8 bytes.

Bit 7 describes the direction the RIF should be read.

0 - from left to right
1 - from right to left

Bits 6-4 is a code for the largest frame accepted on route to the destination.

Answer 6–155.
    c)   There should be at least one Appletalk seed router.

There needs to be at least one seed router to provide the necessary cable-range and zone information. If there is only one, and that router should go down, there would be no way for neighbors to discover appletalk parameters.

Answer 6–156.
    a)   S0/0 and S0/1 of Router_A

The access list that would have to be used is an extended access-list. The extended access-list should always be placed close to the source but not too close!

Assuming that Router_B had serial IP address of 10.1.8.0 and 10.1.12.0 and the following access list:

```
Router_B(config)#access-list 101 deny tcp 10.1.8.0 0.0.7.255 192.16.5.0
  0.0.0.255
Router_B(config)#access-list 101 permit ip any any
```

If this list were placed on the serial interfaces of Router_B, no traffic would ever be denied.

Router_B would exempt itself from the access list. (It's a Cisco thing.)

Answer 6–157.
   c) IP, Banyan, DECnet

If a protocol is not configured to be routed, then the protocol will be bridged, assuming bridging is configured.

Answer 6–158.
   a) The Cisco IOS will be read from flash if a flash exists.
   f) The configuration file will be read from NVRAM.
   h) The baud rate will be set at 9600.

The configuration register is 16 binary bits represented in hexadecimal notation.

15	14	13	12	11	10	9	8	7	6	5	4	3	2	1	0
0	0	1	0	0	0	0	1	0	0	0	0	0	0	1	0

This register configuration would be 0x2102
The last line of the show version command displays the configuration register.

```
Router_C>sh version

Cisco Internetwork Operating System Software
IOS (tm) 3000 Bootstrap Software (IGS-RXBOOT), Version 10.2(8a), RELEASE
  SOFTWARE (fc1)
Copyright (c) 1986-1995 by cisco Systems, Inc.
Compiled Tue 24-Oct-95 15:46 by mkamson
Image text-base: 0x01020000, data-base: 0x00001000
ROM: System Bootstrap, Version 5.2(8a), RELEASE SOFTWARE
Router_C uptime is 1 minute
System restarted by reload
Running default software
cisco 2500 (68030) processor (revision D) with 16380K/2048K bytes of memory.
Processor board serial number 03264288 with hardware revision 00000000
X.25 software, Version 2.0, NET2, BFE and GOSIP compliant.
2 Ethernet/IEEE 802.3 interfaces.
2 Serial network interfaces.
32K bytes of non-volatile configuration memory.
8192K bytes of processor board System flash (Read/Write)

Configuration register is 0x2102
```

Bits 11 and 12 define the baud rate of the console port.

6. Answers

If bit 12 and 11 are set to 0 0 respectively it represents 9600 baud
If bit 12 and 11 are set to 0 1 respectively it represents 4800 baud
If bit 12 and 11 are set to 1 0 respectively it represents 1200 baud
If bit 12 and 11 are set to 1 1 respectively it represents 2400 baud

Bit 6 defines if the configuration file will be loaded from NVRAM

If bit 6 is 0 then the router will load the configuration file from NVRAM
If bit 6 is 1 then the router will not load the configuration file from NVRAM

Bits 3, 2, 1, and 0 (boot field) control booting of the router

If the boot field has a value of 0x0 the router will boot to the ROM monitor mode.

```
Router_C(config)#config-reg 0x2100
Router_C#reload
Proceed with reload? [confirm]
```

Results of the commands above:

```
%SYS-5-RELOAD: Reload requested
System Bootstrap, Version 5.2(8a), RELEASE SOFTWARE
Copyright (c) 1986-1995 by cisco Systems
2500 processor with 16384 Kbytes of main memory
>
```

The greater than prompt above represents the ROM monitor mode.

If the boot field has a value of 0x1 the router will boot from ROM.

The result of changing the configuration register to 2101

```
Router_C(boot)>sh ver
Cisco Internetwork Operating System Software
IOS (tm) 3000 Bootstrap Software (IGS-RXBOOT), Version 10.2(8a), RELEASE
  SOFTWAR
E (fc1)
Copyright (c) 1986-1995 by cisco Systems, Inc.
Compiled Tue 24-Oct-95 15:46 by mkamson
Image text-base: 0x01020000, data-base: 0x00001000

ROM: System Bootstrap, Version 5.2(8a), RELEASE SOFTWARE

Router_C uptime is 1 minute
System restarted by reload
Running default software

cisco 2500 (68030) processor (revision D) with 16380K/2048K bytes of memory.
Processor board serial number 03264288 with hardware revision 00000000
X.25 software, Version 2.0, NET2, BFE and GOSIP compliant.
2 Ethernet/IEEE 802.3 interfaces.
```

```
2 Serial network interfaces.
32K bytes of non-volatile configuration memory.
8192K bytes of processor board System flash (Read/Write)

Configuration register is 0x2101

Router_C(boot)>
```

The above prompt identifies that router has booted from the IOS located in ROM.

If the boot field has a value of 0x2-0xF the following will occur:

If a valid flash memory exists the IOS will be loaded from flash. If no valid flash exists the boot system commands located in the configuration will be used. If there are no boot system commands, the router will attempt to boot from a TFTP server.

The following is the output of a router with a valid flash.

```
Router_C>sh ver
Cisco Internetwork Operating System Software
IOS (tm) 2500 Software (C2500-J-L), Version 11.2(3), RELEASE SOFTWARE (fc2)
Copyright (c) 1986-1996 by cisco Systems, Inc.
Compiled Mon 30-Dec-96 21:28 by ajchopra
Image text-base: 0x0303D144, data-base: 0x00001000

ROM: System Bootstrap, Version 5.2(8a), RELEASE SOFTWARE
ROM: 3000 Bootstrap Software (IGS-RXBOOT), Version 10.2(8a), RELEASE SOFTWARE
  (fc1)

Router_C uptime is 2 minutes
System restarted by reload
System image file is "flash:c2500-~1.bin", booted via flash

cisco 2500 (68030) processor (revision D) with 16384K/2048K bytes of memory.
Processor board ID 03264288, with hardware revision 00000000
Bridging software.
SuperLAT software copyright 1990 by Meridian Technology Corp).
X.25 software, Version 2.0, NET2, BFE and GOSIP compliant.
TN3270 Emulation software (copyright 1994 by TGV Inc).
2 Ethernet/IEEE 802.3 interface(s)
2 Serial network interface(s)
32K bytes of non-volatile configuration memory.
8192K bytes of processor board System flash (Read ONLY)
```

Configuration register is 0x2102

Answer 6–159.
  b) **Router_B**

There are two ways to get to 10.3.0.0. Therefore, we can load balance.

Answer 6–160.
   d)   **All traffic that hits the link will be pass on the link, if the link is up.**

Interesting traffic defines when the link will come up. Once the link is up, all traffic will pass on the link. If you wish to limit traffic on an interface, an access list should be applied to the physical interface.

Example:

```
Router#sh run
Building configuration...

%SYS-5-CONFIG_I: Configured from console by console
Current configuration:
!
version 11.3
no service password-encryption
!
hostname Router
!
interface BRI0
 no ip address
ip access-group 101 out
dialer-group 1
!
ip classless
access-list 101 permit tcp 172.16.10.0 0.0.0.255 any eq smtp
!
dialer-list 1 protocol ip list 101
!
line con 0
line aux 0
line vty 0 4
 login
!
end
```

Answer 6–161.
   c)   **ip route 0.0.0.0 0.0.0.0 192.13.10.1 220**

The Administrative distance of 220 will only affect the "feasibility" of this default route. If another default route were learned with a lesser administrative distance, it would replace this route.

The mask is not an inverse mask. A mask of all 0s is the same thing as saying there are no network bits. If there are no network bits in the address, then all networks will match the address of 0.0.0.0 0.0.0.0. If you use the mask of 255.255.255.255, it means a network of 0.0.0.0. This is why "ip route 0.0.0.0 255.255.255.255 192.13.10.1" is not correct.

Refer to the following example.

```
Router_C#config t
Enter configuration commands, one per line.  End with CNTL/Z.
Router_C[Config]#ip route 0.0.0.0 0.0.0.0 192.13.10.1 220
Router_C[Config]#^Z
Router_C#
%SYS-5-CONFIG_I: Configured from console by consoleping
Protocol [ip]:
Router_C#
Router_C#ping 192.13.20.17

Router_C#sh ip route
Codes: C - connected, S - static, I - IGRP, R - RIP, M - mobile, B - BGP
       D - EIGRP, EX - EIGRP external, O - OSPF, IA - OSPF inter area
       N1 - OSPF NSSA external type 1, N2 - OSPF NSSA external type 2
       E1 - OSPF external type 1, E2 - OSPF external type 2, E - EGP
       i - IS-IS, L1 - IS-IS level-1, L2 - IS-IS level-2, * - candidate default
       U - per-user static route, o - ODR

Gateway of last resort is 192.13.10.1 to network 0.0.0.0

     172.16.0.0/24 is subnetted, 1 subnets
C       172.16.10.0 is directly connected, Ethernet0
C    192.13.10.0/24 is directly connected, Serial0
S*   0.0.0.0/0 [220/0] via 192.13.10.1
```

The following is a ping of the Token Ring interface of Router_B.

```
Type escape sequence to abort.
Sending 5, 100-byte ICMP Echos to 192.13.20.17, timeout is 2 seconds:
!!!!!
Success rate is 100 percent (5/5), round-trip min/avg/max = 4/4/8 ms
```

Now let's try the same thing using ip route 0.0.0.0 255.255.255.255 192.13.10.1

```
Router_C[Config]#no ip route 0.0.0.0 0.0.0.0 192.13.10.1 220
Router_C[Config]#ip route 0.0.0.0 255.255.255.255 192.13.10.1
Router_C[Config]#^Z
Router_C#sh ip route
%SYS-5-CONFIG_I: Configured from console by console
Codes: C - connected, S - static, I - IGRP, R - RIP, M - mobile, B - BGP
       D - EIGRP, EX - EIGRP external, O - OSPF, IA - OSPF inter area
       N1 - OSPF NSSA external type 1, N2 - OSPF NSSA external type 2
       E1 - OSPF external type 1, E2 - OSPF external type 2, E - EGP
       i - IS-IS, L1 - IS-IS level-1, L2 - IS-IS level-2, * - candidate default
       U - per-user static route, o - ODR

Gateway of last resort is not set

     172.16.0.0/24 is subnetted, 1 subnets
C       172.16.10.0 is directly connected, Ethernet0
C    192.13.10.0/24 is directly connected, Serial0
S    0.0.0.0/32 [1/0] via 192.13.10.1
```

6. Answers

```
Router_C#ping 192.13.20.17

Type escape sequence to abort.
Sending 5, 100-byte ICMP Echos to 192.13.20.17, timeout is 2 seconds:
.....
Success rate is 0 percent (0/5)
```

Answer 6–162.
   b) Ethernet link

Router_B is load balancing over its serial links to get to network CAD. Notice that the tick count is 7 with 1 hop.

```
R         CAD [07/01] via        0.0000.00a1.0000,    4s, Se1
                      via        0.0000.00a1.0000,    3s, Se0
```

The tick count for the Serial Link is 6, and the LAN link is 1. The best answer is ethernet. This link could be Token Ring also, but that was not a choice.

Answer 6–163.
   b) It serves as a password.

The command allows read and write access to hosts presenting the SNMP community string myrouters, if access-list 1 permits it; myrouters serves as a password.

Answer 6–164.
   b) Specifies path for spanning tree explorer frames to reduce explorer traffic

Answer 6–165.
   c) Appletalk load shares if the "appletalk maximum-paths" command is configured.

Refer to the output below:

```
Router_B(config)#appletalk maximum-paths 2

Router_B#sh app route
%SYS-5-CONFIG_I: Configured from console by console
Codes: R - RTMP derived, E - EIGRP derived, C - connected,
  A - AURP, S - static, P - proxy
4 routes in internet. Up to 2 parallel paths allowed.

The first zone listed for each entry is its default (primary) zone.

Router_B#sh app route
R Net 95-99 [1/G] via 100.190, 4 sec, Serial0, zone left-ether
C Net 100-105 directly connected, Serial0, zone leftserial
C Net 106-110 directly connected, Serial1, zone rightserial
R Net 111-115 [1/G] via 109.143, 3 sec, Serial1,
                    via 100.190, 4 sec, Serial0, zone bottom-ether
```

Answer 6–166.
   d) Appletalk, IPX

If a protocol is configured for routing, then it will be routed. Only protocols not configured for routing will be bridged.

Answer 6–167.
   c) In complex SRB environments

When a source does not know the location of the destination device, the source will send an explorer packet. There are two types of explorer packets:

All-routes Explorers
An All-routes Explorer, as the name implies, takes all possible routes on its way to the destination. In a complex network this is not a good thing. The amount of traffic generated can be considerable.

Spanning-Tree Explorers
Spanning-Tree Explorers solve this problem by sending packets to a defined group of nodes. The administrator can statically assign interfaces that will forward Spanning-Tree Explorers and assign interfaces that will block them. The administrator could also use the spanning-tree algorithm to automatically set a single route explorer.

Answer 6–168.
   e) None of the above.

Answer 6–169.
   e) The packet will be removed by the Active monitor.

Answer 6–170.
   b) Router_B
   d) Router_D

The effect of defining a Stub or a Totally Stubby area is to "hide" external routes to Internal routers. The routing tables of Backbone routers and ASBRs will still show external networks.

Example:

```
Router_B#sh ip route
Codes: C - connected, S - static, I - IGRP, R - RIP, M - mobile, B - BGP, D -
  EIGRP, EX - EIGRP external, O - OSPF, IA - OSPF inter area, N1 - OSPF NSSA
  external type 1, N2 - OSPF NSSA external type 2, E1 - OSPF external type 1,
  E2 - OSPF external type 2, E - EGP, i - IS-IS, L1 - IS-IS level-1, L2 - IS-IS
  level-2, * - candidate default, U - per-user static route, o - ODR
Gateway of last resort is not set
O E2 145.10.0.0/16 [110/20] via 10.0.8.2, 00:06:09, Serial0
     10.0.0.0/24 is subnetted, 1 subnets
C    10.0.8.0 is directly connected, Serial0
```

6. Answers

Answer 6–171.
   d) 25%

In this example we would have 70 total bytes of header information, for a total frame size of 280 bytes.
70/280 = .25 = 25%

Answer 6–172.
   c) Will be the lower 8 bits of the tunnel source address
   e) May have a conflicting address

Because the address of the node will be the lower 8 bits of the tunnel source address, there could be a conflict with an IP address when there are more than 8 host bits.

Refer to the example below:

```
interface Tunnel0
 no ip address
 tunnel source Serial0/0
 tunnel destination 172.16.10.2
 tunnel mode iptalk
 appletalk iptalk 300 tunnel
!
interface Ethernet0/0
 ip address 172.18.10.2 255.255.255.0
 no ip mroute-cache
 appletalk cable-range 150-159 156.125
 appletalk zone right
 no cdp enable
!
interface Serial0/0
 ip address 172.16.10.1 255.255.255.0
 encapsulation frame-relay

Tunnel0 is up, line protocol is up
  IPTalk information for Tunnel0, IP 0.0.0.0
  AppleTalk address is 300.1, Valid
  AppleTalk zone is "tunnel"
  AppleTalk address gleaning is not supported by hardware
  AppleTalk route cache is not supported by hardware
```

Answer 6–173.
   a) Area 1
   b) Area 2

There are three requirements that must be met before an area can be configured as a stub or totally stubby area:

1. There is only one way out of the area, or if multiple ways do exist, suboptimal paths may be selected.
2. An ASBR can not be located with in a stubby area.
3. Area 0 can not be configured as a stubby area.

Answer 6–174.

a) **IRB conserves address space.**

d) **IRB allows a packet to be received on a routed interface and sent out a bridged interface.**

e) **IRB allows a packet to be received on a bridged interface and sent out a routed interface.**

Answer 6–175.

f) **All of the above**

Answer 6–176.

b) **Adjacent routers**

Routers that are on the same segment become neighbors by using the Hello protocol. Adjacency is then established by exchanging the database. The "show ip ospf int" command will show the adjacent router.

```
Router_C#sh ip ospf int
Serial0 is up, line protocol is up
  Internet Address 172.16.2.2/24, Area 0
  Process ID 100, Router ID 172.16.2.2, Network Type POINT_TO_POINT, Cost: 64
  Transmit Delay is 1 sec, State POINT_TO_POINT,
  Timer intervals configured, Hello 10, Dead 40, Wait 40, Retransmit 5
    Hello due in 00:00:06
  Neighbor Count is 1; Adjacent neighbor count is 1.
    Adjacent with neighbor 172.16.2.1
  Suppress hello for 0 neighbor(s)
Serial1 is up; line protocol is up.
  Internet Address 172.16.1.2/24, Area 0
  Process ID 100, Router ID 172.16.2.2, Network Type POINT_TO_POINT, Cost: 64
  Transmit Delay is 1 sec, State POINT_TO_POINT,
  Timer intervals configured, Hello 10, Dead 40, Wait 40, Retransmit 5
    Hello due in 00:00:02
  Neighbor Count is 1; Adjacent neighbor count is 1.
    Adjacent with neighbor 172.16.1.1
  Suppress hello for 0 neighbor(s)
```

Answer 6–177.

a) **Remove the IPX network number from Serial 0/0**

c) **Configure an IPX internal network number on Router_C**

Refer to the configuration commands below:

```
Router_A(config)#int s0/0
Router_A(config-if)#no ipx network cad
Router_A(config-if)#exit
Router_A(config)#ipx internal-network cad
Router_A(config)#int s0/0
Router_A(config-if)#ipx ipxwan
%IPXWAN Resetting Interface Serial0/0
```

```
Router_A(config-if)#
%LINEPROTO-5-UPDOWN: Line protocol on Interface Serial0/0, changed state to
  down

%LINK-5-CHANGED: Interface Serial0/0, changed state to administratively down
%LINK-3-UPDOWN: Interface Serial0/0, changed state to up
%LINEPROTO-5-UPDOWN: Line protocol on Interface Serial0/0, changed state to up

 Serial0/0 is up, line protocol is up
  IPX address is 0.0000.0ead.0000 [up]
  Delay of this IPX network, in ticks is 18 throughput 0 link delay 0
   Local IPXWAN Node ID:        EAD/Router_A
   Network when IPXWAN master:      0 IPXWAN delay (master owns): 18
   IPXWAN Retry Interval:          20 IPXWAN Retry limit:        3
   IPXWAN Routing negotiated: RIP Unnumbered
   IPXWAN State:             Master: Connect
   State change reason: Received Router Info Rsp as Master
   Last received remote node info: CAD/Router_B
   Client mode disabled, Static mode disabled, Error mode is reset
  IPX SAP update interval is 60 seconds
  IPX type 20 propagation packet forwarding is disabled
  Incoming access list is not set
  Outgoing access list is not set
  IPX helper access list is not set
  SAP GNS processing enabled, delay 0 ms, output filter list is not set
  SAP Input filter list is not set
  SAP Output filter list is not set
  SAP Router filter list is not set
  Input filter list is not set
  Output filter list is not set
```

Answer 6–178.

b) A station that is connected to two separate dual attachment connectors (DACs)

A dual-homed station is a single-attachment station that is connected to two separate dual-attachment connectors for fault tolerance.

Answer 6–179.

d) It sets the interface to the discovery mode to allow discovery of both cable range and zone name.

The result of configuring the cable-range 0-0 command is shown below:
Notice that the interface "learns" its cable range and its zone name.

```
Router_C(config)#appletalk routing
Router_C(config)#int e0
Router_C(config-if)#appletalk cable-range 0-0

Router_C#sh app int
Ethernet0 is up, line protocol is up
  AppleTalk node down, Line protocol is down
  AppleTalk cable range is 100-150
```

```
    AppleTalk address is 128.21, Unknown
    AppleTalk zone is not set.
    AppleTalk port configuration provided by 128.85
    AppleTalk discovery mode is enabled
    AppleTalk address gleaning is disabled
    AppleTalk route cache is disabled, port down

  Router_C#sh app int
  Ethernet0 is up, line protocol is up
    AppleTalk port disabled, Verifying port net information
    AppleTalk cable range is 100-150
    AppleTalk address is 128.21, Valid
    AppleTalk zone is "ccieprep"
    AppleTalk port configuration provided by 128.85
    AppleTalk discovery mode is enabled
    AppleTalk address gleaning is disabled
    AppleTalk route cache is disabled, port initializing

  Router_C#sh app int

  Ethernet0 is up, line protocol is up
    AppleTalk cable range is 100-150
    AppleTalk address is 128.21, Valid
    AppleTalk zone is "ccieprep"
    AppleTalk port configuration provided by 128.85
    AppleTalk discovery mode is enabled
    AppleTalk address gleaning is disabled
    AppleTalk route cache is enabled
```

Answer 6–180.
   b) **Incremental SAP updates should not be configured where non-Cisco systems may exist.**
   e) **Incremental SAP updates would communicate only when a change occurs and contain only the information that has changed.**

Answer 6–181.
   b) **The packet will be removed by Host A.**

Answer 6–182.
   f) **notset**

The console 0 is the password that would be required to log into the router. The user mode allows a user to use most all the show commands. One exception is the show run command, which, if it was allowed, the user would be able to view passwords. All of the above information is the default on a Cisco router. For instance you could change the configuration to allow a user to view the configuration file without the enable password. You could also encrypt all passwords. Stay tuned and we will cover these additional topics.

Answer 6–183.
   c) **They have misconfigured defult gateways.**
   d) **The E0 of Router_C is not configured with a secondary address.**

6. Answers

Answer 6–184.
   a)   **MAC addresses never change.**

The purpose of a transparent bridge (TR) is to use the MAC addresses to determine whether a packet should be forwarded or filtered. The (TR) is the most intelligent device in the TR environment because it is making decisions. The name transparent comes from the fact that "hosts" should be unaware that a bridge exists.

Answer 6–185.
   a)   **Allows communication between Ethernet and Token Ring hosts**
   b)   **Will insert a RIF when communicating from a Transparent Bridge domain to a Source Route Bridge domain**
   c)   **Will remove a RIF when communicating from a Source Route Bridge domain to a Transparent Bridge domain**
   e)   **It may be necessary to configure MTU manually.**

Answer 6–186.
   a)   **There is a central distribution point.**
   c)   **Easier to troubleshoot than a bus topolgy**
   e)   **Requires more cabling than other topologies**

10BaseT is an example of Physical star topology, yet it is a Logical bus topology.

Answer 6–187.
   a)   **MAC of Host A**

This is bridging. It does not make any difference what kind of bridging, it still takes place at Layer 2. MAC addresses are used to determine location. Bridges take frames and pass them along or they filter. A bridge does not insert new MAC addresses into a frame.

Answer 6–188.
   d)   **The TICK count is the same.**
   e)   **The Clock Rate is the same.**

The only way IPX RIP will load balance is to have the same metric over the links. IPX uses TICK count. TICK count is calculated from clock rate. Therefore they would both have to be the same.

The following is the complete configuration of Router_B:

```
Router_B#sh run
Building configuration...

Current configuration:
!
version 11.3
no service password-encryption
!
```

```
hostname Router_B
!
!
ipx routing 0007.7816.fe54
ipx maximum-paths 2
ipx internal-network B1
!
interface Serial0
 no ip address
 no ip mroute-cache
 ipx ipxwan 0 unnumbered Router_B
 ipx nlsp enable
 no fair-queue
!
interface Serial1
 no ip address
 ipx ipxwan 0 unnumbered Router_B
 ipx nlsp enable
 clockrate 4000000
!
interface Serial2
 no ip address
 shutdown
!
interface Serial3
 no ip address
 shutdown
!
interface TokenRing0
 no ip address
 shutdown
!
interface BRI0
 no ip address
 shutdown
!
ip classless
!
ipx router nlsp
!
line con 0
line aux 0
line vty 0 4
 login
!
end
```

Answer 6–189.
  c) **No login would be required to establish a telnet session.**
  d) **The telnet user would not be able to access the privilege mode of Router_B.**

Establishing a telnet session with Router_A no password required, but unable to access the privilege mode because no enable password has been set.

```
Router_A>192.168.5.1
Trying 192.168.5.1 ... Open

Router_B>en
% No password set
Router_B>
```

Answer 6–190.
    c) Default routes
    d) Intra area routes
    e) Inter area routes

The example below will show the inter area routes and the default gateway, if there were additional intra area routes they would also show.

```
Router_A#sh ip
%SYS-5-CONFIG_I: Configured from console by consoleroute
Codes: C - connected, S - static, I - IGRP, R - RIP, M - mobile, B - BGP, D -
    EIGRP, EX - EIGRP external, O - OSPF, IA - OSPF inter area, N1 - OSPF NSSA
    external type 1, N2 - OSPF NSSA external type 2, E1 - OSPF external type 1,
    E2 - OSPF external type 2, E - EGP, i - IS-IS, L1 - IS-IS level-1, L2 - IS-IS
    level-2, * - candidate default, U - per-user static route, o - ODR
Gateway of last resort is 172.16.1.1 to network 0.0.0.0
        172.16.0.0/24 is subnetted, 1 subnets
C       172.16.1.0 is directly connected, Serial0/0
        123.0.0.0/24 is subnetted, 1 subnets
O IA 123.23.23.0 [110/138] via 172.16.1.1, 00:00:21, Serial0/0
O IA 192.168.1.0/24 [110/128] via 172.16.1.1, 00:00:31, Serial0/0
O*IA 0.0.0.0/0 [110/65] via 172.16.1.1, 00:00:36, Serial0/0
```

Answer 6–191.
    a) Keepalives are not being received.

If the serial cable is plugged into the router, and the other end of the serial cable is not plugged in to anything, the interface will go to a down and down state. Because of the proprietary pin out, the "show controller" command will show us the type of cable that is being used.

Example:

```
Router_B#sh int s0
Serial0 is down, line protocol is up
  Hardware is HD64570
  Internet address is 172.16.10.9/24
  MTU 1500 bytes, BW 1544 Kbit, DLY 20000 usec, rely 255/255, load 1/255
  Encapsulation HDLC, loopback not set, keepalive set (10 sec)
  Last input 00:00:00, output 00:00:00, output hang never

Router_B#sh controller s 0
HD unit 0, idb = 0xD4B64, driver structure at 0xD8D00
buffer size 1524  HD unit 0, V.35 DCE
```

Answer 6–192.
  b) **RIF**

Since SRT is configured Host A will set the Routing Information Indicator bit to 1. As a result Source Route Bridges will know that a Routing Information Field (RIF) follows the Source address.

Answer 6–193.
  a) **Router B**

The network layer address never changes as the frame passes through the internetwork. We wouldn't expect the US mail system to change the destination address of the recipient and we don't expect the router to change the address of the destination host.

Answer 6–194.
  e) **Spanning tree protocol is IBM.**

Answer 6–195.
  b) **1**

Since SRT is configured, Host A will set the Routing Information Indicator (RII) bit to 1. The RII bit is the most significant bit of the source MAC address.

Answer 6–196.
  d) **Area Border Router**
  e) **Autonomous System Boundary Router**

ABRs or ASBRs could have the responsibility to summarize or aggregate routes into the backbone. ASBRs would summarize routes into another Autonomous System.

Advantages of summarization are as follows:

- The size of The routing table is reduced on The Backbone router.
- The Backbone router will not have to deal with topology changes outside of Area 0.

Answer 6–197.
  a) **Managed Device**
  b) **Agent**
  c) **Network Management System (NMS)**

Answer 6–198.
  d) **4**

Each station sends a FIN and an ACK bit for a total of four segments. If you have a network analyzer, open a telnet session and then exit the session.

Answer 6–199.
  e) **After the primary has 50% capacity, the secondary will be brought up.**

6. Answers

The back up load command is an interface command. The first parameter describes a percentage of the capacity of the primary link. When that percentage is reached the back up interface will be brought up. The second parameter describes the total percentage of the capacity of the primary and secondary link. When the percentage drops to 5%, in this case, the secondary will be brought down.

Answer 6–200.
   a) **Source quench**

ICMP will send the source quench error. If the protocol is UDP (unreliable) this message will be ignored. TCP (reliable) will slow down the data transfer rate.

Answer 6–201.
   c) **Router_C**

```
Router_C(Config)#bridge irb
Router_C(Config)#bridge 10 protocol dec
Router_C(Config)#bridge 10 route ip
```

The above three steps: enables IRB, assigns the Spanning-Tree protocol of DEC, and enables the BVI to route IP packets to bridge group 10.

Answer 6–202.
   b) **Router_B**
   d) **Router_D**

Internal routers - routers that have their interfaces in the same area
Backbone routers - routers that have at least one interface connected to area 0
Area Border Routers (ABR) - routers that have interfaces attached to multiple areas
Autonomous System Boundary Routers (ASBR) - routers that have interfaces connected to external network (non-OSPF environment or another AS).

Keep in mind that a router can be defined in more than one category. For instance, in our diagram Router_B is an ABR and a Backbone router.

Answer 6–203.
   c) **0630.0011.0190**

The RIF
The RIF is made up of 2 fields the RC and the RD.
The RIF is represented in HEX.

Route Control field (RC)

The following is a sample of an RC:

15	14	13	12	11	10	9	8	7	6	5	4	3	2	1	0
0	0	0	0	1	0	0	0	0	0	1	1				
0				8				3				0			

Bits 15-13 (first 3) bits describe the type of packet:

0xx Specific Route
10x All rings, all routes
11x Spanning Route

Bits 12-8 (the next 5 bits) describe the total length of the RIF represented in bytes.

Bit 7 describes the direction the RIF should be read.

0 means the RIF is read from left to right
1 means the RIF is read from right to left

In the above example the RC has a value of 0830. The 8 signifies the total length of the RIF.

A value of a means that there are three bridges
A value of 8 means that there are two bridges
A value of 6 means there is one bridge

0630.0011.0191.0030

The above is not a legal RIF because the 6 means that the total RIF length is 6 bytes, and yet we can see that it is eight bytes in length. The two bridge numbers are the second and twelfth 1s. Two bridges mean a RIF length of 8 bytes.

Route Descriptor field (RD)

The RD contains Ring and Bridge identifiers. The structure of the Route Descriptor (RD) field is ring bridge, ring bridge, ring bridge, etc. Given the fact that we now know that a frame always ends up on a ring we now know that all RIFs will end with a bridge value of 0!

RIFs always end in zero (0)!

Think about the frame as the frame travels across a bridged network. The frame begins on a ring, then a bridge, then a ring, then a bridge, and continues in this manner until it reaches the destination host, which of course is on a ring.

A frame is never sent to a bridge.

The frame goes to a Token Ring host, which is on a ring.

Answer 6–204.
   d) **IGRP and EIGRP will always automatically redistribute between each other.**

EIGRP and IGRP must be configured with an autonomous system (AS) number. Only when the AS is the same is there automatic redistribution.

Answer 6–205.
   e) **None of the above**

One of the advantages of DLSw is that the RIF is terminated on each end, which can make the token ring environment more scalable. IBM Token Ring has a limitation of eight rings and seven bridges. Since the RIF is terminated the first ring in the RIF will be the virtual ring 10. Which gives us a RIF of:

0630.00ae.0230

HINT: Since DLSw will terminate the RIF it is not required that the virtual rings configured on our routers have the same value. In our case I show a single virtual ring, but in actuality there are two virtual rings configured one on each router. The router on the right could have a value of 10, the router on the left could have a value of 20. This is not the case of RSRB. The virtual ring values must match because the RIF is end-to-end route information.

Answer 6–206.
   a) **Bandwidth**
   b) **Delay**

Answer 6–207.
   a) **TCP/IP header Compression**
   c) **Payload Compression**
   e) **Link Compression**

Answer 6–208.
   a) **The destination address will be that of Workstation B.**
   c) **The source address will be the outbound interface of Device 2.**

The router will forward a packet based upon the destination Layer 3 address. The MAC addresses will change as the packet is forwarded to reflect the next Network Interface Card. The Layer 3 addresses will never change.

```
Router_C>sh int e1
Ethernet1 is up, line protocol is up
   Hardware is Lance, address is 0060.09c3.df61 (bia 0060.09c3.df61)
   Internet address is 10.1.16.1/24
```

The following is a protocol analyzer capture of a ping to the ip address of 172.16.1.2:

```
Ethernet Version II
   Address: 00-80-C7-CA-0A-8A --->00-60-09-C3-DF-61
   Ethernet II Protocol Type: IP
Internet Protocol
   Version(MSB 4 bits): 4
   Header length(LSB 4 bits): 5 (32-bit word)
   Service type: Precd=Routine,Delay=Normal,Thrput=Normal,Reli=Normal
   Total length: 60 (Octets)
   Fragment ID: 11008
   Flags: May be fragmented,Last fragment,Offset=0 (0x00)
   Time to live: 32 seconds/hops
   IP protocol type: ICMP (0x01)
   Checksum: 0xA8A9
   IP address 10.1.16.5 ->172.16.1.2
   No option
IP Internet Control Message Protocol
   Type: Echo Request.
```

Notice in the screen capture above that the destination MAC address is the e1 interface of Router _C but the destination IP address is that of the ultimate destination.

Answer 6–209.
   b) **Router_C would ping Workstation B with a 50% success rate.**

Classful routing protocols only use the set prefixes of 8 bits for a Class A, 16 bits for a Class B and 24 bits for a Class C address. IP RIP is a classful routing protocol and does not communicate the subnet across different major networks. Router_C hears routing updates relating to network 10.0.0.0 from Router_A and Router_B. These updates are sent with the same metric of 1 hop. Therefore Router_C assumes that it can reach the 10 network by going out S0 or S1. When a ping is initiated from Router_C or Workstation C, Router_C will load balance the packets.

Refer to the routing table of Router_C below:

```
Gateway of last resort is not set

     172.16.0.0/24 is subnetted, 2 subnets
C       172.16.1.0 is directly connected, Serial1
C       172.16.2.0 is directly connected, Serial0
R    10.0.0.0/8 [120/1] via 172.16.1.1, 00:00:09, Serial1
                 [120/1] via 172.16.2.1, 00:00:19, Serial0
```

Two pings are shown below:

```
Router_C#ping 10.0.4.1

Type escape sequence to abort.
Sending 5, 100-byte ICMP Echos to 10.0.4.1, timeout is 2 seconds:
U!.!U
Success rate is 40 percent (2/5), round-trip min/avg/max = 4/4/4 ms
Router_C#ping 10.0.4.1

Type escape sequence to abort.
Sending 5, 100-byte ICMP Echos to 10.0.4.1, timeout is 2 seconds:
!U!.!
Success rate is 60 percent (3/5), round-trip min/avg/max = 4/4/4 ms
```

Ten ping probes were successful five times or 50%.

Answer 6–210.
   b) **2**

Because of this limitation Cisco developed the ring group process. A ring group is a collection of Token Ring interfaces that share the same "virtual" target ring number. The maximum number of bridge hops is seven.

6. Answers

Answer 6–211.
   c) **No login would be required to establish a telnet session.**

```
Router_A
Router_A#192.168.5.1
Trying 192.168.5.1 ... Open

Router_B>
```

No password was required to open the telnet session.

Answer 6–212.
   c) **60 seconds**

When communicating over a serial link to another Cisco device, you may want to consider extending this periodic time.

The "ipx sap-interval" command is used to send less frequent updates. The SAP updates can also be changed to incremental using the "ipx sap-incremental" command. An incremental update means that a SAP will be sent only when a change occurs.

Answer 6–213.
   e) **A transparent bridge makes decisions.**

First let's discuss transparent bridging. A transparent bridge is an intelligent device that makes decisions as to whether or not a packet will be forwarded or filtered. This decision is made by comparing MAC addresses with a bridge port assignment. The term "transparent bridging" is derived from the fact that in a perfect environment the end node is unaware that a bridge exists.

A source-route bridge (SRB) is the "dumbest device" on the network. The bridge does not make decisions, its main duty is to supply a bridge ID to the Routing Information Field (RIF).

The token ring card is the intelligent device that reads the RIF. Hence the name SRB implies the source knows the route to the destination.

Answer 6–214.
   c) **64**

The total cost to get to that network is 74. The cost of the ethernet link is 10, thus the cost of the serial link must be 64.

By default, the cost of an OSPF link is 10 to the eighth power divided by the bandwidth of the link.

Answer 6–215.
   c) **172.16.1.1**

The IP address of Ethernet 0 address will be used.

Answer 6–216.
   e) **acknowledgement**

The User Datagram Protocol (UDP) header is used for connectionless, unreliable data transfers and thus requires no acknowledgement field.

Answer 6–217.
   d) **DLCI number (Data Link Connection Identifier)**
   e) **LMI type (Local Management Interface)**

A frame relay switch will announce its DLCI, and many switches can pick up on the LMI used by the router. Ask your carrier for the specific parameters needed. One of the most confusing parameters can be the DLCI. Let's assume you have a PVC NYC - San Francisco. If the carrier says "the DLCI for NYC is 135," configure the San Francisco router with DLCI 135!

Refer to the configuration below:

```
version 11.3
no service password-encryption
!
hostname router_a
!
enable secret 5 $1$.s1R$iaEqZxLnYJo2QlZi8UNaO0
enable password
!
no ip routing
!
interface Ethernet0/0
 no ip address
 no ip route-cache
 no ip mroute-cache
 shutdown
 no cdp enable
!
interface Serial0/0
 no ip address
 encapsulation frame-relay
 no ip route-cache
 no ip mroute-cache
 frame-relay lmi-type cisco
!
interface Serial0/0.1 point-to-point
 ip address 65.62.245.1 255.255.255.0
 no ip route-cache
 no ip mroute-cache
 no cdp enable
 frame-relay interface-dlci 100
!
interface Serial0/0.2 point-to-point
 ip address 210.7.93.1 255.255.255.0
 no ip route-cache
 no ip mroute-cache
```

6. Answers

```
 no cdp enable
 frame-relay interface-dlci 101
!
line con 0
 exec-timeout 0 0
line aux 0
line vty 0 4
 password
 login
!
end
```

Answer 6–218.
   c)   **No election will be held.**

Answer 6–219.
   d)   **Not necessary if there is a single area**

An ABR is defined as having interfaces located in multiple areas. When OSPF is configured networks will be defined as being in an area.

Example:

```
ip ospf 100
network 172.16.0.0 0.0.255.255 area 1
network 10.0.0.0 0.255.255.255 area 0
```

If multiple directly connected networks are configured on the same router, this router will be described as a ABR. Stub areas are areas that have only one way out and are defined by their ABR.

Chapter Seven
Lab Scenarios

The Laboratory or Practical portion of the Cisco Certified Internetworking Expert (CCIE) program is the most rigorous portion of the entire process. The CCIE Practical is two days of intense configuration and troubleshooting.

The CCIE Practical consists of two parts, Configuration and Troubleshooting. This chapter has 19 configurations that may be *similar* to those on your exam. Chapter 8 has 12 for troubleshooting.

On the exam, you will be presented with different scenarios. Each scenario will be assigned a certain point value. At the end of the two days you must have acquired 80 points. Cisco does not reveal much about the possible protocols and scenarios that may come up during your stay. When asked by my students, "What do I study for the Practical?" I respond with several tips.

1) IP is the most widely used protocol in the world, Cisco expects their CCIEs to be very competent with IP. Routing protocols associated with IP could include RIP, RIP version 2, IGRP, EIGRP, OSPF, BGP, EBGP and IS-IS.

2) IPX is the second most widely used protocol in the world. You should expect to see some configuration requirements with Novell's IPX. Routing protocols might include Novell's NLSP.

3) SNA, although old, is still around. Cisco Systems has hundreds of engineers that are former IBM employees. What does this mean? Study SNA. Possible topics would be DLSW+, RSRB, and Serial Tunneling (STUN).

4) Appletalk is slowly being phased out of most networks; however, there is still some lingering in the desktop publishing industry.

5) Miscellaneous protocols such as DECnet, Banyan Vines, CLNP, Apollo, and many more are all possibilities.

6) Cisco proprietary features are always a good bet. Integrated Routing and Bridging (IRB), Concurrent Routing and Bridging (CRB), Hot Standby Routing Protocol (HSRP), and so forth, are examples of proprietary features.

7) Cisco Catalyst Switch products are becoming more and more popular. The Cisco LAN Switching Class (CLSC) is always full. These are indications that more and more of the exam will consist of Catalyst switching products.

According to Cisco Connection Online (http://www.cisco.com), the equipment you will find in the practical consists of 2500, 4000, and 4500 series routers and Catalyst 5000 series switches. You will find several lab scenarios in this chapter dealing with the Catalyst 5000 series products.

The Practical Exam is two days in length and costs $1000 (US dollars). There are several facilities in the world that you may sit for the exam. An updated listing of their locations with contact names and phone numbers can be found at: http/www.cisco.com/warp/public/625/ccie/l.html.

I took the practical in Research Triangle Park, North Carolina. I flew in two days before my scheduled exam to get acclimated. I suggest arriving early, especially if there is the possibility of jet lag.

On the night before my exam I relaxed, did not study, and went to bed early. Enjoy the evening before your first day and get lots of sleep. You won't the night after your first day. The first day will be eight hours of configurations. It is important to understand your time restrictions and to skip those tasks that you are unsure of. You do not want to get bogged down on a task that is worth only several points.

The night after my first day was full of unrest. I did not receive an evaluation of my first day and was left to wonder how I was doing. On the second day, you will be presented with more configurations and troubleshooting. Troubleshooting is discussed in the last chapter. The additional configurations will be done in the morning before lunch. If you have enough points, they send you to lunch. While at lunch the proctor will "break" your network that you have spent the last day and a half configuring. The next chapter will deal with the afternoon of the second day.

Lou Rossi, CCIE

Labs in Chapter 7

Lab Scenario
NAT Translation

All configurations will refer to the diagram below:

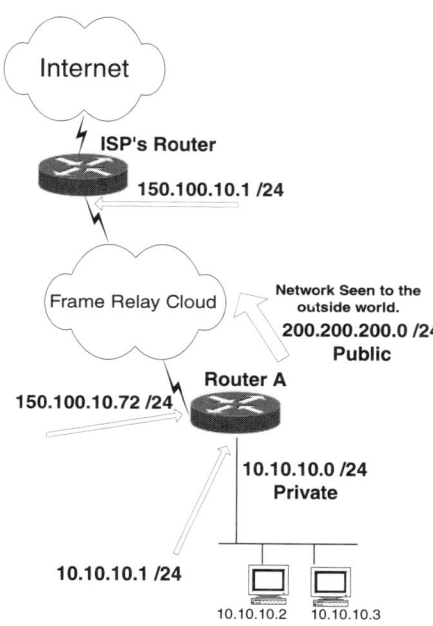

The scenario is as follows:

Our organization is using the private address of 10.10.10.0 /24. Our ISP has assigned the public address of 200.200.200.0 /24 to your organization.

Our goal is to configure Router A to provide us with address translation to go from the private address to the public address. We also want to advertise this public address out to the world.

The configuration commands that accomplish these goals are presented in **bold**.

```
Current configuration:
!
version 11.3
no service password-encryption
!
hostname router_a
!
```

```
enable secret 5 $1$.s1R$iaEqZxLnYJo2QlZi8UNaO0
enable password guess
!
ip nat pool nat-example 200.200.200.1 200.200.200.255 prefix-
    length 24
ip nat inside source list 1 pool nat-example
!
interface Ethernet0/0
 ip address 200.200.200.1 255.255.255.0 secondary
 ip address 10.10.10.1 255.255.255.0
 ip nat inside
!
interface Serial0/0
 ip address 150.100.10.72 255.255.255.0
 ip nat outside
 encapsulation frame-relay
!
interface TokenRing0/0
 no ip address
 shutdown
 ring-speed 16
!
interface FastEthernet1/0
 no ip address
 shutdown
!
router rip
 network 200.200.200.0
 network 150.100.0.0
!
ip classless
no logging buffered
access-list 1 permit 10.10.10.0 0.0.0.255
!
!
line con 0
 exec-timeout 0 0
line aux 0
line vty 0 4
 login
!
end
```

7. Lab Scenarios

Explanation of Router Commands

`ip nat pool`

Defines the pool name of "nat-example." The first public address is 200.200.200.1, and the last address 200.200.200.255. The mask is 255.255.255.0 or /24.

`ip nat inside source`

Applies the access-list 1 to the pool "nat-example"

`ip address 200.200.200.1 255.255.255.0 secondary`

Applies the public address to the e0/0 interface as a secondary address. Since we want to advertise the public address, we must configure the address.

`ip nat inside`

Defines the e0/0 interface as the inside address.

`ip nat outside`

Defines serial 0 as the outside addresses.

`Router rip`
`Network 200.200.200.0`

Because we configure the 200.200.200.0 address as a secondary address, we can advertise it with RIP.

`access-list 1 permit 10.10.10.0 0.0.0.0.255`

Permits the private addresses on the 10.10.10.0 subnet to be translated to the public address.

The following is the actual translation taken after the 10.10.10.1 interface of the router, and the workstation 10.10.10.2 performed a ping of the Serial interface of the ISP's router.

```
router_a#sh ip nat trans
Pro Inside global   Inside local  Outside local  Outside global
—  200.200.200.1     10.10.10.1         —              —
—  200.200.200.2     10.10.10.2         —              —
```

Lab Scenario
BGP External & Internal

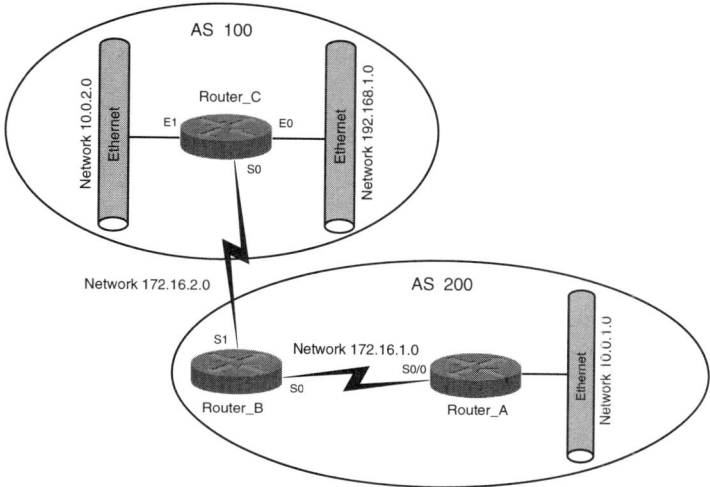

PART I

Router A and Router B reside in Autonomous System 200, with Router B having a serial connection to Router C. Router C resides in Autonomous System 100 (See diagram above.).

Configure Router B and Router C so that they exchange BGP updates to one another (EBGP). Also configure Router A and Router B to exchange BGP updates (IBGP). Verify that all routes are present in all of the routers' routing tables.

PART II

Network 10.0.2.0 should not be advertised to any router in Autonomous System 200. Use any method necessary to ensure that this network is not advertised and verify this by checking the routing table of the Routers A and B in Autonomous System 200.

Solution

In the first part of the lab we must configure EBGP and IBGP. We will start with configuring Router C with the appropriate commands. Assuming that all ip addresses and general setups have been performed, we must first configure the BGP routing protocol. As with any IP routing protocol we begin with the command "Router BGP" followed by the Autonomous System number. Please see the following configuration...

```
version 11.2
!
hostname Router_C
!
```

```
enable secret 5 $1$/rKI$r9ZHrCdxKBFIki8jqlDok1
!
interface Ethernet0
 ip address 192.168.1.1 255.255.255.0
!
interface Ethernet1
 ip address 10.0.2.1 255.255.255.0
!
interface Serial0
 ip address 172.16.2.1 255.255.255.0
 clockrate 4000000
!
interface Serial1
 no ip address
 shutdown
!
router rip
 network 192.168.1.0
 network 10.0.0.0
!
router bgp 100
 redistribute rip
 neighbor 172.16.2.2 remote-as 200
 neighbor 172.16.2.2 distribute-list 1 out
!
no ip classless
access-list 1 permit 192.168.1.0 0.0.0.255
!
!
line con 0
line aux 0
line vty 0 4
 password sa
 login
!
end
```

Please note the neighbor statements under the "router bgp 100" command. In BGP you must identify your neighbors, unlike other IP routing protocols where you simply specify the networks of interfaces on which you would like to advertise.

To satisfy Part II of the lab, we create an access-list that permits only the 192.68.0.0 network, thus denying all other networks, including 10.0.2.0. To apply an access-list to a routing protocol we use the "distribute-list" command, however, with BGP we can actually specify this on the neighbor command, which only restricts updates going to that neighbor. In the event that we were to establish

other neighbors, this distribute list would not apply. The "out" at the end of the command ensures that this access-list is only applied while we are sending updates to the neighbor, not while we are receiving.

We now must configure Router B. Please see the configuration below.

```
Password:
Router_B>en
Password:
Router_B#sh run
Building configuration...

Current configuration:
!
version 11.3
no service password-encryption
!
hostname Router_B
!
enable secret 5 $1$G7z5$NK1ayAgGrd3t1/1F9IBFy.
!
!
interface Serial0
 ip address 172.16.1.1 255.255.255.0
 no ip mroute-cache
 no fair-queue
 clockrate 4000000
!
interface Serial1
 ip address 172.16.2.2 255.255.255.0
!
interface Serial2
 no ip address
 shutdown
!
interface Serial3
 no ip address
 shutdown
!
interface TokenRing0
 no ip address
 shutdown
!
interface BRI0
 no ip address
 shutdown
```

```
!
router bgp 200
 neighbor 172.16.1.2 remote-as 200
 neighbor 172.16.2.1 remote-as 100
!
ip classless
!
!
line con 0
line aux 0
line vty 0 4
 password sa
 login
!
end
```

Router B will have two BGP neighbors, thus requiring two neighbor statements. Each neighbor statement requires the autonomous system number of the neighbor. We use the same series of commands that we used on Router C. We add a second neighbor statement for Router A and specify that it resides in autonomous system 200. Do not be confused that the command reads "remote-as", the fact that 200 is not really a remote AS indicates that this neighbor is an IBGP peer.

The final step will be to configure Router A. Please see the configuration below.

```
Current configuration:
!
version 11.3
no service password-encryption
!
hostname Router_A
!
interface Ethernet0/0
 ip address 10.0.1.1 255.255.255.0
 shutdown
!
interface Serial0/0
 ip address 172.16.1.2 255.255.255.0
 ip rip authentication mode 0
!
interface TokenRing0/0
 no ip address
 shutdown
 ring-speed 16
!
interface FastEthernet1/0
 no ip address
```

```
   shutdown
 !
 router rip
  network 10.0.0.0
 !
 router bgp 200
  neighbor 172.16.1.1 remote-as 200
 !
 ip classless

 line con 0
 line aux 0
 line vty 0 4
  login
 !
 end
```

Router A only has the IBGP neighbor Router B and therefore has a single neighbor statement.

The only thing left to do is to check and make sure there is connectivity. We can verify that EBGP has been established between Router B and C by typing the command "**sh ip bgp neig**".

```
Router_B#sh ip bgp nei
BGP neighbor is 172.16.1.2,  remote AS 200, internal link
 Index 0, Offset 0, Mask 0x0
  BGP version 4, remote router ID 172.16.1.2
  BGP state = Established, table version = 1. up for 00:13:10
  Last read 00:00:10, hold time is 180, keepalive interval is
     60 seconds
  Minimum time between advertisement runs is 5 seconds
  Received 16 messages, 0 notifications, 0 in queue
  Sent 16 messages, 0 notifications, 0 in queue
  Connections established 1; dropped 0
  No. of prefix received 0
Connection state is ESTAB, I/O status: 1, unread input bytes:
     0
Local host: 172.16.1.1, Local port: 179
Foreign host: 172.16.1.2, Foreign port: 11000

Enqueued packets for retransmit: 0, input: 0, saved: 0

Event Timers (current time is 0x7E00F0):
Timer          Starts      Wakeups              Next
Retrans            17           0               0x0
TimeWait            0           0               0x0
AckHold            16           0               0x0
SendWnd             0           0               0x0
KeepAlive           0           0               0x0
```

```
    GiveUp                    0               0             0x0
    PmtuAger                  0               0             0x0
iss: 1637978956   snduna: 1637979271   sndnxt: 1637979271     sndwnd:   16070
irs:  451296618   rcvnxt:  451296933   rcvwnd:         16070  delrcvwnd:    314

    SRTT: 372 ms, RTTO: 1823 ms, RTV: 539 ms, KRTT: 0 ms
    minRTT: 4 ms, maxRTT: 304 ms, ACK hold: 300 ms
    Flags: passive open, nagle, gen tcbs

    Datagrams (max data segment is 1460 bytes):
    Rcvd: 32 (out of order: 0), with data: 16, total data bytes: 314
    Sent: 17 (retransmit: 0), with data: 16, total data bytes: 314

BGP neighbor is 172.16.2.1,   remote AS 100, external link
  Index 1, Offset 0, Mask 0x2
    BGP version 4, remote router ID 192.168.1.1
    BGP state = Established, table version = 1, up for 00:02:21
    Last read 00:00:21, hold time is 180, keepalive interval is
      60 seconds
    Minimum time between advertisement runs is 30 seconds
    Received 5 messages, 0 notifications, 0 in queue
    Sent 5 messages, 0 notifications, 0 in queue
    Connections established 1; dropped 0
    No. of prefix received 0
Connection state is ESTAB, I/O status: 1, unread input bytes:
      0
Local host: 172.16.2.2, Local port: 179
Foreign host: 172.16.2.1, Foreign port: 11000

Enqueued packets for retransmit: 0, input: 0, saved: 0

Event Timers (current time is 0x7E0F44):
Timer           Starts      Wakeups            Next
Retrans              6            0             0x0
TimeWait             0            0             0x0
AckHold              5            0             0x0
SendWnd              0            0             0x0
KeepAlive            0            0             0x0
GiveUp               0            0             0x0
PmtuAger             0            0             0x0

iss: 2290934612   snduna: 2290934718   sndnxt: 2290934718
      sndwnd:   16279
irs: 2813033514   rcvnxt: 2813033620   rcvwnd:         16279
      delrcvwnd:    105

    SRTT: 624 ms, RTTO: 4197 ms, RTV: 1474 ms, KRTT: 0 ms
```

```
minRTT: 8 ms, maxRTT: 400 ms, ACK hold: 300 ms
Flags: passive open, nagle, gen tcbs

Datagrams (max data segment is 1460 bytes):
Rcvd: 10 (out of order: 0), with data: 5, total data bytes:
    105
Sent: 6 (retransmit: 0), with data: 5, total data bytes: 105
```

We verify that Router_B sees both its EBGP neighbor Router_C and its IBGP neighbor Router_A. To verify that updates are actually being sent, we type "sh ip route" on Router_B.

```
Router_B#sh ip route
Codes: C - connected, S - static, I - IGRP, R - RIP,
    M - mobile, B - BGP, D - EIGRP, EX - EIGRP external,
    O - OSPF, IA - OSPF inter area,
    N1 - OSPF NSSA external type 1,
    N2 - OSPF NSSA external type 2
    E1 - OSPF external type 1, E2 - OSPF external type 2,
    E - EGP, i - IS-IS, L1 - IS-IS level-1,
    L2 - IS-IS level-2, * - candidate default
    U - per-user static route, o - ODR

Gateway of last resort is not set

     172.16.0.0/24 is subnetted, 2 subnets
C       172.16.1.0 is directly connected, Serial0
C       172.16.2.0 is directly connected, Serial1
B    192.168.1.0/24 [20/0] via 172.16.2.1, 00:00:40
```

We notice that we are receiving updates from Router_C, and it is advertising 192.168.1.0; however, it is not advertising 10.0.2.0. This confirms that indeed Router_C is sending updates via the EBGP connection, and the distribute list is working.

Lab-Scenario
Policy Routing

The following scenario refers to the diagram below.

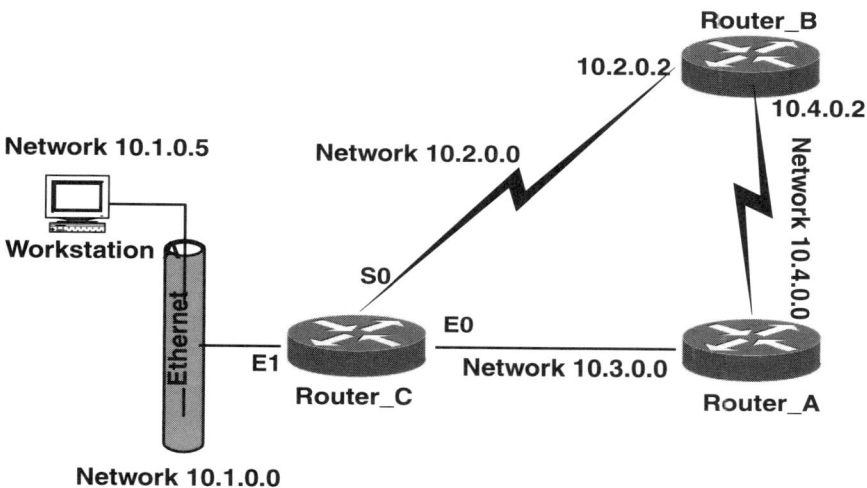

All routers are configured in a single OSPF area. Router_C, based on the cost metric for OSPF, will send all packets with a destination network address of 10.4.0.0 out the E0 interface (See the routing table below.). Configure the network such that all packets destined for network 10.4.0.0 exit the Serial 0 of Router_C.

```
Router_C#sh ip route
Codes: C - connected, S - static, I - IGRP, R - RIP,
    M - mobile, B - BGP, D - EIGRP, EX - EIGRP external,
    O - OSPF, IA - OSPF inter area,
    N1 - OSPF NSSA external type 1,
    N2 - OSPF NSSA external type 2, E1 - OSPF external type 1,
    E2 - OSPF external type 2, E - EGP, i - IS-IS,
    L1 - IS-IS level-1, L2 - IS-IS level-2,
    * - candidate default, U - per-user static route, o - ODR

Gateway of last resort is not set

     10.0.0.0/16 is subnetted, 3 subnets
C       10.2.0.0 is directly connected, Serial0
C       10.3.0.0 is directly connected, Ethernet0
O       10.4.0.0 [110/74] via 10.3.0.1, 00:00:13, Ethernet0
```

7. Lab Scenarios

Solution

One possible solution is to use Policy Based Routing. You must configure a route map to perform policy routing. The router, in lieu of destination routing, will use the route map.

In this scenario, the best route to the destination network 10.4.0.0 is through Ethernet 0. We want to force the traffic through the serial connection.

Step 1
Choose a route map tag. I chose "takeserial."

Step 2
Point the route map to the tag. The sequence number is arbitrary, but you must be consistent. In this example I chose "10."

```
Router_C(config)#route-map takeserial permit ?
  <0-65535>  Sequence to insert to/delete from existing
     route-map entry
```

Step 3
Identify which packet should be route mapped. In our example we will match the ip address of access list 1.

Step 4
Tell the router where to send the matched packet. We will send the packets to Serial 0.

Here is the completed configuration:

```
Current configuration:
!
version 11.2
!
hostname Router_C
!
interface Ethernet0
 ip address 10.3.0.3 255.255.0.0
!
interface Ethernet1
 ip address 10.1.0.3 255.255.0.0
 ip policy route-map takeserial      ←Step 1
!
interface Serial0
 ip address 10.2.0.1 255.255.0.0
 clockrate 38400
!
interface Serial1
 no ip address
 shutdown
```

```
!
router ospf 100
 network 10.0.0.0 0.255.255.255 area 0
!
no ip classless
access-list 1 permit 10.1.0.5
route-map takeserial permit 10       ←Step 2
 match ip address 1                  ←Step 3
 set interface Serial0               ←Step 4
!
line con 0
line aux 0
line vty 0 4
 login
!
end
```

Now we will ping 10.4.0.2 from Workstaton A:

```
Router_C#debug ip policy
Policy routing debugging is on
Router_C#
IP: s=10.1.0.5 (Ethernet1), d=10.4.0.2, len 74, policy match
IP: route map takeserial, item 10, permit
IP: s=10.1.0.5 (Ethernet1), d=10.4.0.2 (Serial0), len 74,
    policy routed
IP: Ethernet1 to Serial0 10.4.0.2
IP: s=10.1.0.5 (Ethernet1), d=10.4.0.2, len 74, policy match
IP: route map takeserial, item 10, permit
IP: s=10.1.0.5 (Ethernet1), d=10.4.0.2 (Serial0), len 74,
    policy routed
IP: Ethernet1 to Serial0 10.4.0.2
IP: s=10.1.0.5 (Ethernet1), d=10.4.0.2, len 74, policy match
IP: route map takeserial, item 10, permit
IP: s=10.1.0.5 (Ethernet1), d=10.4.0.2 (Serial0), len 74,
    policy routed
IP: Ethernet1 to Serial0 10.4.0.2
IP: s=10.1.0.5 (Ethernet1), d=10.4.0.2, len 74, policy match
IP: route map takeserial, item 10, permit
IP: s=10.1.0.5 (Ethernet1), d=10.4.0.2 (Serial0), len 74,
    policy routed
IP: Ethernet1 to Serial0 10.4.0.2
```

7. Lab Scenarios

Lab Scenario
Protocol Translation
X25/TCP

Users working on network 172.16.10.0 need access to applications running on the X25 network as shown in the figure below. Configure your router to provide protocol translation from the TCP Telnet application to the X25 X29 application so users may telnet to these X25 hosts.

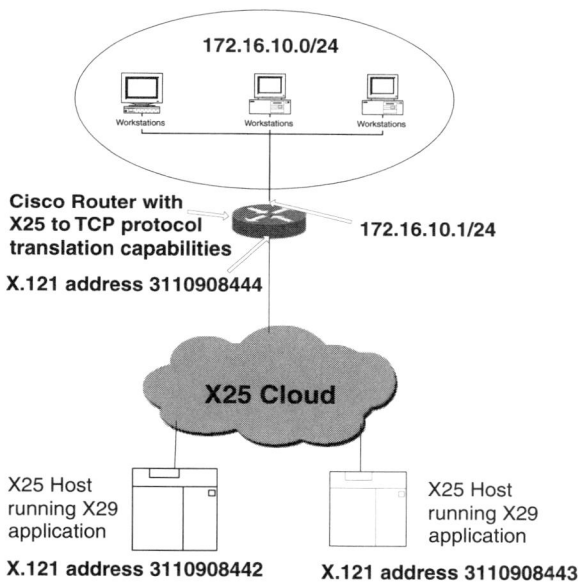

Solution

We must first establish an X25 connection. To do this we will require an X.121 address from our X25 provider. An X25 connection is set up by addressing the interface and specifying the X25 encapsulation type.

We must also set up a TCP/IP connection to our local area network and set aside an IP address for each X25 host that will need connectivity.

The final step is to define the translations. Refer to the configuration below:

```
Current configuration:
!
version 11.2
```

```
!
hostname Router_C
!
x25 routing
!
interface Ethernet0
 ip address 172.16.10.1 255.255.255.0
 shutdown
!
interface Ethernet1
 no ip address
 shutdown
!
interface Serial0
 no ip address
 no ip mroute-cache
 encapsulation x25
 shutdown
 x25 address 311090844
!
interface Serial1
 no ip address
 shutdown
!
no ip classless
!

translate x25 3110908442 tcp 172.16.10.42
translate x25 3110908443 tcp 172.16.10.43
translate tcp 172.16.10.43 x25 311090443
translate tcp 172.16.10.42 x25 311090442
!
line con 0
line aux 0
line vty 0 4
 login
!
end
```

Once we establish X25 and TCP/IP connectivity to the router, it will automatically translate IP traffic going to 172.16.10.42 and 172.16.10.43 into X25 traffic. The destination address will change to the appropriate X25 address. The reverse is true for X25 traffic coming to the router.

Router_C#sh x25 route

```
Number          X.21          CUD          Forward to
   1        3.1109E+09   translation        0 Uses
   2        3.1109E+09   translation        0 Uses
```

Router_C#debug x25 all
X25 packet debugging is on.

When a telnet request is made from 172.16.10.5 to 172.16.10.42:

```
Serial0: X25 O P3 CALL REQUEST (18) 8 lci 1
From(9): 311090844 To(9): 311090442
  Facilities: (0)
  Call User Data (4): 0x01000000 (pad)
Serial0: X25 I P3 CLEAR REQUEST (5) 8 lci 1 cause 0 diag 67
Serial0: X25 O P3 CLEAR CONFIRMATION (3) 8 lci 1
```

Lab Scenario
Fast EtherChannel between Catalyst 5000 Switches

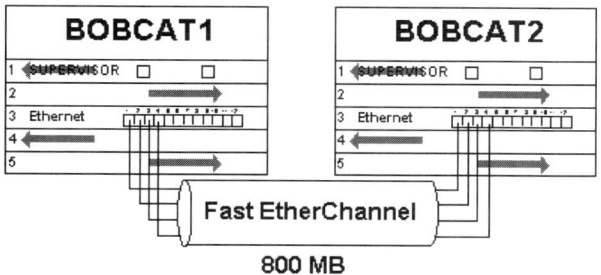

Objective

Configure the Catalyst 5000 switches above to perform Fast EtherChannel between ports 3/1-4. The aggregate bandwidth between switches must be 800 Mbps. Also configure the Fast EtherChannel to trunk all VLANs.

Solution

There are two parts to this configuration, first we must configure the Fast Etherchannel, second we must set the Channel to trunk.

To set up a Fast Etherchannel we must configure each of the ports exactly the same. They must be in the same VLAN, the same spanning tree parameters, the same duplex method, the same speed, and so forth. There is also one other requirement that is difficult to obtain from documentation, ALL PORTS IN THE CHANNEL CANNOT BE TRUNKS. If any of the ports we wish to configure in the Channel are set to trunk the Channel will not work. This does not mean we cannot trunk over the Fast Etherchannel, it simply means we must set up trunking after the Channel has been configured.

Step 1- Verify all ports are configured the same on both switches. We do this using the "show port" and "show spantree" commands. (See below.)

```
BOBCAT1> (enable) show port <Enter>
Port Name          Status      Vlan  Level   Duplex Speed  Type
____ ____ ____     _____   ____  _____  _____ _____  _____

1/1                notconnect 1      normal   half    100 100BaseTX
1/2                notconnect 1      normal   half    100 100BaseTX
3/1                connected  3      normal a-full a-100 10/100BaseTX
3/2                connected  2      normal a-full a-100 10/100BaseTX
3/3                connected  3      normal a-full a-100 10/100BaseTX
3/4                connected  2      normal a-full a-100 10/100BaseTX
3/5                notconnect 2      normal   auto   auto 10/100BaseTX
3/6                notconnect 2      normal   auto   auto 10/100BaseTX
3/7                notconnect 2      normal   auto   auto 10/100BaseTX
```

```
3/8              notconnect 2     normal   auto   auto 10/100BaseTX
3/9              notconnect 2     normal   auto   auto 10/100BaseTX
3/10             notconnect 2     normal   auto   auto 10/100BaseTX
3/11             notconnect 2     normal   auto   auto 10/100BaseTX
3/12             notconnect 2     normal   auto   auto 10/100BaseTX

BOBCAT2> (enable) show port <Enter>
Port Name        Status      Vlan Level   Duplex Speed  Type
____ ____ ____   _____  ____ _____  _____ _____  ____

1/1              notconnect 1     normal   half    100 100BaseTX
1/2              notconnect 1     normal   half    100 100BaseTX
3/1              connected  2     normal a-full  a-100 10/100BaseTX
3/2              connected  2     normal a-full  a-100 10/100BaseTX
3/3              connected  2     normal a-full  a-100 10/100BaseTX
3/4              connected  2     normal a-full  a-100 10/100BaseTX
3/5              notconnect 2     normal   auto   auto 10/100BaseTX
3/6              notconnect 2     normal   auto   auto 10/100BaseTX
3/7              notconnect 2     normal   auto   auto 10/100BaseTX
3/8              notconnect 2     normal   auto   auto 10/100BaseTX
3/9              notconnect 2     normal   auto   auto 10/100BaseTX
3/10             notconnect 2     normal   auto   auto 10/100BaseTX
3/11             notconnect 2     normal   auto   auto 10/100BaseTX
3/12             notconnect 2     normal   auto   auto 10/100BaseTX
```

- Note that ports 3/1-4 are all set to Full-Duplex capabilities on both switches, giving a bandwidth of 200 Mbps per port and an aggregate bandwidth of 800Mbps.

- Also Note that ports 3/1 and 3/3 of BOBCAT1 are in VLAN 3.

```
BOBCAT1> (enable) show spantree 2<Enter>
VLAN 2
Spanning tree enabled
Spanning tree type           ieee

Designated Root              00-10-07-e0-b0-00
Designated Root Priority     32768
Designated Root Cost         0
Designated Root Port         1/0
Root Max Age   20 sec    Hello Time 2  sec    Forward Delay 15 sec

Bridge ID MAC ADDR           00-10-07-e0-e0-00
Bridge ID Priority           32768
Bridge Max Age 20 sec    Hello Time 2  sec    Forward Delay 15 sec


Port     Vlan  Port-State   Cost   Priority  Fast-Start  Group-method
____     ____  _____   ____   _____  _____  _____
3/2      2     forwarding   9      32        disabled
3/4      2     blocking     9      32        disabled
```

```
BOBCAT2> (enable) show spantree 2<Enter>
VLAN 2
Spanning tree enabled
Spanning tree type              ieee

Designated Root                 00-10-07-e0-b0-00
Designated Root Priority        32768
Designated Root Cost            0
Designated Root Port            1/0
Root Max Age    20 sec    Hello Time 2  sec    Forward Delay 15 sec

Bridge ID MAC ADDR              00-10-07-e0-b0-00
Bridge ID Priority              32768
Bridge Max Age 20 sec     Hello Time 2  sec    Forward Delay 15 sec


Port      Vlan   Port-State      Cost    Priority  Fast-Start  Group-method
____      ____   _____      ____    _____  _____  _____
 3/1       2     forwarding       9         32      disabled
 3/2       2     forwarding       9         32      disabled
 3/3       2     forwarding       9         32      disabled
 3/4       2     forwarding       9         32      disabled
```

- Note that BOBCAT2 is the root bridge, and BOBCAT1 is blocking on port 3/1, this is due to the redundancy created by having two ports connected to the same switch, this is normal.

- Also Note that ports 3/1 and 3/3 of BOBCAT1 are not seen when we use the show spantree 2 command, this is due to the fact that ports 3/1 and 3/3 are in VLAN 3.

Step 2- If any of the parameters are not the same we must set them the same. In Step 1 we found out that port 3/2 and 3/4 were in VLAN 2 while 3/1 and 3/3 of BOBCAT1 were in VLAN 3. We must configure these ports to be in the same VLAN, so we chose VLAN 2 and use the set vlan command to configure ports 3/1 and 3/3 in VLAN 2.

```
BOBCAT1> (enable) set vlan 2 3/1,3/3 <Enter>
VLAN 2 modified.
VLAN 3 modified.
VLAN  Mod/Ports
____  _____

3     3/1, 3/3
```

Step 3- Now that all ports are configured the same we can build our channel. We must use the set port channel command as follows.

```
BOBCAT1> (enable) set port channel 3/1-4 <Enter>
Port(s) 3/1-4 channel mode set to on.
BOBCAT1> (enable)
```

and

```
BOBCAT2> (enable) set port channel 3/1-4 <Enter>
Port(s) 3/1-4 channel mode set to on.
BOBCAT2> (enable)
```

Step 4- We now need to verify that the Channel is operational. The show port channel command will show us the status of our Channel.

```
BOBCAT1> (enable)show port channel<Enter>
```

Port	Status	Channel mode	Channel status	Neighbor device	Neighbor	Port
3/1	connected	on	channel	WS-C5000	006047419	3/1
3/2	connected	on	channel	WS-C5000	006047419	3/2
3/3	connected	on	channel	WS-C5000	006047419	3/3
3/4	connected	on	channel	WS-C5000	006047419	3/4

Step 5- Now that the Fast EtherChannel is operational we must configure it to trunk. Because the ports are grouped together in the Channel only one port on each switch need to be configured to trunk and the others will automatically follow.

```
BOBCAT1> (enable) set trunk 3/1 on <Enter>
Port 3/1-4 trunk mode set to on.
5/25/1997,17:53:39:DISL-5:Port 3/1 has become trunk
                5/25/1997,17:53:39:DISL-5:Port 3/2 has become trunk
                5/25/1997,17:53:39:DISL-5:Port 3/3 has become trunk
                5/25/1997,17:53:39:DISL-5:Port 3/4 has become trunk
```

and

```
BOBCAT2> (enable) set trunk 3/1 on <Enter>
Port 3/1-4 trunk mode set to on.
5/25/1997,17:53:39:DISL-5:Port 3/1 has become trunk
                5/25/1997,17:53:39:DISL-5:Port 3/2 has become trunk
                5/25/1997,17:53:39:DISL-5:Port 3/3 has become trunk
                5/25/1997,17:53:39:DISL-5:Port 3/4 has become trunk
```

Step 6- Verify that the Channel is trunking by using the show trunk command. Also verify that the spanning tree protocols view the Fast EtherChannel as a single connection so as not to block on any of the four ports, use the show spantree command.

```
BOBCAT1> (enable) show trunk <Enter>
```

Port	Mode	Status
3/1	on	trunking
3/2	on	trunking
3/3	on	trunking
3/4	on	trunking

```
Port          Vlans allowed on trunk
____          _____

3/1           1-1005
3/2           1-1005
3/3           1-1005
3/4           1-1005

Port          Vlans allowed and active in management domain
____          _____

3/1           1,2,3
3/2           1,2,3
3/3           1,2,3
3/4           1,2,3

Port          Vlans in spanning tree forwarding state and not pruned
____          _____

3/1           1,2,3
3/2           1,2,3
3/3           1,2,3
3/4           1,2,3
```

BOBCAT1> (enable) show spantree 2 <Enter>
```
VLAN 2
Spanning tree enabled
Spanning tree type              ieee

Designated Root                 00-10-07-e0-d0-00
Designated Root Priority        32768
Designated Root Cost            0
Designated Root Port            1/0
Root Max Age   20 sec    Hello Time 2  sec    Forward Delay 15 sec

Bridge ID MAC ADDR              00-10-07-e0-e0-00
Bridge ID Priority              32768
Bridge Max Age 20 sec    Hello Time 2  sec    Forward Delay 15 sec
```

Port	Vlan	Port-State	Cost	Priority	Fast-Start	Group-method
3/1-4	1	forwarding	9	32	disabled	channel

- Notice that ports 3/1-4 now show as a single connection to spanning tree and are not blocking on any ports, unlike step 1 when port 3/2 was blocking.

  You have now successfully configured a Fast EtherChannel and configured it to trunk.

Lab Scenario
Appletalk Configuration

Given the following routing table and diagram, configure all routers.

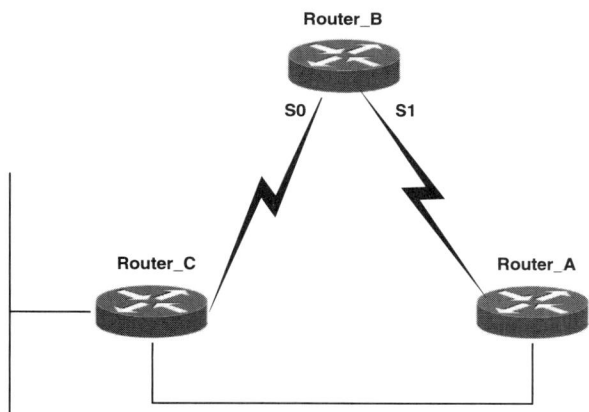

From the diagram and the routing table we can ascertain the following information:

Parallel paths are allowed.

Cable-range 111-115 is one hop away from Router_B by two different paths.

Cable-range is located in the bottom-ether zone.

Cable-range 100-105 is directly connected to the serial 0 of Router_B and it is in the leftserial zone.

Cable-range 106-110 is directly connected to the serial 1 of Router_B and it is in the rightserial zone.

```
Router_B#sh app route
Codes: R - RTMP derived,  E - EIGRP derived, C - connected,
   A - AURP, S - static, P - proxy
4 routes in internet. Up to 2 parallel paths allowed.

The first zone listed for each entry is its default (primary) zone.

R Net 95-99 [1/G] via 100.190, 4 sec, Serial0, zone left-ether
C Net 100-105 directly connected, Serial0, zone leftserial
C Net 106-110 directly connected, Serial1, zone rightserial
R Net 111-115 [1/G] via 109.143, 3 sec, Serial1,
                    via 100.190, 4 sec, Serial0, zone bottom-ether
```

Solution

From the diagram and the routing table we can ascertain the following information:

Parallel paths are allowed.
Cable-range 111-115 is one hop away from Router_B by two different paths.
Cable-range is located in the bottom-ether zone.
Cable-range 100-105 is directly connected to the serial 0 of Router_B, and it is in the leftserial zone
Cable-range 106-110 is directly connected to the serial 1 of Router_B, and it is in the rightserial zone

Router_B

```
hostname Router_B
!
appletalk routing
appletalk maximum-paths 2
!
interface Serial0
 no ip address
 no ip mroute-cache
 appletalk cable-range 100-105 100.37
 appletalk zone leftserial
 no fair-queue
!
interface Serial1
 no ip address
 appletalk cable-range 106-110 106.59
 appletalk zone rightserial
 clockrate 4000000
!
!
line con 0
line aux 0
line vty 0 4
 login
!
end
```

Router_C

```
Router_C#sh run
Building configuration...

Current configuration:
!
version 11.1
service udp-small-servers
service tcp-small-servers
```

```
!
hostname Router_C
!
!
appletalk routing
!
interface Ethernet0
 ip address 172.16.10.1 255.255.255.0
 no ip mroute-cache
 no ip route-cache
 appletalk cable-range 111-115 112.170
 appletalk zone bottom-ether
!
interface Ethernet1
 no ip address
 no ip mroute-cache
 no ip route-cache
 appletalk cable-range 95-99 97.221
 appletalk zone left-ether
!
interface Serial0
 no ip address
 no ip mroute-cache
 no ip route-cache
 appletalk cable-range 100-105 100.190
 appletalk zone leftserial
 clockrate 4000000
!
interface Serial1
 no ip address
 no ip mroute-cache
 no ip route-cache
 shutdown
!
line con 0
line aux 0
 transport input all
line vty 0 4
 login
!
end
```

Router_A

```
Current configuration:
!
```

```
version 11.3
no service password-encryption
!
hostname Router_A
!
!
appletalk routing
!
interface Ethernet0/0
 no ip address
 appletalk cable-range 111-115 111.94
 appletalk zone bottom-ether
!
interface Serial0/0
 no ip address
 no ip mroute-cache
 appletalk cable-range 106-110 109.143
 appletalk zone rightserial
 no fair-queue
!
interface TokenRing0/0
 no ip address
 shutdown
 ring-speed 16
!
interface FastEthernet1/0
 no ip address
 shutdown
!
ip classless
!
!
line con 0
line aux 0
line vty 0 4
 login
!
end
```

Lab Scenario
Hot Standby Routing Protocol (HSRP)

Cisco's Hot Standby Routing Protocol (HSRP) provides Workstation A with a backup router in case its default gateway goes down. HSRP creates a virtual router with a virtual MAC address and a Virtual IP address.

Many students have suggested that Windows 95 has this feature. While it is true that we can add multiple default gateways this feature is only used at boot up time. In other words, the host will ARP for the first default gateway on the list if that ARP fails it will continue down the list.
What happens when the host has successfully found the default gateway and it subsequently dies? The host will need to be re-booted!

HSRP solves this problem because it is dynamic. If the primary router dies the secondary will take over, and the host will never know the difference.

Let's take a look at the following scenario.

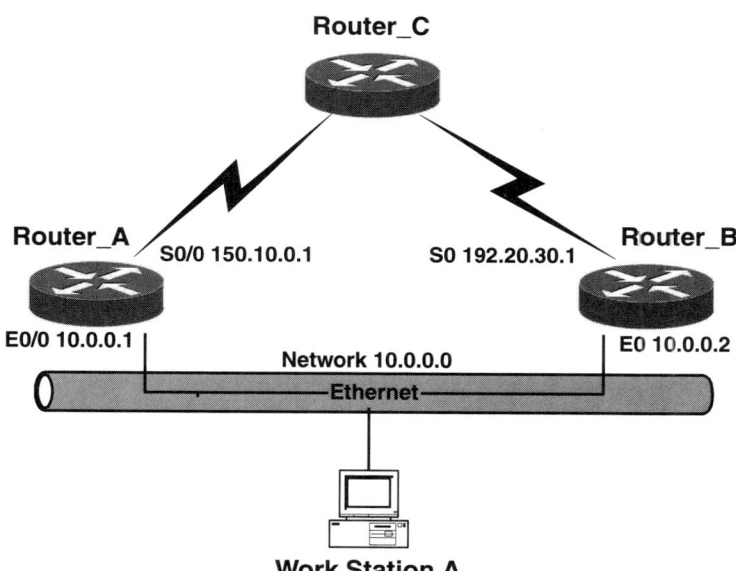

7. Lab Scenarios

Configuration for Router_A

```
version 11.3
no service password-encryption
!
hostname Router_A
!
enable secret 5 $1$.s1R$iaEqZxLnYJo2QlZi8UNaO0
enable password
!
interface Ethernet0/0
 ip address 10.0.0.1 255.0.0.0
 no ip redirects
 standby 1 priority 110
 standby 1 preempt
 standby 1 ip 10.0.0.3
!
interface Serial0/0
 ip address 150.10.0.1 255.255.0.0
 no ip mroute-cache
!
interface TokenRing0/0
 no ip address
 shutdown
 ring-speed 16
!
interface FastEthernet1/0
 no ip address
 shutdown
!
router igrp 100
 network 10.0.0.0
 network 150.10.0.0
!
ip classless
no logging buffered
!
!
line con 0
 exec-timeout 0 0
line aux 0
line vty 0 4
 login
!
end
```

Configuration for Router_B

```
Current configuration:
!
version 11.2
!
hostname Router_B
!
!
!
interface Ethernet0
 ip address 10.0.0.2 255.0.0.0
 no ip redirects
 standby 1 preempt
 standby 1 ip 10.0.0.3
!
interface Ethernet1
 no ip address
 shutdown
!
interface Serial0
 ip address 192.20.30.1 255.255.255.0
!
interface Serial1
 no ip address
 shutdown
!
router igrp 100
 network 10.0.0.0
 network 192.20.30.0
!
no ip classless
!
!
line con 0
line aux 0
line vty 0 4
 login
!
end
```

Configuration for Workstation A

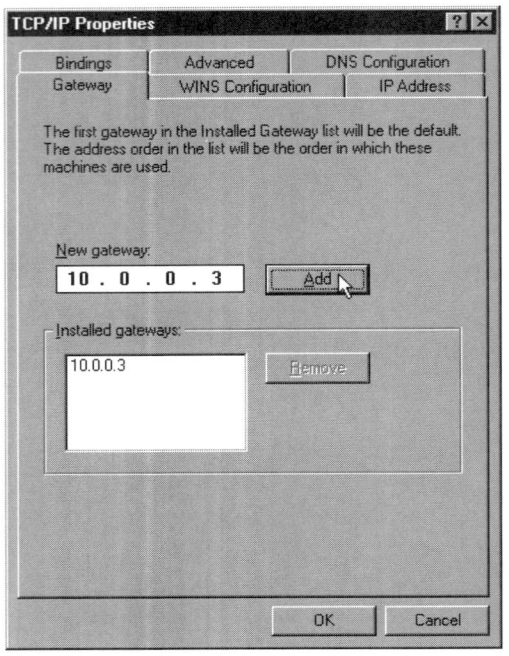 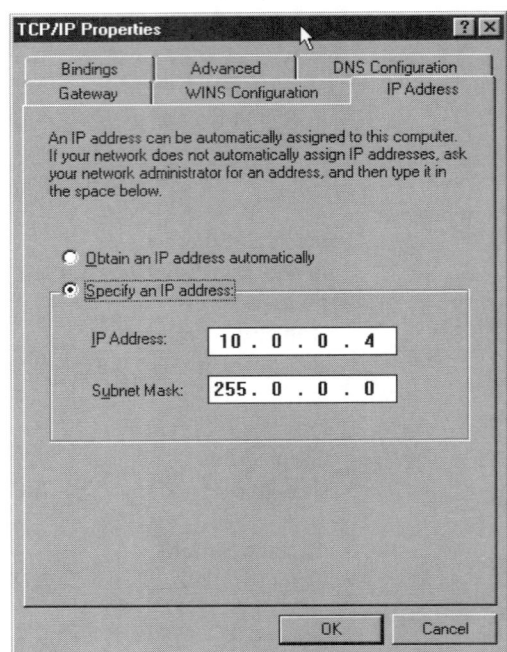

The following is the result of putting the e0/0 interface in "shut" mode.

```
Router_A(config)#int e0/0
Router_A(config-if)#shut
Router_A(config-if)#
%STANDBY-6-STATECHANGE: Standby: 1: Ethernet0/0 state Active
    -> Init
%LINEPROTO-5-UPDOWN: Line protocol on Interface Ethernet0/0,
    changed state to do wn
%LINK-5-CHANGED: Interface Ethernet0/0, changed state to
    administratively down
```

The following is the result of putting the e0/0 interface in "no shut" mode.

```
Router_A(config-if)#no shut
Router_A(config-if)#
%LINEPROTO-5-UPDOWN: Line protocol on Interface Ethernet0/0,
    changed state to up
```

```
%LINK-3-UPDOWN: Interface Ethernet0/0, changed state to up
%STANDBY-6-STATECHANGE: Standby: 1: Ethernet0/0 state Listen
    -> Active
```

The following is the result of a successful ping from workstation A.

```
Router_B#debug ip icmp
ICMP packet debugging is on
Router_B#
ICMP: echo reply sent, src 10.0.0.3, dst 10.0.0.4
ICMP: echo reply sent, src 10.0.0.3, dst 10.0.0.4
ICMP: echo reply sent, src 10.0.0.3, dst 10.0.0.4
ICMP: echo reply sent, src 10.0.0.3, dst 10.0.0.4
Router_B#debug ip icmp
```

Explanation of Router Commands

```
standby 1 priority   110
```

This sets the router's standby HSRP priority as 110, which is higher than the default of 100. Only Router_A contains this comand, which makes Router_A the default active router.

```
standby 1 preempt
```

This comand allows the router to become the active router if its priority is higher than all other routers in the group.

```
standby 1 ip 10.0.0.3
```

This command enables HSRP and establishes 10.0.0.3 as the ip address of the virtual router. The configuration of both routers should include this command.

Lab Scenario
Variable Length Subnet Masking (VLSM)

Given the registered IP address of 199.10.11.0 and the following diagram, address the entire network.

You may **NOT** use:

- Any dynamic host address assignment
- Any unnumbered serial links
- Any Network Address Translation

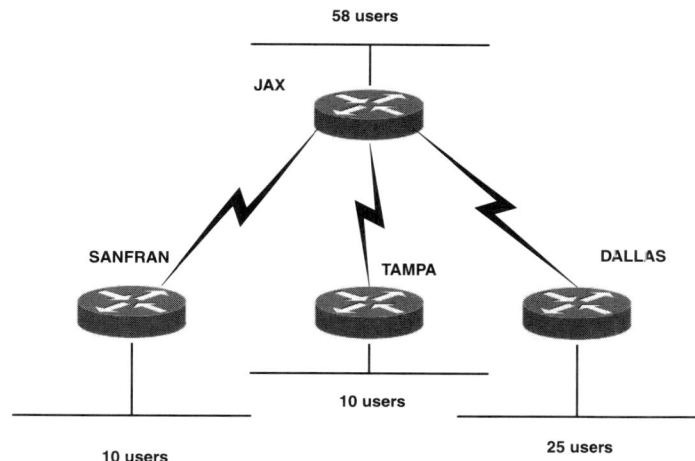

Answer

First of all let's be clear that there are several addressing schemes that could be used. The following is one way. If your solution does not match this one, that does not mean that yours is wrong.

We soon realize that the only way to solve this problem is to use Variable Length Subnet Masking (VLSM).

The serial mask to use is, of course, the 255.255.255.252 mask. The reason is that this mask provides for exactly two IP addresses, which is perfect for our needs. There are only two hosts on a serial connection. As a result of using this mask, we do not waste any addresses.

This solution will be as follows:

> Wire 199.10.11.4 to the JAX-SANFRAN link.
> Wire 199.10.11.8 to the JAX-TAMPA link
> Wire 199.10.11.12 to the JAX-DALLAS link

IP addresses will be assigned as follows:

JAX

S0	199.10.11.5/30	255.255.255.252
S1	199.10.11.9/30	255.255.255.252
S2	199.10.11.13/30	255.255.255.252

At this point we have addressed six interfaces and used the addressing space 199.10.11.4 – 199.10.11.15.

Now let's move on to the LAN interfaces:

SANFRAN

We need to have host addressing space for 10 users. The mask to use would be 255.255.255.240/28. If we were to use the 248 mask, that would only provide for six addresses. The first available wire address we could use with the /28 mask would be 16. What I might do at this point is pick the next wire, which would be 32. This would leave us the lower address of 16-31 for additional serial connections in case our network grows. I could pick the 16 wire for SANFRAN. It is just a matter of preference to keep the lower addresses for the serial connections.

IP address of **E0** for **SANFRAN** will be **199.10.11.33/28.**

TAMPA

The same situation as SANFRAN: the next wire would be 48.

IP address of **E0** for **TAMPA** will be **199.10.11.49/28.**

Now we have burned all the addressing space up to 63, but we also have reserved the space of 16-33.

DALLAS

Our situation here is a little different due to the fact we need to have addressing space for 25 users.

Since the 240 mask only gave us a maximum of 14 users, we will take the 255.255.255.228, which will give us a maximum of 30 host addresses.

The first wire address available that we can use with the 240 mask is 32, but be careful, if there is any place you will screw up VLSM, it's right at this point. We have already used this addressing space at another location, so we will take the wire address of 199.10.11.64.

IP address of **E0** for **DALLAS** will be **199.10.11.65/27.**

JAX

At this location we need addressing space for 58 users. The 240 mask only gave us 30 host addresses, so we will use the 255.255.255.192 mask. This mask will provide up to 62 users.

The first wire address for this mask would be 64, but again, be careful. We already used this space for DALLAS. The next wire is 192.10.11.128.

IP address of **E0** for **JAX** is **192.10.11.129** /27.

Summary

Addresses 199.10.11.4-15 used for serial connections.
Addresses 199.10.11.16-31 not used.
Addresses 199.10.11.32-63 used for SANFRAN & TAMPA.
Addresses 199.10.11.64-95 used for Dallas.
Addresses 199.10.11.96-127 not used.
Addresses 199.10.11.128-191 used for JAX.
Addresses 199.10.11.192 and up not used.

Class C Address Masks

Mask	Network Bits	Host Bits	Number of Networks	Number of Hosts
255.255.255.192	2	6	2	62
255.255.255.224	3	5	6	30
255.255.255.240	4	4	14	14
255.255.255.248	5	3	30	6
255.255.255.252	6	2	62	2

7. Lab Scenarios

Lab Scenario
Configuring DECnet

Given the following diagram, configure DECnet on all three routers.

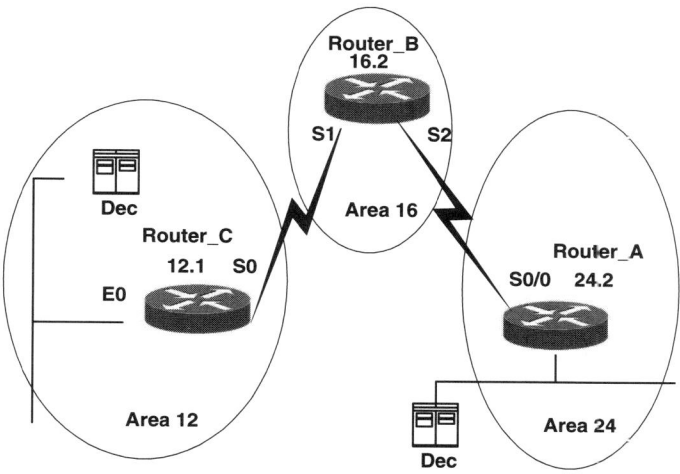

Solution

Router_B

```
Router_B#sh run
Building configuration...

Current configuration:
!
version 11.3
service password-encryption
!
hostname Router_B
enable password 7 020507520E161D245C
!
decnet 0 routing 16.2
decnet 0 node-type area
!
!
interface Serial0
shutdown
 no fair-queue
```

```
!
interface Serial1
 no ip address
 decnet 0 cost 50
 clockrate 56000
!
interface Serial2
 no ip address
decnet 0 cost 50
clockrate 56000
!
interface Serial3
 no ip address
 shutdown
interface TokenRing0
 no ip address
 shutdown
!
interface BRI0
 no ip address

ip classless
!
line con 0
line aux 0
line vty 0 4
 password 7 1306141C0A1C162F3B
 login
!
end
```

Router_C

```
Current configuration:
!
version 11.2
no service password-encryption
no service udp-small-servers
no service tcp-small-servers
!
hostname Router_C
!
decnet routing 12.1
decnet node-type area
```

```
!
!
interface Ethernet0
 no ip address
 shutdown
 decnet cost 15
!
interface Ethernet1
 no ip address
 shutdown
!
interface Serial0
 no ip address
 decnet cost 50
!
interface Serial1
 no ip address
 shutdown
!
no ip classless
!
line con 0
 password cisco
 login
line aux 0
line vty 0 4
 login
!
end
```

Router_B#sh dec nei
```
Net  Node      Interface     MAC address       Flags
0    12.1      Serial1       0000.0000.0000 A
0    24.2      Serial2       0000.0000.0000 A
Router_B#sh dec route
Net 0 Area    Cost   Hops    Next Hop to Node     Expires   Prio
*12            50      1       Serial1 -> 12.1       39     64   A+
*16             0      0       (Local) -> 16.2
*24            50      1       Serial2 -> 24.2       38     64   A+
Net 0 Node    Cost   Hops    Next Hop to Node     Expires   Prio
*(Area)         0      0       (Local) -> 16.2
*16.2           0      0       (Local) -> 16.2
```

Router_A

```
Router_A#sh run
Building configuration...

Current configuration:
!
version 11.3
no service password-encryption
!
hostname Router_A
!
enable secret 5 $1$.s1R$iaEqZxLnYJo2QlZi8UNaO0
enable password ccnaprep
!
ip host router_B 210.7.93.2 65.62.245.1
ip host router_C 65.62.245.2
!
decnet routing 24.2
decnet node-type area
interface Loopback0
 ip address 172.17.10.2 255.255.255.0
!
interface Ethernet0/0
 ip address 172.18.10.2 255.255.255.0
 no ip mroute-cache
decnet cost 50
 no cdp enable
!
interface Serial0/0
 ip address 172.16.10.1 255.255.255.0
 no ip mroute-cache
 decnet cost 50
!
interface TokenRing0/0
 no ip address
 no ip mroute-cache
 shutdown
 ring-speed 16
 no cdp enable
!
interface FastEthernet1/0
 no ip address
 no ip mroute-cache
```

```
 shutdown
 no cdp enable
!
ip classless
!
line con 0
 exec-timeout 0 0
line aux 0
line vty 0 4
 password ccieprep
 login
!
end
```

Router_A#sh dec route

Area	Cost	Hops	Next Hop to Node	Expires	Prio	
*12	100	2	Serial0/0 -> 16.2			
*16	50	1	Serial0/0 -> 16.2	34	64	A+
*24	0	0	(Local) -> 24.2			
Node	Cost	Hops	Next Hop to Node	Expires	Prio	
*(Area)	0	0	(Local) -> 24.2			
*24.2	0	0	(Local) -> 24.2			

Router_A#sh dec nei

Net	Node	Interface	MAC address	Flags
0	16.2	Serial0/0	0000.0000.0000	A

Lab Scenario
Configure IPX

Given the following diagram and routing table, configure IPX on all three routers:

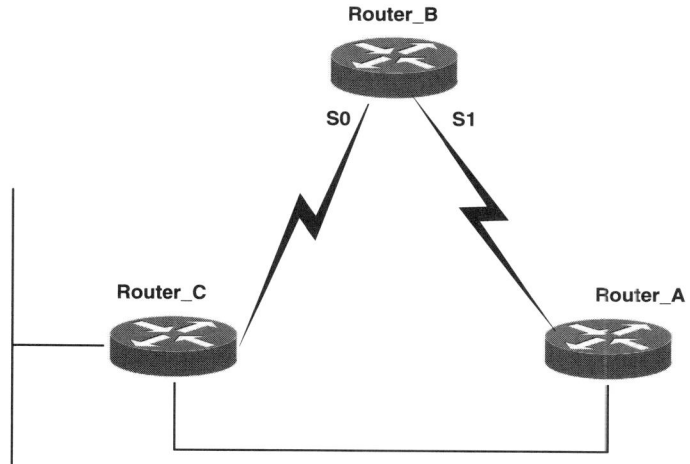

```
Router_B#sh ipx route
Codes: C - Connected primary network,
    c - Connected secondary network, S - Static,
    F - Floating static, L - Local (internal), W - IPXWAN
    R - RIP, E - EIGRP, N - NLSP, X - External, A - Aggregate
    s - seconds, u - uses, U - Per-user static

5 Total IPX routes. Up to 2 parallel paths and 16 hops al-
    lowed.

No default route known.

L         B1 is the internal network
R         A1 [07/01] via        0.0000.00a1.0C00,    3s, Se1
R         C1 [07/01] via        0.0000.00a1.0C00,    3s, Se0
R        CAD [07/01] via        0.0000.00a1.0C00,    4s, Se1
                     via        0.0000.00a1.0C00,    3s, Se0
R        FAD [07/01] via        0.0000.00a1.0C00,    3s, Se0
```

Solution

Given the diagram and the routing table, we can deduce the following:

- Network CAD is the ethernet link on the bottom
- CAD is the only network in the diagram that can be reached by two different paths of the same metric of 7 TICKS and 1 HOP
- Router_B must have maximum paths configured
- Since we have two ways to get to Network CAD and IPX RIP does not load share by default maximum paths must have been configured
- Network FAD is the ethernet on the left. It's the only other network out Serial 0 that is 1 HOP away.
- IPXWAN is configured on all serial links
- The fact there is no IPX networks numbers on the serial links would mean that IPXWAN is configured.
- NLSP is configured on the serial interfaces
- If IPXWAN is configured we must be using NLSP as the routing protocol on the serial interfaces

Router_A

```
hostname Router_A
!
ipx routing 0010.7b15.bd41
ipx internal-network A1
!
interface Ethernet0/0
 no ip address
 %b%ipx network CAD%/b%
!
interface Serial0/0
 no ip address
 no ip mroute-cache
 ipx ipxwan 0 unnumbered Router_A
 ipx nlsp enable
 no fair-queue
!
interface TokenRing0/0
 no ip address
 shutdown
 ring-speed 16
!
interface FastEthernet1/0
 no ip address
 shutdown
!
```

7. Lab Scenarios

```
ip classless
!
line con 0
line aux 0
line vty 0 4
 login
!
end
```

Router_B

```
Router_B#sh run
Building configuration...

Current configuration:
!
version 11.3
no service password-encryption
!
hostname Router_B
!
!
ipx routing 0007.7816.fe54
ipx maximum-paths 2
ipx internal-network B1
!
interface Serial0
 no ip address
 no ip mroute-cache
 ipx ipxwan 0 unnumbered Router_B
 ipx nlsp enable
 no fair-queue
!
interface Serial1
 no ip address
 ipx ipxwan 0 unnumbered Router_B
 ipx nlsp enable
 clockrate 4000000
!
interface Serial2
 no ip address
 shutdown
!
interface Serial3
 no ip address
```

```
 shutdown
!
interface TokenRing0
 no ip address
 shutdown
!
interface BRI0
 no ip address
 shutdown
!
ip classless
!
ipx router nlsp
!
line con 0
line aux 0
line vty 0 4
 login
end
```

Router_C

```
hostname Router_C
!
ipx routing 0060.09c3.df60
ipx internal-network C1
!
interface Ethernet0
 ip address 172.16.10.1 255.255.255.0
 no ip mroute-cache
 no ip route-cache
 ipx network CAD
!
interface Ethernet1
 no ip address
 no ip mroute-cache
 no ip route-cache
 ipx network FAD
!
interface Serial0
 no ip address
 no ip mroute-cache
 no ip route-cache
 ipx ipxwan 0 unnumbered Router_C
 ipx nlsp enable
 clockrate 4000000
```

```
!
interface Serial1
 no ip address
 no ip mroute-cache
 no ip route-cache
 clockrate 4000000
!
no ip classless
!
ipx router nlsp
!
line con 0
line aux 0
 transport input all
line vty 0 4
 login
!
end
```

7. Lab Scenarios

Lab Scenario
Integrated Routing and Bridging

Given the following scenario and diagram configure both Router_B and Router_C:

Route and bridge IP.
Only route Appletalk.

Router_C

```
Appletalk
E0  cable range 100-105
E1 cable range 106-110
E0 & E1 are in the lanzone
S0 cable-range 115-115
S0 zone is leftserial
```

Router_B

```
S1 cable range 120-120
S1 zone rightserial
```

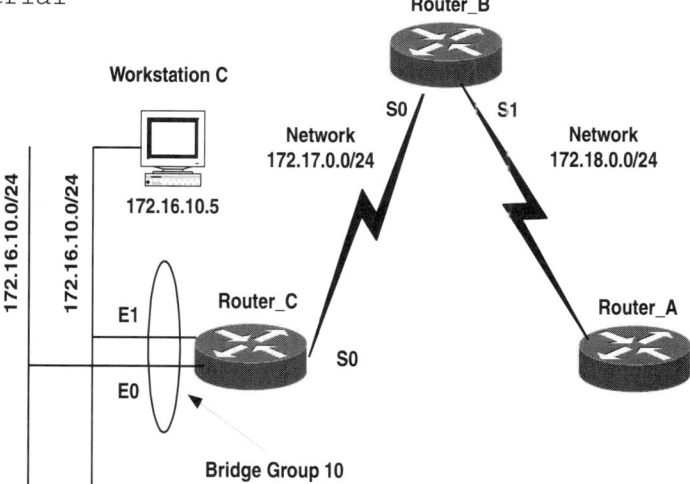

Solution

Router_B

```
<Router_B#sh run
Building configuration...

Current configuration:
!
version 11.3
no service password-encryption
!
```

```
hostname Router_B
!
appletalk routing
!
interface Serial0
 ip address 172.17.1.2 255.255.255.0
 no ip mroute-cache
 appletalk cable-range 115-115 115.229
 appletalk zone leftserial
 no fair-queue
!
interface Serial1
 ip address 172.18.1.2 255.255.255.0
 appletalk cable-range 120-120 120.17
 appletalk zone rightserial
 clockrate 4000000
!
interface Serial2
 no ip address
 shutdown
!
interface Serial3
 no ip address
 shutdown
!
interface TokenRing0
 no ip address
 shutdown
!
interface BRI0
 no ip address
 shutdown
!
router rip
 network 172.17.0.0
!
ip classless
!
!
line con 0
line aux 0
line vty 0 4
 login
!
end
```

Router_C

```
Router_C#sh run
Building configuration...

Current configuration:
!
version 11.2
no service password-encryption
service udp-small-servers
service tcp-small-servers
!
hostname Router_C
!
appletalk routing
!
interface Ethernet0
 no ip address
 no ip route-cache
 no ip mroute-cache
 appletalk cable-range 100-105 103.186
 appletalk zone lanzone
 bridge-group 10
!
interface Ethernet1
 no ip address
 no ip route-cache
 no ip mroute-cache
 appletalk cable-range 106-110 108.131
 appletalk zone lanzone
 bridge-group 10
!
interface Serial0
 ip address 172.17.1.1 255.255.255.0
 no ip route-cache
 no ip mroute-cache
 appletalk cable-range 115-115 115.252
 appletalk zone leftserial
 clockrate 4000000
!
interface Serial1
 no ip address
 no ip route-cache
 no ip mroute-cache
```

```
  shutdown
 !
interface BVI10
 ip address 172.16.10.1 255.255.255.0
 !
router rip
 network 172.17.0.0
 network 172.16.0.0
 !
no ip classless
 !
bridge irb
bridge 10 protocol dec
bridge 10 route ip
bridge 10 route appletalk
no bridge 10 bridge appletalk   ←Turns off Appletalk Bridging
 !
line con 0
line aux 0
 transport input all
line vty 0 4
 login
 !
end
```

Verifying IRB

```
Router_C#sh int e 1 irb

Ethernet1

  Routed protocols on Ethernet1:
   appletalk  ip

  Bridged protocols on Ethernet1:
   clns        decnet      ip          vines
   apollo      ipx         xns

  Software MAC address filter on Ethernet1

Hash Len    Address        Matches  Act       Type

0x00:  0 ffff.ffff.ffff       0 RCV Physical broadcast
0x2A:  0 0900.2b01.0001       0 RCV DEC spanning tree
0x57:  0 0100.5e00.0009       0 RCV IP multicast
0x68:  0 0060.09c3.df61       0 RCV Interface MAC address
```

```
0x69:   0  0060.09c3.df60      0  RCV  Bridge-group Virtual Interface
0xBF:   0  0900.0700.00b8      0  RCV  Appletalk zone
0xC0:   0  0100.0ccc.cccc      0  RCV  CDP
0xC2:   0  0180.c200.0000      0  RCV  IEEE spanning tree
0xF8:   0  0900.07ff.ffff      0  RCV  Appletalk broadcast

    Router_C#sh int bvi10
    BVI10 is up, line protocol is up
      Hardware is BVI, address is 0060.09c3.df60 (bia
         0000.0000.0000)
      Internet address is 172.16.10.1/24
      MTU 1500 bytes, BW 10000 Kbit, DLY 5000 usec, rely 255/255,
         load 1/255
      Encapsulation ARPA, loopback not set, keepalive set (10 sec)
      ARP type: ARPA, ARP Timeout 04:00:00
      Last input never, output never, output hang never
      Last clearing of "show interface" counters never
      Queueing strategy: fifo
      Output queue 0/0, 0 drops; input queue 0/75, 0 drops
      5 minute input rate 0 bits/sec, 0 packets/sec
      5 minute output rate 0 bits/sec, 0 packets/sec
         1087 packets input, 151074 bytes, 0 no buffer
         Received 0 broadcasts, 0 runts, 0 giants, 0 throttles
         0 input errors, 0 CRC, 0 frame, 0 overrun, 0 ignored, 0
         abort
         5726 packets output, 456 bytes, 0 underruns
         0 output errors, 0 collisions, 0 interface resets
         0 output buffer failures, 0 output buffers swapped out
```

The following is a ping from Workstation B

```
    Microsoft(R) Windows 95
       (C)Copyright Microsoft Corp 1981-1995.


    C:\WINDOWS\Desktop>cd\


    C:\>ping 172.17.1.2


    Pinging 172.17.1.2 with 32 bytes of data:

    Reply from 172.17.1.2: bytes=32 time=5ms TTL=254
    Reply from 172.17.1.2: bytes=32 time=5ms TTL=254
    Reply from 172.17.1.2: bytes=32 time=5ms TTL=254
    Reply from 172.17.1.2: bytes=32 time=4ms TTL=254

    C:\>
```

7. Lab Scenarios

Lab Scenario
IP Access Lists

Referring to the diagram and configurations below, configure the router(s) so that:

- Workstation C is not allowed to ping Router_A.
- Workstation C is not allowed to use SNMP to Router_A.
- Workstation C is denied accessing Router_B with any protocol other than Telnet & TFTP.
- Any other traffic not explicitly defined will be denied.

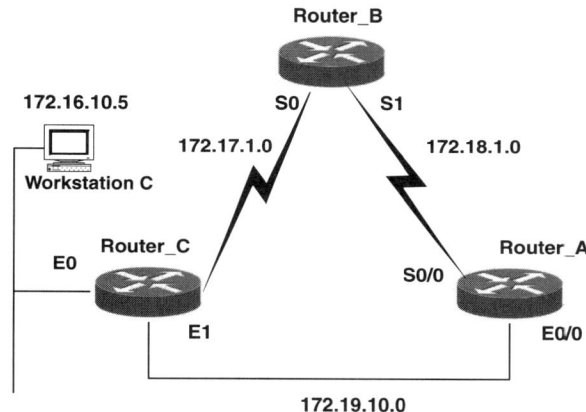

Router_A

```
Router_A#sh run
Building configuration...

Current configuration:
!
version 11.3
no service password-encryption
!
hostname Router_A
!
interface Ethernet0/0
 ip address 172.19.10.2 255.255.255.0
!
interface Serial0/0
 ip address 172.18.1.1 255.255.255.0
!
interface TokenRing0/0
```

```
 no ip address
 shutdown
 ring-speed 16
!
interface FastEthernet1/0
 no ip address
 shutdown
!
router eigrp 16
 network 172.18.0.0
 network 172.19.0.0
!
router rip
 redistribute eigrp 16 metric 1
 network 172.19.0.0
!
ip classless
!
line con 0
line aux 0
line vty 0 4
 login
!
end
```

Router_B

```
Router_B#sh run
Building configuration...

Current configuration:
!
version 11.3
no service password-encryption
service udp-small-servers
service tcp-small-servers
!
hostname Router_B
!
interface Serial0
 ip address 172.17.1.2 255.255.255.0
 no ip route-cache
 no ip mroute-cache
 no fair-queue
```

```
!
interface Serial1
 ip address 172.18.1.2 255.255.255.0
 no ip route-cache
 no ip mroute-cache
 clockrate 4000000
!

router eigrp 16
 redistribute rip metric 1544 10 255 1 1500
 network 172.17.0.0
 network 172.18.0.0
!
router rip
 redistribute eigrp 16 metric 1
 network 172.17.0.0
!
ip classless
!
line con 0
line aux 0
 transport input all
line vty 0
 access-class 12 in
 login
line vty 1 4
 login
!
end
```

Router_C

```
Router_C#sh run
Building configuration...

Current configuration:
!
version 11.2
no service password-encryption
service udp-small-servers
service tcp-small-servers
!
hostname Router_C
!
```

```
appletalk routing
!
interface Ethernet0
 ip address 172.16.10.1 255.255.255.0
 ip access-group 101 in
 no ip route-cache
 no ip mroute-cache
!
interface Ethernet1
 ip address 172.19.10.1 255.255.255.0
 no ip route-cache
 no ip mroute-cache
!
interface Serial0
 ip address 172.17.1.1 255.255.255.0
 no ip route-cache
 no ip mroute-cache
clockrate 4000000
!
interface Serial1
 no ip address
 no ip route-cache
 no ip mroute-cache
 shutdown
!
router rip
 network 172.16.0.0
 network 172.17.0.0
 network 172.19.0.0
no ip classless
!
line con 0
line aux 0
 transport input all
line vty 0 4
 login
!
end
```

Solution

There are two steps in activating an access list.

Step 1: Create the list

Step 2: Place the list on an interface(s) of the appropriate router. (I was told by a very good source that this step is often overlooked by CCIE candidates)

The following is the list:

```
access-list 101 deny    icmp host 172.16.10.5 host 172.18.1.1 echo
access-list 101 deny    icmp host 172.16.10.5 host 172.19.10.2 echo
access-list 101 deny    udp host 172.16.10.5 host 172.19.10.2 eq snmp
access-list 101 deny    udp host 172.16.10.5 host 172.18.1.1 eq snmp
access-list 101 permit ip host 172.16.10.5 host 172.19.10.2
access-list 101 permit ip host 172.16.10.5 host 172.18.1.1
access-list 101 permit tcp any any eq telnet
access-list 101 permit udp any any eq tftp
```

There is no need to deny all protocols from Workstation C to Router_B because the implicit deny all will take care of that.

The last step is the placement of the list.

Place the list on the e0 incoming interface of Router_C as follows:

```
Router_C(config)#int e0
Router_C(config-if)#ip access-group 101 in
```

7. Lab Scenarios

Lab Scenario
Frame Relay and Appletalk Tunneling (Cayman)

Given the following diagram

Configure Router_B as a frame relay switch.
Configure Appletalk with Cayman Tunneling.

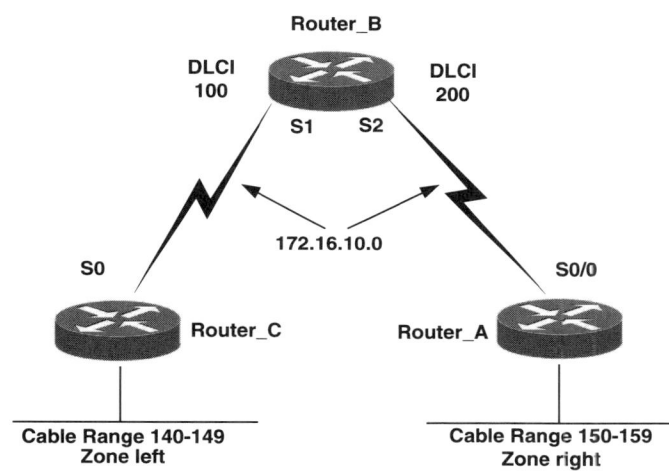

Solution

Router_C

```
Router_C#sh run
Building configuration...

Current configuration:
!
version 11.2
no service password-encryption
no service udp-small-servers
no service tcp-small-servers
!
hostname Router_C
!
enable secret 5 $1$jCQH$nzkHW61Q9ywoAX87xsp9p1
enable password ccnaprep
!
```

7. Lab Scenarios

```
appletalk routing
ipx routing 0060.09c3.df60
!
interface Loopback0
 ip address 172.17.10.1 255.255.255.0
!
interface Tunnel0
 no ip address
 tunnel source Serial0
 tunnel destination 172.16.10.1
 tunnel mode cayman
!
interface Ethernet0
 no ip address
 appletalk cable-range 140-149 148.178
 appletalk zone left
!
interface Ethernet1
 no ip address
 shutdown
!
interface Serial0
 ip address 172.16.10.2 255.255.255.0
 encapsulation frame-relay
 no fair-queue
 cdp enable
 frame-relay lmi-type cisco
!
interface Serial1
 no ip address
 shutdown
!
no ip classless

!
line con 0
line aux 0
line vty 0 4
 password sailing
 login
!
end
```

```
Router_C#sh app route
Codes: R - RTMP derived, E - EIGRP derived, C - connected, A
    - AURP
        S - static  P - proxy
2 routes in internet

The first zone listed for each entry is its default (primary)
    zone.

C Net 140-149 directly connected, Ethernet0, zone left
R Net 150-159 [1/G] via 0.0, 4 sec, Tunnel0, zone right
</routerio>
```

Router_B

```
version 11.3
no service password-encryption
!
hostname Router_B
!
enable secret 5 $1$eZ3D$vnTjKaCLtbSCcMF1mGzZm0
enable password cnaprep
!
ip host a 210.7.93.1
ip host router_a 210.7.93.1
ip host router_c 65.62.245.2
frame-relay switching
isdn switch-type ntt
!
interface Serial0
 no ip address
 no ip mroute-cache
 shutdown
 no fair-queue
 clockrate 4000000
!
interface Serial1
 ip address 65.62.245.3 255.255.255.0
 encapsulation frame-relay
 no ip mroute-cache
 keepalive 15
 clockrate 2000000
 frame-relay lmi-type cisco
 frame-relay intf-type dce
```

```
  frame-relay route 100 interface Serial2 200
!
interface Serial2
 ip address 65.62.245.4 255.255.255.0
 encapsulation frame-relay
 no ip mroute-cache
 keepalive 15
 clockrate 115200
 frame-relay lmi-type cisco
 frame-relay intf-type dce
 frame-relay route 200 interface Serial1 100
!
interface Serial3
 no ip address
 no ip mroute-cache
 shutdown
 no cdp enable
!
interface TokenRing0
 no ip address
 no ip mroute-cache
 shutdown
 no cdp enable
!
interface BRI0
 no ip address
 no ip mroute-cache
 shutdown
 no cdp enable
!
ip classless
!
!
line con 0
 exec-timeout 0 0
line aux 0
line vty 0 4
 password ccieprep
 login
!
end
```

Router_A

```
Router_A#sh run
Building configuration...

Current configuration:
!
version 11.3
no service password-encryption
!
hostname Router_A
!
enable secret 5 $1$.s1R$iaEqZxLnYJo2QlZi8UNaO0
enable password ccnaprep
appletalk routing
ipx routing 0010.7b15.bd41
!
interface Loopback0
 ip address 172.17.10.2 255.255.255.0
!
interface Tunnel0
 no ip address
 tunnel source Serial0/0
 tunnel destination 172.16.10.2
 tunnel mode cayman
!
interface Ethernet0/0
 ip address 172.18.10.2 255.255.255.0
 no ip mroute-cache
 appletalk cable-range 150-159 152.202
 appletalk zone right
no cdp enable
!
interface Serial0/0
 ip address 172.16.10.1 255.255.255.0
 encapsulation frame-relay
 no ip mroute-cache
 cdp enable
 frame-relay lmi-type cisco
!
interface TokenRing0/0
 no ip address
 no ip mroute-cache
 shutdown
```

```
 ring-speed 16
 no cdp enable
!
interface FastEthernet1/0
 no ip address
 no ip mroute-cache
 shutdown
 no cdp enable
!
ip classless
!
line con 0
 exec-timeout 0 0
line aux 0
line vty 0 4
 password ccieprep
 login
!
end


Router_A#sh app route
Codes: R - RTMP derived, E - EIGRP derived, C - connected,
   A - AURP, S - static  P - proxy

2 routes in internet

The first zone listed for each entry is its default (primary)
    zone.

R Net 140-149 [1/G] via 0.0, 7 sec, Tunnel0, zone left
C Net 150-159 directly connected, Ethernet0/0, zone right
```

Notice that when using Cayman tunneling, you must not configure the tunnel with an AppleTalk network address.

When configuring GRE-IP an appletalk address must be used.

LAB Scenario
IGRP Load Balancing

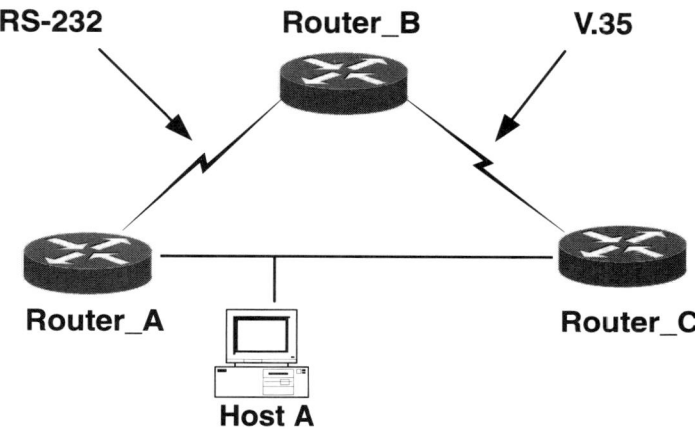

Scenario

Configure IGRP on all routers and take advantage of IGRP's load balancing feature to access Host_A.

Use the major network address of 172.16.0.0 with a mask of 255.255.255.0.
Configure a bandwidth of 128k on the Serial 1 of Router_B
Configure a bandwidth of 64k on the Serial 0 of Router_B
Router_B has the DCE connections.

Solution

The key here is to keep in mind that IGRP will load balance over unequal metrics. To take advantage of this feature we use the variance command.

Router Configurations and routing tables are shown below:

Router_B

```
Router_B#sh run
Building configuration...

Current configuration:
!
```

```
version 11.3
no service password-encryption
service udp-small-servers
service tcp-small-servers
!
hostname Router_B
!
!
ip host r3620 2001 1.1.1.1
ip host r2521 2002 1.1.1.1
ip host r2514 2003 1.1.1.1
!
interface Ethernet0
 no ip address
 shutdown
!
interface Serial0
 ip address 172.16.10.1 255.255.255.0
 bandwidth 64
 no fair-queue
 clockrate 64000
!
interface Serial1
 ip address 172.16.20.1 255.255.255.0
 bandwidth 128
 clockrate 125000
!
router igrp 100
 variance 2
 network 172.16.0.0
!
no ip classless
!
!
line con 0
line 1 8
 transport input all
line aux 0
line vty 0 4
 login
!
end

Router_B#sh ip route
Codes: C - connected, S - static, I - IGRP, R - RIP,
```

```
        M - mobile, B - BGP, D - EIGRP, EX - EIGRP external,
        O - OSPF, IA - OSPF inter area,
        N1 - OSPF NSSA external type 1,
        N2 - OSPF NSSA external type 2, E1 - OSPF external type 1,
        E2 - OSPF external type 2, E - EGP, i - IS-IS,
        L1 - IS-IS level-1, L2 - IS-IS level-2,
         * - candidate default, U - per-user static route, o - ODR

    Gateway of last resort is not set

         172.16.0.0/24 is subnetted, 3 subnets
    I        172.16.30.0 [100/80225] via 172.16.20.2, 00:01:11,
         Serial1
                            [100/158350] via 172.16.10.2, 00:00:08,
         Serial0
    C        172.16.20.0 is directly connected, Serial1
    C        172.16.10.0 is directly connected, Serial0
```

Router_A

```
    Router_A#sh run
    Building configuration...

    Current configuration:
    !
    version 11.3
    no service password-encryption
    !
    hostname Router_A
    !
    interface Ethernet0/0
     ip address 172.16.30.1 255.255.255.0
    !
    interface Serial0/0
     ip address 172.16.10.2 255.255.255.0
     no ip mroute-cache
    !
    interface TokenRing0/0
     no ip address
     shutdown
     ring-speed 16
    !
    interface FastEthernet1/0
     no ip address
```

```
  shutdown
 !
 router igrp 100
  network 172.16.0.0
 !
 ip classless
 !
 !
 line con 0
 line aux 0
 line vty 0 4
  login
 !
 end

 Router_A#sh ip route
 Codes: C - connected, S - static, I - IGRP, R - RIP,
    M - mobile, B - BGP, D - EIGRP, EX - EIGRP external,
    O - OSPF, IA - OSPF inter area
   N1 - OSPF NSSA external type 1,
   N2 - OSPF NSSA external type 2, E1 - OSPF external type 1,
   E2 - OSPF external type 2, E - EGP, i - IS-IS,
   L1 - IS-IS level-1, L2 - IS-IS level-2,
    * - candidate default, U - per-user static route, o - ODR

 Gateway of last resort is not set

      172.16.0.0/24 is subnetted, 3 subnets
 C      172.16.30.0 is directly connected, Ethernet0/0
 I      172.16.20.0 [100/8576] via 172.16.30.3, 00:00:53,
     Ethernet0/0
 C      172.16.10.0 is directly connected, Serial0/0
```

Router_C

```
 Router_C#sh run
 Building configuration...

 Current configuration:
 !
 version 11.2
 no service password-encryption
 no service udp-small-servers
```

```
no service tcp-small-servers
!
hostname Router_C
!
!
!
interface Ethernet0
 ip address 172.16.30.3 255.255.255.0
!
interface Ethernet1
 no ip address
 shutdown
!
interface Serial0
 ip address 172.16.20.2 255.255.255.0
 ip rip authentication mode 0
!
interface Serial1
 no ip address
 shutdown
!
router igrp 100
 network 172.16.0.0
!
no ip classless
!
!
line con 0
line aux 0
line vty 0 4
 login
!
end

Router_C#sh ip route
Codes: C - connected, S - static, I - IGRP, R - RIP,
   M - mobile, B - BGP, D - EIGRP, EX - EIGRP external,
   O - OSPF, IA - OSPF inter area
  N1 - OSPF NSSA external type 1,
  N2 - OSPF NSSA external type 2
  E1 - OSPF external type 1, E2 - OSPF external type 2,
   E - EGP, i - IS-IS, L1 - IS-IS level-1,
   L2 - IS-IS level-2, * - candidate default
   U - per-user static route, o - ODR
```

```
Gateway of last resort is not set

     172.16.0.0/24 is subnetted, 3 subnets
C       172.16.30.0 is directly connected, Ethernet0
C       172.16.20.0 is directly connected, Serial0
I       172.16.10.0 [100/8576] via 172.16.30.1, 00:00:06,
     Ethernet0
```

Lab Scenario
Reverse Telnet

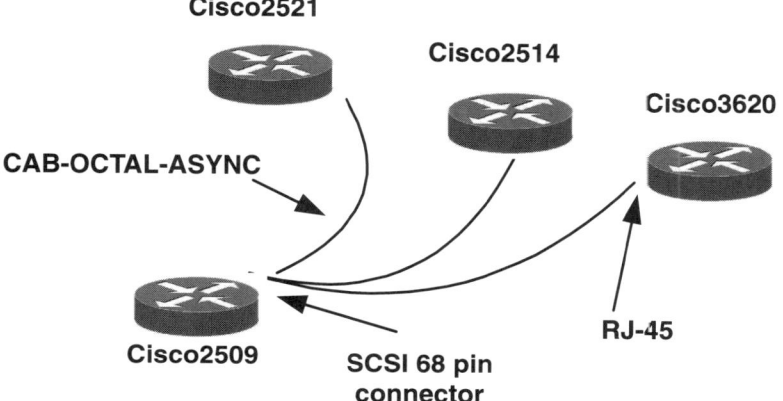

Working with several routers at once can be fun, but it can get kind of tiring going back and forth with console cables to all the routers.

Reverse telnet is a very "neat" way to access several routers from one port. This is done through a Cisco Access Server, in my case a 2509. This router is equipped with a 68-pin SCSI connector. The cable shown is an Asynchronous Breakout cable (CAB_OCTAL_ASYNC) with 8 RJ-45s (8 pin).

The RJ-45s get connected to the console port of each router. The lines of the cable are numbered 1 through 8. Take note of these numbers and what router they are attached to. You will need to know this when the host table is configured.

Each of these 8 RJ-45 connectors provide us with a TTY connection.

```
r2509#sh line
   Tty Typ      Tx/Rx      A Modem  Roty AccO AccI  Uses    Noise
                Overruns
*   0 CTY                  -   -      -    -    -     2       0    0/0
*   1 TTY    9600/9600     -   -      -    -    -     1       0    0/0
*   2 TTY    9600/9600     -   -      -    -    -     1       1    0/0
    3 TTY    9600/9600     -   -      -    -    -     0       0    0/0
    4 TTY    9600/9600     -   -      -    -    -     0       0    0/0
    5 TTY    9600/9600     -   -      -    -    -     0       0    0/0
    6 TTY    9600/9600     -   -      -    -    -     0       0    0/0
    7 TTY    9600/9600     -   -      -    -    -     0       0    0/0
    8 TTY    9600/9600     -   -      -    -    -     0       0    0/0
    9 AUX    9600/9600     -   -      -    -    -     0       0    0/0
   10 VTY                  -   -      -    -    -     0       0    0/0
   11 VTY                  -   -      -    -    -     0       0    0/0
   12 VTY                  -   -      -    -    -     0       0    0/0
   13 VTY                  -   -      -    -    -     0       0    0/0
   14 VTY                  -   -      -    -    -     0       0    0/0
```

Once you have the cabling complete, the only remaining task is to configure the 2509 for reverse telnet. Two lines are all that is needed.

1. Create a loopback interface.

2. Specify which protocol to use when connecting to a line.

The command "transport input all" will allow several different protocols including Telnet.

All the necessary lines are in bold.

```
r2509#sh run
Building configuration...

Current configuration:
!
version 11.1
service udp-small-servers
service tcp-small-servers
!
hostname r2509
!
interface Loopback0
 ip address 1.1.1.1 255.255.255.0
!
interface Ethernet0
 no ip address
 shutdown
!
interface Serial0
 no ip address
 shutdown
 no fair-queue
!
interface Serial1
 no ip address
 shutdown
!
no ip classless
!
line con 0
line 1 8
 transport input all
line aux 0
line vty 0 4
```

```
  login
  !
  end
```

Create a host table

```
r2509(config)#ip host r2514 2002 1.1.1.1
r2509(config)#ip host r3620 2003 1.1.1.1
r2509(config)#ip host r2521 2001 1.1.1.1
```

2000 indicates the TCP port for telnet protocol.

This cable has each of the eight breakout lines numbered:

Breakout line 1 is plugged into the console port of the 2521.
Breakout line 2 is plugged into the console port of the 2514.
Breakout line 3 is plugged into the console port of the 3620.

This line number is added to the port number, hence 2001, 2002 and 2003.

Now it becomes a simple task of configuring several routers from a single point, which is of course the console port of the 2509.

```
r2509#telnet r2514
Trying r2514 (1.1.1.1, 2002)... Open

r2514(config)
```

So if you are ever in a situation where you have to configure several routers quick, under a lot of stress, remember Reverse Telnet, it might come in handy!

7. Lab Scenarios

Lab Scenario
ATM LAN Emulation

Using ATM LAN Emulation (LANE), configure trunking on Switches A and B such that there is connectivity for all VLAN traffic.

ATM LANE Cloud

Solution

Step 1- Create a LANE plan and worksheet.

To configure LANE, ELANs must be defined. There will be one ELAN per VLAN. This ELAN will carry a particular VLAN's traffic, which will be mapped by the user. In this case there are two VLANs, therefore there will be two ELANs. I have created ELANs, ELAN_10 and ELAN_20. Your ELAN may be different. An ELAN can be named anything and is case sensitive. The LANE plan and worksheet will identify the locations of all the LANE components that are required. See diagram below.

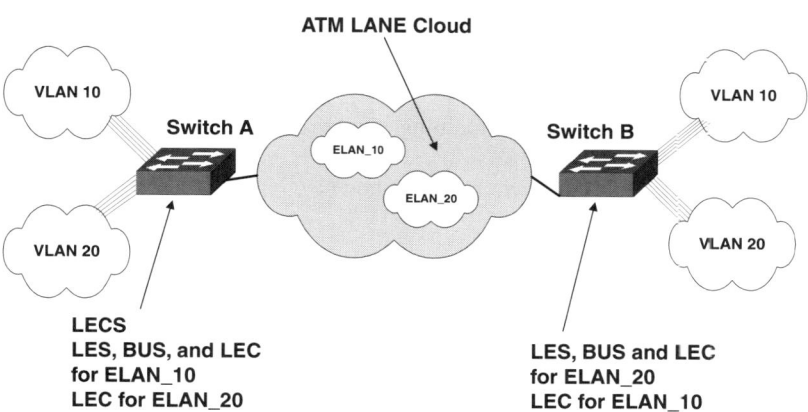

Notice that Switch_A will be configured as the LAN Emulation Configuration Server (LECS). It will also be configured as the LAN Emulation Server (LES), Broadcast and Unknown Server (BUS), and LAN Emulation Client (LEC) for ELAN_10. For connectivity to ELAN_20, Switch_A will also be configured as a LEC for ELAN_20.

Notice that Switch_B will be configured as the LES, BUS, and LEC for ELAN_20. For connectivity to ELAN_10, Switch_B will also be configured as a LEC of ELAN_10.

Step 2 – Configure the LEC, LES, and BUS.

To configure a LEC, the command "lane client ethernet [VLAN #] [ELAN name]" must be used. This command maps a VLAN to an ELAN.

To configure the LES and BUS, the command "lane server-bus [ELAN name]" must be used. This command should be placed on a different sub-interface than the LEC for performance reasons. Please also note that the LES and BUS will always be placed together.

See the configurations for Switch_A and Switch_B.

Step 3 – Configure the LECS

The LECS is simply a database with the ATM addresses of all the LES in the ATM cloud. The command sequence shown below willl set up the database.

```
        lane database ATM_Cloud
name ELAN_10 server-atm-address 47.00918100000000905FF4A001.00905FF49C41.0B
name ELAN_20 server-atm-address 47.00918100000000905FF4A001.00905AE34C11.15
```

The ATM address can be found by using "show lane server".

The last part of this step will be to enable the LECS. The LECS must be configured on a major interface. The command "lane config [database-name]" on the ATM interface will enable the LECS.

Traffic will now traverse the ATM cloud, remaining in its respective VLAN.

The configurations for Switch_A and Switch_B are shown:

Switch_A

```
        version 11.2
        !
        hostname Switch_A
        !
        !
        !
```

```
      lane database ATM_Cloud
name ELAN_10 server-atm-address 47.00918100000000905FF4A001.00905FF49C41.0B
name ELAN_20 server-atm-address 47.00918100000000905FF4A001.00905FAC3E41.15
      !
      interface ATM0
       atm preferred phy A
       atm pvc 1 0 5 qsaal
       atm pvc 2 0 16 ilmi
       lane config auto-config-atm-address
       lane config database nfl
      !
      interface ATM0.10 multipoint
       lane client ethernet 10 ELAN_10
      !
      interface ATM0.11 multipoint
      lane server-bus ethernet ELAN_10

      interface ATM0.20 multipoint
       lane client ethernet 20 ELAN_20
      !
      !
      line con 0
      line vty 0 4
       no login
      !
      end

      Switch_A#
```

Switch_B

```
      !
      version 11.2
      !
      hostname Switch_B
      !
      !
      interface ATM0
       atm preferred phy A
       atm pvc 1 0 5 qsaal
       atm pvc 2 0 16 ilmi
      !
      interface ATM0.10 multipoint
       lane client ethernet 10 ELAN_10
```

```
!
interface ATM0.20 multipoint
 lane client ethernet 20 ELAN_20
!
interface ATM0.21 multipoint
 lane server-bus ethernet ELAN_20
!
line con 0
line vty 0 4
 no login
!
end

Switch_A#
```

To verify the configuration of the two LES, two LEC, and the LECS, the "show lane config" command can be used on the switch that is the LECS (See below.).

```
Switch_A#sh lane config
LE Config Server ATM0 config table: ATM_Cloud
Admin: up  State: operational
LECS Mastership State: active master
list of global LECS addresses (38 seconds to update):
47.00918100000000905FF4A001.00905FF49C43.00  <——— me
ATM Address of this LECS:
     47.00918100000000905FF4A001.00905FF49C43.00 (auto)
 vcd  rxCnt  txCnt  callingParty
2723     1      1   47.00918100000000905FF4A001.00905FF49C40.A LEC
2731     0      0   47.00918100000000905FF4A001.00905FAC3E40.14 LEC
2732     5      5   47.00918100000000905FF4A001.00905FF49C41.0B LES
     ELAN_10 0 active
2744     4      4   47.00918100000000905FF4A001.00905FAC3E41.15 LES
     ELAN_20 0 active
cumulative total number of unrecognized packets received so far: 0
cumulative total number of config requests received so far: 23940
cumulative total number of config failures so far: 14413
    cause of last failure: no configuration
    culprit for the last failure:
    47.00918100000000905FF4A001.00905FAC3E41.15
```

Lab Scenario
Configuring DECnet

Configure DECnet in the following network.

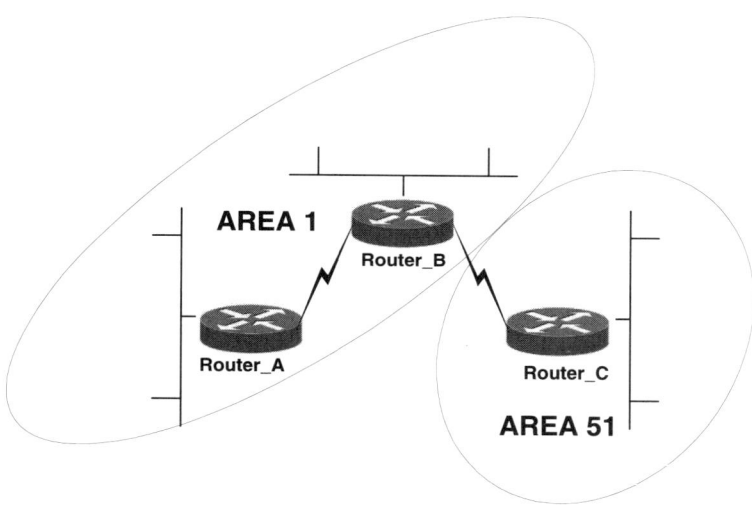

Solution

Step 1- Create an addressing scheme.

In the diagram, the area numbers 1 and 51 are given, therefore only node addresses need to be decided upon. In DECnet routing, the router only receives one address. You do not need to put an address on each interface. The addresses we used are below, your addresses may vary.

Router_A	1.2
Router_B	1.1
Router_C	51.1

The interfaces and DTE-DCE relationships are shown in the following diagram:

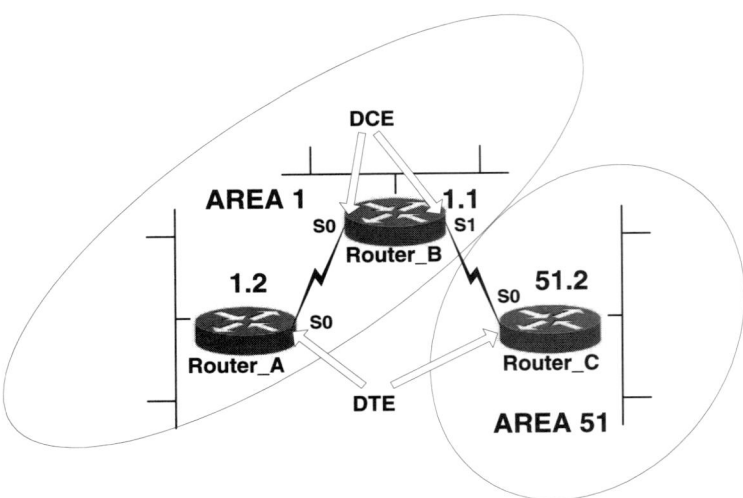

To assign an address to a DECnet Router use the "decnet routing [node-address]" command. This will assign an addresss; however, the router needs to be configured with the proper node-type. There are two types of DECnet routers, Level 1 and Level 2. A Level 1 router is a DECnet router that only communicates with nodes in its area. The diagram indicates that only Router_A is a Level 1 router. A Level 2 router is a DECnet router that can exchange updates with local nodes and nodes that reside in other areas. Notice that in the diagram Router_B and Router_C connect to nodes that are in different areas than their respective area. Router_B and Router_C are Level 2 routers.

On a Cisco Router the default node-type is "routing-iv", this is a Level 1 router. In the network given, there are two routers that need to be configured for Level 2 routing, Router_B and Router_C. To change the default node-type, use the "decnet node-type area" command. This will configure the router for Level 2 routing.

The final step in configuring DECnet is to set the DECnet cost on an interface. The command "decnet cost [cost value]" will set the cost value and enable DECnet on the interface. There is no default DECnet cost value. This value will most likely be inversely proportional to the bandwidth, i.e. the higher the bandwidth, the lower the cost. Please notice in the configurations below that the cost is lower on the Ethernet interfaces.

Router_A's Configuration

```
Router_A#sh run
Building configuration...

Current configuration:
```

```
!
version 11.3
no service password-encryption
!
hostname Router_A
!
enable secret 5 $1$.s1R$iaEqZxLnYJo2QlZi8UNaO0
enable password ccnaprep
!
!
decnet routing 1.2
decnet node-type routing-iv
!
!
interface Ethernet0/0
 ip address 172.16.10.2 255.255.255.0
 decnet cost 5
!
interface Serial0/0
 ip address 172.16.11.1 255.255.255.0
 decnet cost 25
!
interface TokenRing0/0
 no ip address
 no ip mroute-cache
 shutdown
 ring-speed 16
!
interface FastEthernet1/0
 no ip address
 no ip mroute-cache
 shutdown
 no cdp enable
!
ip classless
!
!
!
line con 0
 exec-timeout 0 0
line aux 0
line vty 0 4
 password ccieprep
 login
!
```

```
end

Router_A#
```

The Routing Table of Router_A

```
Router_A#sh dec route
   Node        Cost   Hops         Next Hop to Node        Ex-
     pires   Prio
*(Area)          25      1         Serial0/0 -> 1.1
*1.1             25      1         Serial0/0 -> 1.1
     43      64   V+
*1.2              0      0             (Local) -> 1.2
Router_A#
```

Router_B's Configuration

```
Router_B#sh run
Building configuration...

Current configuration:
!
version 11.3
no service password-encryption
service udp-small-servers
service tcp-small-servers
!
hostname Router_B
!
!
decnet routing 1.1
decnet node-type area
!
!
interface Loopback0
 ip address 1.1.1.1 255.255.255.0
!
interface Ethernet0
 ip address 172.16.12.1 255.255.255.0
 decnet cost 5
!
interface Serial0
 ip address 172.16.13.1 255.255.255.0
 decnet cost 25
```

```
 no fair-queue
 clockrate 2000000
!
interface Serial1
 ip address 172.16.13.1 255.255.255.0
 decnet cost 25
 clockrate 2000000
!
no ip classless
!
!
!
line con 0
line 1 8
 transport input all
line aux 0
line vty 0 4
 login
!
end

Router_B#
```

Router_B's Routing Table

```
Router_B#sh dec route
  Area         Cost   Hops    Next Hop to Node      Expires  Prio
  *1              0      0     (Local) -> 1.1
  *51            25      1     Serial0 -> 51.1          37      64   A+

  Node         Cost   Hops    Next Hop to Node      Expires  Prio
  *(Area)         0      0     (Local) -> 1.1
  *1.1            0      0     (Local) -> 1.1
  *1.2           25      1     Serial1 -> 1.2           34      64   V
Router_B#
```

Router C's Configuration

```
Router_C#sh run
Building configuration...

Current configuration:
```

```
!
version 11.2
no service password-encryption
no service udp-small-servers
no service tcp-small-servers
!
hostname Router_C
!
!
!
decnet routing 51.1
decnet node-type area
!
!
interface Ethernet0
 ip address 172.16.14.1 255.255.255.0
 decnet cost 5
!
interface Ethernet1
 no ip address
 shutdown
!
interface Serial0
 ip address 172.16.15.1 255.255.255.0
 decnet cost 25
 no fair-queue
!
interface Serial1
 no ip address
 shutdown
!
no ip classless
!
!
!
line con 0
line aux 0
line vty 0 4
 login
!
end

Router_C#
```

Router C's Routing Table

```
Router_C#sh dec route
   Area        Cost   Hops    Next Hop to Node      Expires   Prio
*1             25     1        Serial0 -> 1.1          37       64   A+
*51             0     0        (Local) -> 51.1
   Node        Cost   Hops    Next Hop to Node      Expires   Prio
*(Area)         0     0        (Local) -> 51.1
*51.1           0     0        (Local) -> 51.1
Router_C#
```

7. Lab Scenarios

Lab Scenario
Configure EIGRP with RIP Redistribution

Given the diagram below, configure entire network with EIGRP. Router_C is to use IP RIP only.

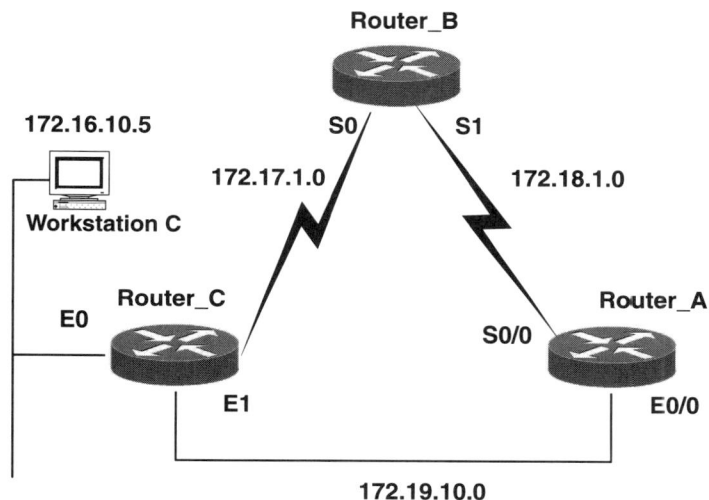

Solution

Router_A

```
Router_A#sh run
Building configuration...

Current configuration:
!
version 11.3
no service password-encryption
!
hostname Router_A
!
interface Ethernet0/0
 ip address 172.19.10.2 255.255.255.0
!
interface Serial0/0
 ip address 172.18.1.1 255.255.255.0
```

```
!
interface TokenRing0/0
 no ip address
 shutdown
 ring-speed 16
!
interface FastEthernet1/0
 no ip address
 shutdown
!
router eigrp 16
 network 172.18.0.0
 network 172.19.0.0
!
router rip
 redistribute eigrp 16 metric 1
 network 172.19.0.0
!
ip classless
!
line con 0
line aux 0
line vty 0 4
 login
!
end
```

Router_A#sh ip route
```
Codes: C - connected, S - static, I - IGRP, R - RIP,
   M - mobile, B - BGP, D - EIGRP, EX - EIGRP external,
   O - OSPF, IA - OSPF inter area
  N1 - OSPF NSSA external type 1,
  N2 - OSPF NSSA external type 2
  E1 - OSPF external type 1,
  E2 - OSPF external type 2, E - EGP, i - IS-IS,
  L1 - IS-IS level-1, L2 - IS-IS level-2,
   * - candidate default, U - per-user static route, o - ODR

Gateway of last resort is not set

D    172.17.0.0/16 [90/2681856] via 172.18.1.2, 02:53:39,
     Serial0/0
R    172.16.0.0/16 [120/1] via 172.19.10.1, 00:00:12,
     Ethernet0/0
     172.19.0.0/16 is variably subnetted, 2 subnets, 2 masks
C       172.19.10.0/24 is directly connected, Ethernet0/0
D       172.19.0.0/16 is a summary, 02:53:39, Null0
```

```
        172.18.0.0/16 is variably subnetted, 2 subnets, 2 masks
D          172.18.0.0/16 is a summary, 02:54:24, Null0
C          172.18.1.0/24 is directly connected, Serial0/0
```

Router_B

```
Router_B#sh run
Building configuration...

Current configuration:
!
version 11.3
no service password-encryption
service udp-small-servers
service tcp-small-servers
!
hostname Router_B
!
interface Serial0
 ip address 172.17.1.2 255.255.255.0
 no ip route-cache
 no ip mroute-cache
 no fair-queue
!
interface Serial1
 ip address 172.18.1.2 255.255.255.0
 no ip route-cache
 no ip mroute-cache
 clockrate 4000000
!
!
router eigrp 16
 redistribute rip metric 1544 10 255 1 1500
 network 172.17.0.0
 network 172.18.0.0
!
router rip
 redistribute eigrp 16 metric 1
 network 172.17.0.0
!
ip classless
access-list 50 permit 172.16.50.4
!
line con 0
```

```
line aux 0
 transport input all
line vty 0
 access-class 12 in
 login
line vty 1 4
 login
!
end

Router_B#sh ip route
Codes: C - connected, S - static, I - IGRP, R - RIP,
   M - mobile, B - BGP, D - EIGRP, EX - EIGRP external,
   O - OSPF, IA - OSPF inter area,
   N1 - OSPF NSSA external type 1,
   N2 - OSPF NSSA external type 2
   E1 - OSPF external type 1, E2 - OSPF external type 2,
    E - EGP, i - IS-IS, L1 - IS-IS level-1,
   L2 - IS-IS level-2, * - candidate default
    U - per-user static route, o - ODR

Gateway of last resort is not set

     172.17.0.0/16 is variably subnetted, 2 subnets, 2 masks
C       172.17.1.0/24 is directly connected, Serial0
D       172.17.0.0/16 is a summary, 02:48:42, Null0
R     172.16.0.0/16 [120/1] via 172.17.1.1, 00:00:05, Serial0
D     172.19.0.0/16 [90/2195456] via 172.18.1.1, 02:48:42,
      Serial1
     172.18.0.0/16 is variably subnetted, 2 subnets, 2 masks
D       172.18.0.0/16 is a summary, 02:48:42, Null0
C       172.18.1.0/24 is directly connected, Serial1
```

Router_C

```
Router_C#sh run
Building configuration...

Current configuration:
!
version 11.2
no service password-encryption
service udp-small-servers
service tcp-small-servers
```

```
!
hostname Router_C
!
interface Ethernet0
 ip address 172.16.10.1 255.255.255.0
 ip access-group 101 in
 no ip route-cache
 no ip mroute-cache
!
interface Ethernet1
 ip address 172.19.10.1 255.255.255.0
 no ip route-cache
 no ip mroute-cache
!
interface Serial0
 ip address 172.17.1.1 255.255.255.0
 no ip route-cache
 no ip mroute-cache
clockrate 4000000
!
interface Serial1
 no ip address
 no ip route-cache
 no ip mroute-cache
 shutdown
!
router rip
 network 172.16.0.0
 network 172.17.0.0
 network 172.19.0.0
!
no ip classless
!
!
line con 0
line aux 0
 transport input all
line vty 0 4
 login
!
end
```

```
Router_C#sh ip route
Codes: C - connected, S - static, I - IGRP, R - RIP,
   M - mobile, B - BGP, D - EIGRP, EX - EIGRP external,
   O - OSPF, IA - OSPF inter area
  N1 - OSPF NSSA external type 1,
  N2 - OSPF NSSA external type 2
  E1 - OSPF external type 1, E2 - OSPF external type 2,
   E - EGP, i - IS-IS, L1 - IS-IS level-1,
  L2 - IS-IS level-2, * - candidate default,
   U - per-user static route, o - ODR

Gateway of last resort is not set

     172.16.0.0/24 is subnetted, 1 subnets
C       172.16.10.0 is directly connected, Ethernet0
     172.17.0.0/24 is subnetted, 1 subnets
C       172.17.1.0 is directly connected, Serial0
R    172.18.0.0/16 [120/1] via 172.17.1.2, 00:00:16, Serial0
                    [120/1] via 172.19.10.2, 00:00:21,
     Ethernet1
     172.19.0.0/24 is subnetted, 1 subnets
C       172.19.10.0 is directly connected, Ethernet1
```

Lab Scenario
Frame Relay and IPX Tunneling (GRE)

Given the following diagram, configure IPX on the ethernet link of Router_A and Router_C only. Provide full connectivity using Router_B as a frame relay switch.

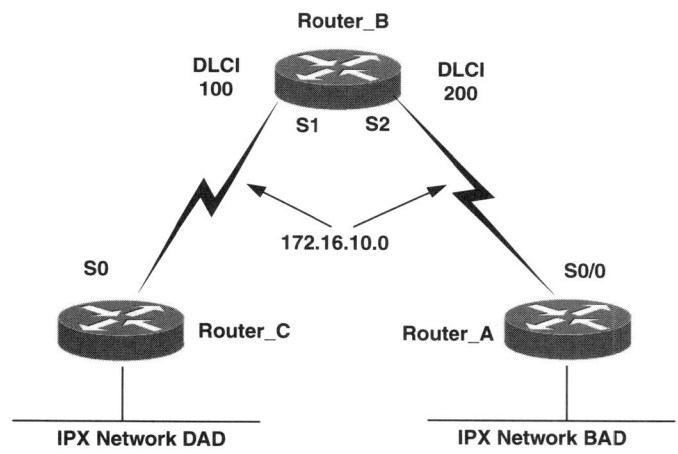

Solution

Router_B

```
hostname Router_B
enable secret 5 $1$eZ3D$vnTjKaCLtbSCcMF1mGzZm0
enable password ccnaprep
!

frame-relay switching
isdn switch-type ntt
!
interface Serial0
 no ip address
 no ip mroute-cache
 shutdown
 no fair-queue
 clockrate 4000000
!
```

```
interface Serial1
  encapsulation frame-relay
 no ip mroute-cache
 keepalive 15
 clockrate 2000000
 frame-relay lmi-type cisco
 frame-relay intf-type dce
 frame-relay route 100 interface Serial2 200
!
interface Serial2
 encapsulation frame-relay
frame-relay lmi-type ansi
 no ip mroute-cache
 keepalive 15
 clockrate 115200
 frame-relay intf-type dce
 frame-relay route 200 interface Serial1 100
!
interface Serial3
 no ip address
 no ip mroute-cache
 shutdown
 no cdp enable
!
interface TokenRing0
 no ip address
 no ip mroute-cache
 shutdown
 no cdp enable
!
interface BRI0
 no ip address
 no ip mroute-cache
 shutdown
 no cdp enable
!
ip classless
!
line con 0
 exec-timeout 0 0
line aux 0
line vty 0 4
 password ccieprep
 login
end
```

Router_C

```
Current configuration:
!
version 11.2
no service password-encryption
no service udp-small-servers
no service tcp-small-servers
!
hostname Router_C
!
enable secret 5 $1$jCQH$nzkHW61Q9ywoAX87xsp9p1
enable password ccnaprep
!
ipx routing 0060.09c3.df60

interface Tunnel0
 no ip address
 ipx network CAD
 tunnel source Serial0
 tunnel destination 172.16.10.1
!
interface Ethernet0
 ipx network DAD
!
interface Ethernet1
 no ip address
 shutdown
!
interface Serial0
 ip address 172.16.10.2 255.255.255.0
 encapsulation frame-relay
 no fair-queue
!
interface Serial1
 no ip address
 shutdown
!
no ip classless

line con 0
line aux 0
line vty 0 4
 password sailing
 login
```

```
!
end
```

Router_A

```
Current configuration:
!
version 11.3
no service password-encryption
!
hostname Router_A
!
enable secret 5 $1$.s1R$iaEqZxLnYJo2QlZi8UNaO0
enable password ccnaprep
!

ipx routing 0010.7b15.bd41
!
interface Tunnel0
 no ip address
 ipx network CAD
 tunnel source Serial0/0
 tunnel destination 172.16.10.2
interface Ethernet0/0
  no ip mroute-cache
 ipx network BAD
 no cdp enable
!
interface Serial0/0
 ip address 172.16.10.1 255.255.255.0
 encapsulation frame-relay
 no ip mroute-cache
 frame-relay lmi-type ansi
!
interface TokenRing0/0
 no ip address
 no ip mroute-cache
 shutdown
 ring-speed 16
 no cdp enable
!
interface FastEthernet1/0
 no ip address
```

```
 no ip mroute-cache
 shutdown
 no cdp enable
!
ip classless
no cdp run
!
line con 0
 exec-timeout 0 0
line aux 0
line vty 0 4
 password ccieprep
 login
!
end
```

Full connectivity

```
Router_A#sh ipx route
Codes: C - Connected primary network,
   c - Connected secondary network, S - Static,
   F - Floating static, L - Local (internal), W - IPXWAN
   R - RIP, E - EIGRP, N - NLSP, X - External, A - Aggregate
   s - seconds, u - uses, U - Per-user static

3 Total IPX routes. Up to 1 parallel paths and 16 hops al-
    lowed.

No default route known.

C        BAD (NOVELL-ETHER),  Et0/0
C        CAD (TUNNEL),        Tu0
R        DAD [151/01] via      CAD.0060.09c3.df60,   32s, Tu0
```

Chapter Eight
Trouble-Shooting LAB Scenarios

Congratulations. You have made it through the challenging written exam and completed the first day and a half of the practical with enough points to continue to the final step, troubleshooting. Trouble-shooting, in my opinion, is the easiest portion of the practical exam. Your job in this portion is to restore your routers and switches back to their original state. You do not have to fix anything that you could not get to work in the first portion of the exam.

In this final chapter, you will be presented with several troubleshooting scenarios. You will have an arsenal of "show" commands to help you identify problems, so be familiar with them. Remember not to troubleshoot anything that was never working in the first place. I found myself wanting to fix those tasks I had almost completed earlier. This will just take time away from the task at hand.

You will be required to document the "bugs" you have found, so be sure to take careful notes of those problems you encountered. Simply telling the proctor everything is fixed will not be accepted. Once you believe you have fixed all the problems, check again. I recommend that you let the proctor end your trouble-shooting section. Take all the time that is given to you, and double check every routing table and every interface for a possible overlooked mistake.

We all wish you luck with your pursuit and hope you have to endure this excruciating exam only once!

Lou Ross ¡ CCIE

8. Trouble Shooting Scenarios

Trouble-Shooting Scenario 1

Suppose you connect to the console port of a router with your terminal emulation program and you have "garbage" on the screen.

The solution to this problem is quite easy if you understand the configuration register. The configuration register consists of 16 bits.

Binary:

15	14	13	12	11	10	9	8	7	6	5	4	3	2	1	0
0	0	1	0	0	0	0	1	0	0	0	0	0	0	1	0

Hex:

2	1	0	2

Bits 12 and 11 are related to baud rate.

If bit 12 and 11 are set to 0 0 respectively, it represents 9600 baud.
If bit 12 and 11 are set to 0 1 respectively, it represents 4800 baud.
If bit 12 and 11 are set to 1 0 respectively, it represents 1200 baud.
If bit 12 and 11 are set to 1 1 respectively, it represents 2400 baud.

Because we are receiving "garbage" on the screen, there will be no way to log in to the router to change the configuration register.

There is no way to change the configuration register since your terminal emulation software is not set for the correct baud rate, therefore you will have to change YOUR terminal to the routers baud rate.

If you do not know what that baud rate is, you will have to guess and try several settings until you get it right. Remember that there are only four values for the console baud rate: 1200, 2400, 4800, and 9600. Assuming that you had your terminal set to 9600 to begin with, there are only three other possible values!

With the RISC-based routers, the situation is a little different. RISC-based routers run a different version of ROM monitor software. It is possible to set the baud rate to any value from 1200 to 115200, thus giving us more possible values.

8. Trouble Shooting Scenarios

Possible Baud Rates for Non-Risc Based Routers	Possible Baud Rates for RISC based Routers
1200 Baud	1200 Baud
2400 Baud	2400 Baud
2800 Baud	4800 Baud
9600 Baud	9600 Baud
-	19,200 Baud
-	28,800 Baud
-	33,600 Baud
-	56,000 Baud
-	115,200 Baud

Once you have "matched" the baud rate, the configuration register can be changed with the "*config-register*" command as shown below:

```
Router_C(config)#config-register 0x2142
```

8. Trouble Shooting Scenarios

Trouble-Shooting Scenario 2

Problem

You come back from lunch and you are no longer able to log in to your router; someone has changed your password.

Solution

First and foremost you must have physical access to the router to perform password recovery.

The configuration register's bit 6 defines whether or not the configuration file will be loaded from NVRAM. We do not want to apply the configuration file in NVRAM since we do not know the password contained in the file.

If bit 6 is 0 the router will load the configuration file from NVRAM.
If bit 6 is 1 the router will not load the configuration file from NVRAM.

Configuration Register represented in Decimal:

15	14	13	12	11	10	9	8	7	6	5	4	3	2	1	0
0	0	1	0	0	0	0	1	0	0	0	0	0	0	1	0

The Configuration Register represented in Hexadecimal:

2	1	0	2

The following are the steps to recover from a lost password.

1. Turn the router off and on. Within 60 seconds issue the break sequence of your terminal emulation package. If you are using HyperTerminal the sequence is <ctrl><break>.

2. You will now be in ROM monitor mode, indicated by the ">" prompt. Our goal here is to turn bit 6 on. If the configuration register is set to 0x2102, we will want to change the register to 0x2142. To determine the current configuration register setting use the following command:

        >e/s 2000002

    To change the register:

        >o/r 0x2142

8. Trouble Shooting Scenarios

To re-initialize the router:

```
>i
```

3. After the router prompt appears, get into the privileged mode and copy the backup configuration file to RAM.

4. Get into the configuration mode and set your new password.

5. Use the "config-register" command to change the configuration register back to the original setting.

6. Perform a no-shut on all interfaces

7. Copy the running configuration to NVRAM

All of the steps are in **bold**

```
System Bootstrap, Version 5.2(8a), RELEASE SOFTWARE
Copyright (c) 1986-1995 by cisco Systems
2500 processor with 16384 Kbytes of main memory

Abort at 0x10EA87C (PC) break sequence issued here
>e/s2000002
2000002: 2102 use q to quit the examine mode
>o/r0x2142
>i

System Bootstrap, Version 5.2(8a), RELEASE SOFTWARE
Copyright (c) 1986-1995 by cisco Systems
2500 processor with 16384 Kbytes of main memory

F3: 7564496+94188+304272 at 0x3000060

        <output eliminated>

        — System Configuration Dialog —

At any point you may enter a question mark '?' for help.
Use ctrl-c to abort configuration dialog at any prompt.
Default settings are in square brackets '[]'.
Would you like to enter the initial configuration dialog? [yes]: n
Press RETURN to get started!

%LINK-3-UPDOWN: Interface Ethernet0, changed state to up
```

```
%LINK-3-UPDOWN: Interface Ethernet1, changed state to up
%LINK-3-UPDOWN: Interface Serial0, changed state to down
%LINK-3-UPDOWN: Interface Serial1, changed state to down
%LANCE-5-COLL: Unit 0, excessive collisions. TDR=6
%LINEPROTO-5-UPDOWN: Line protocol on Interface Ethernet0, changed
state to down

%LINEPROTO-5-UPDOWN: Line protocol on Interface Ethernet1, changed
state to down

%LINEPROTO-5-UPDOWN: Line protocol on Interface Serial0, changed
state to down
%LINEPROTO-5-UPDOWN: Line protocol on Interface Serial1, changed
state to down
%SYS-5-RESTART: System restarted —
Cisco Internetwork Operating System Software
IOS (tm) 2500 Software (C2500-J-L), Version 11.2(3), RELEASE SOFT-
WARE (fc2)
Copyright (c) 1986-1996 by cisco Systems, Inc.
Compiled Mon 30-Dec-96 21:28 by ajchopra
%LINK-5-CHANGED: Interface Ethernet0, changed state to administra-
tively down
%LINK-5-CHANGED: Interface Ethernet1, changed state to administra-
tively down
%LINK-5-CHANGED: Interface Serial0, changed state to administra-
tively down
%LINK-5-CHANGED: Interface Serial1, changed state to administra-
tively down
Router>en

Router#copy start run

atlanta#

atlanta#config t
Enter configuration commands, one per line.  End with CNTL/Z.
atlanta(config)#enable secret password
atlanta(config)#config-reg 0x2102

atlanta(config)#int e0
atlanta(config-if)#no shut

atlanta(config)#int e1
atlanta(config-if)#no shut

atlanta(config-if)#int s0
atlanta(config-if)#no shut
```

```
atlanta(config)#int s1
atlanta(config-if)#no shut
atlanta(config-if)#

atlanta#
%SYS-5-CONFIG_I: Configured from console by console
atlanta#copy run start
Building configuration...
[OK]
atlanta#
```

Trouble-Shooting Scenario 3

Everything was working fine before I went to lunch. Refer to the output of the various show commands:

```
Router_C#sh int s0
Serial0 is up, line protocol is up
  Hardware is HD64570
  Internet address is 192.68.5.49/28
  MTU 1500 bytes, BW 1544 Kbit, DLY 20000 usec, rely 255/255,
    load 1/255
  Encapsulation HDLC, loopback not set, keepalive set (10
    sec)
  Last input 00:00:01, output 00:00:02, output hang never
  Last clearing of "show interface" counters never
  Input queue: 0/75/0 (size/max/drops); Total output drops: 0
  Queueing strategy: weighted fair
  Output queue: 0/64/0 (size/threshold/drops)
    Conversations  0/1 (active/max active)
    Reserved Conversations 0/0 (allocated/max allocated)
  5 minute input rate 0 bits/sec, 0 packets/sec
  5 minute output rate 0 bits/sec, 0 packets/sec
    19 packets input, 1056 bytes, 0 no buffer
    Received 19 broadcasts, 0 runts, 0 giants
    0 input errors, 0 CRC, 0 frame, 0 overrun, 0 ignored, 0
    abort
    22 packets output, 1697 bytes, 0 underruns
    0 output errors, 0 collisions, 2 interface resets
    0 output buffer failures, 0 output buffers swapped out
    2 carrier transitions
    DCD=up  DSR=up  DTR=up  RTS=up  CTS=up
Router_C#ping 192.68.5.50

Type escape sequence to abort.
Sending 5, 100-byte ICMP Echos to 192.68.5.50, timeout is 2
    seconds:
!!!!!
Success rate is 100 percent (5/5), round-trip min/avg/max =
    4/4/4 ms
Router_C#sh cdp nei det
_____
Device ID: R1
Entry address(es):
  IP address: 192.68.5.66
```

```
Platform: cisco 2521,   Capabilities: Router
Interface: Serial1,   Port ID (outgoing port): Serial1
Holdtime : 168 sec

Version :
Cisco Internetwork Operating System Software
IOS (tm) 2500 Software (C2500-JS-L), Version 11.3(1), RELEASE
     SOFTWARE (fc1)
Copyright (c) 1986-1997 by cisco Systems, Inc.
Compiled Mon 15-Dec-97 18:28 by richardd


_____

Device ID: R1
Entry address(es):
  IP address: 192.68.5.50
Platform: cisco 2521,   Capabilities: Router
Interface: Serial0,   Port ID (outgoing port): Serial0
Holdtime : 168 sec

Version :
Cisco Internetwork Operating System Software
IOS (tm) 2500 Software (C2500-JS-L), Version 11.3(1), RELEASE
     SOFTWARE (fc1)
Copyright (c) 1986-1997 by cisco Systems, Inc.
Compiled Mon 15-Dec-97 18:28 by richardd

Router_C#sh controller s 0
HD unit 0, idb = 0xB6BCC, driver structure at 0xBA810
buffer size 1524  HD unit 0, V.35 DCE cable, clockrate
     2000000
cpb = 0x2, eda = 0x2140, cda = 0x2000
RX ring with 16 entries at 0x4022000
00 bd_ptr=0x2000 pak=0x0BB6C8 ds=0x40258E8 status=80
     pak_size=0
00 bd_ptr=0x2000 pak=0x0BB6C8 ds=0x40258E8 status=80
     pak_size=0
```

But on your return from lunch you have lost connectivity:

```
Router_C#ping 192.68.5.50

Type escape sequence to abort.
Sending 5, 100-byte ICMP Echos to 192.68.5.50, timeout is 2
     seconds:
.....
```

```
Success rate is 0 percent (0/5)

Router_C#sh int s0
Serial0 is down, line protocol is down
  Hardware is HD64570
  Internet address is 192.68.5.49/28
  MTU 1500 bytes, BW 1544 Kbit, DLY 20000 usec, rely 255/255,
    load 1/255
  Encapsulation HDLC, loopback not set, keepalive set (10
    sec)
  Last input 00:02:56, output 00:02:56, output hang never
  Last clearing of "show interface" counters never
  Input queue: 0/75/0 (size/max/drops); Total output drops: 0
  Queueing strategy: weighted fair
  Output queue: 0/64/0 (size/threshold/drops)
    Conversations  0/1 (active/max active)
    Reserved Conversations 0/0 (allocated/max allocated)
  5 minute input rate 0 bits/sec, 0 packets/sec
  5 minute output rate 0 bits/sec, 0 packets/sec
    75 packets input, 4886 bytes, 0 no buffer
    Received 70 broadcasts, 0 runts, 0 giants
    1 input errors, 1 CRC, 0 frame, 0 overrun, 0 ignored, 1
    abort
    78 packets output, 5418 bytes, 0 underruns
    0 output errors, 0 collisions, 9 interface resets
    0 output buffer failures, 0 output buffers swapped out
    6 carrier transitions
    DCD=down  DSR=down  DTR=down  RTS=down  CTS=down

Router_C#sh controller s 0
HD unit 0, idb = 0xB6BCC, driver structure at 0xBA810
buffer size 1524  HD unit 0, No cable, clockrate 2000000
cpb = 0x2, eda = 0x2140, cda = 0x2000
RX ring with 16 entries at 0x4022000
00 bd_ptr=0x2000 pak=0x0BBA60 ds=0x4026658 status=80
    pak_size=0
01 bd_ptr=0x2014 pak=0x0BB894 ds=0x4025FA0 status=80
    pak_size=0
```

Even though show controller reports that there is no cable you can clearly see that the cable is plugged in but just to be safe you tighten the screws a little more, but to no avail!

What's is the problem?

Answer: The cable is plugged in upside down.

Cisco has a proprietary 60-pin symmetrical cable. Because it is symmetrical it can be plugged in upside down very easily, and it looks fine. There is only one problem…it doesn't work!

A good trouble-shooting technique is to look for the obvious first. If show controllers does not show a cable, look at the cable and check its orientation!

You only have so much time to complete the LAB; you don't want to waste your time by missing the obvious!

Trouble-Shooting Scenario 4

Problem: Upon returning from lunch you log into the router, and immediately you are logged out!

You suspect that your console and vty timeout has been changed to one second, making it impossible to stay logged into the router.

Solutions

I have provided a couple of solutions. If all your lines have a one-second time-out, then solution 3 is the way to go!

Solution 1 - Try to telnet to the router and change the configuration. If the vty port has been also changed, go to solution 2.

Solution 2 - Try to connect to the AUX port and change the configuration. If the AUX port has also been changed go to solution 3.

Solution 3 - **TYPE FAST!**

Keep on tapping the down arrow key (or any key that will not perform a function) to prevent a timeout while at the same time you change the console or the telnet timeout. (This might take some practice.)

Example

```
Router_C con0 is now available

Press RETURN to get started.

Router_C>en
Password:
Router_C#config t
Enter configuration commands, one per line.  End with CNTL/Z.
Router_C(config)#line 0
Router_C(config-line)#exec-timeout 0 0
Router_C(config-line)#
```

During the time I was keying in the above commands, I was tapping the down arrow key.

Solution 4 - Create an additional vty connection and connect through this port.

The steps are as follows:

1. Turn the router off, turn the router on, and within 60 seconds, issue the break sequence of your terminal emulation package. If you are using hyperterminal, that would be <ctrl><pause>.
2. You will now be in ROM monitor mode indicated by the > prompt. Our goal here is to turn bit 6 on so, if the configuration register is set to 0x2102, we want to change the register to 0x2142. To determine the current configuration register setting use the following command:

```
>e/s 2000002
     To change the register:
>o/r 0x2142
To re-initialize the router
>I
```

3. After the router prompt appears log into the privileged mode
4. Create vty 5
5. Telnet to the router on connection 5
6. Copy start to run
7. Change the exec time-out
8. Save your configuration

Create vty 5

```
Router_C(config)#line vty 5
Router_C(config-line)#no login
```

Telnet to vty 5

Attempt 1

```
Router_A>telnet 172.16.1.2
Trying 172.16.1.2 ... Open
User Access Verification

Password:
< key <cntrl>-<shift>-<6> then <x> to suspend the session
```

Attempt 2

```
Router_A>telnet 172.16.1.2 create another session without
     logging into previous session
Trying 172.16.1.2 ... Open

User Access Verification

Password:
```

```
< key <cntrl>-<shift>-<6> then <x>
```

Attempt 3

```
Router_A telnet 172.16.1.2
Trying 172.16.1.2 ... Open

User Access Verification

Password:
< key <cntrl>-<shift>-<6> then <x>
```

Attempt 4

```
Router_A>telnet 172.16.1.2
Trying 172.16.1.2 ... Open

User Access Verification

Password:
< key <cntrl>-<shift>-<6> then <x>
```

Attempt 5

```
Router_A>telnet 172.16.1.2
Trying 172.16.1.2 ... Open

User Access Verification

Password:
< key <cntrl>-<shift>-<6> then <x>
```

Attempt 6 will be successful because this session will connect to vty 5

```
Router_A>telnet 172.16.1.2
Trying 172.16.1.2 ... Open
```

Router_C# copy run start

8. Trouble Shooting Scenarios

Trouble-Shooting Scenario 5

Problem: Upon return from lunch you boot up your router and you see the following:

```
Cisco Internetwork Operating System Software
IOS (tm) 3000 Bootstrap Software (IGS-RXBOOT), Version
     10.2(8a), RELEASE SOFTWARE (fc1)
Copyright (c) 1986-1995 by cisco Systems, Inc.
Compiled Tue 24-Oct-95 15:46 by mkamson
Image text-base: 0x01020000, data-base: 0x00001000

cisco 2500 (68030) processor (revision D) with 16380K/2048K
     bytes of memory.
Processor board serial number 03264288 with hardware revision
     00000000
X.25 software, Version 2.0, NET2, BFE and GOSIP compliant.
2 Ethernet/IEEE 802.3 interfaces.
2 Serial network interfaces.
32K bytes of non-volatile configuration memory.
8192K bytes of processor board System flash (Read/Write)

Press RETURN to get started!

Router(boot)>
```

A **show flash** command gives the following results:

```
Router(boot)>sh flash

System flash directory:
No files in System flash
[0 bytes used, 8388608 available, 8388608 total]
8192K bytes of processor board System flash (Read/Write)

Router(boot)>
```

To summarize our problem, we have lost the IOS in flash.

Let's take a look at two possible solutions. There are other ways to go about solving this problem; these are just two methods. Solution 2 really doesn't completely solve the problem because we are still left with an empty flash.

8. Trouble Shooting Scenarios

Solution 1

Copy the IOS from a TFTP server using the **copy tftp flash** command.

Once connectivity to the TFTP server has been established, we are ready to proceed:

```
Router(boot)#copy tftp flash

System flash directory:
No files in System flash
[0 bytes used, 8388608 available, 8388608 total]
Address or name of remote host [172.16.10.5]?
Source file name? 2500.111
Destination file name [2500.111]?
Accessing file '2500.111' on 172.16.10.5...
Loading 2500.111 from 172.16.10.5 (via Ethernet0): ! [OK]

Device needs erasure before copying new file
Erase flash device before writing? [confirm]

Copy '2500.111' from server
  as '2500.111' into Flash WITH erase? [yes/no]y
Erasing device... eeeeeeeeeeeeeeeeeeeeeeeeeeeeeeee ...erased
Loading 2500.111 from 172.16.10.5 (via Ethernet0):
        !!!!!!!!!!!!!!!!!!!!!!!!!.!!!!
!!!!!!!!!!!!..!!!!!!!!!!!!!!!!!!!!!!!!!!!.!!!!!!!!!!!!!!!!!!!!!!!!!!!!!!!!!!!!!!!!!!
!!!!!!!!!!!!!!!!!!!!!!!!!!!!!!!!!!!!!!!!!!!!!!!!!!!!!!!!!!!!!!!!!!!!!!!!!!!!!!!!!!!!
!!!!!!!!!!!!!!!!!!!!!!!!!!!!!!!!!!!!!!!!!!!!!!!!!!!!!!!!!!!!!!!!!!!!!!!!!!!!!!!!!!!!
!!!..!!!!!!!!!!!!!!!!!!!!!!!!!!!!!!!!!!!!!!!!!!!!!!!!!!!!!!!!!!!!!!!!!!!!!!!!!!!!!!!
!!!!!!!!!!!!!!!!!!!!!!!!!!!!!!!!!!!!!!!!!!!!!!!!!!!!!!!!!!!!!!!!!!!!!!!!!!!!!!!!!!!!
!!!!!!!!!!!!!!!!!!!!!!!!!!!!!!!!!!!!!!!!!!!!!!!!!!!!!!!!!!!!!!!!!!!!!!!!!!!!!!!!!!!!
!!!!!!!!!!!!!!!!!!!!!!!!!!!!!!!!!!!!!!!!!!!!!!!!!!!!!!!!!!!!!!!!!!!!!!!!!!!!!!!!!!!!
!!!!!!!!!!!!!!!!!!!!!!!!!!!!!!!!!!!!!!!!!!!!!!!!!!!!!!!!!!!!!!!!!!!!!!!!!!!!!!!!!!!!
!!!!!!!!!!!!!!!!!!!!!!!!!!!!!!!!!!!!!!!!!!!!!!!!!!!!!!!!!!!!!!!!!!!!!!!!!!!!!!!!!!!!
!!!!!!!!!!!!!!!!!!!!!!!!!!!!!!!!!!!!!!!!!!!!!!!!!!!!!!!!!!!!!!!!!!!!!!!!!!!!!!!!!!!!
!!!!!!!!!!!!!!!!!!!!!!!!!!!!!!!!!!!!!!!!!!!!!!!!!!!!!!!!!!!!!!!!!!!!!!!!!!!!!!!!!!!!
!!!!!!!!!!!!!!!!!!!!!!!!!!!!!!!!!!!!!!!!!!!!!!!!!!!!!!!!!!!!!!!!!!!!!!!!!!!!!!!!!!!!
!!!!!!!!!!!!!!!!!!!!!!!!!!!!!!!!!!!!!!!!!!!!!!!!!!!!!!!!!!!!!!!!!!!!!!!!!!!!!!!!!!!!
!!!!!!!!!!!!!!!!!!!!!!!!!!!!!!!!!!!!!!!!!!!!!!!!!!!!!!!!!!!!!!!!!!!!!!!!!!!!!!!!!!!!
!!!!!!!!!!!!!!!!!!!!!!!!!!!!!!!!!!!!!!!!!!!!!!!!!!!!!!!!!!!!!!!!!!!!!!!!!!!!!!!!!!!!
[OK - 7048408/8388608 bytes]

Verifying checksum...  OK (0xC8D2)
```

Flash copy took 0:05:49 [hh:mm:ss]

Router(boot)#sh flash

System flash directory:
File Length   Name/status
  1   7048408   2500.111
[7048472 bytes used, 1340136 available, 8388603 total]
8192K bytes of processor board System flash (Read/Write)

Router(boot)#reload
Proceed with reload? [confirm]

Router>en
Router#sh ver
Cisco Internetwork Operating System Software
IOS (tm) 3000 Software (IGS-J-L), Version 11.1(11), RELEASE
    SOFTWARE (fc1)
Copyright (c) 1986-1997 by cisco Systems, Inc.
Compiled Mon 21-Apr-97 16:40 by dschwart
Image text-base: 0x03038D60, data-base: 0x00C01000

ROM: System Bootstrap, Version 5.2(8a), RELEASE SOFTWARE
ROM: 3000 Bootstrap Software (IGS-RXBOOT), Version 10.2(8a),
    RELEASE SOFTWARE (fc1)

Router uptime is 1 minute
System restarted by reload
System image file is "flash:2500.111", booted via flash

cisco 2500 (68030) processor (revision D) with 16384K/2048K
    bytes of memory.
Processor board ID 03264288, with hardware revision 00000000
Bridging software.
SuperLAT software copyright 1990 by Meridian Technology
    Corp).
X.25 software, Version 2.0, NET2, BFE and GOSIP compliant.
TN3270 Emulation software (copyright 1994 by TGV Inc).
2 Ethernet/IEEE 802.3 interfaces.
2 Serial network interfaces.
32K bytes of non-volatile configuration memory.
8192K bytes of processor board System flash (Read ONLY)

Configuration register is 0x2102

8. Trouble Shooting Scenarios

Solution 2

Use the manual "netboot" feature to load the Cisco IOS from a TFTP server.

This solution also requires that there is connectivity to a TFTP server, the difference is that the IOS is loaded into RAM, which effectively turns this 2500 into a run from RAM router, which is not a good idea, considering the RAM available in a 2500.

```
>b 2500.111 172.16.10.5

Loading 2500.111 .from 172.16.10.5 (via Ethernet0):
     !!!!!!!!!!!!!!!!!!!!!!!!!!!!!!
!!!!!!!!!!!!!!!!!!!!!!!!!!!!!!!!!!!!!!!!!!!!!!!!!!!!!!!!!!!!!!!!!!!!!!!!!!!!!!!!!!!!
!!!!!!!!!!!!!!!!!!!!!!!!!!!!!!!!!!!!!!!!!!!!!!!!!!!!!!!!!!!!!!!!!!!!!!!!!!!!!!!!!!!!!
!!!!!!!!!!!!!!!!!!!!!!!!!!!!!!!!!!!!!!!!!!!!!!!!!!!!!!!!!!!!!!!!!!!!!!!!!!!!!!!!!!!!!
!!!!!!!!!!!!!!!!!!!!!!!!!!!!!!!!!!!!!!!!!!!!!!!!!!!!!!!!!!!!!!!!!!!!!!!!!!!!!!!!!!!!!
!!!!!!!!!!!!!!!!!!!!!!!!!!!!!!!!!!!!!!!!!!!!!!!!!!!!!!!!!!!!!!!!!!!!!!!!!!!!!!!!!!!!!
!!!!!!!!!!!!!!!!!!!!!!!!!!!!!!!!!!!!!!!!!!!!!!!!!!!!!!!!!!!!!!!!!!!!!!!!!!!!!!!!!!!!!
!!!!!!!!!!!!!!!!!!!!!!!!!!!!!!!!!!!!!!!!!!!!!!!!!!!!!!!!!!!!!!!!!!!!!!!!!!!!!!!!!!!!!
!!!!!!!!!!!!!!!!!!!!!!!!!!!!!!!!!!!!!!!!!!!!!!!!!!!!!!!!!!!!!!!!!!!!!!!!!!!!!!!!!!!!!
!!!!!!!!!!!!!!!!!!!!!!!!!!!!!!!!!!!!!!!!!!!!!!!!!!!!!!!!!!!!!!!!!!!!!!!!!!!!!!!!!!!!!
!!!!!!!!!!!!!!!!!!!!!!!!!!!!!!!!!!!!!!!!!!!!!!!!!!!!!!!!!!!!!!!!!!!!!!!!!!!!!!!!!!!!!
!!!!!!!!!!!!!!!!!!!!!!!!!!!!!!!!!!!!!!!!!!!!!!!!!!!!!!!!!!!!!!!!!!!!!!!!!!!!!!!!!!!!!
!!!!!!!!!!!!!!!!!!!!!!!!!!!!!!!!!!!!!!!!!!!!!!!!!!!!!!!!!!!!!!!!!!!!!!!!!!!!!!!!!!!!!
!!!!!!!!!!!!!!!!!!!!!!!!!!!!!!!!!!!!!!!!!!!!!!!!!!!!!!!!!!!!!!!!!!!!!!!!!!!!!!!!!!!!!
!!!!!!!!!!!!!!!!!!!!!!!!!!!!!!!!!!!!!!!!!!!!!!!!!!!!!!!!!!!!!!!!!!!!!!!!!!!!!!!!!!!!!
!!!!!!!!!!!!!!!!!!!!!!!!!!!!!!!!!!!!!!!!!!!!!!!!!!!!!!!!!!!!!!!!!!!!!!!!!!!!!!!!!!!!!
!!!!!!!!!!!!!!!!!!!!!!!!!!!!!!!!!!!!!!!!!!!!!!!!!!!!!!!!!!!!!!!!!!!!!!!!!!!!!!!!!
[OK - 7048408/16150494 bytes]
F3: 6839160+209216+267328 at 0x1000


            Restricted Rights Legend

Use, duplication, or disclosure by the Government is
subject to restrictions as set forth in subparagraph
(c) of the Commercial Computer Software - Restricted
Rights clause at FAR sec. 52.227-19 and subparagraph
(c) (1) (ii) of the Rights in Technical Data and Computer
Software clause at DFARS sec. 252.227-7013.

            cisco Systems, Inc.
            170 West Tasman Drive
            San Jose, California 95134-1706
```

```
Cisco Internetwork Operating System Software
IOS (tm) 3000 Software (IGS-J-L), Version 11.1(11), RELEASE
     SOFTWARE (fc1)
Copyright (c) 1986-1997 by cisco Systems, Inc.
Compiled Mon 21-Apr-97 16:40 by dschwart
Image text-base: 0x00001448, data-base: 0x0064E2C0


cisco 2500 (68030) processor (revision D) with 16384K/2048K
     bytes of memory.
Processor board ID 03264288, with hardware revision 00000000
Bridging software.
SuperLAT software copyright 1990 by Meridian Technology
     Corp).
X.25 software, Version 2.0, NET2, BFE and GOSIP compliant.
TN3270 Emulation software (copyright 1994 by TGV Inc).
2 Ethernet/IEEE 802.3 interfaces.
2 Serial network interfaces.
32K bytes of non-volatile configuration memory.
8192K bytes of processor board System flash (Read/Write)

Router>en
Router#sh flash

System flash directory:
No files in System flash
[0 bytes used, 8388608 available, 8388608 total]
```

8. Trouble Shooting Scenarios

Trouble-Shooting Scenario 6

Upon your return from lunch you notice the following:

```
System Bootstrap, Version 5.2(8a), RELEASE SOFTWARE
Copyright (c) 1986-1995 by cisco Systems
2500 processor with 16384 Kbytes of main memory

Loading cisco2-2500 ... [timed out]

File read failed — Time out
```

Solution

The above message is an indication that the boot field value of the configuration register is set to "2," and the platform is a 2500. The IOS was not present in flash, and the router is attempting a default netboot. (which is very rarely used).

From ROM mode we will obtain the IOS using the "boot system" command. Keep in mind that this procedure does NOT copy the IOS into flash. The IOS will be loaded into RAM. Of course this will only work when you have connectivity to the TFTP server.

```
Router(boot)(config)#boot ?
  bootstrap   Bootstrap image file
  buffersize  Specify the buffer size for netbooting a config
     file
  host        Router-specific config file
  network     Network-wide config file
  system      System image file

Router(boot)(config)#boot system ?
  WORD   Configuration filename
  flash  Boot from flash memory
  mop    Boot from a Decnet MOP server
  rcp    Boot from a server via rcp
  rom    Boot from rom
  tftp   Boot from a tftp server

Router(boot)(config)#boot system tftp ?
  WORD   Configuration filename

Router(boot)(config)#boot system tftp 2500.111
Router(boot)(config)#boot system tftp 2500.111 ?
  A.B.C.D  Address from which to download the boot config
     file
  <cr>
```

8. Trouble Shooting Scenarios

```
Router(boot)(config)#boot system tftp 2500.111   172.16.10.5
Router(boot)(config)#^Z
Router(boot)#wri
Warning: Attempting to overwrite an NVRAM configuration written
by a full system image. This bootstrap software does not support
the full configuration command set. If you write memory now, some
     configuration commands may be lost.
Overwrite the previous NVRAM configuration?[confirm]
####[OK]
Router(boot)#reload
Proceed with reload? [confirm]

Router(boot)#reload

System configuration has been modified. Save? [yes/no]: y
####[OK]

System Bootstrap, Version 5.2(8a), RELEASE SOFTWARE
Copyright (c) 1986-1995 by cisco Systems
Proceed with reload? [confirm]
2500 processor with 16384 Kbytes of main memory
Loading 2500.111 .from 172.16.10.5 (via Ethernet0):
     !!!!!!!!!!!!!!!!!!!!!!!!!!!!!
!!!!!!!!!!!!!!!!!!!!!!!!!!!!!!!!!!!!!!!!!!!!!!!!!!!!!!!!!!!!!!!!!!!!!!!!!!
!!!!!!!!!!!!!!!!!!!!!!!!!!!!!!!!!!!!!!!!!!!!!!!!!!!!!!!!!!!!!!!!!!!!!!!!!!
!!!!!!!!!!!!!!!!!!!!!!!!!!!!!!!!!!!!!!!!!!!!!!!!!!!!!!!!!!!!!!!!!!!!!!!!!!
!!!!!!!!!!!!!!!!!!!!!!!!!!!!!!!!!!!!!!!!!!!!!!!!!!!!!!!!!!!!!!!!!!!!!!!!!!
!!!!!!!!!!!!!!!!!!!!!!!!!!!!!!!!!!!!!!!!!!!!!!!!!!!!!!!!!!!!!!!!!!!!!!!!!!
!!!!!!!!!!!!!!!!!!!!!!!!!!!!!!!!!!!!!!!!!!!!!!!!!!!!!!!!!!!!!!!!!!!!!!!!!!
!!!!!!!!!!!!!!!!!!!!!!!!!!!!!!!!!!!!!!!!!!!!!!!!!!!!!!!!!!!!!!!!!!!!!!!!!!
!!!!!!!!!!!!!!!!!!!!!!!!!!!!!!!!!!!!!!!!!!!!!!!!!!!!!!!!!!!!!!!!!!!!!!!!!!
!!!!!!!!!!!!!!!!!!!!!!!!!!!!!!!!!!!!!!!!!!!!!!!!!!!!!!!!!!!!!!!!!!!!!!!!!!
!!!!!!!!!!!!!!!!!!!!!!!!!!!!!!!!!!!!!!!!!!!!!!!!!!!!!!!!!!!!!!!!!!!!!!!!!!
!!!!!!!!!!!!!!!!!!!!!!!!!!!!!!!!!!!!!!!!!!!!!!!!!!!!!!!!!!!!!!!!!!!!!!!!!!
!!!!!!!!!!!!!!!!!!!!!!!!!!!!!!!!!!!!!!!!!!!!!!!!!!!!!!!!!!!!!!!!!!!!!!!!!!
!!!!!!!!!!!!!!!!!!!!!!!!!!!!!!!!!!!!!!!!!!!!!!!!!!!!!!!!!!!!!!!!!!!!!!!!!!
!!!!!!!!!!!!!!!!!!!!!!!!!!!!!!!!!!!!!!!!!!!!!!!!!!!!!!!!!!!!!!!!!!!!!!!!!!
!!!!!!!!!!!!!!!!!!!!!!!!!!!!!!!!!!!!!!!!!!!!!!!!!!!!!!!!!!!!!!!!!!!!!!!!!!
!!!!!!!!!!!!!!!!!!!!!!!!!!!!!!!!!!!!!!!!!!!!!!!!!!!!!!!!!!!!!!!!!!!!!!!!
[OK - 7048408/16150314 bytes]
F3: 6839160+209216+267328 at 0x1000

          Restricted Rights Legend
```

```
            cisco Systems, Inc.
            170 West Tasman Drive
            San Jose, California 95134-1706


Cisco Internetwork Operating System Software
IOS (tm) 3000 Software (IGS-J-L), Version 11.1(11), RELEASE
    SOFTWARE (fc1)
Copyright (c) 1986-1997 by cisco Systems, Inc.
Compiled Mon 21-Apr-97 16:40 by dschwart
Image text-base: 0x00001448, data-base: 0x0064E2C0


cisco 2500 (68030) processor (revision D) with 16384K/2048K
    bytes of memory.
Processor board ID 03264288, with hardware revision 00000000
Bridging software.
SuperLAT software copyright 1990 by Meridian Technology
    Corp).
X.25 software, Version 2.0, NET2, BFE and GOSIP compliant.
TN3270 Emulation software (copyright 1994 by TGV Inc).
2 Ethernet/IEEE 802.3 interfaces.
2 Serial network interfaces.
32K bytes of non-volatile configuration memory.
8192K bytes of processor board System flash (Read/Write)
```

Press RETURN to get started!

```
%LINK-3-UPDOWN: Interface Ethernet0, changed state to up
%LINK-3-UPDOWN: Interface Ethernet1, changed state to up
%LINK-3-UPDOWN: Interface Serial0, changed state to up
%LINK-3-UPDOWN: Interface Serial1, changed state to down
%LINEPROTO-5-UPDOWN: Line protocol on Interface Ethernet0,
    changed state to up
%LINEPROTO-5-UPDOWN: Line protocol on Interface Ethernet1,
    changed state to up
%LINEPROTO-5-UPDOWN: Line protocol on Interface Serial0,
    changed state to up
%LINEPROTO-5-UPDOWN: Line protocol on Interface Serial1,
```

```
        changed state to down
%LINEPROTO-5-UPDOWN: Line protocol on Interface Ethernet1,
      changed state to down

%LINEPROTO-5-UPDOWN: Line protocol on Interface Serial0,
      changed state to down
%SYS-5-CONFIG_I: Configured from memory by console
%SYS-5-RESTART: System restarted —
Cisco Internetwork Operating System Software
IOS (tm) 3000 Software (IGS-J-L), Version 11.1(11), RELEASE
      SOFTWARE (fc1)
Copyright (c) 1986-1997 by cisco Systems, Inc.
Compiled Mon 21-Apr-97 16:40 by dschwart
%LINK-5-CHANGED: Interface Ethernet1, changed state to admin-
      istratively down
%LINK-5-CHANGED: Interface Serial0, changed state to adminis-
      tratively down
%LINK-5-CHANGED: Interface Serial1, changed state to adminis-
      tratively down

Router>sh flash

System flash directory:
No files in System flash
[0 bytes used, 8388608 available, 8388608 total]
8192K bytes of processor board System flash (Read/Write)
```

The router has loaded the IOS from the TFTP server directly into RAM. To load the IOS into flash you must use the "copy tftp flash" command.

Trouble-Shooting Scenario 7

Given the following diagram, routing table, and the fact that A1, B1 and C1 are internal networks, find the solution to the following scenarios:

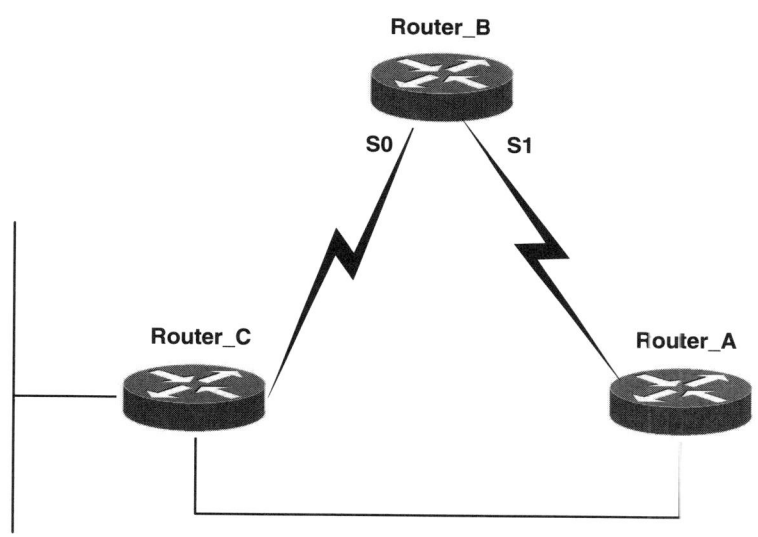

```
Router_B#sh ipx route
Codes: C - Connected primary network,
   c - Connected secondary network, S - Static,
   F - Floating static, L - Local (internal), W - IPXWAN,
   R - RIP, E - EIGRP, N - NLSP, X - External, A - Aggregate,
   s - seconds, u - uses, U - Per-user static

5 Total IPX routes. Up to 2 parallel paths and 16 hops al-
     lowed.

No default route known.

L          B1 is the internal network
R          A1 [07/01] via          0.0000.00a1.0000,    3s, Se1
R          C1 [07/01] via          0.0000.00a1.0000,    3s, Se0
R         CAD [07/01] via          0.0000.00a1.0000,    4s, Se1
                      via          0.0000.00a1.0000,    3s, Se0
R         FAD [07/01] via          0.0000.00a1.0000,    3s, Se0
```

Trouble-Shooting Scenario 1

Upon return from lunch, you discover that the routing table of Router_B has changed.

Examine the router table below. Assume that all links are in the Up and Up state.

What has changed and how would you remedy the situation?

```
Router_B#sh ipx route
Codes: C - Connected primary network,
    c - Connected secondary network, S - Static,
    F - Floating static, L - Local (internal), W - IPXWAN
    R - RIP, E - EIGRP, N - NLSP, X - External, A - Aggregate,
    s - seconds, u - uses, U - Per-user static

5 Total IPX routes. Up to 2 parallel paths and 16 hops al-
    lowed.

No default route known.

L       B1 is the internal network
R       A1 [1312/02] via          0.0000.00c1.0000,    26s, Se0
R       C1 [1311/01] via          0.0000.00c1.0000,    26s, Se0
R      CAD [1311/01] via          0.0000.00c1.0000,    26s, Se0
R      FAD [1311/01] via          0.0000.00c1.0000,    26s, Se0
```

Trouble-Shooting Scenario 2

Now assume the following routing table of Router_B. What is wrong, and what are the steps to remedy the situation?

```
Router_B#sh
%SYS-5-CONFIG_I: Configured from console by consoleipx route
Codes: C - Connected primary network,
    c - Connected secondary network, S - Static,
    F - Floating static, L - Local (internal), W - IPXWAN
    R - RIP, E - EIGRP, N - NLSP, X - External, A - Aggregate
    s - seconds, u - uses, U - Per-user static

5 Total IPX routes. Up to 1 parallel paths and 16 hops al-
    lowed.

No default route known.
```

```
L           B1 is the internal network
R           A1 [1312/02] via      0.0000.00c1.0000,   34s, Se0
R           C1 [1311/01] via      0.0000.00c1.0000,   35s, Se0
R          CAD [1311/01] via      0.0000.00c1.0000,   35s, Se0
R          FAD [1311/01] via      0.0000.00c1.0000,   35s, Se0
```

Solution

In both scenarios our problem is that we have lost our redundant path to network CAD.
CAD must be the network on the bottom because that is the only network that could possibly have
the same metric from the perspective of Router_B.

In the first scenario there are two parallel paths permitted but only one is being taken.
IPX will not load share unless the metric to the destination is exactly the same. Therefore, someone
has changed the clock rate on Serial 1 to something other than the clock rate Serial 0.

The clock rate must match because we are using IPXWAN on the serial links. How do you know
IPXWAN is configured? There is no IPX network number on the serial links. IPXWAN requires that
there be no IPX network number. IPX RIP and IPX EIGRP requires a network number on the serial
links.

In the second scenario someone has removed the "ipx maximum-paths 2" command. We know this
because the routing table shows only one parallel path permitted.

Trouble-Shooting Scenario 8

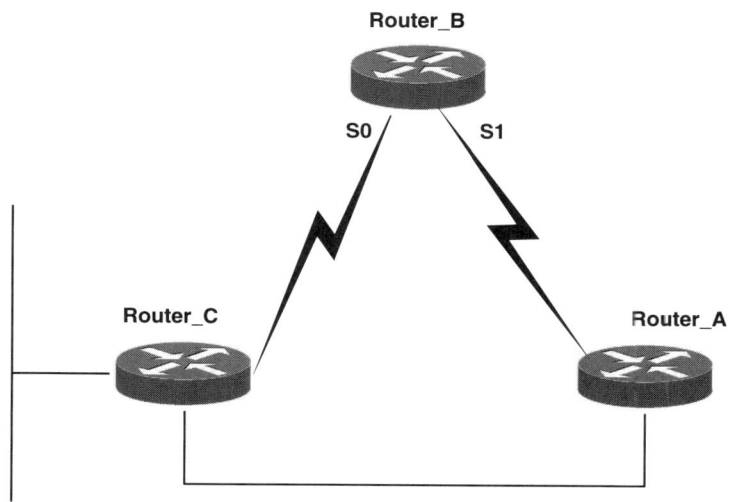

Given the diagram and the routing table below, solve the three scenarios.

```
Router_B#sh app route
Codes: R - RTMP derived, E - EIGRP derived, C - connected,
    A - AURP, S - static  P - proxy
4 routes in internet. Up to 2 parallel paths allowed.

The first zone listed for each entry is its default (primary)
    zone.

C Net 100-100 directly connected, Serial0, zone leftserial
C Net 110-110 directly connected, Serial1, zone rightserial
R Net 200-210 [1/G] via 100.209, 5 sec, Serial0,
                    via 110.153, 3 sec, Serial1, zone
    bottom_ether
R Net 300-310 [1/G] via 100.209, 5 sec, Serial0, zone
    left_ether
```

Scenario 1

```
Router_B#sh app route
Codes: R - RTMP derived, E - EIGRP derived, C - connected,
    A - AURP, S - static  P - proxy
```

```
4 routes in internet

The first zone listed for each entry is its default (primary)
    zone.

C Net 100-100 directly connected, Serial0, zone leftserial
C Net 110-110 directly connected, Serial1, zone rightserial
R Net 200-210 [1/G] via 110.153, 0 sec, Serial1, zone
    bottom_ether
R Net 300-310 [1/G] via 100.209, 3 sec, Serial0, zone
    left_ether
```

What changed, and how would you correct it?

Scenario 2

```
Ethernet0/0 is up, line protocol is up
   AppleTalk node down, Port configuration error
   AppleTalk cable range is 200-210
   AppleTalk address is 203.92, Invalid
   AppleTalk zone is "ether-bottom"
   AppleTalk address gleaning is disabled
   AppleTalk route cache is disabled, port initializing
```

What changed, and how would you correct it?

Scenario 3

```
Router_C#sh app int s0
Serial0 is up, line protocol is up
   AppleTalk node down, Port configuration error
   AppleTalk cable range is 101-101
   AppleTalk address is 101.50, Invalid
   AppleTalk zone is not set.
   AppleTalk address gleaning is not supported by hardware
   AppleTalk route cache is not initialized
```

What changed, and how would you correct it?

Solution 1

The "maximum paths" command has been removed from the configuration. The routing table now shows only one way to get to cable-range 300-310.

```
Router_B(config)#appletalk maximum-paths 2
```

Solution 2

The Zone Name should be "bottom_ether".
Due to the fact that an appletalk interface can exist in more than a single zone, you must remove the incorrect zone.

```
Router_A(config)#int e0/0
Router_A(config-if)#no app zone ether-bottom
Router_A(config-if)#app zone bottom_ether
Router_A(config-if)#shut
Router_A(config-if)#
%AT-6-CONFIGOK: Ethernet0/0: AppleTalk interface enabled;
     verified by 207.49
```

Solution 3

The cable-range was incorrectly set to 101-101.

```
Router_C(config)#int s0
Router_C(config-if)#app cable-range 100-100
Router_C(config-if)#app zone leftserial

Router_C#
%AT-6-CONFIGOK: Serial0: AppleTalk port enabled; verified by
     100.250
```

8. Trouble Shooting Scenarios

Trouble-Shooting Scenario 9

Upon returning from lunch you notice that there is a problem with the routing table. Given the diagram and the routing table below, determine the problem.

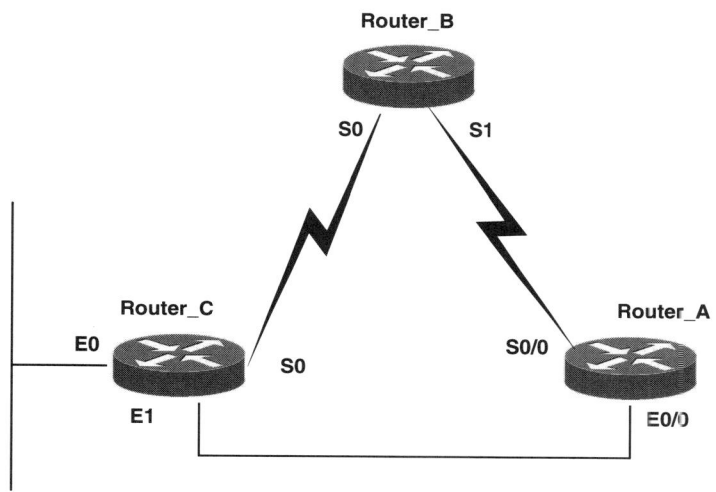

```
Router_B#sh ip route
Codes: C - connected, S - static, I - IGRP, R - RIP,
    M - mobile, B - BGP, D - EIGRP, EX - EIGRF external,
    O - OSPF, IA - OSPF inter area,
    N1 - OSPF NSSA external type 1,
    N2 - OSPF NSSA external type 2
    E1 - OSPF external type 1, E2 - OSPF external type 2,
    E - EGP, i - IS-IS, L1 - IS-IS level-1,
    L2 - IS-IS level-2, * - candidate default
    U - per-user static route, o - ODR

Gateway of last resort is not set
      172.17.0.0/24 is subnetted, 1 subnets
C        172.17.1.0 is directly connected, Serial0
R     172.16.0.0/16 [120/1] via 172.18.1.1, 00:00:08, Serial1
R     172.19.0.0/16 [120/1] via 172.18.1.1, 00:00:08, Serial1
      172.18.0.0/24 is subnetted, 1 subnets
C        172.18.1.0 is directly connected, Serial1
```

Given the Router configurations below determine the solution.

8. Trouble Shooting Scenarios

Router_B

```
Router_B#sh run
Building configuration...

Current configuration:
!
version 11.3
no service password-encryption
!
hostname Router_B
!
!
appletalk routing
!
interface Serial0
 ip address 172.17.1.2 255.255.255.0
 no ip mroute-cache
 appletalk cable-range 115-115 115.229
 appletalk zone leftserial
 no fair-queue
!
interface Serial1
 ip address 172.18.1.2 255.255.255.0
 appletalk cable-range 120-120 120.17
 appletalk zone rightserial
 clockrate 4000000
!
interface Serial2
 no ip address
 shutdown
!
interface Serial3
 no ip address
 shutdown
!
interface TokenRing0
 no ip address
 shutdown
!
interface BRI0
 no ip address
 shutdown
!
```

```
router rip
 network 172.17.0.0
 network 172.18.0.0
!
ip classless
!
!
line con 0
line aux 0
line vty 0 4
 login
!
end
```

Router_C

```
Router_C#sh run
Building configuration...

Current configuration:
!
version 11.2
no service password-encryption
service udp-small-servers
service tcp-small-servers
!
hostname Router_C
!
appletalk routing
!
interface Ethernet0
 ip address 172.16.10.1 255.255.255.0
 no ip route-cache
 no ip mroute-cache
 appletalk cable-range 100-105 103.186
 appletalk zone lanzone
 bridge-group 10
!
interface Ethernet1
 ip address 172.19.10.1 255.255.255.0
 no ip route-cache
 no ip mroute-cache
 appletalk cable-range 106-110 108.131
 appletalk zone lanzone
```

8. Trouble Shooting Scenarios

```
 bridge-group 10
!
interface Serial0
 ip address 172.17.1.1 255.255.255.0
 no ip route-cache
 no ip mroute-cache
 appletalk cable-range 115-115 115.252
 appletalk zone leftserial
 clockrate 4000000
!
interface Serial1
 no ip address
 no ip route-cache
 no ip mroute-cache
 shutdown
!
router rip
 redistribute igrp 16 metric 2
 network 172.17.0.0
!
router igrp 16
 network 172.16.0.0
 network 172.19.0.0
!
no ip classless
!
bridge 10 protocol dec
!
line con 0
line aux 0
 transport input all
line vty 0 4
 login
!
end
```

Router_A

```
Router_A#sh run
Building configuration...

Current configuration:
!
version 11.3
```

```
no service password-encryption
!
hostname Router_A
!
interface Ethernet0/0
 ip address 172.19.10.2 255.255.255.0
!
interface Serial0/0
 ip address 172.18.1.1 255.255.255.0
!
interface TokenRing0/0
 no ip address
 shutdown
 ring-speed 16
!
interface FastEthernet1/0
 no ip address
 shutdown
!
router rip
 redistribute igrp 16 metric 0
 network 172.18.0.0
!
router igrp 16
 network 172.19.0.0
!
ip classless
!

line con 0
line aux 0
line vty 0 4

 login
!
end
```

Solution

The default metrics used by Router_A and Router_C are forcing Router_B to take the long way around to get to Network 172.16.0.0

The solution is to set the default metrics appropriately.

```
Router_A[Config-router)#redistribute igrp 16 metric 2
Router_C[Config-router)#redistribute igrp 16 metric 1
```

The statements above will give Router_B a more accurate perspective of the topology.

```
Router_B#sh ip route
Codes: C - connected, S - static, I - IGRP, R - RIP,
   M - mobile, B - BGP, D - EIGRP, EX - EIGRP external,
   O - OSPF, IA - OSPF inter area,
  N1 - OSPF NSSA external type 1,
  N2 - OSPF NSSA external type 2, E1 - OSPF external type 1,
  E2 - OSPF external type 2, E - EGP, i - IS-IS,
  L1 - IS-IS level-1, L2 - IS-IS level-2,
   * - candidate default, U - per-user static route, o - ODR

Gateway of last resort is not set

     172.17.0.0/24 is subnetted, 1 subnets
C       172.17.1.0 is directly connected, Serial0
R     172.16.0.0/16 [120/1] via 172.17.1.1, 00:00:00, Serial0
R     172.19.0.0/16 [120/1] via 172.17.1.1, 00:00:00, Serial0
     172.18.0.0/24 is subnetted, 1 subnets
C       172.18.1.0 is directly connected, Serial1
```

The following configuration change will accomplish load sharing:

```
Router_A[Config-router)#redistribute igrp 16 metric 1
Router_C[Config-router)#redistribute igrp 16 metric 1

Router_B#sh ip route
Codes: C - connected, S - static, I - IGRP, R - RIP,
   M - mobile, B - BGP, D - EIGRP, EX - EIGRP external,
   O - OSPF, IA - OSPF inter area
  N1 - OSPF NSSA external type 1,
  N2 - OSPF NSSA external type 2
  E1 - OSPF external type 1, E2 - OSPF external type 2,
   E - EGP, i - IS-IS, L1 - IS-IS level-1,
  L2 - IS-IS level-2, * - candidate default
   U - per-user static route, o - ODR

Gateway of last resort is not set

     172.17.0.0/24 is subnetted, 1 subnets
C       172.17.1.0 is directly connected, Serial0
```

```
R     172.16.0.0/16 [120/1] via 172.17.1.1, 00:00:27, Serial0
                     [120/1] via 172.18.1.1, 00:00:12, Serial1
R     172.19.0.0/16 [120/1] via 172.17.1.1, 00:00:27, Serial0
                     [120/1] via 172.18.1.1, 00:00:12, Serial1
      172.18.0.0/24 is subnetted, 1 subnets
C        172.18.1.0 is directly connected, Serial1
```

Trouble-Shooting Scenario 10

Upon return from lunch you notice something strange!

```
Router_B#telnet Router_A
Trying Router_A (192.13.10.10)... Open

User Access Verification

Password:
Router_B>

Router_B#sh sess
Conn Host              Address            Byte  Idle Conn Name
*   1 router_a          192.13.10.10          0     0 router_a
```

- What is the problem?
- What is the most likely cause of the problem?
- What is the solution to our dilemma?

Explanation

The problem is that when a telnet session is initiated from Router_B to Router_A, we end up back at Router_B!

The most likely cause is a misconfigured host table.

The solution is to correct the host table. Make sure that the address used to identify Router_A is actually an interface of Router_A.

Review the configurations below and make the necessary changes.

Router_B

```
Router_B#sh run
Building configuration...

Current configuration:
!
version 11.3
no service password-encryption
hostname Router_B
!
ip host Router_A 192.13.10.10 172.16.10.1
interface Serial0
 ip address 192.13.10.10 255.255.255.252
 no ip mroute-cache
 no fair-queue
```

```
 clockrate 4000000
!
interface Serial1
 no ip address
 shutdown
!
interface Serial2
 no ip address
 shutdown
!
interface Serial3
 no ip address
 shutdown
!
interface TokenRing0
 ip address 20.20.20.1 255.255.255.0 secondary
 ip address 172.16.11.1 255.255.255.0
 bandwidth 4000000
 ring-speed 16
!
interface BRI0
 no ip address
 shutdown
!
router rip
 network 192.13.10.0
 network 20.0.0.0
 network 192.13.20.0
!
ip classless
!
line con 0
line aux 0
line vty 0 4
 password ccna
 login
!
end
```

Router_A

```
Router_A#sh run
Building configuration...

Current configuration:
```

```
!
version 11.2
no service password-encryption
no service udp-small-servers
no service tcp-small-servers
!
hostname Router_A
!
interface Ethernet0
 ip address 172.16.10.1 255.255.255.0
!
interface Ethernet1
 no ip address
 shutdown
!
interface Serial0
 ip address 192.13.10.9 255.255.255.252
 no fair-queue

interface Serial1
 no ip address
 shutdown
!
router rip
 network 192.13.10.0
 network 172.16.0.0
!
ip classless
ip route 0.0.0.0 255.255.255.255 192.13.10.1
!
line con 0
line aux 0
line vty 0 4
 login
!
end
```

The following configuration line of Router_A

```
ip host Router_A 192.13.10.10 172.16.10.1
```

Should be:

```
ip host Router_A 192.13.10.9 172.16.10.1
```

Trouble-Shooting Scenario 11

Given the following diagram, routing table, and configurations; find 2 configuration errors.

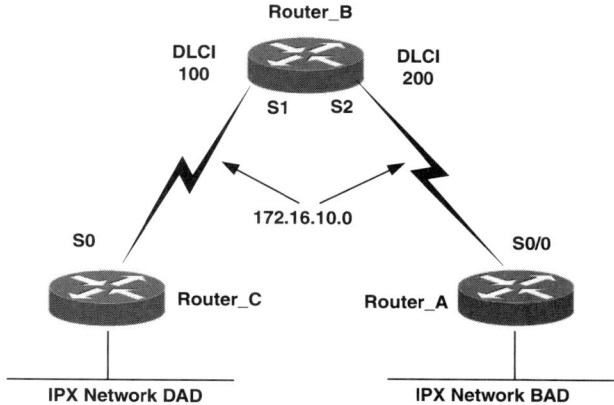

When you come back from lunch you notice that you no longer have complete connectivity.

```
Router_A#sh ipx route
Codes: C - Connected primary network,
    c - Connected secondary network, S - Static,
    F - Floating static, L - Local (internal), W - IPXWAN
    R - RIP, E - EIGRP, N - NLSP, X - External, A - Aggregate
    s - seconds, u - uses, U - Per-user static

3 Total IPX routes. Up to 1 parallel paths and 16 hops al-
    lowed.

No default route known.

C        BAD (NOVELL-ETHER),   Et0/0
C        CAD (TUNNEL),         Tu0
```

Router_C

```
Current configuration:
!
version 11.2
no service password-encryption
no service udp-small-servers
no service tcp-small-servers
```

```
!
hostname Router_C
!
enable secret 5 $1$jCQH$nzkHW61Q9ywoAX87xsp9p1
enable password ccnaprep
!

ipx routing 0060.09c3.df60
!
interface Tunnel0
 no ip address
 ipx network FAD
 tunnel source Serial0
 tunnel destination 172.16.10.2
!
interface Ethernet0
 ipx network DAD
!
interface Ethernet1
 no ip address
 shutdown
!
interface Serial0
 ip address 172.16.10.2 255.255.255.0
 encapsulation frame-relay
 no fair-queue
!
interface Serial1
 no ip address
 shutdown
!
no ip classless
!
line con 0
line aux 0
line vty 0 4
 password sailing
 login

!
end
```

Router_A

```
Router_A#sh run
Building configuration...

Current configuration:
!
version 11.3
no service password-encryption
!
hostname Router_A
!
enable secret 5 $1$.s1R$iaEqZxLnYJo2QlZi8UNaO0
enable password ccnaprep
!
ipx routing 0010.7b15.bd41
!
interface Tunnel0
 no ip address
 ipx network CAD
 tunnel source Serial0/0
 tunnel destination 172.16.10.2
interface Ethernet0/0
  no ip mroute-cache
 ipx network BAD
 no cdp enable
!
interface Serial0/0
 ip address 172.16.10.1 255.255.255.0
 encapsulation frame-relay
 no ip mroute-cache
 frame-relay lmi-type ansi
!
interface TokenRing0/0
 no ip address
 no ip mroute-cache
 shutdown
 ring-speed 16
 no cdp enable
!
interface FastEthernet1/0
 no ip address
 no ip mroute-cache
 shutdown
```

8. Trouble Shooting Scenarios

```
 no cdp enable
 !
ip classless
no cdp run
 !
line con 0
 exec-timeout 0 0
line aux 0
line vty 0 4
 password ccieprep
 login
 !
end
```

Solution

The two errors are:

The IPX address of both tunnels must be the same. Make them both FAD or CAD.

The Tunnel destination address of Router_C was pointing to its own Serial 0 interface. It should be the remote serial interface of Router_A.

I purposely used two different LMI for each router. This would not be a problem because the LMI is just between the local router and the local switch, in this case between Router_A and Router_B and between Router_C and Router_B.

Trouble-Shooting Lab 12

The following is a continuous stream of output from a single router.

What is the problem?
What is the solution?

```
       Router_B#sh run
Building configuration...

Current configuration:
!
version 11.3
no service password-encryption
!
hostname Router_B
!
enable secret 5 $1$F1L/$o6UBu.eE0dr0WGXR6ahPM0
enable password ccie
!
interface Serial0
 ip address 172.1.1.1 255.255.0.0
 no ip mroute-cache
!
interface Serial1
 no ip address
 shutdown
!
interface Serial2
 no ip address
 shutdown
!
interface Serial3
 no ip address
 shutdown
!
interface TokenRing0
 no ip address
 shutdown
!
interface BRI0
 no ip address
 shutdown
!
```

8. Trouble Shooting Scenarios

```
router igrp 10
 redistribute connected
 network 172.1.0.0
!
ip classless
!
!
line con 0
line aux 0
line vty 0 4
 password ccnaprep
 login
!
end


Router_B#copy run start
Building configuration...
[OK]
Router_B#reload
Proceed with reload? [confirm]

%SYS-5-RELOAD: Reload requested
System Bootstrap, Version 11.0(10c)XB1, PLATFORM SPECIFIC
     RELEASE SOFTWARE (fc1)

Copyright (c) 1986-1997 by cisco Systems
2500 processor with 6144 Kbytes of main memory

F3: 8679016+110272+475336 at 0x3000060

               Restricted Rights Legend

Use, duplication, or disclosure by the Government is
subject to restrictions as set forth in subparagraph
(c) of the Commercial Computer Software - Restricted
Rights clause at FAR sec. 52.227-19 and subparagraph
(c) (1) (ii) of the Rights in Technical Data and Computer
Software clause at DFARS sec. 252.227-7013.

             cisco Systems, Inc.
             170 West Tasman Drive
             San Jose, California 95134-1706

Cisco Internetwork Operating System Software
```

```
IOS (tm) 2500 Software (C2500-JS-L), Version 11.3(1), RELEASE
    SOFTWARE (fc1)
Copyright (c) 1986-1997 by cisco Systems, Inc.
Compiled Mon 15-Dec-97 18:28 by richardd
Image text-base: 0x03047DB8, data-base: 0x00001000

cisco 2521 (68030) processor (revision K) with 6144K/2048K
    bytes of memory.
Processor board ID 06170381, with hardware revision 00000003
Bridging software.
X.25 software, Version 3.0.0.
SuperLAT software copyright 1990 by Meridian Technology
    Corp).
TN3270 Emulation software.
Basic Rate ISDN software, Version 1.0.
1 Token Ring/IEEE 802.5 interface(s)
2 Serial network interface(s)
2 Low-speed serial(sync/async) network interface(s)
1 ISDN Basic Rate interface(s)
32K bytes of non-volatile configuration memory.
16384K bytes of processor board System flash (Read ONLY)
        — System Configuration Dialog —-

At any point you may enter a question mark '?' for help.
Use ctrl-c to abort configuration dialog at any prompt.
Default settings are in square brackets '[]'.
Would you like to enter the initial configuration dialog?
    [yes]: n

Press RETURN to get started!

%LINK-3-UPDOWN: Interface BRI0, changed state to up
%LINK-3-UPDOWN: Interface Serial0, changed state to down
%LINK-3-UPDOWN: Interface Serial1, changed state to down
%LINK-3-UPDOWN: Interface Serial2, changed state to down
%LINK-3-UPDOWN: Interface Serial3, changed state to down
%LINEPROTO-5-UPDOWN: Line protocol on Interface BRI0, changed
    state to down
%LINEPROTO-5-UPDOWN: Line protocol on Interface BRI0:1,
    changed state to down
%LINEPROTO-5-UPDOWN: Line protocol on Interface BRI0:2,
    changed state to down
%LINEPROTO-5-UPDOWN: Line protocol on Interface Serial0,
    changed state to down
%LINEPROTO-5-UPDOWN: Line protocol on Interface Serial1,
```

```
          changed state to down
%LINEPROTO-5-UPDOWN: Line protocol on Interface Serial2,
     changed state to down
%LINEPROTO-5-UPDOWN: Line protocol on Interface Serial3,
     changed state to down
%LINEPROTO-5-UPDOWN: Line protocol on Interface TokenRing0,
     changed state to down
%SYS-5-RESTART: System restarted —
Cisco Internetwork Operating System Software
IOS (tm) 2500 Software (C2500-JS-L), Version 11.3(1), RELEASE
     SOFTWARE (fc1)
Copyright (c) 1986-1997 by cisco Systems, Inc.
Compiled Mon 15-Dec-97 18:28 by richardd
%LINK-5-CHANGED: Interface BRI0, changed state to administra-
     tively down
%LINK-5-CHANGED: Interface Serial0, changed state to adminis-
     tratively down
%LINK-5-CHANGED: Interface Serial1, changed state to adminis-
     tratively down
%LINK-5-CHANGED: Interface Serial2, changed state to adminis-
     tratively down
%LINK-5-CHANGED: Interface Serial3, changed state to adminis-
     tratively down
%LINK-5-CHANGED: Interface TokenRing0, changed state to ad-
     ministratively down
Router>
```

Explanation

The problem is that the running configuration was saved to NVRAM. Yet, when the router was rebooted the configuration was not loaded into RAM. Does the configuration file still exist?

Answer: Yes

Where is the configuration file?

Answer: NVRAM

If the configuration file is saved in NVRAM, why did it not load into RAM?

Answer: The number 6 bit of the configuration register was set to 1.

Upon further examination of the router we see the following:

```
Router>en
Router#sh ver
Cisco Internetwork Operating System Software
IOS (tm) 2500 Software (C2500-JS-L), Version 11.3(1), RELEASE
```

```
      SOFTWARE (fc1)
Copyright (c) 1986-1997 by cisco Systems, Inc.
Compiled Mon 15-Dec-97 18:28 by richardd
Image text-base: 0x03047DB8, data-base: 0x00C01000

ROM: System Bootstrap, Version 11.0(10c)XB1, PLATFORM SPE-
     CIFIC RELEASE SOFTWARE
(fc1)
BOOTFLASH: 3000 Bootstrap Software (IGS-BOOT-R), Version
     11.0(10c)XB1, PLATFORM
SPECIFIC RELEASE SOFTWARE (fc1)

Router uptime is 21 minutes
System restarted by reload
System image file is "flash:c2500-js-1.113-1", booted via
     flash

cisco 2521 (68030) processor (revision K) with 6144K/2048K
     bytes of memory.
Processor board ID 06170381, with hardware revision 00000003
Bridging software.
X.25 software, Version 3.0.0.
SuperLAT software copyright 1990 by Meridian Technology
     Corp).
TN3270 Emulation software.
Basic Rate ISDN software, Version 1.0.
1 Token Ring/IEEE 802.5 interface(s)
2 Serial network interface(s)
2 Low-speed serial(sync/async) network interface(s)
1 ISDN Basic Rate interface(s)
32K bytes of non-volatile configuration memory.
16384K bytes of processor board System flash (Read ONLY)
```

Configuration register is 0x2142

Router#

Since the configuration register has a value of 0x2142, the router will ignore the configuration file stored in NVRAM and boot with no configuration file.

Solution

Change the configuration register to 0x2102.

```
Router#config t
Enter configuration commands, one per line.  End with CNTL/Z.
Router(config)#config-reg 0x2102
```

Now, when the router reloads, the configuration file will be loaded into RAM.

Appendix A
CISCO Certification Career Paths

Cisco has announced several new certifications. I will attempt to explain what tests are required to achieve each certification and what is the best way to gain the knowledge needed for each one of the exams.

Changes are very often made to Cisco's certification programs and exams, so it is always best to check their site for the latest information.

They say a picture is worth a thousand words, so here goes:

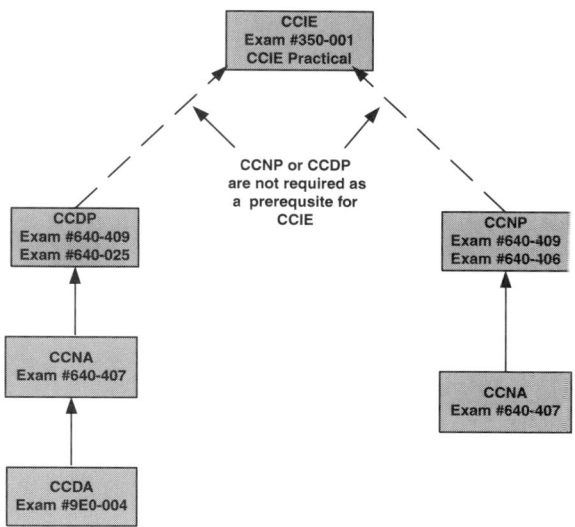

There are a couple of ways you can look at these certifications.

For most people being introduced to Cisco, CCNA will be the first step towards CCIE. Then the tracks can be followed in order to the final goal of CCIE.

If you have plenty of experience and attended most of the classes you may want to forget about the other certifications and go right for CCIE. CCNA, CCNP, CCDA and CCDP are not required to obtain CCIE.

My recommendation is of course to take an instructor lead class, I have been a teacher for 30 years so I may be a bit prejudice. I have listed all the classes below.

During the course of your normal workday, if you do not get "hands on" Cisco router experience, you will need a LAB to practice your configuration skills.

Maybe your company will consider putting a LAB in for you and your group. This may seem a bit extreme but nothing will flatten the learning curve like a LAB that you can "play" in.

CCIEprep.com does have a virtual LAB set up, check out CCIEprep.com for details on accessing this LAB.

If you have the time and wish to join myself in the CCIEprep.com LAB please send me email at lrossisr@ar-inc.com to schedule a time.

CCNP Track
Cisco Certified Network Professional

Cisco Certified Network Associate

EXAM: #640-407 (CCNA-EXAM) $100.00

As this time, this exam consists of 70 questions and has a 90 minute time limit:

Most of these questions are extracted from the ICRC course.

Recommendation:

Take the ICRC class, this will cover the vast majority of the exam. ICRC covers Appletalk but there is no Appletalk on the CCNA exam.

Cisco also suggests a booklet entitled High-Performance Solutions for Desktop Connectivity, this booklet costs $100.00.

Cisco also recommends the (ITM) Internetworking Technology Multimedia CD-ROM course the cost for this CD is $95.00

CCIEprep.com has just recently opened up CCNAprep.com that will help you prepare for the CCNA exam.

Check the following URL for further information:

http://www.cisco.com/warp/public/10/wwtraining/certprog/lan/programs/ccna_course.html#train

Cisco Certified Network Professional

EXAM: #640-409 (Foundation R/S Exam) $200.00

This exam encompasses the following three areas:

Advanced Cisco Router Configuration Exam (ACRC) #640-403 $100.00
Cisco LAN Switch Configuration Exam (CLSC) #640-404 $100.00
Configuring, Monitoring and Troubleshooting Dial-up Services (CMTD) #640-405 $100.00

So you have a choice take the Foundation R/S exam or take the above three exams.

EXAM: #640-406 (Cisco Internetworking Troubleshooting-CIT) $100.00

Recommendation:
Take the instructor lead classes.

CCDP Track
Cisco Certified Design Professional

Cisco Certified Design Associate

EXAM: #9E0-004

The Cisco Design Specialist has been changed to Designing Cisco Networks (DCN)

There is no instructor lead class for this exam.
There is a DCN -CD (TRN-100065) you can purchase from Cisco for $385 that will provide you
with the information required to pass this exam.

Cisco Certified Design Professional

EXAM: #640-407 (CCNA-EXAM) $100.00

EXAM: #640-409 (Foundation R/S Exam) $200.00

This exam encompasses the following three areas:

Advanced Cisco Router Configuration Exam (ACRC) #640-403 $100.00
Cisco LAN Switch Configuration Exam (CLSC) #640-404 $100.00
Configuring, Monitoring and Troubleshooting Dial-up Services (CMTD) #640-405 $100.00
So you have a choice take the Foundation R/S exam or take the above three exams.

EXAM: #640-025 (Cisco Internetwork Design) $100.00

Check the following URL for more information:
http://www.cisco.com/warp/public/10/wwtraining/certprog/lan/programs/ccdp_course.html#train

Recommendation:
Take the instructor-lead classes.

CCIE
Cisco Certified Internetworking Expert

CCIE practical $1000
EXAM: #350-001 (Cisco Certified Internetworking Expert-CCIE) $200.00

CCIE certification at this time does not require any of the other certifications.
This exam is 2 hours long and consists of 100 questions
The only two requirements are the CCIE exam and the two day practical exam.

The two day practical exam is more than a test of how much you know it is also a test of how you work under pressure and how fast can you work!

Recommendation:

Take the ICRC, ACRC, CLSC, and the CIT classes.
Learn Token Ring, SRB and DLSW.
Experience, experience and experience.

The last recommendation is of course to remain a CCIEprep subscriber.
CCIEprep will help you prepare for all the written exams as well as provide you with the required LAB scenarios to help you pass the two day practical exam.
All of our questions are coded.

The third character will tip off the certification to which the question is applicable.

Examples:

xxNx for CCNA
xxPx for CCNP
xxDx for CCDA & CCDP
All questions are possible CCIE questions.

Training through questions and explanations is fun!

Knowledge is power, power is independence!

Good Luck

Lou Rossi Sr.

Appendix B
Quantity of Questions by Code

There are a total of 600 questions in this book. Each question is coded as a particular Category, Protocol and Certification (see the Code Key for details).

Code Key — Following is an explanation of the code letters in brackets that follow each question.

1st Character: Category.

A	ATM
B	Bridging
C	Cisco specific
E	Ethernet
F	Frame relay
I	FDDI
N	ISDN
O	OSI model
P	PPP
R	Routing
S	Switching
T	Token ring
X	X.25
x	Not applicable

2nd Character: Protocol.

A	Appletalk
I	IP
L	Dial on Demand (or CMTD Exam)
N	NLSP
O	OSPF
X	IPX
x	Not applicable

3rd Character: Certification for which the question will help you prepare.

D CCDA & CCDP — Cisco Design Specialist Exam #9E0-004
Cisco Internetwork Design #640-025

N CCNA Exam #640-407

P CCNP
Advanced Cisco Router Configuration (ACRC) Exam #640-403
Cisco LAN Switch Configuration (CLSC) Exam #640-404
Cisco Monitoring and Troubleshooting Dial-up Services Exam #640-405
Cisco Internetworking Troubleshooting (CIT) Exam #640-406

4th Character (x): Reserved for future use.

As an example, when you come across a question coded "BXDx", it signifies a question that will help you gain the CCDA or CCDP certification and covers Bridging of the IPX protocol.

Since all of the questions that are posted at **CCIEprep.com** are modeled after those that could also appear on the CCIE written test, we will not assign a specific code for this exam.

As the need arises, we will add appropriate designations to this coding system.

In the future you will be able to request a practice test on-line, based on this code system. For example you may wish to build a model exam that contains 25 IP related questions or you may want a mix of IP and IPX questions.

This Appendix contains an analysis of the number of questions that fall into each Category, Protocol, and Certification and their combinations.

Categories

There are 3 questions (0.5%) marked as Category "A" — ATM
Within this group of questions there are:

Protocols
3 (0.5%) also marked as Protocol "x" — Not applicable

Certifications
3 (0.5%) also marked as Certification "D" — CCDA & CCDP

There are 15 questions (2.5%) marked as Category "B" — Bridging
Within this group of questions there are:

Protocols
15 (2.5%) also marked as Protocol "x" — Not applicable

Certifications
1 (0.2%) also marked as Certification "N" — CCNA
14 (2.3%) also marked as Certification "P" — CCNP

There are 152 questions (25.3%) marked as Category "C" — Cisco-specific
Within this group of questions there are:

Protocols
2 (0.3%) also marked as Protocol "A" — Appletalk
15 (2.5%) also marked as Protocol "I" — IP
10 (1.7%) also marked as Protocol "L" — Dial on Demand (or CMTD Exam)
2 (0.3%) also marked as Protocol "X" — IPX
123 (20.5%) also marked as Protocol "x" — Not applicable

Certifications
15 (2.5%) also marked as Certification "D" — CCDA & CCDP
55 (9.2%) also marked as Certification "N" — CCNA
82 (13.7%) also marked as Certification "P" — CCNP

There are 5 questions (0.8%) marked as Category "E" — Ethernet
Within this group of questions there are:

Protocols
5 (0.8%) also marked as Protocol "x" — Not applicable

Certifications
2 (0.3%) also marked as Certification "N" — CCNA
3 (0.5%) also marked as Certification "P" — CCNP

There are 12 questions (2.0%) marked as Category "F" — Frame Relay
Within this group of questions there are:

Protocols
6 (1.0%) also marked as Protocol "I" — IP
6 (1.0%) also marked as Protocol "x" — Not applicable

Certifications
10 (1.7%) also marked as Certification "N" — CCNA
2 (0.3%) also marked as Certification "P" — CCNP

There are 5 questions (0.8%) marked as Category "I" — FDDI
Within this group of questions there are:
Protocols
5 (0.8%) also marked as Protocol "x" — Not applicable

Certifications
5 (0.8%) also marked as Certification "P" — CCNP

There are 7 questions (1.2%) marked as Category "N" — ISDN
Within this group of questions there are:
> *Protocols*
> 6 (1.0%) also marked as Protocol "L" — Dial on Demand (or CMTD Exam)
> 1 (0.2%) also marked as Protocol "x" — Not applicable
>
> *Certifications*
> 1 (0.2%) also marked as Certification "D" — CCDA & CCDP
> 6 (1.0%) also marked as Certification "P" — CCNP

There are 33 questions (5.5%) marked as Category "O" — OSI Model
Within this group of questions there are:
> *Protocols*
> 33 (5.5%) also marked as Protocol "x" — Not applicable
>
> *Certifications*
> 29 (4.8%) also marked as Certification "N" — CCNA
> 4 (0.7%) also marked as Certification "P" — CCNP

There are 5 questions (0.8%) marked as Category "P" — PPP
Within this group of questions there are:
> *Protocols*
> 4 (0.7%) also marked as Protocol "L" — Dial on Demand (or CMTD Exam)
> 1 (0.2%) also marked as Protocol "x" — Not applicable
>
> *Certifications*
> 5 (0.8%) also marked as Certification "P" — CCNP

There are 130 questions (21.7%) marked as Category "R" — Routing
Within this group of questions there are:
> *Protocols*
> 11 (1.8%) also marked as Protocol "A" — Appletalk
> 48 (8.0%) also marked as Protocol "I" — IP
> 3 (0.5%) also marked as Protocol "N" — NLSP
> 18 (3.0%) also marked as Protocol "O" — OSPF
> 21 (3.5%) also marked as Protocol "X" — IPX
> 29 (4.8%) also marked as Protocol "x" — Not applicable
>
> *Certifications*
> 11 (1.8%) also marked as Certification "D" — CCDA & CCDP
> 44 (7.3%) also marked as Certification "N" — CCNA
> 75 (12.5%) also marked as Certification "P" — CCNP

There are 115 questions (19.2%) marked as Category "S" — Switching
Within this group of questions there are:
> *Protocols*
> 115 (19.2%) also marked as Protocol "x" — Not applicable

Appendix B

Certifications
2 (0.3%) also marked as Certification "N" — CCNA
113 (18.8%) also marked as Certification "P" — CCNP

There are 35 questions (5.8%) marked as Category "T" — Token Ring
Within this group of questions there are:
Protocols
35 (5.8%) also marked as Protocol "x" — Not applicable

Certifications
35 (5.8%) also marked as Certification "P" — CCNP

There are 5 questions (0.8%) marked as Category "X"— X.25
Within this group of questions there are:
Protocols
2 (0.3%) also marked as Protocol "I" — IP
23 (0.5%) also marked as Protocol "x" — Not applicable

Certifications
5 (0.8%) also marked as Certification "P" — CCNP

There are 78 questions (13.0%) marked as Category "x" — Not applicable — X.25
Within this group of questions there are:
Protocols
20 (3.3%) also marked as Protocol "I" — IP
43 (7.2%) also marked as Protocol "L" — Dial on Demand (or CMTD Exam)
15 (2.5%) also marked as Protocol "x" — Not applicable

Certifications
10 (1.7%) also marked as Certification "D" — CCDA & CCDP
18 (3.0%) also marked as Certification "N" — CCNA
50 (8.3%) also marked as Certification "P" — CCNP

Protocols

There are 13 questions (2.2%) marked as Protocol "A" — Appletalk
Within this group of questions there are:
Categories
2 (0.3%) also marked as Category "C" — Cisco-specific
11 (1.8%) also marked as Category "R" — Routing

Certifications
2 (0.3%) also marked as Certification "D" — CCDA & CCDP
1 (0.2%) also marked as Certification "N" — CCNA
10 (1.7%) also marked as Certification "P" — CCNP

There are 91 questions (15.2%) marked as Protocol "I" — IP
Within this group of questions there are:

Categories

15 (2.5%) also marked as Category "C" — Cisco-specific
6 (1.0%) also marked as Category "F" — Frame Relay
48 (8.0%) also marked as Category "R" — Routing
2 (0.3%) also marked as Category "X" — X.25
20 (3.3%) also marked as Category "x" — Not applicable

Certifications

6 (1.0%) also marked as Certification "D" — CCDA & CCDP
45 (7.5%) also marked as Certification "N" — CCNA
40 (6.7%) also marked as Certification "P" — CCNP

There are 63 questions (10.5%) marked as Protocol "L" — Dial on Demand (or CMTD Exam) — Dial on Demand (or CMTD Exam)
Within this group of questions there are:

Categories

10 (1.7%) also marked as Category "C" — Cisco-specific
6 (1.0%) also marked as Category "N" — ISDN
4 (0.7%) also marked as Category "P" — PPP
43 (7.2%) also marked as Category "x" — Not applicable

Certifications

63 (10.5%) also marked as Certification "P" — CCNP

There are 3 questions (0.5%) marked as Protocol "N" — NLSP
Within this group of questions there are:

Categories

3 (0.5%) also marked as Category "R" — Routing

Certifications

3 (0.5%) also marked as Certification "P" — CCNP

There are 18 questions (3.0%) marked as Protocol "O" — OSPF
Within this group of questions there are:

Categories

18 (3.0%) also marked as Category "R" — Routing

Certifications

18 (3.0%) also marked as Certification "P" — CCNP

There are 23 questions (3.8%) marked as Protocol "X" — IPX
Within this group of questions there are:

Categories

2 (0.3%) also marked as Category "C" — Cisco-specific
21 (3.5%) also marked as Category "R" — Routing

Appendix B

Certifications
2 (0.3%) also marked as Certification "D" — CCDA & CCDP
6 (1.0%) also marked as Certification "N" — CCNA
15 (2.5%) also marked as Certification "P" — CCNP

There are 389 questions (64.8%) marked as Protocol "x" — Not applicable
Within this group of questions there are:
Categories
3 (0.5%) also marked as Category "A" — ATM
15 (2.5%) also marked as Category "B" — Bridging
123 (20.5%) also marked as Category "C" — Cisco-specific
5 (0.8%) also marked as Category "E" — Ethernet
6 (1.0%) also marked as Category "F" — Frame Relay
5 (0.8%) also marked as Category "I" — FDDI
1 (0.2%) also marked as Category "N" — ISDN
33 (5.5%) also marked as Category "O" — OSI Model
1 (0.2%) also marked as Category "P" — PPP
29 (4.8%) also marked as Category "R" — Routing
115 (19.2%) also marked as Category "S" — Switching
35 (5.8%) also marked as Category "T" — Token Ring
3 (0.5%) also marked as Category "X"— X.25
15 (2.5%) also marked as Category "x" — Not applicable

Certifications
30 (5.0%) also marked as Certification "D" — CCDA & CCDP
109 (18.2%) also marked as Certification "N" — CCNA
250 (41.7%) also marked as Certification "P" — CCNP

Certifications

There are 40 questions (6.7%) marked as Certification "D" — CCDA & CCDP
Within this group of questions there are:
Categories
3 (0.5%) also marked as Category "A" — ATM
15 (2.5%) also marked as Category "C" — Cisco-specific
1 (0.2%) also marked as Category "N" — ISDN
11 (1.8%) also marked as Category "R" — Routing
10 (1.7%) also marked as Category "x" — Not applicable

Protocols
2 (0.3%) also marked as Protocol "A" — Appletalk
6 (1.0%) also marked as Protocol "I" — IP
2 (0.3%) also marked as Protocol "X" — IPX
30 (5.0%) also marked as Protocol "x" — Not applicable

There are 161 questions (26.8%) marked as Certification "N" — CCNA
Within this group of questions there are:

Categories
1 (0.2%) also marked as Category "B" — Bridging
55 (9.2%) also marked as Category "C" — Cisco-specific
2 (0.3%) also marked as Category "E" — Ethernet
10 (1.7%) also marked as Category "F" — Frame Relay
29 (4.8%) also marked as Category "O" — OSI Model
44 (7.3%) also marked as Category "R" — Routing
2 (0.3%) also marked as Category "S" — Switching
18 (3.0%) also marked as Category "x" — Not applicable

Protocols
1 (0.2%) also marked as Protocol "A" — Appletalk
45 (7.5%) also marked as Protocol "I" — IP
6 (1.0%) also marked as Protocol "X" — IPX
109 (18.2%) also marked as Protocol "x" — Not applicable

There are 399 questions (66.5%) marked as Certification "P" — CCNP
Within this group of questions there are:

Categories
14 (2.3%) also marked as Category "B" — Bridging
82 (13.7%) also marked as Category "C" — Cisco-specific
3 (0.5%) also marked as Category "E" — Ethernet
2 (0.3%) also marked as Category "F" — Frame Relay
5 (0.8%) also marked as Category "I" — FDDI
6 (1.0%) also marked as Category "N" — ISDN
4 (0.7%) also marked as Category "O" — OSI Model
5 (0.8%) also marked as Category "P" — PPP
75 (12.5%) also marked as Category "R" — Routing
113 (18.8%) also marked as Category "S" — Switching
35 (5.8%) also marked as Category "T" — Token Ring
5 (0.8%) also marked as Category "x" — Not applicable — X.25
50 (8.3%) also marked as Category "x" — Not applicable

Protocols
10 (1.7%) also marked as Protocol "A" — Appletalk
40 (6.7%) also marked as Protocol "I" — IP
63 (10.5%) also marked as Protocol "L" — Dial on Demand (or CMTD Exam)
3 (0.5%) also marked as Protocol "N" — NLSP
18 (3.0%) also marked as Protocol "O" — OSPF
15 (2.5%) also marked as Protocol "X" — IPX
250 (41.7%) also marked as Protocol "x" — Not applicable

Appendix B

Appendix B

Bibliography

Ballew, Scott M. *Managing IP Networks with Cisco Routers*, O'Reilly. Cambridge, Mass. 1997

Bates, Regis J. and Gregory, Donald W. *Voice and Data Communications Handbook*. McGraw-Hill. New York, NY. 1998

Black, Uyless *ATM Volume III: Internetworking with ATM*. Prentice Hall. Upper Saddle River, NJ. 1998

Cisco Systems, Inc. *Cisco CCIE Fundamentals: Network Design and Case Studies*. Macmillan Technical Publishing. Indianapolis, IN. 1998

Cisco Systems, Inc. *Cisco IOS Bridging and IBM Network Solutions*. Macmillan Technical Publishing. Indianapolis, IN. 1998

Cisco Systems, Inc. *Cisco IOS Configuration Fundamentals*. Macmillan Technical Publishing. Indianapolis, IN. 1998

Cisco Systems, Inc. *Cisco IOS Network Security*. Macmillan Technical Publishing. Indianapolis, IN. 1998

Cisco Systems, Inc. *Cisco IOS Network Security*. Macmillan Technical Publishing. Indianapolis, IN. 1998

Cisco Systems, Inc. *Cisco IOS Solutions for Network Protocols Volume I:IP*. Macmillan Technical Publishing. Indianapolis, IN. 1998

Cisco Systems, Inc. *Cisco IOS Solutions for Network Protocols Volume II:IPX, Appletalk, and More*. Macmillan Technical Publishing. Indianapolis, IN. 1998

Cisco Systems, Inc. *Cisco IOS Switching Services*. Macmillan Technical Publishing. Indianapolis, IN. 1998

Cisco Systems, Inc. *Cisco IOS Wide Area Networking Solutions*. Macmillan Technical Publishing. Indianapolis, IN. 1998

Bibliography

Cisco Systems, Inc. *Cisco Router Configuration*. Macmillan Technical Publishing. Indianapolis, IN. 1998

Cisco Systems, Inc. *Internetworking Technology Handbook*. New Riders Publishing. Indianapolis, IN. 1997

Cisco Systems, Inc. *IOS Dial Solutions*. Macmillan Technical Publishing. Indianapolis, IN. 1998

Cisco Systems, Inc. Website at http://www.cisco.com

Comer, Douglas E. *Internetworking with TCP/IP Vol1:Principles, Protocols, and Architectur,e Third Edition*. Prentice Hall. Englewood Cliffs, NJ. 1995

Halabi, Bassam. Cisco Systems, Inc. *Internet Routing Architectures*, New Riders Publishing. Indianapolis, IN. 1997

Johnson, Howard W. *Fast Ethernet Dawn of a New Network*. Prentice Hall. Upper Saddle River, NJ. 1996

Lewis, Chris. *Cisco TCP/IP Routing Professional Reference*. McGraw-Hill. New York, N.Y. 1998

Perlman, Radia. *Interconnections: Bridges and Routers*. Addison-Wesley. Reading, Mass. 1992

Siyan, Karanjit. *Netware The Professional Reference Second Edition*. New Riders Publishing. Indianapolis, IN. 1993

Stevens, Richard W. *TCP/IP Illustrated, Volume 1 The Protocols*. Addison-Wesley. Reading, Mass. 1994

Bibliography

Introducing

CCNA Boot Camp

If you're serious about CCNA, here's the program that can turn you into a Cisco Certified Network Associate in just five days!

It ain't easy! It ain't cheap! But if you work hard at this Boot Camp, your networking career will instantly be on the fast track! This course consists of five days of intensive, hands-on training that will provide qualified students with the skills needed to pass the CCNA exam.

Who will be the instructor? Lou Rossi Sr., Certified Cisco Systems Instructor

Is this class certified from Cisco? No.

How many students in a class? Class size will be limited to 12. (Cisco Certified Courses have a class size of 24.)

When will I take the exam? On Friday, the last day of class, or you can receive a voucher and take the test at any time.

Suppose I fail the exam? You may sit in on a future class at no additional charge, assuming you were present during the entire course time. Students who repeat the Boot Camp will be responsible for all transportation, food, and lodging expenses.

What does the tuition include? Hotel (First Class Accommodations) • Breakfast, Lunch & Dinner • Transportation to and from Airport • Transportation to and from Testing Center • Testing Fee

How much does it cost to attend the CCNA Boot Camp? $4495.00

If I own CCIEprep.com Study Guide or I am a subscriber to CCNAprep.com or CCIEprep.com, will I receive a discount? Yes. all those who own this book will receive a $100 discount. *CCIEprep.com* website subscribers save even more - 12-month subscribers will receive a $300 discount; all 6-month CCIE and all CCNA subscribers will receive a $200 discount. Maximum discount $300.

Can anyone take this course? If you are interested, please contact Lou Rossi, Sr. (lrossisr@ar-inc.com) so that we may set up a pre-qualification phone conversation. Knowledge of the OSI model will be required as a pre-requisite.

What course materials will I receive? Each student will receive copies of Lou Rossi's *CCNA Study Guide* and *High Speed Desktop Solutions* from Cisco.

CCNA Boot Camp Schedule 1999
January 11-15 • Jacksonville, FL
February 15-19 • Honolulu, HI
March 8-12 • San Francisco, CA
April 12-16 • Tallahassee, FL
May 10-14 • Raleigh, NC
June 7-11 • New York, NY
July 12-16 • Boston, MA
August 9-13 • Atlanta, GA
September 13-17 • Orlando FL
October 11-15 • Miami, FL
November 1-5 • Colorado Springs, CO
December 13-17 • New York, NY

Other camps will be added. Please contact Lou Rossi, Sr. by e-mail for details or to register:

lrossisr@ar-inc.com

Single-User License Agreement

The CCIEprep.com Study Guide, Volume 1 and Beachfront Quizzer (the "PRODUCT") contain proprietary software, data and information owned by Genium Publishing Corporation ("GENIUM") and its licensors. Your right to use the PRODUCT is governed by the terms and conditions of this Agreement.

You are granted a non-exclusive and non-transferable single-user license to use the PRODUCT on your computer, provided that it is not used in any network, file server, multiple CPU, other multi-user, bulletin board, or remotely accessible arrangement, where more than one user at a time has access to the PRODUCT, unless GENIUM has granted you a multi-user license.

You may make one copy of the PRODUCT for back-up purposes only, and you must maintain an accurate record as to the location of the back-up at all times.

You may not use, copy, decompile, disassemble, reverse engineer, modify, reproduce, create derivative works, transmit, distribute, sublicense, store in a database or retrieval system of any kind, rent or transfer the PRODUCT, or any portion thereof, in any form or by any means (including electronically or otherwise) except as expressly provided for in this License Agreement. All rights in the PRODUCT not expressly granted herein are reserved by GENIUM and its licensors.

You may not reproduce or otherwise use any material retrieved from or contained in the PRODUCT in any work, either paper or electronic, that you intend to publish, without prior written permission from GENIUM.

Limited Warranty: The PRODUCT is licensed "as is." It is the user's responsibility to determine the suitability of the PRODUCT for the user's particular purposes. The information contained in the PRODUCT was prepared and presented with reasonable care, and is based upon the most reliable information available to the authors. However, GENIUM, its licensors and the authors make no warranties, express or implied, as to the results to be obtained by any person or entity from the use of the PRODUCT and/or any information or data included therein. GENIUM, its licensors and the authors make no express or implied warranties of merchantability or fitness for a particular purpose or use with respect to the PRODUCT.

Limited Warranty for Disc: GENIUM warrants that the physical disc on which the PRODUCT is recorded is free from defects in materials and workmanship under normal use and service for a period of ninety (90) days from the date of purchase. In the event of a defect in the disc, GENIUM will replace the disc. The entire and exclusive remedy under this warranty shall be limited to replacement of a defective disc.

Limitation of Liability: Neither GENIUM, its licensors, nor the authors shall be liable for any indirect, special or consequential damages, such as but not limited to, loss of anticipated profits or benefits, resulting from the use or inability to use the PRODUCT even if any of them has been advised of the possibility of such damages. Some states do not allow the exclusion or limitation of indirect, special or consequential damages, so the above limitation may not apply to you.

This License Agreement is effective until terminated. It will terminate if you fail to comply with any term or condition of this License Agreement. Upon termination, you are obligated to return to GENIUM the PRODUCT together with any copy thereof and to purge all copies of the PRODUCT included in all your servers and computer facilities.

This License Agreement constitutes the entire agreement between the parties relating to the PRODUCT. The terms of any Purchase Order shall have no effect on the terms of this License Agreement. Failure of GENIUM to insist at any time on strict compliance with this License Agreement shall not constitute a waiver of any rights under this License Agreement. This License Agreement shall be construed and governed in accordance with the laws of the State of New York. If any provision of this License Agreement is held to be contrary to law, the remaining provisions will remain in full force and effect.

Genium Publishing Corporation
One Genium Plaza
Schenectady, NY 12304

CCIE Prep.com

STUDY GUIDE

VOLUME 1

ADDENDUM

Chapter Six
CCIE

Addendum

The last 58 CCIE-topic questions were inadvertently omitted from Chapter Six, and are included here. The questions that follow should have appeared starting on page 81 of Chapter Six. The answers for these questions were not omitted and appear on pages 128-144 of Chapter Six.

Question 6–162. [RXPx] IPX network CAD is a/an: (Choose the best answer.)
(Refer to the following diagram and routing table.)

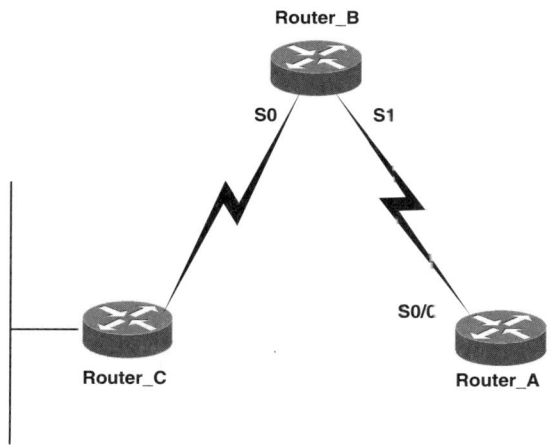

```
Router_B#sh ipx route
Codes: C - Connected primary network,
  c - Connected secondary network, S - Static,
  F - Floating static, L - Local (internal), W - IPXWAN
  R - RIP, E - EIGRP, N - NLSP, X - External, A - Aggregate
  s - seconds, u - uses, U - Per-user static

5 Total IPX routes. Up to 2 parallel paths and 16 hops allowed.

No default route known.

L          B1 is the internal network
R          A1 [07/01] via         0.0000.00a1.0C00,      3s, Se1
R          C1 [07/01] via         0.0000.00a1.0C00,      3s, Se0
R          CAD [07/01] via        0.0000.00a1.0000,      4s, Se1
                       via        0.0000.00a1.0000,      3s, Se0
R          FAD [07/01] via        0.0000.00a1.0000,      3s, Se0
```

a) Fast serial Link
b) Ethernet link
c) Slow serial link
d) X25
e) None of the above

Question 6–163. [CxPx] What is the purpose of the "myrouter" in the following command?

```
snmp-server community myrouter RW 1
```

a) It identifies an autonomous system of routers named myrouters.
b) It serves as a password.
c) It will allow all routers with the name myrouters read and write access.
d) It is just used as a tag to identify community.
e) None of the above.

Question 6–164. [BxPx] Which of the following describes the function of spanning tree for SRB?

a) Causing the bridge to go in a blocking state as to avoid broadcasts
b) Specifies path for spanning tree explorer frames to reduce explorer traffic
c) Transparently bridges instead of SRB
d) There is no such thing as Spanning tree in SRB network.
e) To assure that there is only one unique way to pass data through the bridged circuit

Question 6–165. [RAFx] Which of the following are true?

a) Appletalk does not load share.
b) Appletalk load shares by default.
c) Appletalk load shares if the "appletalk maximum-paths" command is configured.
d) Appletalk load shares if the "appletalk load-balance" command is used.
e) None of the above.

Question 6–166. [BxPx] Given the following router configuration, which of the following protocols would be routed?

```
version 11.1
service udp-small-servers
service tcp-small-servers
!
hostname Router_C
!
no ip routing
appletalk routing
ipx routing 0060.09c3.df60
ipx internal-network C1
!
interface Ethernet0
  ip address 10.1.1.1 255.255.255.0
  no ip mroute-cache
  no ip route-cache
  appletalk cable-range 111-115 112.170
  appletalk zone bottom-ether
  ipx network CAD
  bridge-group 1
```

```
!
interface Ethernet1
 ip address 10.1.2.1 255.255.255.0
 no ip mroute-cache
 no ip route-cache
 appletalk cable-range 95-99 97.221
 appletalk zone left-ether
 ipx network FAD
 bridge-group 1
!
interface Serial0
 ip address 10.1.3.1 255.255.255.0
 no ip mroute-cache
 no ip route-cache
 appletalk cable-range 100-105 100.190
 appletalk zone leftserial
 ipx ipxwan 0 unnumbered Router_C
 clockrate 1200
 bridge-group 1
!
interface Serial1
 no ip address
 no ip mroute-cache
 no ip route-cache
 shutdown
 clockrate 4000000
!
no ip classless
!
ipx router nlsp
!
bridge 1 protocol dec
bridge 1 priority 1
!
line con 0
line aux 0
 transport input all
line vty 0 4
 login
!
end
```

a) IP, IPX, Appletalk
b) IPX, IP
c) IP, IPX, DECNET
d) Appletalk, IPX
e) No routing will take place because bridging is configured.

Question 6–167. [TxPx] Enabling forwarding of spanning-tree explorers is recommended: (Choose the best answer.)

a) In all transparent bridged (TB) networks
b) In all SRB environments
c) In complex SRB environments
d) In all SR/TLB environments
e) Is never recommended.

Question 6–168. [CxPx] Which of the following is true as it pertains to the ip unnumbered command?

a) This command can not be used on an ethernet interface.
b) ip unnumbered must be configured on both sides of the serial link.
c) All routers within the topology must be Cisco.
d) An unnumbered interface can be pinged.
e) None of the above.

Question 6–169. [TxPx] If Host A sends a packet to Host B over token ring: Host A dies after transmitting, and Host B is not active:

a) The packet will time out.
b) The packet will be removed by Host A.
c) The NVRAM of Host B will remove the packet.
d) The packet will "die" when it reaches the terminator.
e) The packet will be removed by the Active monitor.

Question 6–170. [ROPx] If all possible stub areas were defined, and assuming all Cisco defaults, what Routers or Router would see External Type 2 networks?

a) Router_A
b) Router_B
c) Router_C
d) Router_D
e) None of the above

Question 6–171. [xxPx] Assume that there are 210 bytes of data, that there are seven layers of encapsulation and each of these layers contains a header of 10 bytes. What percentage of the entire frame contains header information? (Choose the best answer.)

a) 10%
b) 15%
c) 20%
d) 25%
e) 33%

Question 6–172. [CxPx] When using IPTALK encapsulation on a tunnel interface, which of the following are true as it pertains to the AppleTalk node address?

a) Will be dynamically assigned
b) Will be statically configured
c) Will be the lower 8 bits of the tunnel source address
d) Will be lower 8 bits of the tunnel destination address
e) May have a conflicting address

Question 6–173. [ROPx] Which of the following areas could be defined as Stubby or Totally Stubby? (Refer to the following diagram.)

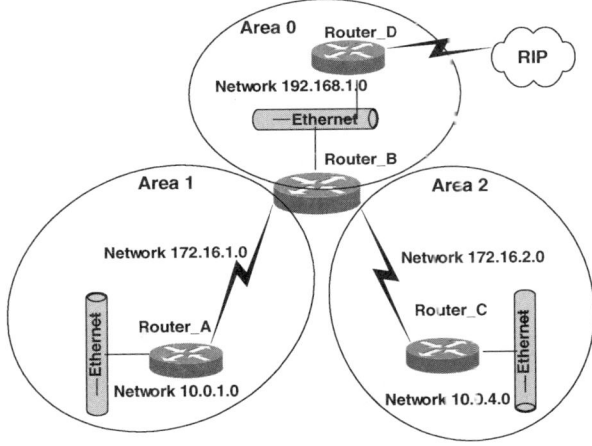

a) Area 1
b) Area 2
c) Area 3
d) None of the above
e) All of the above

Question 6–174. [CxPx] A unique advantage of Integrated Routing and Bridging (IRB) over other bridging techniques is: (Choose all that apply.)

a) IRB conserves address space.
b) IRB allows different protocols to be routed and bridged in the same box.
c) IRB allows the same protocol to be routed and bridged in the same box.
d) IRB allows a packet to be received on a routed interface and sent out a bridged interface.
e) IRB allows a packet to be received on a bridged interface and sent out a routed interface.

Question 6–175. [CxPx] Cisco supports routing services over which of the following interface types?

  a) Token Ring
  b) FDDI
  c) Ethernet
  d) Synchronous Serial
  e) Asynchronous Serial
  f) All of the above

Question 6–176. [ROPx] If OSPF routers have the same topological databases they are called?

  a) Neighbor routers
  b) Adjacent routers
  c) Designated routers
  d) Area Border routers
  e) Backbone routers

Question 6–177. [RXPx] Given the following configuration of Router_A, which of the following tasks must be performed to configure IPX WAN?

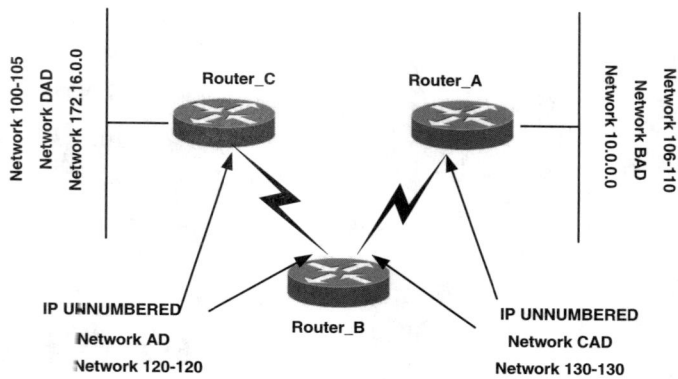

```
Router_C#sh run
Building configuration...

Current configuration:
!
version 11.2
!
hostname Router_C
!
!
appletalk routing
ipx routing 0060.09c3.df60
```

```
!
interface Ethernet0
 ip address 172.16.1.1 255.255.255.0
 appletalk cable-range 100-105 103.243
 appletalk zone right
 ipx network DAD
!
interface Ethernet1
 no ip address
 shutdown
!
interface Serial0
 ip unnumbered Ethernet0
 appletalk cable-range 120-120 120.17
 appletalk zone left
 ipx network AD
 clockrate 56000
!
interface Serial1
 no ip address
 shutdown
!
router igrp 100
 network 172.16.0.0
!
no ip classless
!!
line con 0
line aux 0
line vty 0 4
 login
!
end

Router_B#sh run
Building configuration...

Current configuration:
!
version 11.3
no service password-encryption
!
hostname Router_B
!
!
appletalk routing
ipx routing 0007.7816.fe54
!
interface Loopback0
```

```
 ip address 172.17.1.1 255.255.255.0
!
interface Serial0
 ip unnumbered Loopback0
 no ip mroute-cache
 appletalk cable-range 130-130 130.81
 appletalk zone right
 ipx network CAD
 no fair-queue
!
interface Serial1
 ip unnumbered Loopback0
 appletalk cable-range 120-120 120.125
 appletalk zone left
 ipx network AD
!
interface Serial2
 no ip address
 shutdown
!
interface Serial3
 no ip address
 shutdown
!
interface TokenRing0
 no ip address
 shutdown
!
interface BRI0
 no ip address
 shutdown
!
router igrp 100
 network 172.17.0.0
!
ip classless
!
!
!
!
!
line con 0
line aux 0
line vty 0 4
 login
!
end

Router_A#sh run
```

```
Building configuration...

Current configuration:
!
version 11.3
no service password-encryption
!
hostname Router_A
!
!
appletalk routing
ipx routing 0010.7b15.bd41
!
interface Ethernet0/0
 ip address 10.1.1.1 255.255.255.0
 appletalk cable-range 106-110 106.17
 appletalk zone left
 ipx network BAD
!
interface Serial0/0
 ip unnumbered Ethernet0/0
 no ip mroute-cache
 appletalk cable-range 130-130 130.37
 appletalk zone right
 ipx network CAD
 clockrate 56000
!
interface TokenRing0/0
 no ip address
 shutdown
 ring-speed 16
!
interface FastEthernet1/0
 no ip address
 shutdown
!
router igrp 100
 network 10.0.0.0
!
ip classless
!!
line con 0
line aux 0
line vty 0 4
 login
!
end
```

a) Remove the IPX network number from Serial 0/0
b) Remove the IPX network number from Ethernet 0/0
c) Configure an IPX internal network number on Router_C
d) Assign a default tick count to S0/0
e) All of the above

Question 6–178. [IxPx] Which of the following describe a FDDI Dual-homed station?

a) A station that has two FDDI NICs installed
b) A station that is connected to two separate dual attachment connectors (DACs)
c) A station that is connected to the primary ring twice
d) A station that is connected to both the primary and the secondary ring
e) None of the above

Question 6–179. [CAPx] Which is true of the appletalk cable-range 0-0 command?

a) It is a global configuration command.
b) It sets the interface cable range to 0-0.
c) An appletalk zone command would still be required.
d) It sets the interface to the discovery mode to allow discovery of both cable range and zone name.
e) No such command.

Question 6–180. [CxPx] Which of the following are true as they relate to IPX EIGRP and Incremental SAP updates?

a) Incremental SAP updates should be configured on all interfaces.
b) Incremental SAP updates should not be configured where non-Cisco systems may exist.
c) Incremental SAP updates would need to be configured on WAN links.
d) Incremental SAP updates are sent every 10 minutes by default.
e) Incremental SAP updates would communicate only when a change occurs and contain only the information that has changed.

Question 6–181. [TxPx] If Host A sends a packet to Host B over token ring, and Host B is not active:

a) The packet will time out.
b) The packet will be removed by Host A.
c) The NVRAM of Host B will remove the packet.
d) The packet will "die" when it reaches the terminator.
e) The packet will be removed by the token monitor.

Question 6–182. [CxPx] What is the password required to access the non-privileged or user mode from the Console Port? (Refer to the following configuration.)

```
Router_B#sh run
Building configuration...

Current configuration:
```

```
!
version 11.3
no service password-encryption
!
hostname Router_B
!
enable secret 5 $1$4Rzs$i9EC6.trjXdJe0pO6dpZm0
enable password Secret
!
ip host toronto 196.60.26.1
!
interface Serial0
 ip address 192.168.5.1 255.255.255.0
!
interface Serial1
 ip address 192.168.10.2 255.255.255.0
!
interface Serial2
 no ip address
 shutdown
!
interface Serial3
 no ip address
 shutdown
!
interface TokenRing0
 no ip address
 shutdown
!
interface BRI0
 no ip address
 shutdown
!
router rip
 network 196.60.26.0
!
ip classless
!
!
line con 0
 password notset
line aux 0
line vty 0 4
 password nologin
 login
!
end
```

a) No password has beer set.
b) No login will be permitted.
c) Secret
d) Secret 5
e) nologin
f) notset
g) Can not be determined.

Question 6–183. [xIPx] What are two reasons why these two workstations might not be able to ping each other? (Choose the best answers.)

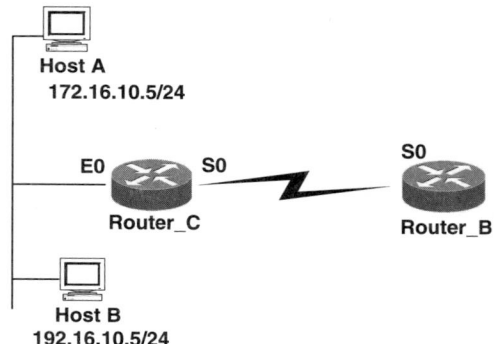

Host A
172.16.10.5/24

EO Router_C SO Router_B SO

Host B
192.16.10.5/24

a) They have the same host address.
b) They have different IP encapsulation methods.
c) They have misconfigured defult gateways.
d) The E0 of Router_C is not configured with a secondary address.
e) None of the above. Since both Workstations are on the same physical wire, they must be able to ping each other.

Question 6–184. [BxFx] Workstation A sends a frame to Workstation B. The devices shown are transparent bridges. Which of the following are true? (Choose all that apply) (Refer to the diagram below.)

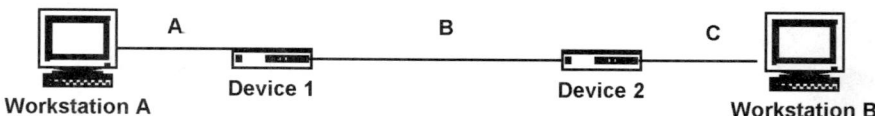

Workstation A A Device 1 B Device 2 C Workstation B

a) MAC addresses never change.
b) Only source MAC address will change as the frame traverses the network.
c) Only destination MAC address will change as the frame traverses the network.
d) Both the source and destination MAC address will change as the frame traverses the network.
e) Not enough information given.

Question 6–185. [TxPx] Which of the following is true of Source Route Translational Bridging (SR/TLB)? (Choose all that apply.)

a) Allows communication between Ethernet and Token Ring hosts
b) Will insert a RIF when communicating from a Transparent Bridge domain to a Source Route Bridge domain
c) Will remove a RIF when communicating from a Source Route Bridge domain to a Transparent Bridge domain
d) Multiple paths may exist between SRB and TB domains.
e) It may be necessary to configure MTU manually.

Question 6–186. [xxPx] Which of the following describes a Star topology?

a) There is a central distribution point.
b) A linear transmission media
c) Easier to troubleshoot than a bus topolgy
d) All nodes are directly attached to the media.
e) Requires more cabling than other topologies

Question 6–187. [TxPx] When Host A sends a frame to Host B what is the source MAC address on Host B's Token Ring segment?

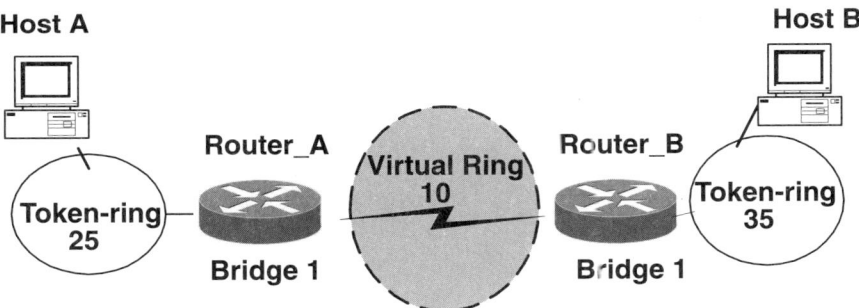

a) MAC of Host A
b) MAC of Host B
c) Serial MAC of Router A
d) Ethernet MAC of Router B
e) Ethernet MAC of Router A

Question 6–188. [RXPx] What must be true of the two serial links of Router_B? (Choose all that apply.) (Refer to the following diagram and routing table.)

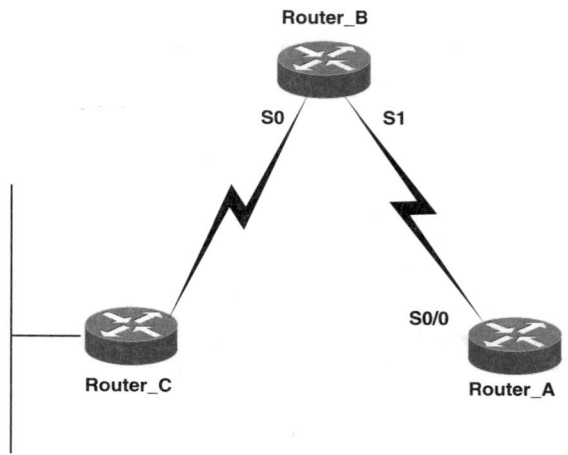

```
Router_B#sh ipx route
Codes: C - Connected primary network,
   c - Connected secondary network, S - Static,
   F - Floating static, L - Local (internal), W - IPXWAN
   R - RIP, E - EIGRP, N - NLSP, X - External, A - Aggregate
   s - seconds, u - uses, U - Per-user static

5 Total IPX routes. Up to 2 parallel paths and 16 hops allowed.

No default route known.

L         B1 is the internal network
R         A1 [07/01] via        0.0000.00a1.0000,    3s, Se1
R         C1 [07/01] via        0.0000.00a1.0000,    3s, Se0
R        CAD [07/01] via        0.0000.00a1.0000,    4s, Se1
                     via        0.0000.00a1.0000,    3s, Se0
R        FAD [07/01] via        0.0000.00a1.0000,    3s, Se0
```

a) They have the same bandwidth.
b) They have the same HOP count.
c) The TTL is the same.
d) The TICK count is the same.
e) The Clock Rate is the same.

Question 6–189. [CxPx] Which of the following are true? (Choose all that apply.) (Refer to the following configuration.)

```
Current configuration:
!
version 11.3
no service password-encryption
!
hostname Router_B
!
!
ip host toronto 196.60.26.1
!
interface Serial0
 ip address 192.168.5.1 255.255.255.0
!
interface Serial1
 ip address 192.168.10.2 255.255.255.0
!
interface Serial2
 no ip address
 shutdown
!
interface Serial3
 no ip address
 shutdown
!
interface TokenRing0
 no ip address
 shutdown
!
interface BRI0
 no ip address
 shutdown
!
router rip
 network 196.60.26.0
!
ip classless
!
!
line con 0
line aux 0
line vty 0 4
 no login
!
end
```

a) "no login" would be the password used for a telnet session.
b) A telnet session could not be established to Router_B.
c) No login would be required to establish a telnet session.
d) The telnet user would not be able to access the privilege mode of Router_B.
e) None of the above.

Question 6–190. [ROPx] If all possible stubby areas were defined, and assuming all Cisco defaults, what type of networks could an internal router see?

a) External Type 1
b) External Type 2
c) Default routes
d) Intra area routes
e) Inter area routes

Question 6–191. [CxPx] Which of the following are reasons why a serial link might go to the up and down state?

a) Keepalives are not being received.
b) The cable is not plugged into the router
c) The cable is not plugged into the CSU/DSU
d) The CSU/DSU is powered down
e) All of the above

Question 6–192. [BxPx] Assume Source Route Bridging (SRB) is configured and Host A knows the location of Host B and sends a frame to Host B. Within the frame, what follows Host A's MAC address? Refer to the following diagram.

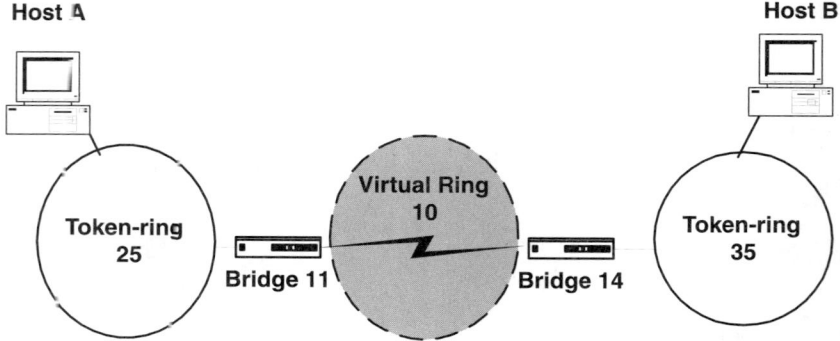

a) Data
b) RIF
c) Host B's layer 3 address
d) Host A's Layer 3 address
e) Can not be determined

Question 6–193. [RIPx] Host A and Host B are running the TCP/IP protocol, Router A and Router B are connected together using a X.25 serial connection. When Host A transmits to Host B, what will be the destination address in the Network header? (Refer to the following diagram.)

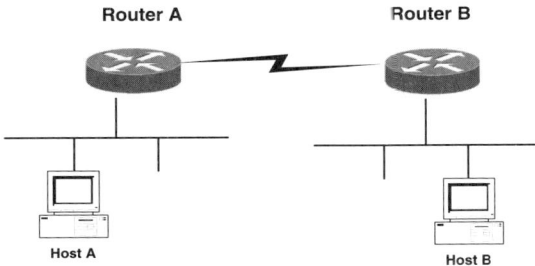

a) Router B
b) Router A
c) Host B
d) Because it's using X.25 there will be no Network header.
e) None of the above.

Question 6–194. [TxPx] Which of the following is true of Source Route Bridging?

a) Spanning tree protocol used can be IEEE 802.1d.
b) Spanning tree protocol used can be DEC.
c) The bridge is the only device that knows the route to the destination.
d) Source Route bridges must have a unique number.
e) Spanning tree protocol is IBM.

Question 6–195. [TxPx] Assume Source Route Bridging (SRB) is configured and Host A knows the location of Host B and sends a frame to Host B. What is the value of the most significant bit of the source MAC address? Refer to the following diagram.

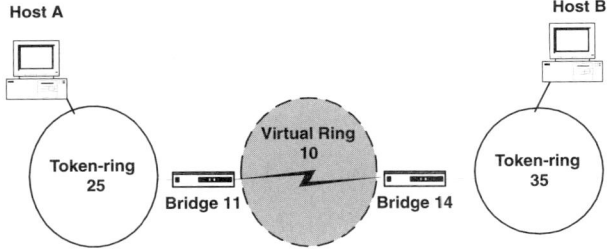

a) 0
b) 1
c) Can not be determined

Question 6–196. [ROPx] Which of the following routers would be configured for summarization?

    a) Internal
    b) Backbone
    c) External
    d) Area Border Router
    e) Autonomous System Boundary Router

Question 6–197. [xIPx] Name the three components of Simple Network Management Protocol (SMNP).

    a) Managed Device
    b) Agent
    c) Network Management System (NMS)
    d) Management Information Base (MIB)
    e) Tag Information Base (TIF)

Question 6–198. [RIPx] It takes three segments to initiate a TCP connection-oriented session. How many does it take to terminate the session?

    a) 1
    b) 2
    c) 3
    d) 4
    e) 0, just disconnect the link.

Question 6–199. [RIPx] The command backup load 50 10 means:

    a) After the primary link goes down, within 50 seconds the back up will be brought up.
    b) After the primary link has come back up there will be a 10-second waiting period before
       the secondary is taken down.
    c) After the primary has 50/255 % capacity, the secondary will be brought up.
    d) After the primary has 10/255% capacity, the secondary will be taken down.
    e) After the primary has 50% capacity, the secondary will be brought up.

Question 6–200. [RIPx] Which one of the following is an error that a router may generate when it receives datagrams at a pace faster than it can process?

    a) Source quench
    b) TTF (Tick Too Fast)
    c) BECN
    d) TTL error
    e) FECN

Question 6–201. [CxPx] Refer to the following diagram. The BVI should be configured on:

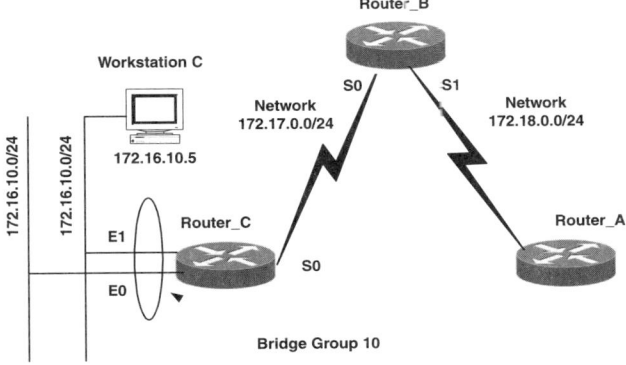

a) Router_A
b) Router_B
c) Router_C
d) Router_C and Router_B
e) All routers

Question 6–202. [ROPx] Which of the following routers would be defined as backbone routers? (Refer to the following diagram.)

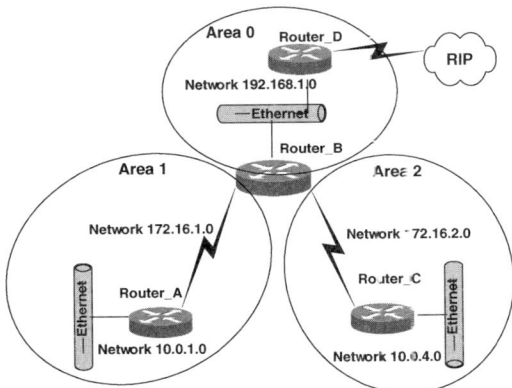

a) Router_A
b) Router_B
c) Router_C
d) Router_D
e) None of the above

Question 6–203. [TxPx] Which of the following is a possible "legal RIF"? (Choose all that apply.)

a) 0630.0011.0191.0030
b) 0630.0011.0191
c) 0630.0011.0190
d) 0630.0011 0191.0030
e) 0830.0011 0191.0031

Question 6–204. [CxPx] Which of the following statements is false?

a) IGRP is a Distance Vector routing protocol.
b) IGRP and EIGRP use the same metrics.
c) IGRP communicates the whole routing table to its neighbors.
d) IGRP and EIGRP will always automatically redistribute between each other.
e) EIGRP is NOT a Link State routing protocol.

Question 6–205. [TxPx] Assume Data Link Switching (DLSw) is configured and Host A sends a frame to Host B. Which one of the following would be the RIF at Host B? Refer to the following diagram.

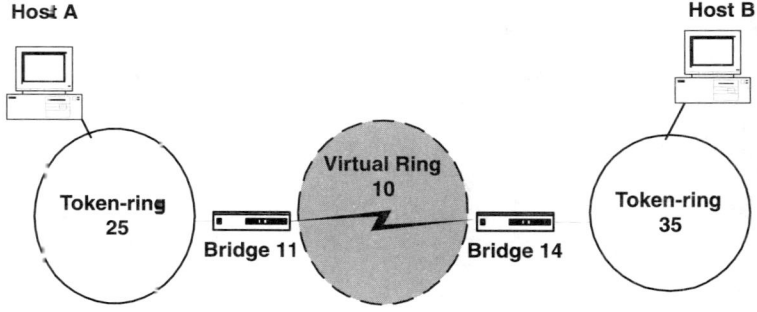

a) 0630.019b.00ae.0230
b) 2511.1014.3500
c) 0830.2511.1014.3500
d) 0830.019b.00ae.0230
e) None of the above

Question 6–206. [CxPx] IGRP uses by default which of the following as part of the metric?

a) Bandwidth
b) Delay
c) Load
d) Reliability
e) Hop count
f) Presentation

Question 6–207. [CxPx] What are the three types of serial compression methods? (Choose three.)

a) TCP/IP header Compression
b) IPX header & trailer
c) Payload Compression
d) Compress Compression (used for damaged links)
e) Link Compression

Question 6–208. [RxPx] Workstation A sends a frame to Workstation B. The devices shown are routers. Which of the following are true of the Layer 2 addresses at reference point C? (Choose all that apply.) (Refer to the diagram below.)

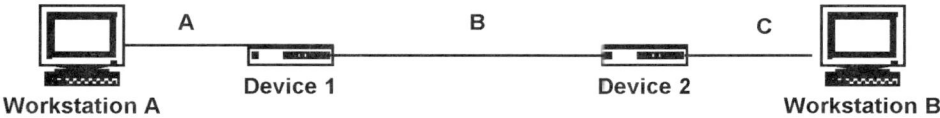

a) The destination address will be that of Workstation B.
b) The source address will be that of Workstation A.
c) The source address will be the outbound interface of Device 2.
d) Routers do not use Layer 2 addresses so they never change.
e) Not enough information is given.

Question 6–209. [RIPx] Assuming IP RIP is the routing protocol used for all networks on all routers: (Refer to the following diagram.)

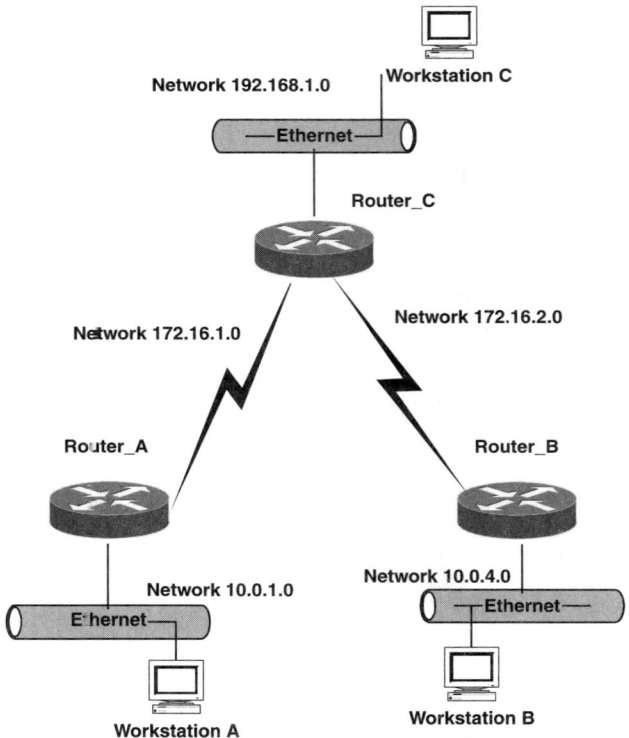

a) Router_C would ping Workstation B with a 100% success rate.
b) Router_C would ping Workstation B with a 50% success rate.
c) Router_C would ping Workstation B with a 0% success rate.
d) Router_C would ping Workstation A with a 100% success rate.
e) Router_C would ping Workstation A with a 0% success rate.

Question 6–210. [TxPx] IBM Token Ring chips can process how many ring numbers?

a) 1
b) 2
c) 7
d) 13
e) Unlimited

Question 6–211. [CxPx] Which of the following are true? (Refer to the following configuration.)

```
Current configuration:
!
version 11.3
no service password-encryption
!
hostname Router_B
!
enable secret 5 $1$53Qx$oxT6JVmrL6.z7vg2LFnX1/
enable password arg
!
ip host toronto 196.60.26.1
!
interface Serial0
 ip address 192.168.5.1 255.255.255.0
!
interface Serial1
 ip address 192.168.10.2 255.255.255.0
!
interface Serial2
 no ip address
 shutdown
!
interface Serial3
 no ip address
 shutdown
!
interface TokenRing0
 no ip address
 shutdown
!
interface BRI0
 no ip address
 shutdown
!
router rip
 network 196.60.26.0
!
ip classless
!
!
line con 0
line aux 0
line vty 0 4
 no login
!
end
```

a) "no login" would be the password used for a telnet session.
b) A telnet session could not be established to Router_B.
c) No login would be required to establish a telnet session.
d) Secret would be the password used to establish a telnet session.
e) None of the above.

Question 6–212. [RXPx] IPX SAPs are periodical. They are sent every

a) 10 seconds
b) 30 seconds
c) 60 seconds
d) 90 seconds
e) Depends on the type of SAP.

Question 6–213. [BxPx] Which of the following is true?

a) A transparent bridge simply supplies a bridge ID to the bridged packet.
b) A source-route bridge filters packets based upon MAC-addresses.
c) A transparent bridge end node knows the location of all devices in relation to the bridge or bridges.
d) A source-route bridge end node is unaware that a bridge exists.
e) A transparent bridge makes decisions.

Question 6–214. [RIPx] What is the OSPF cost of the serial link with the address of 10.4.0.2?

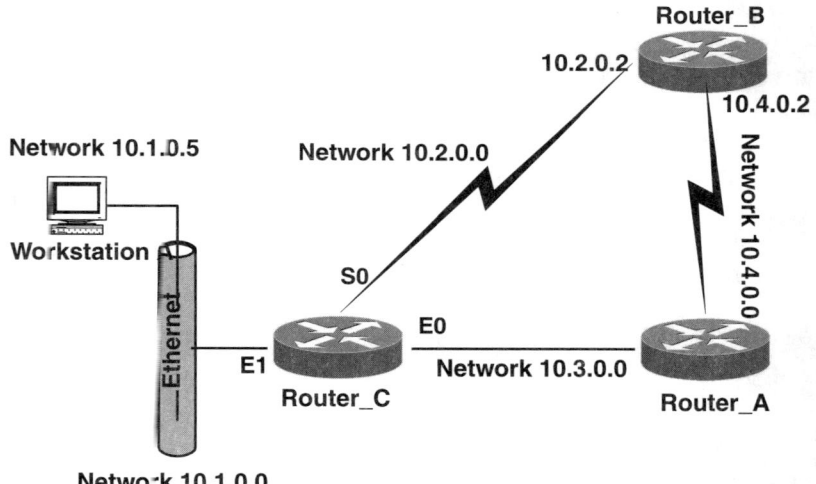

```
Current configuration:
!
version 11.2
```

```
!
hostname Router_C
!
interface Ethernet0
 ip address 10.3.0.3 255.255.0.0
!
interface Ethernet1
 ip address 10.1.0.3 255.255.0.0
 ip policy route-map thisway
!
interface Serial0
 ip address 10.2.0.1 255.255.0.0
 clockrate 38400
!
interface Serial1
 no ip address
 shutdown
!
router ospf 100
 network 10.0.0.0 0.255.255.255 area 0
!
no ip classless
access-list 1 permit 10.1.0.5
route-map thisway permit 10
 match ip address 1
 set interface Serial0
!
line con 0
line aux 0
line vty 0 4
 login
!
end

Router_C#sh ip route
Codes: C - connected, S - static, I - IGRP, R - RIP, M - mobile,
   B - BGP, D - EIGRP, EX - EIGRP external, O - OSPF,
   IA - OSPF inter area, N1 - OSPF NSSA external type 1,
   N2 - OSPF NSSA external type 2, E1 - OSPF external type 1,
   E2 - OSPF external type 2, E - EGP, i - IS-IS,
   L1 - IS-IS level-1, L2 - IS-IS level-2, * - candidate default
   U - per-user static route, o - ODR
```

```
Gateway of last resort is not set

     10.0.0.0/16 is subnetted, 3 subnets
C         10.2.0.0 is directly connected, Serial0
C         10.3.0.0 is directly connected, Ethernet0
O         10.4.0.0 [110/74] via 10.3.0.1, 00:00:13, Ethernet0
```

a) 10
b) 74
c) 64
d) 110
e) Can't be determined.

Question 6–215. [CxPx] What is the IP address used for the serial interface of Router_C when communication takes place? (Refer to the following diagram and configurations.)

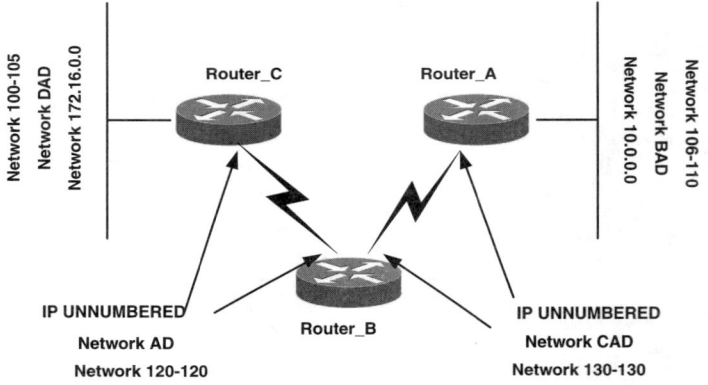

```
Router_C#sh run
Building configuration...

Current configuration:
!
version 11.2
!
hostname Router_C
!
!
appletalk routing
ipx routing 0060.09c3.df60
!
interface Ethernet0
  _p address 172.16.1.1 255.255.255.0
  appletalk cable-range 100-105 103.243
```

```
 appletalk zone right
 ipx network DAD
!
interface Ethernet1
 no ip address
 shutdown
!
interface Serial0
 ip unnumbered Ethernet0
 appletalk cable-range 120-120 120.17
 appletalk zone left
 ipx network AD
 clockrate 56000
!
interface Serial1
 no ip address
 shutdown
!
router igrp 100
 network 172.16.0.0
!
no ip classless
!!
line con 0
line aux 0
line vty 0 4
 login
!
end

          Router_B#sh run
Building configuration...

Current configuration:
!
version 11.3
no service password-encryption
!
hostname Router_B
!
!
appletalk routing
ipx routing 0007.7816.fe54
!
interface Loopback0
 ip address 172.17.1.1 255.255.255.0
!
interface Serial0
 ip unnumbered Loopback0
```

```
 no ip mroute-cache
 appletalk cable-range 130-130 130.81
 appletalk zone right
 ipx network CAD
 no fair-queue
!
interface Serial1
 ip unnumbered Loopback0
 appletalk cable-range 120-120 120.125
 appletalk zone left
 ipx network AD
!
interface Serial2
 no ip address
 shutdown
!
interface Serial3
 no ip address
 shutdown
!
interface TokenRing0
 no ip address
 shutdown
!
interface BRI0
 no ip address
 shutdown
!
router igrp 100
 network 172.17.0.0
!
ip classless
!
!
!
!
!
line con 0
line aux 0
line vty 0 4
 login
!
end

Router_A#sh run
Building configuration...

Current configuration:
!
```

```
version 11.3
no service password-encryption
!
hostname Router_A
!
!
appletalk routing
ipx routing 0010.7b15.bd41
!
interface Ethernet0/0
 ip address 10.1.1.1 255.255.255.0
 appletalk cable-range 106-110 106.17
 appletalk zone left
 ipx network BAD
!
interface Serial0/0
 ip unnumbered Ethernet0/0
 no ip mroute-cache
 appletalk cable-range 130-130 130.37
 appletalk zone right
 ipx network CAD
 clockrate 56000
!
interface TokenRing0/0
 no ip address
 shutdown
 ring-speed 16
!
interface FastEthernet1/0
 no ip address
 shutdown
!
router igrp 100
 network 10.0.0.0
!
ip classless
!!
line con 0
line aux 0
line vty 0 4
 login
!
end
```

a) No IP address will be used.
b) 120.120.120.17
c) 172.16.1.1
d) 127.0.0.1
e) 172.1.16.1

Question 6–216. [RIPx] Which of the following fields is NOT part of a User Datagram Protocol (UDP) Segment?

a) source port
b) destination port
c) length
d) checksum
e) acknowledgement

Question 6–217. [FxPx] Which of the following may be required to configure Frame Relay? (Choose all that apply.)

a) X.121 address
b) Frame Relay Switch Type
c) SPID number (Service Profile Identifier)
d) DLCI number (Data Link Connection Identifier)
e) LMI type (Local Management Interface)

Question 6–218. [ROPx] Suppose a new router is introduced into an OSPF topology with a priority of 1. Which one of the following would be true?

a) An election will be held to elect a new DR.
b) An election will be held to elect a new BDR.
c) No election will be held.
d) The new router will become the DR.
e) The new router will become the BDR.

Question 6–219. [ROPx] An area border router (ABR) is:

a) A router with all interfaces in the same area
b) A router with all interfaces in the backbone
c) Not necessary with stub areas configured
d) Not necessary if there is a single area
e) Must be configured with the "ip ospf abr" command